College Success

SENIOR CONTRIBUTING AUTHOR
AMY BALDWIN, UNIVERSITY OF CENTRAL ARKANSAS

ISBN: 978-1-951693-18-3

OpenStax
Rice University
6100 Main Street MS-375
Houston, Texas 77005

To learn more about OpenStax, visit https://openstax.org.
Individual print copies and bulk orders can be purchased through our website.

©**2020 Rice University.** Textbook content produced by OpenStax is licensed under a Creative Commons Attribution 4.0 International License (CC BY 4.0). Under this license, any user of this textbook or the textbook contents herein must provide proper attribution as follows:

- If you redistribute this textbook in a digital format (including but not limited to PDF and HTML), then you must retain on every page the following attribution:
  "Access for free at openstax.org."
- If you redistribute this textbook in a print format, then you must include on every physical page the following attribution:
  "Access for free at openstax.org."
- If you redistribute part of this textbook, then you must retain in every digital format page view (including but not limited to PDF and HTML) and on every physical printed page the following attribution:
  "Access for free at openstax.org."
- If you use this textbook as a bibliographic reference, please include https://openstax.org/details/books/college-success in your citation.

For questions regarding this licensing, please contact support@openstax.org.

Trademarks
The OpenStax name, OpenStax logo, OpenStax book covers, OpenStax CNX name, OpenStax CNX logo, OpenStax Tutor name, Openstax Tutor logo, Connexions name, Connexions logo, Rice University name, and Rice University logo are not subject to the license and may not be reproduced without the prior and express written consent of Rice University. XANEDU and the XanEdu Logo are trademarks of Xanedu Publishing, Inc. The XANEDU mark is registered in the United States, Canada, and the European Union. These trademarks may not be used without the prior and express written consent of XanEdu Publishing, Inc.

HARDCOVER BOOK ISBN-13	978-1-951693-16-9
B&W PAPERBACK BOOK ISBN-13	978-1-951693-18-3
DIGITAL VERSION ISBN-13	978-1-951693-17-6
ORIGINAL PUBLICATION YEAR	2020

10 9 8 7 6 5 4 3 2 1

Printed by

XanEdu

4750 Venture Drive, Suite 400
Ann Arbor, MI 48108
800-562-2147
www.xanedu.com

OpenStax

OpenStax provides free, peer-reviewed, openly licensed textbooks for introductory college and Advanced Placement® courses and low-cost, personalized courseware that helps students learn. A nonprofit ed tech initiative based at Rice University, we're committed to helping students access the tools they need to complete their courses and meet their educational goals.

Rice University

OpenStax, OpenStax CNX, and OpenStax Tutor are initiatives of Rice University. As a leading research university with a distinctive commitment to undergraduate education, Rice University aspires to path-breaking research, unsurpassed teaching, and contributions to the betterment of our world. It seeks to fulfill this mission by cultivating a diverse community of learning and discovery that produces leaders across the spectrum of human endeavor.

Philanthropic Support

OpenStax is grateful for our generous philanthropic partners, who support our vision to improve educational opportunities for all learners.

Laura and John Arnold Foundation	Leon Lowenstein Foundation, Inc.
Chegg, Inc.	The Maxfield Foundation
Arthur and Carlyse Ciocca Charitable Foundation	Burt and Deedee McMurtry
Ann and John Doerr	Michelson 20MM Foundation
Bill & Melinda Gates Foundation	National Science Foundation
Girard Foundation	The Open Society Foundations
Google Inc.	Jumee Yhu and David E. Park III
The William and Flora Hewlett Foundation	Brian D. Patterson USA-International Foundation
The Hewlett-Packard Company	The Bill and Stephanie Sick Fund
Rusty and John Jaggers	Robin and Sandy Stuart Foundation
The Calvin K. Kazanjian Economics Foundation	The Stuart Family Foundation
Charles Koch Foundation	Tammy and Guillermo Treviño

TABLE OF CONTENTS

Preface 1

1 Exploring College 7

1.1 Why College? 9
1.2 The First Year of College Will Be an Experience 15
1.3 College Culture and Expectations 18
1.4 How Can This Book And This Course Help? 30

2 Knowing Yourself as a Learner 33

2.1 The Power to Learn 34
2.2 The Motivated Learner 38
2.3 It's All in the Mindset 49
2.4 Learning Styles 56
2.5 Personality Types and Learning 60
2.6 Applying What You Know about Learning 65
2.7 The Hidden Curriculum 69

3 Managing Your Time and Priorities 73

3.1 The Benefits of Time Management 74
3.2 Time Management in College 76
3.3 Procrastination: The Enemy Within 81
3.4 How to Manage Time 85
3.5 Prioritization: Self-Management of What You Do and When You Do It 91
3.6 Goal Setting and Motivation 101
3.7 Enhanced Strategies for Time and Task Management 105

4 Planning Your Academic Pathways 115

4.1 Defining Values and Setting Goals 117
4.2 Planning Your Degree Path 123
4.3 Making a Plan 137
4.4 Managing Change and the Unexpected 143

5 Reading and Notetaking 151

5.1 The Nature and Types of Reading 153
5.2 Effective Reading Strategies 156
5.3 Taking Notes 169

6 Studying, Memory, and Test Taking   191

- **6.1** Memory   192
- **6.2** Studying   201
- **6.3** Test Taking   210

7 Thinking   221

- **7.1** What Thinking Means   223
- **7.2** Creative Thinking   224
- **7.3** Analytical Thinking   233
- **7.4** Critical Thinking   236
- **7.5** Problem-Solving   240
- **7.6** Metacognition   242
- **7.7** Information Literacy   246

8 Communicating   255

- **8.1** An Overview of Communication   256
- **8.2** Purpose of Communication   260
- **8.3** Communication and Technology   261
- **8.4** The Context of Communication   271
- **8.5** Barriers to Effective Communication   277

9 Understanding Civility and Cultural Competence   283

- **9.1** What Is Diversity, and Why Is Everybody Talking About It?   284
- **9.2** Categories of Diversity   299
- **9.3** Navigating the Diversity Landscape   305
- **9.4** Inclusivity and Civility: What Role Can I Play?   315

10 Understanding Financial literacy   319

- **10.1** Personal Financial Planning   321
- **10.2** Savings, Expenses, and Budgeting   327
- **10.3** Banking and Emergency Funds   333
- **10.4** Credit Cards and Other Debt   341
- **10.5** Education Debt: Paying for College   345
- **10.6** Defending against Attack: Securing Your Identity and Accounts   355

11 Engaging in a Healthy Lifestyle   365

- **11.1** Taking Care of Your Physical Health   367
- **11.2** Sleep   374
- **11.3** Taking Care of Your Emotional Health   379
- **11.4** Taking Care of Your Mental Health   383

11.5 Maintaining Healthy Relationships 388
11.6 Your Safety 393

12 Planning for Your Future 403

12.1 Why Worry about a Career While I'm in College? 404
12.2 Your Map to Success: The Career Planning Cycle 410
12.3 Where Can You Go from Here? 432

A Conducting and Presenting Research 435

B Recommended Readings 445

C Activities and Artifacts From the Book 447

Index 455

Preface

Welcome to *College Success*, an OpenStax resource. This textbook was written to increase student access to high-quality learning materials, maintaining highest standards of academic rigor at little to no cost.

About OpenStax

OpenStax is a nonprofit based at Rice University, and it's our mission to improve student access to education. Our first openly licensed college textbook was published in 2012, and our library has since scaled to over 35 books for college and AP® courses used by hundreds of thousands of students. OpenStax Tutor, our low-cost personalized learning tool, is being piloted in college courses throughout the country. Through our partnerships with philanthropic foundations and our alliance with other educational resource organizations, OpenStax is breaking down the most common barriers to learning and empowering students and instructors to succeed.

About OpenStax Resources

Customization

College Success is licensed under a Creative Commons Attribution 4.0 International (CC BY) license, which means that you can distribute, remix, and build upon the content, as long as you provide attribution to OpenStax and its content contributors.

Because our books are openly licensed, you are free to use the entire book or pick and choose the sections that are most relevant to the needs of your course. Feel free to remix the content by assigning your students certain chapters and sections in your syllabus, in the order that you prefer. You can even provide a direct link in your syllabus to the sections in the web view of your book.

Instructors also have the option of creating a customized version of their OpenStax book. The custom version can be made available to students in low-cost print or digital form through their campus bookstore. Visit the Instructor Resources section of your book page on openstax.org for more information.

Art Attribution in *College Success*

In *College Success*, most art contains attribution to its title, creator or rights holder, host platform, and license within the caption. For art that is openly licensed, anyone may reuse the art as long as they provide the same attribution to its original source. Some art has been provided through permissions and should only be used with the attribution or limitations provided in the credit. If art contains no attribution credit, it may be reused without attribution.

Errata

All OpenStax textbooks undergo a rigorous review process. However, like any professional-grade textbook, errors sometimes occur. Since our books are web based, we can make updates periodically when deemed pedagogically necessary. If you have a correction to suggest, submit it through the link on your book page on openstax.org. Subject matter experts review all errata suggestions. OpenStax is committed to remaining transparent about all updates, so you will also find a list of past errata changes on your book page on openstax.org.

Format

You can access this textbook for free in web view or PDF through openstax.org, and for a low cost in print.

About *College Success*

College Success is designed to meet the course needs of a one-semester course, workshop, or seminar for first year experience or college transition students. FYE programs vary greatly according to institution, so the textbook has been developed to cover the most common concepts, and the open license and flexible formats provide many opportunities for coordinators, instructional designers, and faculty to tailor the material for their needs.

This book is an invitation—an invitation to students to step boldly into their college experience. *College Success* addresses the evolving challenges and opportunities of today's diverse students. The intensive development work leveraged expertise from hundreds of FYE coordinators and faculty across the country. It highlights resources available to students as they embark on new roads of independence and responsibility. Students engage in careful self-analysis and research-based strategies to identify their strengths, challenges, and aptitudes. While they explore study skills and learning methods, they are continually asked to apply the concepts in reading, writing, and thinking exercises, which build both a solid base for classroom discussion and a portfolio they can augment throughout their college career. Recognizing the ubiquity of technology and social media, the authors address relevant information and advice where appropriate throughout the text. The material is rooted in motivation, growth-mindset, and resilience; student readers will feel seen and involved as they continually encounter one of the textbook's core themes: "real-life" doesn't stop when college starts.

Student engagement and self-analysis are reflected in each section through applications and activities. Student reflection and opinions can be captured directly in the text, online, or in worksheets provided through the ancillary package.

The diversity and intersectionality of students was considered in every example, context, and application, and the text's active surveys and detailed profiles make student voices a key element of the reading.

Interconnected topics are acknowledged and built upon, demonstrating that no element of college learning and growth occurs in isolation. The result is a cumulative, more complete understanding, which better prepares students to meet the multi-dimensional challenges of higher education.

Openly licensed and free in all digital formats, the text provides unparalleled flexibility in its use, customization, and accessibility for faculty and students. The book is provided at no cost in online, pdf, epub, Kindle, and other formats. It is also available in print for a very low price.

Robust instructor ancillaries will support faculty and course designers with teaching notes, additional exercises, worksheet versions of the in-text activities, lecture slides, and assessment items.

Features

- **Student Profiles:** The voices of real students inform every chapter. These students grapple with the same concepts, from improving study skills to embracing diversity, and through their experiences and successes we share important stories.
- **Get Connected:** Apps, websites and tech opportunities that our experts recommend to help students better face the challenges of college and life beyond the classroom.
- **Analysis and Applications:** Peppered through every chapter are opportunities for students to reflect on concepts, try out processes, and apply what they're learning.
- **Career Connection:** How can the material in each chapter help the student once they leave the

classroom? Features at the end of every chapter help students apply what they've learned to work life.
- **Where Do You Go From Here?:** Each chapter gives students the opportunity to dig in deeper and hone their research skills by choosing one topic for a closer look.

Student Surveys and Results

Chapters begin and end with a survey, posing questions that will get readers engaged in considering their own level of connection and understanding of the chapter's concept, from time management to personal finance to career planning. The close of each chapter revisits the survey, helping students gauge how their understanding has evolved.

Student survey results are gathered anonymously and will be regularly provided to adopters as part of the instructor resources. (See below for more information on instructor resources.) In the future, the surveys will be assignable and the results viewable on an individual-course basis. For the survey results featured in the textbook, hundreds of students from a diverse array of colleges and universities provided their feedback to inform future students taking the course.

Estimated Module Completion Time

Each section of College Success includes an estimate of the average time needed to read through the material, work on the activities and applications, and—where necessary—explore external websites or watch videos. Each student will engage the material differently, and faculty will likely prioritize or assign certain components over others. As a result, the actual time students spend will vary greatly. OpenStax will periodically update these estimates based on user feedback. As with all other elements of the text, these estimates may be adjusted by instructors (or deleted completely) based on addition or removal of material or activities.

Additional Resources

Student and Instructor Resources

We've compiled additional resources for both students and instructors, including Getting Started Guides, lecture slides, and a Test Bank.

The most robust of these is the Instructor Resource Manual, developed by author Amy Baldwin based on extensive experience and requests from faculty reviewers and survey respondents. For each chapter, the IRM will contain:

- Detailed teaching suggestions
- Bloom's Taxonomy matrix, indicating the alignment of each chapter activity and application to the level of Bloom's it fulfills.
- Overarching "big picture" questions from the chapter
- Topical and cumulative case scenario activities, which present a realistic situation based on the concepts, and ask students to respond via writing or another method. These may be adapted and assigned by instructors.

Instructor resources require a verified instructor account, which you can apply for when you log in or create your account on openstax.org. Instructor and student resources are typically available within a few months after the book's initial publication. Take advantage of these resources to supplement your OpenStax book.

Community Hubs

OpenStax partners with the Institute for the Study of Knowledge Management in Education (ISKME) to offer

Community Hubs on OER Commons—a platform for instructors to share community-created resources that support OpenStax books, free of charge. Through our Community Hubs, instructors can upload their own materials or download resources to use in their own courses, including additional ancillaries, teaching material, multimedia, and relevant course content. We encourage instructors to join the hubs for the subjects most relevant to your teaching and research as an opportunity both to enrich your courses and to engage with other faculty.

To reach the Community Hubs, visit www.oercommons.org/hubs/OpenStax.

Technology Partners

As allies in making high-quality learning materials accessible, our technology partners offer optional low-cost tools that are integrated with OpenStax books. To access the technology options for your text, visit your book page on openstax.org.

About the Authors
Senior Contributing Author

Amy Baldwin, University of Central Arkansas

Amy Baldwin has dedicated her entire career to supporting students in their successful transition to college. She wrote the first, groundbreaking student success textbook for community colleges and for first-generation students. After 18 years as an award winning community college professor, she now serves as Director of the Department of Student Transitions at the University of Central Arkansas. This unique blend of experience provides perspective on two critical student and faculty populations, which she has brought to this book and her extensive work with Complete College America, Achieving the Dream, and the Developmental Education Initiative.

Amy and her husband Kyle live in Arkansas and have two children, Emily and Will.

Contributing Authors

Lisa August, Canisius College
James Bennett, Herzing University
Larry Buland, Metropolitan Community College
Sabrina Mathues, Brookdale Community College
Susan Monroe, Northern Virginia Community College
MJ O'Leary, Wellness Multiplied
Ann Pearson, San Jacinto College
Joshua Troesh, El Camino College
Margit Misangyi Watts, University of Hawai'i at Manoa

Reviewers

Nagash Clarke, Washtenaw Community College
Laura Crisp, Pellissippi State Community College
Abbie Finnegan, Des Moines Area Community College
Kim Fragopoulos, University of Massachusetts-Boston
Maria Galyon, Jefferson Community & Technical College
Kimberly A. Griffith, Bristol Community College
Anna Howell, Portland Community College

Sarah Howard, The Ohio State University
Stacy L. Hurley, Baltimore County Community College
Dawn Lee, Charleston Southern University
Gail Malone, South Plains College
Kim Martin, Chemeketa Community College
Sherri Powell, Shawnee State University
Bobby E. Roberts, Jr., Savannah State University
Laila M. Shishineh, University of Maryland, Baltimore County
Shavecca M. Snead, Albany State University
Jason Smethers, University of Tennessee, Knoxville
Angela C. Thering, SUNY Buffalo State
Antione D. Tomlin, Anne Arundel Community College
Jessica Traylor, Gordon State College
Makeda K. Turner, University of Michigan
Dave Urso, Blue Ridge Community College
Margit Misangyi Watts, University of Hawaii at Manoa
Ann Wolf, New Mexico Highlands University

Figure 1.1

Chapter Outline

1.1 Why College?
1.2 The First Year of College Will Be an Experience
1.3 College Culture and Expectations
1.4 How Can This Book And This Course Help?

Introduction

Student Survey

How do you feel about your ability to meet the expectations of college? These questions will help you determine how the chapter concepts relate to you right now. As we are introduced to new concepts and practices, it can be informative to reflect on how your understanding changes over time. We'll revisit these questions at the end of the chapter to see whether your feelings have changed. Take this quick survey to figure it out, ranking questions on a scale of 1 – 4, 1 meaning "least like me" and 4 meaning "most like me."

Don't be concerned with the results. If your score is low, you will most likely gain even more from this book.

1. I am fully aware of the expectations of college and how to meet them.
2. I know why I am in college and have clear goals that I want to achieve.
3. Most of the time, I take responsibility for my learning new and challenging concepts.
4. I feel comfortable working with faculty, advisors, and classmates to accomplish my goals.

You can also take the Chapter 1 survey (https://openstax.org/l/collegesurvey01) anonymously online.

STUDENT PROFILE

"As students transitioning to college, responsibility is an inherent component of self-advocacy. As someone accepted on full funding to a 4-year university, but whose life's circumstances disallowed attending college until years later, I used to dream of a stress-free college life. The reality is, college can be a meaningful place, but it can also be challenging and unpredictable. The key is to *be your own best advocate*, because no one else is obliged to advocate on your behalf.

"When I began my community college studies, I knew what I wanted to do. Cybersecurity was my passion, but I had no understanding of how credits transfer over to a 4-year university. This came to haunt me later, after I navigated the complex processes of transferring between two different colleges. Not everyone involved volunteers information. It is up to you, the student, to be the squeaky wheel so you can get the grease. Visit office hours, make appointments, and schedule meetings with stakeholders so that you are not just buried under the sheaf of papers on someone's desk."

—**Mohammed Khalid**, University of Maryland

About this Chapter

In this chapter, you will learn about what you can do to get ready for college. By the time you complete this chapter, you should be able to do the following:

- Recognize the purpose and value of college.
- Describe the transitional experience of the first year of college.
- Discuss how to handle college culture and expectations.
- Identify resources in this text and on your campus for supporting your college success.

Reginald	Madison
Reginald has, after much thought and with a high level of family support, decided to enroll in college. It has been a dream in the making, as he was unable to attend immediately after high school graduation. Instead, he worked several years in his family's business, got married, had a son, and then decided that he didn't want to spend the rest of his life regretting that he didn't get a chance to follow his dreams of becoming a teacher. Because it has been almost a decade since he sat in a classroom, he is worried about how he will fit in as an adult learner returning to college. Will his classmates think he is too old? Will his professors think he is not ready for the challenges of college work? Will his family get tired of his long nights at the library and his new priorities? There is so much Reginald is unsure of, yet he knows it's a step in the right direction.	It has been only three months since Madison graduated from high school. She graduated in the top 10 percent of her class, and she earned college credit while in high school. She feels academically prepared, and she has a good sense of what degree she wants to earn. Since Madison was 5 years old, she's wanted to be an engineer because she loved building things in the backyard with her father's tools. He always encouraged her to follow her dreams, and her whole family has been supportive of her hobbies and interests. However, Madison is concerned that her choice of major will keep her from dance, creative writing, and other passions. Furthermore, Madison is heading to a distant college with no other people she knows. Will she be able to find new friends quickly? Will her engineering classes crush her or motivate her to complete college? Will she be able to explore other interests? Madison has a lot on her mind, but she aims to face these challenges head-on.

While Reginald and Madison have had different experiences before and certainly have different motivations for enrolling in college, they have quite a bit in common. They are both committed to this new chapter in their lives, and they are both connected to their families in ways that can influence their commitment to this pursuit. What they don't know just yet—because they haven't started their classes—is that they will have even more in common as they move through each term, focus on a major, and plan for life after graduation. And they have a lot in common with you as well because you are in a similar position—starting the next chapter of the rest of your life.

In this chapter, you will first learn more about identifying the reason you are in college. This is an important first step because knowing your *why* will keep you motivated. Next, the chapter will cover the transitions that you may experience as a new college student. Then, the chapter will focus on how you can acclimate to the culture and meeting the expectations—all of which will make the transition to a full-fledged college student easier. Finally, the chapter will provide you with strategies for overcoming the challenges that you may face by providing information about how to find and access resources.

1.1 Why College?

Estimated completion time: 22 minutes.

Questions to consider:

- Why are you in college?
- What are the rewards and value of a college degree?
- Why this course?

This chapter started with the profiles of two students, Reginald and Madison, but now we turn to who you are and why you are in college. Starting this chapter with *you*, the student, seems to make perfect sense. Like Reginald and Madison, you are probably full of emotions as you begin this journey toward a degree and the fulfillment of a dream. Are you excited about meeting new people and *finally* getting to take classes that interest you? Are you nervous about how you are going to handle your courses and all the other activities that come along with being a college student? Are you thrilled to be making important decisions about your future? Are you worried about making the right choice when deciding on a major or a career? All these thoughts, even if contradictory at times, are normal. And you may be experiencing several of them at the same time.

Figure 1.2 Decision-making about college and our future can be challenging, but with self-analysis and support, you can feel more confident and make the best choices.

Why Are You in College?

We know that college is not mandatory—like kindergarten through 12th grade is—and it is not free. You have made a *choice* to commit several years of hard work to earn a degree or credential. In some cases, you may have had to work really hard to get here by getting good grades and test scores in high school and earning money to pay for tuition and fees and other expenses. Now you have more at stake and a clearer path to achieving your goals, but you still need to be able to answer the question.

To help answer this question, consider the following questioning technique called "The Five Whys" that was originally created by Sakichi Toyoda, a Japanese inventor, whose strategy was used by the Toyota Motor Company to find the underlying cause of a problem. While your decision to go to college is not a problem, the exercise is helpful to uncover your underlying purpose for enrolling in college.

The process starts with a "Why" question that you want to know the answer to. Then, the next four "Why" questions use a portion of the previous answer to help you dig further into the answer to the original question. Here is an example of "The Five Whys," with the first question as "Why are you in college?" The answers and their connection to the next "Why" question have been underlined so you can see how the process works.

While the example is one from a student who knows what she wants to major in, this process does not require that you have a specific degree or career in mind. In fact, if you are undecided, then you can explore the "why" of your indecision. Is it because you have lots of choices, or is it because you are not sure what you really want out of college?

The Five Whys in Action

Why are you in college?	I am in college to earn a degree in speech pathology.
Why do you want to earn a degree in speech pathology?	I want to be able to help people who have trouble speaking.
Why do you want to help people who have trouble speaking?	I believe that people who have trouble speaking deserve a life they want.
Why do you feel it is important that people who have trouble speaking deserve a life they want?	I feel they often have needs that are overlooked and do not get treated equally.
Why do you want to use your voice to help these people live a life they deserve?	I feel it is my purpose to help others achieve their full potential despite having physical challenges.

Do you see how this student went beyond a standard answer about the degree that she wants to earn to connecting her degree to an overall purpose that she has to help others in a specific way? Had she not been instructed to delve a little deeper with each answer, it is likely that she would not have so quickly articulated that deeper purpose. And that understanding of "why" you are in college—beyond the degree you want or the job you envision after graduation—is key to staying motivated through what will most likely be some challenging times

How else does knowing your "why," or your deeper reason for being in college, help you? According to Angela Duckworth (2016), a researcher on *grit*—what it takes for us to dig in deep when faced with adversity and continue to work toward our goal—knowing your purpose can be the booster to grit that can help you succeed.[1] Other research has found that people who have a strong sense of purpose are less likely to experience stress and anxiety (Burrown, 2013)[2] and more likely to be satisfied in their jobs (Weir, 2013).[3] Therefore, being able to answer the question "Why are you in college?" not only satisfies the person asking, but it also has direct benefits to your overall well-being.

---

1   Duckworth, A. (2016). *Grit: The Power and Passion of Perseverance*. NY: Simon & Schuster.
2   Burrow, A.L. & Hill, P.L. (2013). Derailed by diversity? Purpose buffers the relationship between ethnic composition on trains and passenger negative mood. *Personality and Psychology Bulletin*, 39 (12), 1610-1619. https://doi.org/10.1177/0146167213499377.
3   Weir, K. (2013). More than job satisfaction: Psychologists are discovering what makes work meaningful--and how to create value in any job. *American Psychological Association*, 44 (11), 39.

ACTIVITY

Try "The Five Whys" yourself in the table below to help you get a better sense of your purpose and to give you a worthy answer for anyone who asks you "Why are you in college?"

The Five Whys: Your Turn

Why are you in college?	I am in college to . . .
Why do you . . .	I . . .
Why do you . . .	I . . .
Why do you . . .	I . . .
Why do you . . .	I . . .

What Are the Rewards and Value of a College Degree?

Once you have explored your "why" for enrolling in college, it may be worth reviewing what we know about the value of a college degree. There is no doubt you know people who have succeeded in a career without going to college. Famous examples of college dropouts include Bill Gates (the cofounder and CEO of Microsoft) and Ellen DeGeneres (comedian, actor, and television producer, among her many other roles). These are two well-known, smart, talented people who have had tremendous success on a global scale. They are also not the typical profile of a student who doesn't finish a degree. For many students, especially those who are first-generation college students, a college degree helps them follow a career pathway and create a life that would not have been possible without the credential. Even in this time of rapid change in all kinds of fields, including technology and education, a college degree is still worth it for many people.

Consider the following chart that shows an average of lifetime earnings per level of education. As you can see, the more education you receive, the greater the increase in your average lifetime earnings. Even though a degree costs a considerable amount of money on the front end, if you think about it as an investment in your future, you can see that college graduates receive a substantial return on their investment. To put it into more concrete terms, let's say you spend $100,000 for a four-year degree (*Don't faint! That is the average sticker cost of a four-year degree at a public university if you include tuition, fees, room, and board*). The return on investment (ROI) over a lifetime, according to the information in the figure below, is 1,500%! You don't have to be a financial wizard to recognize that 1,500% return is fantastic.

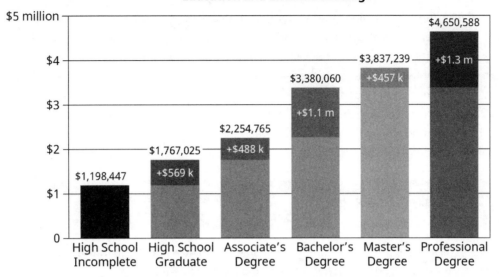

Source: Current Population Survey, U.S. Census Bureau; Help Wanted, The Georgetown University Center on Education and the Workforce. Figures are in 2008 dollars.

Figure 1.3 Every education level brings with it potential for greater lifetime earnings. These are simply averages and may not apply to all career types and individuals. For clarity, the "professional degree," attaining the highest earnings, refers to degrees such as those given to doctors or lawyers. Monetary values are in 2008 dollars. (Credit: based on data provided by Georgetown Center on Education and the Workforce)

Making more money over time is not the only benefit you can earn from completing a college degree. College graduates are also more likely to experience the following:

- **Greater job satisfaction.** That's right! College graduates are more likely to get a job that they like or to find that their job is more enjoyable than not.
- **Better job stability.** Employees with college degrees are more likely to find and keep a job, which is comforting news in times of economic uncertainty.
- **Improved health and wellness.** College graduates are less likely to smoke and more likely to exercise and maintain a healthy weight.
- **Better outcomes for the next generation.** One of the best benefits of a college degree is that it can have positive influences for the graduate's immediate family and the next generations.

One last thing: There is some debate as to whether a college degree is needed to land a job, and there are certainly jobs that you can get without a college degree. However, there are many reasons that a college degree can give you an edge in the job market. Here are just a few reasons that graduating with a degree is still valuable:

- More and more entry-level jobs will require a college degree. According to Georgetown University's Center on Education and the Workforce, in 2020, 35% of jobs will require a college degree.[4]
- A credential from a college or university still provides assurance that a student has mastered the material. Would you trust a doctor who never went to medical school to do open-heart surgery on a close relative? No, we didn't think so.
- College provides an opportunity to develop much-needed soft skills. The National Association of Colleges

---

4   Carnevale, A.P., Smith, N., & Strohl, J. (2013). Recover: Job growth and education requirements through 2020. Georgetown University's Center on Education and the Workforce. Retrieved from https://cew.georgetown.edu/cew-reports/recovery-job-growth-and-education-requirements-through-2020/.

and Employers has identified eight career-readiness competencies that college students should develop: critical thinking/problem solving, oral/written communication, teamwork/collaboration, digital technology, leadership, professionalism/work ethic, career management, and global/intercultural fluency.[5] There are few occasions that will provide you the opportunity to develop all of these skills in a low-stakes environment (i.e., without the fear of being fired!). You will learn all of this *and* more in your classes. Seems like a great opportunity, doesn't it? If you find yourself asking the question "What does *this* course have to do with my major?" or "Why do I have to take *that*?" challenge yourself to learn more about the course and look for connections between the content and your larger educational, career, and life goals.

ANALYSIS QUESTION

In what ways will earning a college degree be valuable to you now and in the future? Be sure to describe the financial, career, and personal benefits to earning a college degree.

Why This Course?

Now that you have considered why you are in college and why a college degree may be valuable to you, it's time to focus on why you are reading this book. Most likely, you are enrolled in a course that is helping you learn about college and how to make the most of it. You may be asking yourself "Why am I taking this course?" or even "Why do I have to read this book?" Answers to the first question may vary, depending on your college's requirements for first-year students. Nevertheless, you are probably taking this course because your college believes that it will *help you succeed in college and beyond*. Likewise, the reason your professor has assigned this book is because it has been designed to give you the best information about how to make your transition to college a little smoother. If you are not convinced just yet of the value of this course and its content, consider the following questions that you will be encouraged to answer as you learn about how to succeed in college:

- What will college expect of me in terms of skills, habits, and behaviors, and how can I develop them to ensure that I am successful?
- What do I need to know about how to navigate the process of completing a college degree?
- How can I ensure that I develop worthy long-term goals, and how best can I meet those goals?

These questions are designed to assist you in the transition from high school, or the workforce, to the new world of college. And this won't be the last monumental transition that you will experience. For example, you will experience a new job more than once in your life, and you may experience the excitement and challenge of moving to a new house or a new city. You can be assured that transitions will require that you identify what you need to get through them and that you will experience some discomfort along the way. It wouldn't be such a great accomplishment without a little uncertainty, doubt, and self-questioning. To help you, the next section speaks specifically to transitions for the purpose of making your next steps a little smoother.

---

5   National Association of Colleges and Employers. (2019). Career readiness defined. Retrieved from https://www.naceweb.org/career-readiness/competencies/career-readiness-defined/.

1.2 The First Year of College Will Be an Experience

Estimated completion time: 14 minutes.

Questions to consider:

- How will you adjust to college?
- What are the common college experiences you will have?

Adjustments to College Are Inevitable

College not only will expand your mind, but it may also make you a little uncomfortable, challenge your identity, and at times, make you doubt your abilities. It is hard to truly learn anything without getting messy. This is what education does: it transforms us. For that to happen, however, means that we will need to be open to the transformation and allow the changes to occur. *Flexibility*, *transition*, and *change* are all words that describe what you will experience. Laurie Hazard and Stephanie Carter (2018)[6] use the word *adjustment*. Hazard and Carter (2018) believe there are six adjustment areas that first-year college students experience: academic, cultural, emotional, financial, intellectual, and social. Of course, you won't go through these adjustments all at once or even in just the first year. Some will take time, while others may not even feel like much of a transition. Let's look at them in brief as a way of preparing for the road ahead:

- *Academic adjustment.* No surprises here. You will most likely—depending on your own academic background—be faced with the increased demands of learning in college. This could mean that you need to spend more time learning to learn and using those strategies to master the material.
- *Cultural adjustment.* You also will most likely experience a cultural adjustment just by being in college because most campuses have their own language (*syllabus*, *registrar*, and *office hours*, for example) and customs. You may also experience a cultural adjustment because of the diversity that you will encounter. Most likely, the people on your college campus will be different than the people at your high school—or at your workplace.
- *Emotional adjustment.* Remember the range of emotions presented at the beginning of the chapter? Those will likely be present in some form throughout your first weeks in college and at stressful times during the semester. Knowing that you may have good days and bad—and that you can bounce back from the more stressful days—will help you find healthy ways of adjusting emotionally.
- *Financial adjustment.* Most students understand the investment they are making in their future by going to college. Even if you have all your expenses covered, there is still an adjustment to a new way of thinking about what college costs and how to pay for it. You may find that you think twice about spending money on entertainment or that you have improved your skills in finding discounted textbooks.
- *Intellectual adjustment.* Experiencing an intellectual "a-ha!" moment is one of the most rewarding parts of college, right up there with moving across the graduation stage with a degree in hand. Prepare to be surprised when you stumble across a fascinating subject or find that a class discussion changes your life. At the very least, through your academic work, you will learn to think differently about the world around you and your place in it.
- *Social adjustment.* A new place often equals new people. But in college, those new relationships can have even more meaning. Getting to know professors not only can help you learn more in your classes, but it can also help you figure out what career pathway you want to take and how to get desired internships and jobs. Learning to reduce conflicts during group work or when living with others helps build essential

---

6 Hazard, L., & Carter, S. (2018). A framework for helping families understand the college transition. *E-Source for College Transitions*, 16(1), 13-15.

workplace and life skills.

The table Six Areas of Adjustment for First-Year College Students provides a succinct definition for each of the areas as well as examples of how you can demonstrate that you have adjusted. Think about what you have done so far to navigate these transitions in addition to other things you can do to make your college experience a successful one.

	Academic	Cultural	Emotional	Financial	Intellectual	Social
What Is It?	Students will take a more active role in their learning than they had to in high and have the ability to meet the increasing demands of change.	Students will interact with others of various cultures, religious beliefs, sexual identities and orientations, ages, and abilities.	Students will need to be prepared for the stressors of college and develop habits and behaviors to cope with these changes.	Students will need to demonstrate basic financial literacy, an understanding of the cost of college, and methods of paying for those costs.	Students will have the opportunity to join an academic community that includes classmates, faculty, support personnel, and administrators.	Students will be faced with shifts in their relationships, finding a new peer group and handling the pressure of fitting in.
Students exhibit it when they:	• Take an active role in learning. • Attain college-level learning strategies. • Are open to feedback and change. • Make adjustments to learning strategies as needed.	• Accept and welcome differences in others. • Recognize the include of their own cultural identity. • Seek opportunities to explore other cultures.	• Readily handle the stressors of college life. • Develop emotional coping strategies. • Seek support from campus resources.	• Manage money independently. • Recognize the costs of college. • Explore job and aid opportunities.	• Engage in intellectual discussions. • Are open to new ideas, subject areas, and career choices. • Integrate new ideas into belief systems.	• Join a club or organization. • Form supportive, healthy relationships. • Understand the impact of peer pressure. • Manage conflict in relationships.

Figure 1.4 **Six Areas of Adjustment for First-Year College Students** Based on work by Laurie Hazard, Ed.D., and Stephanie Carter, M.A.

"Experiencing an intellectual 'a-ha!' moment is one of the most rewarding parts of college, right up there with moving across the graduation stage with a degree in hand."

ANALYSIS QUESTION

Which of the six areas of adjustment do you think will be the least challenging for you, and which do you think will be most challenging? What can you do now to prepare for the more challenging transitions?

WHAT STUDENTS SAY

1. How confident are you that your high school and/or work experience have prepared you academically for college?
    a. Extremely confident
    b. Confident
    c. Somewhat confident
    d. Not very confident
2. When you experience a college-related challenge and are not really sure how to solve it, what best describes the action you're likely to take?
    a. I will likely persist and persevere until I figure it out.
    b. I will likely try to solve the problem, but if it is really difficult, I will simply move on to something else.
    c. I will likely ask my parents or friends for advice.
    d. I will likely seek help from resources on campus.
3. Rank the following in terms of how much stress you feel in these situations (1 being the least amount of stress and 6 being the most amount of stress):
    a. The amount of work required in all of my courses
    b. The fact that I know hardly anyone
    c. My ability to handle all of my obligations
    d. Making good grades so I can continue to stay in college
    e. My concern that I may not belong in college
    f. All of the above are equally stressful

You can also take the anonymous What Students Say (https://openstax.org/l/collegesurvey1-5) surveys to add your voice to this textbook. Your responses will be included in updates.

Students offered their views on these questions, and the results are displayed in the graphs below.

How confident are you that your high school and/or work experience have prepared you academically for college?

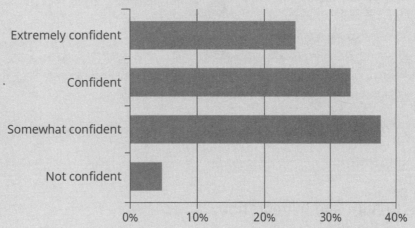

Figure 1.5

When you experience a college-related challenge and are not really sure how to solve it, what best describes the action you're likely to take?

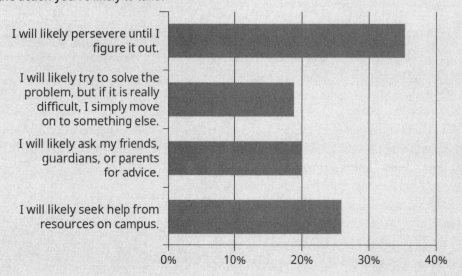

Figure 1.6

Rank the following in terms of how much stress you feel in these situations (1 being the least amount of stress and 6 being the most amount of stress). (Graph displays the percentage of students who ranked the choice highest, indicating the most amount of stress.)

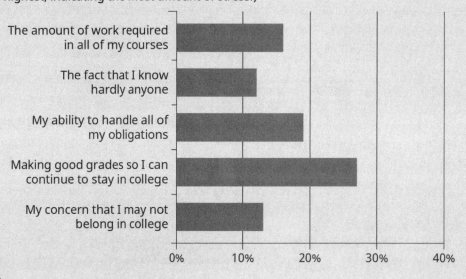

Figure 1.7

1.3 College Culture and Expectations

Estimated completion time: 32 minutes.

Table 1.1

Questions to consider:

- What language and customs do you need to know to succeed in college?
- What is your responsibility for learning in college?
- What resources will you use to meet these expectations?
- What are the common challenges in the first year?

College Has Its Own Language and Customs

Going to college—even if you are not far from home—is a cultural experience. It comes with its own language and customs, some of which can be confusing or confounding at first. Just like traveling to a foreign country, it is best if you prepare by learning what words mean and what you are expected to say and do in certain situations.

Let's first start with the language you may encounter. In most cases, there will be words that you have heard before, but they may have different meanings in a college setting. Take, for instance, "office hours." If you are not in college, you would think that it means the hours of a day that an office is open. If it is your dentist's office, it may mean Monday through Friday from 8 a.m. to 5 p.m. In college, "office hours" can refer to the specific hours a professor is in her office to meet with students, and those hours may be only a few each day: for example, Mondays and Wednesdays from 1 p.m. until 3 p.m.

"Syllabus" is another word that you may not have encountered, but it is one you will soon know very well. A syllabus is often called the "contract of the course" because it contains information about what to expect—from the professor and the student. It is meant to be a roadmap for succeeding in the class. Understanding that office hours are for you to ask your professor questions and the syllabus is the guide for what you will be doing in the class can make a big difference in your transition to college. The table on Common College Terms, has a brief list of other words that you will want to know when you hear them on campus.

Common College Terms, What They Mean, and Why You Need to Know

Term	What It Means	Why You Need to Know
Attendance policy	A policy that describes the attendance and absence expectations for a class	Professors will have different attendance expectations. Read your syllabus to determine which ones penalize you if you miss too many classes.
Final exam	A comprehensive assessment that is given at the end of a term	If your class has a final exam, you will want to prepare for it well in advance by reading assigned material, taking good notes, reviewing previous tests and assignments, and studying.
Learning	The process of acquiring knowledge	In college, most learning happens *outside* the classroom. Your professor will only cover the main ideas or the most challenging material in class. The rest of the learning will happen on your own.

Table 1.2

Common College Terms, What They Mean, and Why You Need to Know

Term	What It Means	Why You Need to Know
Office hours	Specific hours professor is in the office to meet with students	Visiting your professor during office hours is a good way to get questions answered and to build rapport.
Plagiarism	Using someone's words, images, or ideas as your own, without proper attribution	Plagiarism carries much more serious consequences in college, so it is best to speak to your professor about how to avoid it and review your student handbook's policy.
Study	The process of using learning strategies to understand and recall information	Studying in college may look different than studying in high school in that it may take more effort and more time to learn more complex material.
Syllabus	The contract of a course that provides information about course expectations and policies	The syllabus will provide valuable information that your professor will assume you have read and understood. Refer to it first when you have a question about the course.

Table 1.2

ACTIVITY

The language that colleges and universities use can feel familiar but mean something different, as you learned in the section above, and it can also seem alien, especially when institutions use acronyms or abbreviations for buildings, offices, and locations on campus. Terms such as "quad" or "union" can denote a location or space for students. Then there may be terms such as "TLC" (The Learning Center, in this example) that designate a specific building or office. Describe a few of the new terms you have encountered so far and what they mean. If you are not sure, ask your professor or a fellow student to define it for you.

In addition to its own language, higher education has its own way of doing things. For example, you may be familiar with what a teacher did when you were in high school, but do you know what a professor does? It certainly seems like they fulfill a very similar role as teachers in high school, but in college professors' roles are often much more diverse. In addition to teaching, they may also conduct research, mentor graduate students, write and review research articles, serve on and lead campus committees, serve in regional and national organizations in their disciplines, apply for and administer grants, advise students in their major, and serve as sponsors for student organizations. You can be assured that their days are far from routine. See the Table on Differences between High School Teachers and College Professors for just a few differences between high school teachers and college professors.

Differences between High School and College Faculty

High School Faculty	College Faculty
Often have degrees or certifications in teaching in addition to degrees in subject matter	Most likely have not even taken a course in teaching as part of their graduate program
Responsibilities include maximizing student learning and progress in a wide array of areas	Responsibilities include providing students with content and an assessment of their mastery of the content
Are available before or after school or during class if a student has a question	Are available during office hours or by appointment if a student needs additional instruction or advice
Communicate regularly and welcome questions from parents and families about a student's progress	Cannot communicate with parents and families of students without permission because of the Federal Educational Rights and Privacy Act (FERPA)

The relationships you build with your professors will be some of the most important ones you create during your college career. You will rely on them to help you find internships, write letters of recommendation, nominate you for honors or awards, and serve as references for jobs. You can develop those relationships by participating in class, visiting during office hours, asking for assistance with coursework, requesting recommendations for courses and majors, and getting to know the professor's own academic interests. One way to think about the change in how your professors will relate to you is to think about the nature of relationships you have had growing up. In Figure 1.X: You and Your Relationships Before College you will see a representation of what your relationships probably looked like. Your family may have been the greatest influencer on you and your development.

"The relationships you build with your professors will be some of the most important ones during your college career."

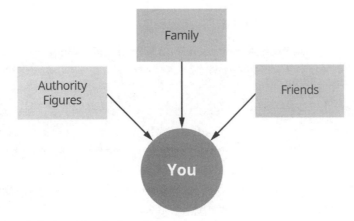

Figure 1.8 You and Your Relationships Before College.

In college, your networks are going to expand in ways that will help you develop other aspects of yourself. As described above, the relationships you will have with your professors will be some of the most important. But they won't be the only relationships you will be cultivating while in college. Consider the Figure on You and Your Relationships during College and think about how you will go about expanding your network while you are completing your degree.

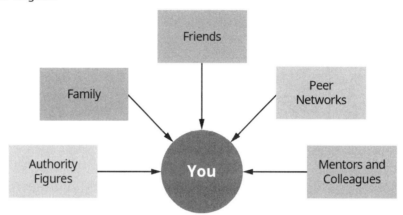

Figure 1.9 You and Your Relationships During College

Your relationships with authority figures, family, and friends may change while you are in college, and at the very least, your relationships will expand to peer networks—not friends, but near-age peers or situational peers (e.g., a first-year college student who is going back to school after being out for 20 years)—and to faculty and staff who may work alongside you, mentor you, or supervise your studies. These relationships are important because they will allow you to expand your network, especially as it relates to your career. As stated earlier, developing relationships with faculty can provide you with more than just the benefits of a mentor. Faculty often review applications for on-campus jobs or university scholarships and awards; they also have connections with graduate programs, companies, and organizations. They may recommend you to colleagues or former classmates for internships and even jobs.

Other differences between high school and college are included in the table about Differences between High School and College. Because it is not an exhaustive list of the differences, be mindful of other differences you may notice. Also, if your most recent experience has been the world of work or the military, you may find that there are more noticeable differences between those experiences and college.

Differences between High School and College

	High School	College	Why You Need to Know the Difference
Grades	Grades are made up of frequent tests and homework, and you may be able to bring up a low initial grade by completing smaller assignments and bonuses.	Grades are often made up of fewer assignments, and initial low grades may keep you from earning high course grades at the end of the semester.	You will need to be prepared to earn high grades on all assignments because you may not have the opportunity to make up for lost ground.

Differences between High School and College

	High School	College	Why You Need to Know the Difference
Learning	Learning is often done in class with the teacher guiding the process, offering multiple ways to learn material and frequent quizzes to ensure that learning is occurring.	Learning happens mostly outside of class and on your own. Faculty are responsible for assigning material and covering the most essential ideas; you are responsible for tracking and monitoring your learning progress.	You will need to practice effective learning strategies on your own to ensure that you are mastering material at the appropriate pace.
Getting Help	Your teachers, parents, and a counselor are responsible for identifying your need for help and for creating a plan for you to get help with coursework if you need it. Extra assistance is usually reserved for students who have an official diagnosis or need.	You will most likely need help to complete all your courses successfully even if you did not need extra help in high school. You will be responsible for identifying that you need it, accessing the resources, and using them.	Because the responsibility is on you, not parents or teachers, to get the help you need, you will want to be aware of when you may be struggling to learn material. You then will need to know *where* the support can be accessed on campus or where you can access support online.
Tests and Exams	Tests cover small amounts of material and study days or study guides are common to help you focus on what you need to study. If you paid attention in class, you should be able to answer all the questions.	Tests are fewer and cover more material than in high school. If you read all the assigned material, took good notes in class, and spent time practicing effective study techniques, you should be able to answer all the questions.	This change in how much material and the depth of which you need to know the material is a shock for some students. This may mean you need to change your strategies dramatically to get the same results.

Table 1.3

Some of What You Will Learn Is "Hidden"

Many of the college expectations that have been outlined so far may not be considered common knowledge, which is one reason that so many colleges and universities have classes that help students learn what they need to know to succeed. The term, which was coined by sociologists,[7] describes unspoken, unwritten, or unacknowledged (hence, *hidden*) rules that students are expected to follow that can affect their learning. To

---

7   P.P. Bilbao, P. I. Lucido, T. C. Iringan and R. B. Javier. (2008). *Curriculum Development*.

illustrate the concept, consider the situation in the following activity.

ACTIVITY

Situation: Your history syllabus indicates that, on Tuesday, your professor is lecturing on the chapter that covers the stock market crash of 1929.

This information sounds pretty straightforward. Your professor lectures on a topic and you will be there to hear it. However, there are some unwritten rules, or hidden curriculum, that are not likely to be communicated. Can you guess what they may be? Take a moment to write at least one potential unwritten rule.

1. What is an unwritten rule about what you should be doing before attending class?
   _____
2. What is an unwritten rule about what you should be doing in class?
   _____
3. What is an unwritten rule about what you should be doing after class?
   _____
4. What is an unwritten rule if you are not able to attend that class?
   _____

Some of your answers could have included the following:

Before class: *Read the assigned chapter, take notes, record any questions you have about the reading.*

During class: *Take detailed notes, ask critical thinking or clarifying questions, avoid distractions, bring your book and your reading notes.*

After class: *Reorganize your notes in relation to your other notes, start the studying process by testing yourself on the material, make an appointment with your professor if you are not clear on a concept.*

Absent: *Communicate with the professor, get notes from a classmate, make sure you did not miss anything important in your notes.*

The expectations before, during, and after class, as well as what you should do if you miss class, are often unspoken because many professors assume you already know and do these things or because they feel you should figure them out on your own. Nonetheless, some students struggle at first because they don't know about these habits, behaviors, and strategies. But once they learn them, they are able to meet them with ease.

Learning Is Your Responsibility

As you may now realize by reviewing the differences between high school and college, learning in college is your responsibility. Before you read about the how and why of being responsible for your own learning, complete the Activity below.

ACTIVITY

For each statement, circle the number that best represents you, with 1 indicating that the statement is least like you, and 5 indicating that the statement is most like you.

Most of the time, I can motivate myself to complete tasks even if they are boring or challenging.				
1	2	3	4	5
I regularly work hard when I need to complete a task no matter how small or big the task may be.				
1	2	3	4	5
I use different strategies to manage my time effectively and minimize procrastination to complete tasks.				
1	2	3	4	5
I regularly track my progress completing work and the quality of work I do produce.				
1	2	3	4	5
I believe how much I learn and how well I learn is my responsibility.				
1	2	3	4	5

Table 1.4

Were you able to mark mostly 4s and 5s? If you were even able to mark at least one 4 or 5, then you are well on your way to taking responsibility for your own learning. Let's break down each statement in the components of the ownership of learning:

- **Motivation.** Being able to stay motivated while studying and balancing all you have to do in your classes will be important for meeting the rest of the components.
- **Deliberate, focused effort.** Taking ownership of learning will hinge on the effort that you put into the work. Because most learning in college will take place outside of the classroom, you will need determination to get the work done. And there will be times that the work will be challenging and maybe even boring, but finding a way to get through it when it is not exciting will pay in the long run.
- **Time and task management.** You will learn more about strategies for managing your time and the tasks of college in a later chapter, but without the ability to control your calendar, it will be difficult to block out the time to study.
- **Progress tracking.** A commitment to learning must include monitoring your learning, knowing not only what you have completed (*this is where a good time management strategy can help you track your tasks*), but also the quality of the work you have done.

Taking responsibility for your learning will take some time if you are not used to being in the driver's seat.

However, if you have any difficulty making this adjustment, you can and should reach out for help along the way.

What to Expect During the First Year

While you may not experience every transition within your first year, there are rhythms to each semester of the first year and each year you are in college. Knowing what to expect each month or week can better prepare you to take advantage of the times that you have more confidence and weather through the times that seem challenging. Review the table on First-Year College Student Milestones. There will be milestones each semester you are in college, but these will serve as an introduction to what you should expect in terms of the rhythms of the semester.

First-Year College Student Milestones for the First Semester

August	September	October	November	December
Expanding social circles	Completing first test and projects	Feeling more confident about abilities	Balancing college with other obligations	Focusing on finishing strong
Experiencing homesickness or imposter syndrome	Earning "lower-than-usual" grades or not meeting personal expectations	Dealing with relationship issues	Staying healthy and reducing stress	Handling additional stress of the end of the semester
Adjusting to the pace of college	Learning to access resources for support	Planning for next semester and beyond	Thinking about majors and degrees	Thinking about the break and how to manage changes

Table 1.5 While each student's first semester will differ, you will likely experience some of the following typical college milestones.

The first few weeks will be pretty exhilarating. You will meet new people, including classmates, college staff, and professors. You may also be living in a different environment, which may mean that a roommate is another new person to get to know. Overall, you will most likely feel both excited and nervous. You can be assured that even if the beginning of the semester goes smoothly, your classes will get more challenging each week. You will be making friends, learning who in your classes seem to know what is going on, and figuring your way around campus. You may even walk into the wrong building, go to the wrong class, or have trouble finding what you need during this time. But those first-week jitters will end soon. Students who are living away from home for the first time can feel homesick in the first few weeks, and others can feel what is called "imposter syndrome," which is a fear some students have that they don't belong in college because they don't have the necessary skills for success. Those first few weeks sound pretty stressful, but the stress is temporary.

After the newness of college wears off, reality will set in. You may find that the courses and assignments do not seem much different than they did in high school (more on that later), but you may be in for a shock when you get your graded tests and papers. Many new college students find that their first grades are lower than they expected. For some students, this may mean they have earned a B when they are used to earning As, but for many students, it means they may experience their first *failing or almost-failing grades* in college because they have not used active, effective study strategies; instead, they studied how they did in high school, which is often insufficient. This can be a shock if you are not prepared, but it doesn't have to devastate you if you are willing to use it as a wake-up call to do something different.

By the middle of the semester, you'll likely feel much more confident and a little more relaxed. Your grades are improving because you started going to tutoring and using better study strategies. You are looking ahead, even beyond the first semester, to start planning your courses for the next term. If you are working while in college, you may also find that you have a rhythm down for balancing it all; additionally, your time management skills have likely improved.

By the last few weeks of the semester, you will be focused on the increasing importance of your assignments and upcoming finals and trying to figure out how to juggle that with the family obligations of the impending holidays. You may feel a little more pressure to prepare for finals, as this time is often viewed as the most stressful period of the semester. All of this additional workload and need to plan for the next semester can seem overwhelming, but if you plan ahead and use what you learn from this chapter and the rest of the course, you will be able to get through it more easily.

Don't Do It Alone

Think about our earlier descriptions of two students, Reginald and Madison. What if they found that the first few weeks were a little harder than they had anticipated? Should they have given up and dropped out? Or should they have talked to someone about their struggles? Here is a secret about college success that not many people know: successful students seek help. They use resources. And they do that as often as necessary to get what they need. Your professors and advisors will expect the same from you, and your college will have all kinds of offices, staff, and programs that are designed to help. This bears calling out again: *you need to use those resources*. These are called "help-seeking behaviors," and along with self-advocacy, which is speaking up for your needs, they are essential to your success. As you get more comfortable adjusting to life in college, you will find that asking for help is easier. In fact, you may become really good at it by the time you graduate, just in time for you to ask for help finding a job! Review the table on Issues, Campus Resources, and Potential Outcomes for a few examples of times you may need to ask for help. See if you can identify where on campus you can find the same or a similar resource.

Issues, Campus Resources, and Potential Outcomes

Type	Issue	Campus Resource	Potential Outcome
Academic	You are struggling to master the homework in your math class.	The campus tutoring center	A peer or professional tutor can walk you through the steps until you can do them on your own.

Table 1.6

Issues, Campus Resources, and Potential Outcomes

Type	Issue	Campus Resource	Potential Outcome
Health	You have felt extremely tired over the past two days and now you have a cough.	The campus health center	A licensed professional can examine you and provide care.
Social	You haven't found a group to belong to. Your classmates seem to be going in different directions and your roommate has different interests.	Student organizations and interest groups	Becoming a member of a group on campus can help you make new friends.
Financial	Your scholarship and student loan no longer cover your college expenses. You are not sure how to afford next semester.	Financial aid office	A financial aid counselor can provide you with information about your options for meeting your college expenses.

Table 1.6

APPLICATION

Using a blank sheet of paper, write your name in the center of the page and circle it. Then, draw six lines from the center (see example in the figure below) and label each for the six areas of adjustment that were discussed earlier. Identify a campus resource or strategy for making a smooth adjustment for each area.

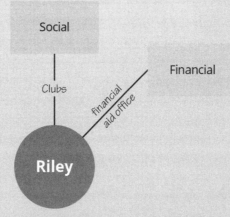

Figure 1.10 For each of the six adjustment areas mentioned above—Academic, Cultural, Emotional, Financial, Intellectual, and Social—identify a campus resource or strategy that will aid you in making a smooth adjustment.

Common Challenges in the First Year

It seems fitting to follow up the expectations for the first year with a list of common challenges that college students encounter along the way to a degree. If you experience any—or even all—of these, the important point here is that you are not alone and that you can overcome them by using your resources. Many college students have felt like this before, and they have survived—even thrived—despite them because they were able to identify a strategy or resource that they could use to help themselves. At some point in your academic career, you may do one or more of the following:

1. **Feel like an imposter.** There is actually a name for this condition: imposter syndrome. Students who feel like an imposter are worried that they don't belong, that someone will "expose them for being a fake." This feeling is pretty common for anyone who finds themselves in a new environment and is not sure if they have what it takes to succeed. Trust the professionals who work with first-year college students: you *do* have what it takes, and you *will* succeed. Just give yourself time to get adjusted to everything.
2. **Worry about making a mistake.** This concern often goes with imposter syndrome. Students who worry about making a mistake don't like to answer questions in class, volunteer for a challenging assignment, and even ask for help from others. Instead of avoiding situations where you may fail, embrace the process of learning, which includes—is even dependent on—making mistakes. The more you practice courage in these situations and focus on what you are going to learn from failing, the more confident you become about your abilities.
3. **Try to manage everything yourself.** Even superheroes need help from sidekicks and mere mortals. Trying to handle everything on your own every time an issue arises is a recipe for getting stressed out. There will be times when you are overwhelmed by all you have to do. This is when you will need to ask for and allow others to help you.
4. **Ignore your mental and physical health needs.** If you feel you are on an emotional rollercoaster and you cannot find time to take care of yourself, then you have most likely ignored some part of your mental and physical well-being. What you need to do to stay healthy should be non-negotiable. In other words, your sleep, eating habits, exercise, and stress-reducing activities should be your highest priorities.
5. **Forget to enjoy the experience.** Whether you are 18 years old and living on campus or 48 years old starting back to college after taking a break to work and raise a family, be sure to take the time to remind yourself of the joy that learning can bring.

GET CONNECTED

Which apps help you meet the expectations of college? Will you be able to meet the expectations of being responsible for your schedule and assignments?

- My Study Life (https://www.mystudylife.com) understands how college works and provides you with a calendar, to-do list, and reminders that will help you keep track of the work you have to do.

How can you set goals and work toward them while in college?

- The Strides (https://www.stridesapp.com) app provides you with the opportunity to create SMART (Specific, Measureable, Attainable, Relevant, and Time bound) goals and track daily habits. These daily habits will add up over time toward your goals.

What can you do to develop your learning skills?

- Lumosity (https://www.lumosity.com/en/) is a brain-training app that can help you build the thinking and learning skills you will need to meet learning challenges in college. If you want to test your memory and attention—and build your skills—take the fit test and then play different games to improve your fitness.

How can you develop networks with people in college?

- LinkedIn (https://www.linkedin.com) is a professional networking app that allows you to create a profile and network with others. Creating a LinkedIn account as a first-year college student will help you create a professional profile that you can use to find others with similar interests.
- Internships.com (https://www.internships.com) provides information, connections, and support to help your career planning and activities. Even if you are not planning an internship right away, you may find some useful and surprising ideas and strategies to motivate your approach.

1.4 How Can This Book And This Course Help?

Estimated completion time: 6 minutes.

Questions to consider:

- How will you be able to develop your purpose?
- In what ways will you be able to create strategies for your success?
- What other resources can you use to help you succeed?

As Reginald and Madison go through their college experiences and create a balance between their academic and personal lives, their stories, no doubt, will diverge. But you can be assured that each of them will demonstrate grit, the ability to stay focused on a goal over the long-term, along the way. As Duckworth (2016) has said, it takes passion and perseverance to be gritty. It also takes resilience, or the ability to bounce back from adversity. The challenges you face will certainly stretch you, but if you have these three things—purpose, strategies, and resources—you will be more likely to bounce back, even become stronger in the process. This book has been designed with these things in mind.

Develop Your "Why"

This chapter began with the suggestion to explore why you are in college or, more simply, what your purpose is. This course—and this book—will help you continue to refine your answer and create a map for your journey to fulfill your purpose. The features in this book that help you develop your purpose include the following:

- Student Survey Questions: Each chapter opens with several questions that provide you with a snapshot on how you feel about the chapter content. How does this feature help you develop purpose? It allows you to develop better self-awareness, which will in turn help you build an awareness of your purpose.
- Analysis Questions: These questions are included throughout each chapter. Consider them "pauses" to help you reflect on what you have read and how to incorporate the information into your own journey.

Refine Your Strategies for Success

Purpose by itself may illuminate the pathway forward, but it will take strategies to help you complete your journey. Think of the strategies you will learn in this course as tools you will need along the way to completing your degree. The following features provide you with an opportunity to practice and refine strategies for success:

- Application Questions: Any time you are asked to *apply* what you are learning in the chapters, you are improving your skills. Look for them throughout and take some time to stop, think, and use the skill.
- Activities: As you read, you will also have the opportunity to interact with the content. They give you the chance to refine the strategies that will help you succeed in college.
- Career Connection: This feature allows you to consider how the skills you are developing for college connect to your future career. Making these connections will help you appreciate the deeper importance of them.

Use Your Resources

In addition to developing strategies for succeeding in your academic and future professional career, you will find that this course will point out the resources you may need to obtain more tools or refuel your desire to continue along the pathway. No one succeeds at anything by oneself. The features related to resources will certainly help you find ways to fill up your toolkit of information.

- Get Connected: Despite its ability to distract us from the work we need to do, technology can help you accomplish your day-to-day tasks with relative ease. This feature offers suggestions for apps and websites that can help you build skills or just keep track of due dates!
- Where Do You Go from Here?: The skills and habits you are building now will serve you well in your future endeavors. This feature is designed to help you dig deeper into the chapter content and refine your research skills. It also asks that you find ways to connect what you are learning now to your life and career.

All of these features, in addition to the content, will help you see yourself for who you are and provide opportunities to develop in ways that will make reaching your goal a little easier. Will it be challenging at times? Yes, it will. Will it take time to reflect on those challenges and find better ways to learn and reach your goals? Most definitely. But the effort you put into completing your college degree will result in the confidence you will gain from knowing that anything you set your mind to do—and you work hard for—can be accomplished.

Summary

This chapter provides an introduction to the transition to college by first asking "Why?" Understanding why you are in college and what a college degree can do for you is the foundation of making a smooth transition. These transitional experiences are part of being in college, and this chapter provides you with information about what to expect and how to handle the changes you will go through. Next, the chapter discusses college culture and how to understand the customs and language of higher education. The chapter ends with resources throughout the text that can help you practice skills and dive deeper into the topics.

Rethinking

Revisit the questions you answered at the beginning of the chapter, and consider one option you learned in this chapter that might change your answer to them.

1. I am fully aware of the expectations of college and how to meet them.
2. I know why I am in college and have clear goals that I want to achieve.
3. Most of the time, I take responsibility for my learning new and challenging concepts.
4. I feel comfortable working with faculty, advisors, and classmates to accomplish my goals.

Where do you go from here?

Making the transition into college smoother for you can have long-term benefits. What have you learned about in this chapter that you want to know more about that could help you? Choose topics from the list below or create your own, and then create an annotated bibliography of three to five reliable sources that provide information about your topic.

- What is the long-term value of a college degree?
- What is the "hidden curriculum," and how can knowing about it help you succeed in college?
- What learning strategies are the most effective?
- What kinds of resources and services do colleges now offer that help students' personal development?

Figure 2.1 *The School of Athens* by Raphael, a fresco in the Vatican, is thought to depict many of the greatest figures in Greek philosophy, including Plato and Aristotle as well as Nicomachus and Averroes. (Credit: Wikimedia Commons / Public Domain)

Chapter Outline

2.1 The Power to Learn
2.2 The Motivated Learner
2.3 It's All in the Mindset
2.4 Learning Styles
2.5 Personality Types and Learning
2.6 Applying What You Know about Learning
2.7 The Hidden Curriculum

Introduction

Student Survey

How do you feel about your learning abilities? Take this quick survey to figure it out, ranking questions on a scale of 1–4, 1 meaning "least like me" and 4 meaning "most like me." These questions will help you determine how the chapter concepts relate to you right now. As you are introduced to new concepts and practices, it can be informative to reflect on how your understanding changes over time. We'll revisit these questions at the end of the chapter to see whether your feelings have changed.

1. Learning for me is easy. I don't even have to think about it.
2. I have a preferred learning style.
3. If I can't learn something right away, I have difficulty staying with it.
4. I think my teachers are the most significant aspect of my learning.

You can also take the Chapter 2 survey (https://openstax.org/l/collegesurvey02) anonymously online.

STUDENT PROFILE

"When I came to college, I was a great STEM student. I knew the best ways to study for understanding the complexity of cellular mechanisms, but I had no idea how to study for classes where I would need to draw upon political theory or even how to memorize vocabulary words for language classes. Since I am now a humanities student studying Russian, I learned the hard way that you cannot study for every class the same way.

"For my first Russian vocabulary quiz, I studied almost 14 hours because I could not remember the words no matter how hard I tried. I was studying the Russian textbook the same way that I would study for a Chemistry or Biology class: to simply read the chapter or vocabulary list over and over again. I knew that I could not afford to be this time-inefficient for the entire semester, so I asked my professor for some tips on how to study for her class. Now, I start studying three days before each quiz by making flash cards the first day, studying the words from Russian to English the second day, and then studying the words from English to Russian by writing them down the third day. This new method is not one that works well for every class, but that's the beauty of it! I am a better learner because I have found ways to use a more diverse range of studying tactics."

— **Gabby Kennedy**, Baylor University

About This Chapter

In this chapter you will learn about the art of learning itself, as well as how to employ strategies that enable you to learn more efficiently.

After reading this chapter, you should be able to do the following:

- Discover the different types of learning and your learning practices.
- Make informed and effective learning choices in regards to personal engagement and motivation.
- Identify and apply the learning benefits of a growth mindset.
- Evaluate and make informed decisions about learning styles and learning skills.
- Recognize how personality type models influence learning and utilize that knowledge to improve your own learning.
- Identify the impact of outside circumstances on personal learning experiences and develop strategies to compensate for them.
- Recognize the presence of the "hidden curriculum" and how to navigate it.

2.1 The Power to Learn

Estimated completion time: 18 minutes.

Questions to consider:

- What actually happens to me when I learn something?
- Am I aware of different types of learning?
- Do I approach studying or practicing differently depending on the desired outcome?

Welcome to one of the most empowering chapters in this book! While each chapter focuses on showing you clear paths to success as a student, this one deals specifically with what is at the core of being a student: the act of learning.

We humans have been obsessed with how we learn and understand things since ancient times. Because of this, some of our earliest recorded philosophies have tried to explain how we take in information about the world around us, how we acquire new knowledge, and even how we can be certain what we learn is correct. This obsession has produced a large number of theories, ideas, and research into how we learn. There is a great deal of information out there on the subject—some of it is very good, and some of it, while well intentioned, has been a bit misguided.

Because of this obsession with learning, over the centuries, people have continually come up with new ideas about how we acquire knowledge. The result has been that commonly held "facts" about education have been known to change frequently. Often, what was once thought to be the newest, greatest discovery about learning was debunked later on. One well-known example of this is that of corporal punishment. For most of the time formal education has existed in our society, educators truly believed that beating students when they made a mistake actually helped them learn faster. Thankfully, *birching* (striking someone with a rod made from a birch tree) has fallen out of favor in education circles, and our institutions of learning have adopted different approaches. In this chapter, not only will you learn about current learning theories that are backed by neuroscience (something we did not have back in the days of birching), but you will also learn other learning theories that did not turn out to be as effective or as thoroughly researched as once thought. That does not mean those ideas about learning are useless. Instead, in these cases you find ways to separate the valuable parts from the myths to make good learning choices.

> **"Research has shown that one of the most influential aids in learning is an understanding about learning itself."**

What Is the Nature of Learning?

To begin with, it is important to recognize that learning is work. Sometimes it is easy and sometimes it is difficult, but there is always work involved. For many years people made the error of assuming that learning was a passive activity that involved little more than just absorbing information. Learning was thought to be a lot like copying and pasting words in a document; the student's mind was blank and ready for an instructor to teach them facts that they could quickly take in. As it turns out, learning is much more than that. In fact, at its most rudimentary level, it is an actual process that physically changes our brains. Even something as simple as learning the meaning of a new word requires the physical alteration of neurons and the creation of new paths to receptors. These new electrochemical pathways are formed and strengthened as we utilize, practice, or remember what we have learned. If the new skill or knowledge is used in conjunction with other things we have already learned, completely different sections of the brain, our nerves, or our muscles may be tied in as a part of the process. A good example of this would be studying a painting or drawing that depicts a scene from a story or play you are already familiar with. Adding additional connections, memories, and mental associations to things you already know something about expands your knowledge and understanding in a way that cannot be reversed. In essence, it can be said that every time we learn something new we are no longer the same.

In addition to the physical transformation that takes place during learning, there are also a number of other factors that can influence how easy or how difficult learning something can be. While most people would assume that the ease or difficulty would really depend on what is being learned, there are actually several other factors that play a greater role.

In fact, research has shown that one of the most influential factors in learning is a clear understanding about learning itself. This is not to say that you need to become neuroscientists in order to do well in school, but instead, knowing a thing or two about learning and how we learn in general can have strong, positive results for your own learning. This is called *metacognition* (i.e., thinking about thinking).

Some of the benefits to how we learn can be broken down into different areas such as

- attitude and motivation toward learning,
- types of learning,
- methods of learning, and
- your own preferences for learning.

In this chapter you will explore these different areas to better understand how they may influence your own learning, as well as how to make conscious decisions about your own learning process to maximize positive outcomes.

All Learning Is Not the Same

The first, fundamental point to understand about learning is that there are several types of learning. Different kinds of knowledge are learned in different ways. Each of these different types of learning can require different processes that may take place in completely different parts of our brain.

For example, simple memorization is a form of learning that does not always require deeper understanding. Children often learn this way when they memorize poems or verses they recite. An interesting example of this can be found in the music industry, where there have been several hit songs sung in English by vocalists who do not speak English. In these cases, the singers did not truly understand what they were singing, but instead they were taught to memorize the sounds of the words in the proper order.

Figure 2.2 Learning has many levels and forms. For example, collaborative learning and showing your work require different skills and produce different results than reading or notetaking on your own. (Credit: StartUpStockPhotos / Pexels)

Memorizing sounds is a very different type of learning than, say, acquiring a deep understanding of Einstein's general theory of relativity.

Notice in the comparative examples of music and physics that the different levels of learning are being defined by what they allow you to know or do. When classifying learning in this way, people usually agree on six different levels of learning. In this next section we will take a detailed look at each of these.

In the table below, the cells in the left column each contain one of the main levels of learning, categorized by what the learning allows you to do. To the right of each category are the "skill acquired" and a set of real-world examples of what those skills might be as applied to a specific topic. This set of categories is called Bloom's Taxonomy, and it is often used as a guide for educators when they are determining what students should learn within a course.

Category of Learning	Skill acquired	Example 1: Musical ability	Example 2: Historical information on Charles the Bald
Create	Produce new or original work	Compose a piece of music	Write a paper on Charles that draws a new conclusion about his reign
Evaluate	Justify or support an idea or decision	Make critical decisions about the notes that make up a melody—what works, what doesn't, and why	Make arguments that support the idea that Charles was a good ruler
Analyze	Draw connections	Play the specific notes that are found in the key of A	Compare and contrast the historical differences between the reign of Charles and his grandfather, Charlemagne
Apply	Use information in new ways	Use knowledge to play several notes that sound good together	Use the information to write a historical account on the reign of Charles
Understand/ Comprehend	Explain ideas or concepts	Understand the relationship between the musical notes and how to play each on a musical instrument	Explain the historical events that enabled Charles to become Emperor
Remember	Recall facts and basic concepts	Memorize notes on a musical scale	Recall that Charles the Bald was Holy Roman Emperor from 875–877 CE

Table 2.1

A review of the above table shows that actions in the left column (or what you will be able to do with the new knowledge) has a direct influence over what needs to be learned and can even dictate the type of learning approach that is best. For example, *remembering* requires a type of learning that allows the person basic memorization. In the case of Charles the Bald and his reign, it is simply a matter of committing the dates to memory. When it comes to *understanding and comprehension*, being able to explain how Charles came to power requires not only the ability to recall several events, but also for the learner to be able to understand the cause and effect of those events and how they worked together to make Charles emperor. Another example would be the ability to *analyze*. In this particular instance the information learned would not only be about Charles, but also about other rulers, such as Charlemagne. The information would have to be of such a depth that the learner could compare the events and facts about each ruler.

When you engage in any learning activity, take the time to understand what you will do with the knowledge once you have attained it. This can help a great deal when it comes to making decisions on how to go about it. Using flashcards to help memorize angles does not really help you solve problems using geometry formulas. Instead, practicing problem-solving with the actual formulas is a much better approach. The key is to make certain the learning activity fits your needs.

2.2 The Motivated Learner

Estimated completion time: 29 minutes.

Questions to consider:

- How do different types of motivation affect my learning?
- What is resilience and grit?
- How can I apply the Uses and Gratification Theory to make decisions about my learning?
- How do I prevent negative bias from hindering learning?

In this section, you will continue to increase your ability as an informed learner. Here you will explore how much of an influence motivation has on learning, as well as how to use motivation to purposefully take an active role in any learning activity. Rather than passively attempting to absorb new information, you will learn how to make conscious decisions about the methods of learning you will use (based on what you intend to do with the information), how you will select and use learning materials that are appropriate for your needs, and how persistent you will be in the learning activity.

There are three main motivation concepts that have been found to directly relate to learning. Each of these has been proven to mean the difference between success and failure. You will find that each of these is a strong tool that will enable you to engage with learning material in a way that not only suits your needs, but also gives you ownership over your own learning processes.

Resilience and Grit

While much of this chapter will cover very specific aspects about the act of learning, in this section, we will present different information that may at first seem unrelated. Some people would consider it more of a personal outlook than a learning practice, and yet it has a significant influence on the ability to learn.

What we are talking about here is called grit or resilience. Grit can be defined as personal perseverance toward a task or goal. In learning, it can be thought of as a trait that drives a person to keep trying until they succeed. It is not tied to talent or ability, but is simply a tendency to not give up until something is finished or accomplished.

Figure 2.3 U.S. Army veteran and captain of the U.S. Invictus team, Will Reynolds, races to the finish line. (Credit: DoD News / Flickr / Attribution 2.0 Generic (CC-BY 2.0))

The study showed that grit and perseverance were better predictors of academic success and achievement than talent or IQ.

This personality trait was defined as "grit" by the psychologist Angela Duckworth.[1] In a 2007 study Duckworth and colleagues found that individuals with high grit were able to maintain motivation in learning tasks despite failures. The study examined a cross section of learning environments, such as GPA scores in Ivy League universities, dropout rates at West Point, rankings in the National Spelling Bee, and general educational attainment for adults. What the results showed was that grit and perseverance were better predictors of academic success and achievement than talent or IQ.

Applying Grit

The concept of grit is an easy one to dismiss as something taken for granted. In our culture, we have a number of sayings and aphorisms that capture the essence of grit: "If at first you do not succeed, try, try again," or the famous quote by Thomas Edison: "Genius is one percent inspiration, ninety-nine percent perspiration."

The problem is we all understand the concept, but actually applying it takes work. If the task we are trying to complete is a difficult one, it can take a lot of work.

The first step in applying grit is to adopt an attitude that looks directly to the end goal as the only acceptable outcome. With this attitude comes an acceptance that you may not succeed on the first attempt—or the nineteenth attempt. Failed attempts are viewed as merely part of the process and seen as a very useful way to gain knowledge that moves you toward success. An example of this would be studying for an exam. In your first attempt at studying you simply reread the chapters of your textbook covered in the exam. You find that while this reinforces some of the knowledge you have gained, it does not ensure you have all the information you will need to do well on the test. You know that if you simply read the chapters yet again, there is no guarantee you are going to be any more successful. You determine that you need to find a different approach.

---

1 Duckworth, A.L.; Peterson, C.; Matthews, M.D.; Kelly, D.R. (June 2007). "Grit: Perseverance and passion for long-term goals". *Journal of Personality and Social Psychology*. **92** (6): 1087–1101. doi:10.1037/0022-3514.92.6.1087. PMID 17547490.

In other words, your first attempt was not a complete failure, but it did not achieve the end goal, so you try again with a different method.

On your second try, you copy down all of the main points onto a piece of paper using the section headlines from the chapters. After a short break you come back to your list and write down a summary of what you know about each item on your list. This accomplishes two things: first, you are able to immediately spot areas where you need to learn more, and second, you can check your summaries against the text to make certain what you know is correct and adequate. In this example, while you may not have yet achieved complete success, you will have learned what you need to do next.

In true grit fashion, for your next try, you study those items on your list where you found you needed a bit more information, and then you go through your list again. This time you are able to write down summaries of all the important points, and you are confident you have the knowledge you need to do well on the exam. After this, you still do not stop, but instead you change your approach to use other methods that keep what you have learned fresh in your mind.

Keeping Grit in Mind: Grit to GRIT

The concept of grit has been taken beyond the original studies of successful learning. While the concept of grit as a personality trait was originally recognized as something positive in all areas of activity, encouraging grit became very popular in education circles as a way to help students become more successful. In fact, many of those that were first introduced to grit through education have begun applying it to business, professional development, and their personal lives. Using a grit approach and working until the goal is achieved has been found to be very effective in not only academics, but in many other areas.[2]

The *New York Times* best-selling author Paul G. Stoltz has taken grit and turned it into an acronym (GRIT) to help people remember and use the attributes of a grit mindset.[3] His acronym is Growth, Resilience, Instinct, and Tenacity. Each of these elements is explained in the table below.

Growth	Your propensity to seek and consider new ideas, additional alternatives, different approaches, and fresh perspectives
Resilience	Your capacity to respond constructively and ideally make use of all kinds of adversity
Instinct	Your gut-level capacity to pursue the right goals in the best and smartest ways
Tenacity	The degree to which you persist, commit to, stick with, and go after whatever you choose to achieve

Table 2.2 The GRIT acronym as outlined by Paul G. Stoltz

There is one other thing to keep in mind when it comes to applying grit (or GRIT) to college success. The same sort of persevering approach can not only be used for individual learning activities, but can be applied to your entire degree. An attitude of tenacity and "sticking with it" until you reach the desired results works just as

---

2   Neisser, U.; Boodoo, G.; Bouchard, T.J.; Boykin, A.W.; Brody, N.; et al. (1996). "Intelligence: Knowns and unknowns" (PDF). *American Psychologist.* **51** (2): 77–101. doi:10.1037/0003-066x.51.2.77.
3   Stoltz, Paul G. (2014). "GRIT The New Science of What It Takes To Persevere, Flourish, Succeed". ClimbStrong Press

well for graduation as it does for studying for an exam.

How Do You Get Grit?

A quick Internet search will reveal that there are a large number of articles out there on grit and how to get it. While these sources may vary in their lists, most cover about five basic ideas that all touch upon concepts emphasized by Duckworth. What follows is a brief introduction to each. Note that each thing listed here begins with a verb. In other words, it is an activity for you to do and keep doing in order to build grit.

1. Pursue what interests you.

Personal interest is a great motivator! People tend to have more grit when pursuing things that they have developed an interest in.

2. Practice until you can do it, and then keep practicing.

The idea of practicing has been applied to every skill in human experience. The reason everyone seems to be so fixated with practice is because it is effective and there is no "grittier" activity.

3. Find a purpose in what you do.

Purpose is truly the driver for anything we pursue. If you have a strong purpose in any activity, you have reason to persist at it. Think in terms of end goals and why doing something is worth it. Purpose answers the question of "Why should I accomplish this?"

4. Have hope in what you are doing.

Have hope in what you are doing and in how it will make things different for you or others. While this is somewhat related to purpose, it should be viewed as a separate and positive overall outlook in regard to what you are trying to achieve. Hope gives value to purpose. If purpose is the goal, hope is why the goal is worth attaining at all.

5. Surround yourself with gritty people.

Persistence and tenacity tend to rub off on others, and the opposite does as well. As social creatures we often adopt the behaviors we find in the groups we hang out with. If you are surrounded by people that quit early, before achieving their goals, you may find it acceptable to give up early as well. On the other hand, if your peers are all achievers with grit, you will tend to exhibit grit yourself.

APPLICATION

Get a Grit Partner

It is an unfortunate statistic that far too many students who begin college never complete their degree. Over the years a tremendous amount of research has gone into why some students succeed while others do not. After reading about grit, you will probably not be surprised to learn that the research has shown it to not only be a major contributor of learning but to be one of the strongest factors contributing to student graduation.

While that may seem obvious since, by definition, grit is a tendency to keep going until you reach your goal, there was something very significant that turned up in the details of a study conducted by American College Testing (also known as ACT). ACT is a nonprofit organization that administers the college admissions test by the same name, and they have been looking at over 50 years of student persistence data to figure out why some students complete college while others do not. What they have found is that the probability a student will stay in college is tied directly to social connections.[4] In other words, students that found someone they connected with and that provided a sense of accountability dramatically increased their grit. It did not matter if the person was another student, an instructor, or someone else. What did matter is that they felt a strong motivation to keep working, even when their college experience was at its most difficult. It has been surmised that from a psychological perspective, the extra grit comes from not wanting to disappoint the person they have connected with. Regardless of the reason, the data show that having a grit partner is one of the most effective ways to statistically increase your chances of graduation.

A grit partner does not have to be a formal relationship. Your partner can simply be a classmate—someone that you can talk with. It can be an instructor you admire or someone else that you establish a connection with. It can even be a family member who will encourage you—someone you do not want to disappoint. What you are looking for is someone who will help motivate you, either by their example or by their willingness to give you a pep talk when you need it. The key is that it is someone you respect and who will encourage you to do well in school.

Right now, think about someone who could be your grit partner. Keep in mind that you may not have the same grit partner throughout your entire college experience. You may begin with another classmate but later find that a school staff member steps into the role. Later, as you near graduation, you may find that your favorite instructor motivates you more to do well in school than anyone else. Regardless, the importance of finding the social connection that helps your grit is important.

Uses and Gratification Theory and Learning

In the middle of the last century, experts held some odd beliefs that we might find exceptionally strange in our present age. For example, many scholars were convinced that not only was learning a passive activity, but that mass media such as movies, television, and newspapers held significant control over us as individuals. The thinking at that time was that we were helpless to think for ourselves or make choices about learning or the media we consumed. The idea was that we just simply ingested information fed to us and we were almost completely manipulated by it.

What changed this way of thinking was a significant study on audience motivations for watching different political television programs.[5] The study found that not only did people make decisions about what information they consumed, but they also had preferences in content and how it was delivered. In other words, people were active in their choices about information. What is more important is that the research began to show that our own needs, goals, and personal opinions are bigger drivers for our choices in

---

4   King, David R., NduM, Edwin, Can Psychosocial Factors Predict First-to Second Year College Retention Above and Beyond Standard Variables, ACT (2017) https://www.act.org/content/dam/act/unsecured/documents/R1656-psychosocial-factors-retention-2017-12.pdf
5   Blumler, J. G., & McQuail, D. (1969). *Television in politics: Its uses and influence*. University of Chicago Press.

information than anything else. This gave rise to what became known as the Uses and Gratification Theory (UGT).

Figure 2.4 Concept maps, or idea clusters, are used to gather and connect ideas. The exercise of creating, recreating, and improving them can be an excellent way to build and internalize a deeper knowledge of subjects. (Credit: Johnny Goldstien / Flickr / Attribution 2.0 Generic (CC-BY 2.0))

At first, personal choices about television programs might seem a strange topic for a chapter on learning, but if you think about it, learning at its simplest is the consumption of information to meet a specific need. You choose to learn something so you can attain certain goals. This makes education and UGT a natural fit.

Applying UGT to education is a *learner-centered* approach that focuses on helping you take control of how and what you learn. Not only that, but it gives you a framework as an informed learner and allows you to choose information and learning activities with the end results in mind. The next section examines UGT a little more closely and shows how it can be directly applied to learning.

The Uses and Gratification Model

The Uses and Gratification model is how people are thought to react according to UGT. It considers individual behavior and motivation as the primary driver for media consumption. In education this means that the needs of the learner are what determine the interaction with learning content such as textbooks, lectures, and other information sources. Since any educational program is essentially content and delivery (the same as with any media), the Uses and Gratification model can be applied to meet student needs, student satisfaction, and student academic success. This is something that is not recognized in many other learning theories since they begin with the premise that it is learning content and how it is delivered that influences the learner more than the learner's own wants and expectations.

The main assumption of the Uses and Gratification model is that media consumers will seek out and return to specific media sources based on a personal need. For learners this is exceptionally useful since it gives an insight and the ability to positively influence their own motivations, expectations, and the perceived value of their education.

Figure 2.5 The Uses and Gratification model indicates that people will actively seek out and integrate specific media into their lives. (Credit: Garry Knight / Flickr / Attribution 2.0 Generic (CC-BY 2.0))

If you understand the key concepts of the Uses and Gratification model, you can make informed decisions about your own learning: how you learn, which materials you use to learn, and what motivates you to learn. An illustration of this was found in the example given in the previous section on grit. There, a series of exam study activities were presented—first reading the appropriate chapters, then making a list of chapter concepts and reviewing what was known, then returning to learn the information needed to fill the gaps. Each activity was chosen by the learner based on how well it fit their needs to help reach the goal of doing well on an exam.

Here we should offer a brief word of caution about being wary when choosing materials and media. There is a great deal of misleading and inaccurate information presented via the Internet and social media. Making informed decisions about your learning and the material you consume includes checking sources and avoiding information that is not credible.

> **"We are able to consciously make learning choices based on our own identified needs and what we hope to gain by that learning."**

In his book *Key Themes in Media Theory*,[6] Dan Laughey presents the UGT model according to its original authors as a single sentence that divides each area of influence into the following concerns:

1. Social and psychological origins of …
2. needs, which generate …
3. expectations of …
4. the mass media or other sources, which lead to …
5. differential patterns of media exposure, resulting in …
6. needs gratification and …
7. other unintended consequences.

Taken as a list or a single sentence, this can be a bit overwhelming to digest. There are many things being said

---

6   Dan Laughey, (2007). Key Themes in Media Theory, Open University Press

at the same time, and they may not all be immediately clear. To better understand what each of the "areas of concern" are and how they can impact learning, each has been separated and explained in the table below.

Area of Concern	What it means for you	How it applies to learning	Real-world example
1. Social and psychological origins of ...	Your motivations, not only as a student but as a person, and both the social and psychological factors that influence you	This can be everything from the original motivation behind enrolling in school in the first place, down to more specific goals like why you want to learn to write and communicate well.	A drive to be self-supporting and to take on a productive role in society.
2. needs, which generate ...	Better job, increased income, satisfying career, prestige	This can include the area of study you select and the school you choose to attend.	Pursuing a degree to seek a career in a field you enjoy.
3. expectations of ...	Expectation and perception (preconceived and continuing) of educational material	What you expect to learn to fulfill goals and meet needs.	Understanding what you need to accomplish the smaller goals. An example would be "study for an exam."
4. the mass media or other sources, which lead to...	The content and learning activities of the program	Selection of content aimed at fulfilling needs. Results are student satisfaction, perceived value, and continued enrollment.	Choosing which learning activities to use (e.g., texts, watch videos, research alternative content, etc.).
5. differential patterns of media exposure, resulting in ...	Frequency and level of participation	How you engage with learning activities and how often. Results are student satisfaction and perceived value, and continued enrollment.	When, how often, and how much time you spend in learning activities.

Table 2.3

Area of Concern	What it means for you	How it applies to learning	Real-world example
6. needs gratification and ...	Better job, increased income, satisfying career, prestige, more immediate goals like pass an exam, earn a good grade, etc.	Needs fulfillment and completion of goals.	Learning activities that meet your learning needs, including fulfillment of your original goals.
7. other unintended consequences.	Increased skills and knowledge, entertainment, social involvement and networking	Causes positive loop-back into 4, 5, and 6, reinforcing those positive outcomes.	Things you learn beyond your initial goals.

Table 2.3

What to Do with UGT

On the surface, UGT may seem overly complex, but this is due to its attempt to capture everything that influences how and why we take in information. At this point in your understanding, the main thing to focus on is the bigger idea that our motivations, our end goals, and our expectations are what drive us to learn. If we are aware of these motivations, we can use them to make influential decisions about what we learn and how we learn.

One of the things that will become apparent as you continue reading this chapter and doing the included activities is that all of it fits within the UGT model. Everything about learning styles, your own attitude about learning, how you prefer to learn, and what you get out of it are covered in UGT. Being familiar with it gives you a way to identify and apply everything else you will learn about learning. As you continue in this chapter, rather than looking at each topic as a stand-alone idea, think about where each fits in the Uses and Gratification model. Does it influence your motivations, or does it help you make decisions about the way you learn? This way UGT can provide a way for you to see the value and how to apply everything you learn from this point forward and for every learning experience along the way.

If you were going to define how UGT applies to learning with a few quick statements, it would look something like this:

UGT asks:

- What is it that motivates you to learn something?
- What need does it fulfill?
- What do you expect to have happen with certain learning activities?
- How can you choose the right learning activities to better ensure you meet your needs and expectations?
- What other things might result from your choices?

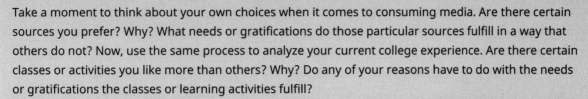

ANALYSIS QUESTION

Take a moment to think about your own choices when it comes to consuming media. Are there certain sources you prefer? Why? What needs or gratifications do those particular sources fulfill in a way that others do not? Now, use the same process to analyze your current college experience. Are there certain classes or activities you like more than others? Why? Do any of your reasons have to do with the needs or gratifications the classes or learning activities fulfill?

After you have answered those questions, you can always step beyond mere analysis and determine what you could change to make the classes or activities you enjoy less better fulfill your needs.

Combating Negative Bias

In addition to being a motivated learner through the use of grit and UGT, there is a third natural psychological tendency you should be aware of. It is a tendency that you should guard against. Ignoring the fact that it exists can not only adversely affect learning, but it can set up roadblocks that may prevent you from achieving many goals. This tendency is called *negative bias*.

Negative bias is the psychological trait of focusing on the negative aspects of a situation rather than the positive. An example of this in a learning environment would be earning a 95 percent score on an assignment but obsessing over the 5 percent of the points that were missed. Another example would be worrying and thinking negative thoughts about yourself over a handful of courses where you did not do as well as in others—so much so that you begin to doubt your abilities altogether.

Figure 2.6 Some level of worry and concern is natural, but an overwhelming amount of negative thoughts about yourself, including doubt in your abilities and place in school, can impede your learning and stifle your success. You can develop strategies to recognize and overcome these feelings. (Credit: Inzmam Kahn / Pexels)

Unfortunately, this is a human tendency that can often overwhelm a student. As a pure survival mechanism it does have its usefulness in that it reminds us to be wary of behaviors that can result in undesirable outcomes.

Imagine that as a child playing outside, you have seen dozens if not hundreds of bees over the years. But once, out of all those other times, you were stung by a single bee. Now, every time you see a bee you recall the sting, and you now have a negative bias toward bees in general. Whenever possible you avoid bees altogether.

It is easy to see how this psychological system could be beneficial in those types of situations, but it can be a hindrance in learning since a large part of the learning process often involves failure on early attempts. Recognizing this is a key to overcoming negative bias. Another way to combat negative bias is to purposefully focus on successes and to acknowledge earlier attempts that fail as just a part of the learning.

What follows are a few methods for overcoming negative bias and negative self-talk. Each focuses on being aware of any negative attitude or emphasizing the positive aspects in a situation.

- **Be aware of any negative bias.** Keep an eye out for any time you find yourself focusing on some negative aspect, whether toward your own abilities or on some specific situation. Whenever you recognize that you are exhibiting a negative bias toward something, stop and look for the positive parts of the experience. Think back to what you have learned about grit, how any lack of success is only temporary, and what you have learned that gets you closer to your goal.
- **Focus on the positive before you begin.** While reversing the impact of negative bias on your learning is helpful, it can be even more useful to prevent it in the first place. One way to do this is to look for the positives before you begin a task. An example of this would be receiving early feedback for an assignment you are working on. To accomplish this, you can often ask your instructor or one of your classmates to look over your work and provide some informal comments. If the feedback is positive then you know you are on the right track. That is useful information. If the feedback seems to indicate that you need to make a number of corrections and adjustments, then that is even more valuable information, and you can use it to greatly improve the assignment for a much better final grade. In either case, accurate feedback is what you really want most, and both outcomes are positive for you.
- **Keep a gratitude and accomplishment journal.** Again, the tendency to recall and overemphasize the negative instances while ignoring or forgetting about the positive outcomes is the nature of negative bias. Sometimes we need a little help remembering the positives, and we can prompt our memories by keeping a journal. Just as in a diary, the idea is to keep a flowing record of the positive things that happen, the lessons you learned from instances that were "less than successful," and all accomplishments you make toward learning. In your journal you can write or paste anything that you appreciated or that has positive outcomes. Whenever you are not feeling up to a challenge or when negative bias is starting to wear on you, you can look over your journal to remind yourself of previous accomplishments in the face of adversity.

ANALYSIS QUESTION

Building the Foundation

In this section you read about three major factors that contribute to your motivation as a learner: grit and perseverance, your own motivations for learning (UGT), and the pitfalls of negative bias. Now it is time to do a little self-analysis and reflection.

Which of these three areas do you feel strongest in? Are you a person that naturally has grit, or do you better understand your own motivations for learning (using UGT)? Do you struggle with negativity bias, or is it something that you rarely have to deal with?

Determine in which of these areas you are strongest, and think about what things make you so strong. Is it a positive attitude (you always see the glass as half full as opposed to half empty), or do you know exactly why you are in college and exactly what you expect to learn?

After you have analyzed your strongest area, then do the same for the two weaker ones. What makes you susceptible to challenges in these areas? Do you have a difficult time sticking with things or possibly focus too much on the negative? Look back at the sections on your two weakest areas, and put together a plan for overcoming them. For each one, choose a behavior you intend to change and think of some way you will change it.

2.3 It's All in the Mindset

Estimated completion time: 14 minutes.

Questions to consider:

- What is a growth mindset, and how does it affect my learning?
- What are performance goals versus learning goals?

In the previous sections of this chapter you have focused on a number of concepts and models about learning. One of the things they all have in common is that they utilize different approaches to education by presenting new ways to think about learning. In each of these, the common element has been a better understanding of yourself as a learner and how to apply what you know about yourself to your own learning experience. If you were to distill all that you have learned in this chapter so far down to a single factor, it would be about using your mindset to your best advantage. In this next section, you will examine how all of this works in a broader sense by learning about the significance of certain mindsets and how they can hinder or promote your own learning efforts.

Figure 2.7 Many fields of study and work create intersections of growth and fixed mindset. People may feel great ability to grow and learn in some areas, like art and communication, but feel more limited in others, such as planning and financials. Recognizing these intersections will help you approach new topics and tasks. (Credit: mentatdgt / Pexels)

Performance vs. Learning Goals

As you have discovered in this chapter, much of our ability to learn is governed by our motivations and goals. What has not yet been covered in detail has been how sometimes hidden goals or mindsets can impact the learning process. In truth, we all have goals that we might not be fully aware of, or if we are aware of them, we might not understand how they help or restrict our ability to learn. An illustration of this can be seen in a comparison of a student that has *performance*-based goals with a student that has *learning*-based goals.

If you are a student with strict performance goals, your primary psychological concern might be to appear intelligent to others. At first, this might not seem to be a bad thing for college, but it can truly limit your ability to move forward in your own learning. Instead, you would tend to play it safe without even realizing it. For example, a student who is strictly performance-goal-oriented will often only says things in a classroom discussion when they think it will make them look knowledgeable to the instructor or their classmates. For example, a performance-oriented student might ask a question that she knows is beyond the topic being covered (e.g., asking about the economics of Japanese whaling while discussing the book *Moby Dick* in an American literature course). Rarely will they ask a question in class because they actually do not understand a concept. Instead they will ask questions that make them look intelligent to others or in an effort to "stump the teacher." When they do finally ask an honest question, it may be because they are more afraid that their lack of understanding will result in a poor performance on an exam rather than simply wanting to learn.

If you are a student who is driven by learning goals, your interactions in classroom discussions are usually quite different. You see the opportunity to share ideas and ask questions as a way to gain knowledge quickly. In a classroom discussion you can ask for clarification immediately if you don't quite understand what is being discussed. If you are a person guided by learning goals, you are less worried about what others think since you are there to learn and you see that as the most important goal.

Another example where the difference between the two mindsets is clear can be found in assignments and other coursework. If you are a student who is more concerned about performance, you may avoid work that is challenging. You will take the "easy A" route by relying on what you already know. You will not step out of your comfort zone because your psychological goals are based on approval of your performance instead of being motivated by learning.

This is very different from a student with a learning-based psychology. If you are a student who is motivated by learning goals, you may actively seek challenging assignments, and you will put a great deal of effort into using the assignment to expand on what you already know. While getting a good grade is important to you, what is even more important is the learning itself.

If you find that you sometimes lean toward performance-based goals, do not feel discouraged. Many of the best students tend to initially focus on performance until they begin to see the ways it can restrict their learning. The key to switching to learning-based goals is often simply a matter of first recognizing the difference and seeing how making a change can positively impact your own learning.

What follows in this section is a more in-depth look at the difference between performance- and learning-based goals. This is followed by an exercise that will give you the opportunity to identify, analyze, and determine a positive course of action in a situation where you believe you could improve in this area.

WHAT STUDENTS SAY

1. In the past, did you feel like you had control over your own learning?
   a. No. Someone has always dictated how and what I learned.
   b. Yes. I always look for ways to take control of what and how I learned.
   c. I am uncertain. I never thought about it before.
2. Have you ever heard of learning styles or do you know your own learning style?
   a. No. I have never heard of learning styles.
   b. Yes. I have heard of learning styles and know my own.
   c. Yes. I have heard of learning styles, but I don't think they're accurate or relate to me.
3. Which factors other than intelligence do you think have the greatest influence on learning?
   a. Motivation
   b. Perseverance
   c. Understanding how I learn
   d. Good teachers and support

You can also take the anonymous What Students Say (https://openstax.org/l/collegesurvey1-5) surveys to add your voice to this textbook. Your responses will be included in updates.

Students offered their views on these questions, and the results are displayed in the graphs below.

In the past, did you feel like you had control over your own learning?

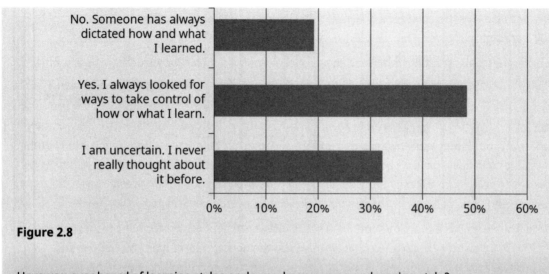

Figure 2.8

Have you ever heard of learning styles or do you know your own learning style?

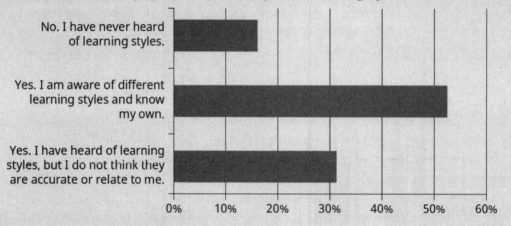

Figure 2.9

Which factors other than intelligence do you think have the greatest influence on learning?

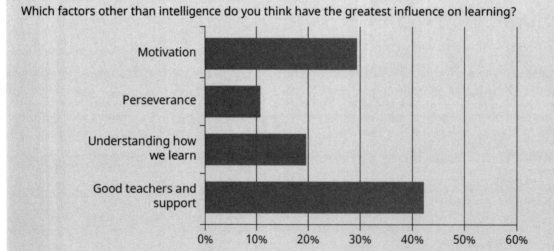

Figure 2.10

Fixed vs. Growth Mindset

The research-based model of these two mindsets and their influence on learning was presented in 1988 by Carol Dweck.[7] In Dr. Dweck's work, she determined that a student's perception about their own learning accompanied by a broader goal of learning had a significant influence on their ability to overcome challenges and grow in knowledge and ability. This has become known as the Fixed vs. Growth Mindset model. In this model, the *performance*-goal-oriented student is represented by the *fixed* mindset, while the *learning*-goal-oriented student is represented by the *growth* mindset.

In the following graphic, based on Dr. Dweck's research, you can see how many of the components associated with learning are impacted by these two mindsets.

---

7   Dweck, C.S. & Leggett, E.L. (1988). A Social-Cognitive Approach to Motivation and Personality

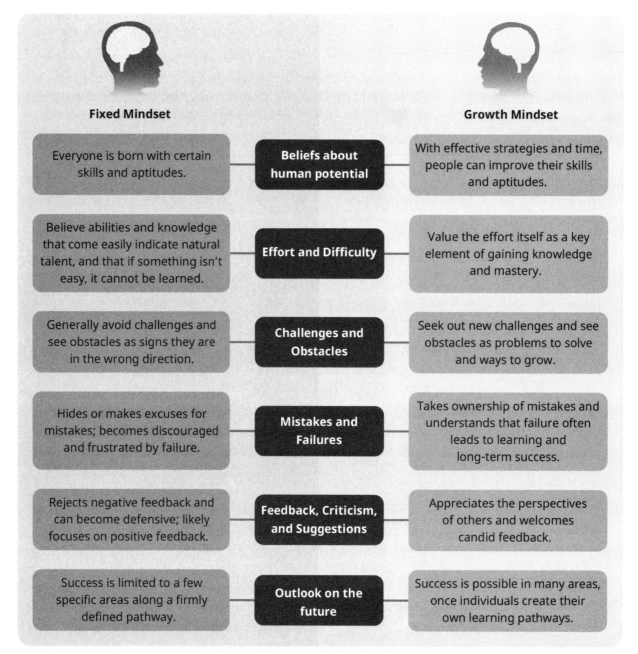

Figure 2.11 The differences between fixed and growth mindset are clear when aligned to key elements of learning and personality. (Credit: Based on work by Dr. Carol Dweck)

The Growth Mindset and Lessons About Failing

Something you may have noticed is that a growth mindset would tend to give a learner grit and persistence. If you had learning as your major goal, you would normally keep trying to attain that goal even if it took you multiple attempts. Not only that, but if you learned a little bit more with each try you would see each attempt as a success, even if you had not achieved complete mastery of whatever it was you were working to learn.

With that in mind, it should come as no surprise that Dr. Dweck found that those people who believed their abilities could change through learning (growth vs. a fixed mindset) readily accepted learning challenges and persisted despite early failures.

Improving Your Ability to Learn

As strange as it may seem, research into fixed vs. growth mindsets has shown that if you believe you can learn something new, you greatly improve your ability to learn. At first, this may seem like the sort of feel-good advice we often encounter in social media posts or quotes that are intended to inspire or motivate us (e.g., *believe in yourself!*), but in looking at the differences outlined between a fixed and a growth mindset, you can see how each part of the growth mindset path would increase your probability of success when it came to learning.

ACTIVITY

Very few people have a strict fixed or growth mindset all of the time. Often we tend to lean one way or another in certain situations. For example, a person trying to improve their ability in a sport they enjoy may exhibit all of the growth mindset traits and characteristics, but they find themselves blocked in a fixed mindset when they try to learn something in another area like computer programming or arithmetic.

In this exercise, do a little self-analysis and think of some areas where you may find yourself hindered by a fixed mindset. Using the outline presented below, in the far right column, write down how you can change your own behavior for each of the parts of the learning process. What will you do to move from a fixed to a growth mindset? For example, say you were trying to learn to play a musical instrument. In the *Challenges* row, you might pursue a growth path by trying to play increasingly more difficult songs rather than sticking to the easy ones you have already mastered. In the *Criticism* row, you might take someone's comment about a weakness in timing as a motivation for you to practice with a metronome. For *Success of others* you could take inspiration from a famous musician that is considered a master and study their techniques.

Whatever it is that you decide you want to use for your analysis, apply each of the Growth characteristics to determine a course of action to improve.

Parts of the learning process	Growth characteristic	What will you do to adopt a growth mindset?
Challenges	Embraces challenges	
Obstacles	Persists despite setbacks	
Effort	Sees effort as a path to success	
Criticism	Learns from criticism	
Success of Others	Finds learning and inspiration in the success of others	

Table 2.4

2.4 Learning Styles

Estimated completion time: 24 minutes.

Questions to consider:

- What are learning styles, and do they really work?
- How do I take advantage of learning styles in a way that works for me?

- How can I combine learning styles for better outcomes?
- What opportunities and resources are available for students with disabilities?

Several decades ago, a new way of thinking about learning became very prominent in education. It was based on the concept that each person has a preferred way to learn. It was thought that these preferences had to do with each person's natural tendencies toward one of their senses. The idea was that learning might be easier if a student sought out content that was specifically oriented to their favored sense. For example, it was thought that a student who preferred to learn visually would respond better to pictures and diagrams.

Over the years there were many variations on the basic idea, but one of the most popular theories was known as the VAK model. VAK was an acronym for the three types of learning, each linked to one of the basic senses thought to be used by students: visual, aural, and kinesthetic. What follows is an outline of each of these and the preferred method.

- **Visual:** The student prefers pictures, images, and the graphic display of information to learn. An example would be looking at an illustration that showed how to do something.
- **Aural:** The student prefers sound as a way to learn. Examples would be listening to a lecture or a podcast.
- **Kinesthetic:** The student prefers using their body, hands, and sense of touch. An example would be doing something physical, such as examining an object rather than reading about it or looking at an illustration.

The Truth about Learning Styles

In many ways these ideas about learning styles made some sense. Because of this, educators encouraged students to find out about their own learning styles. They developed tests and other techniques to help students determine which particular sense they preferred to use for learning, and in some cases learning materials were produced in multiple ways that focused on each of the different senses. That way, each individual learner could participate in learning activities that were tailored to their specific preferences.

While it initially seemed that dividing everyone by learning styles provided a leap forward in education, continued research began to show that the fixation on this new model might not have been as effective as it was once thought. In fact, in some cases, the way learning styles were actually being used created roadblocks to learning. This was because the popularization of this new idea brought on a rush to use learning styles in ways that failed to take into account several important aspects that are listed below:

- A person does not always prefer the same learning style all the time or for each situation. For example, some learners might enjoy lectures during the day but prefer reading in the evenings. Or they may prefer looking at diagrams when learning about mechanics but prefer reading for history topics.
- There are more preferences involved in learning than just the three that became popular. These other preferences can become nearly impossible to make use of within certain styles. For example, some prefer to learn in a more social environment that includes interaction with other learners. Reading can be difficult or restrictive as a group effort. Recognized learning styles beyond the original three include: **social** (preferring to learn as a part of group activity), **solitary** (preferring to learn alone or using self-study), or **logical** (preferring to use logic, reasoning, etc.).
- Students that thought they were limited to a single preferred learning style found themselves convinced that they could not do as well with content that was presented in a way that differed from their style.[8] For example, a student that had identified as a visual learner might feel they were at a significant disadvantage when listening to a lecture. Sometimes they even believed they had an even greater

---

8 Harold Pashler, Mark McDaniel, Doug Rohrer and Robert Bjork. *Learning Styles: Concepts and Evidence*. Psychological Science in the Public Interest, Vol. 9, No. 3 (December 2008).

impairment that prevented them from learning that way at all.
- Some forms of learning are extremely difficult in activities delivered in one style or another. Subjects like computer programming would be almost impossible to learn using an aural learning style. And, while it is possible to read about a subject such as how to swing a bat or how to do a medical procedure, actually applying that knowledge in a learning environment is difficult if the subject is something that requires a physical skill.

Knowing and Taking Advantage of Learning Styles in a Way That Works for You

The problem with relying on learning styles comes from thinking that just one defines your needs. Coupling what you know about learning styles with what you know about UGT can make a difference in your own learning. Rather than being constrained by a single learning style, or limiting your activities to a certain kind of media, you may choose media that best fit your needs for what you are trying to learn at a particular time.

Following are a couple of ways you might combine your learning style preference with a given learning situation:

- You are trying to learn how to build something but find the written instructions confusing so you watch a video online that shows someone building the same thing.
- You have a long commute on the bus but reading while riding makes you dizzy. You choose an aural solution by listening to pre-recorded podcasts or a mobile device that reads your texts out loud.

These examples show that by recognizing and understanding what different learning styles have to offer, you can use the techniques that are best suited for you and that work best under the circumstances of the moment. You may also find yourself using two learning styles at the same time - as when you watch a live demonstration or video in which a person shows you how to do something while verbally explaining what you are being shown. This helps to reinforce the learning as it utilizes different aspects of your thinking. Using learning styles in an informed way can improve both the speed and the quality of your learning.

GET CONNECTED

Finding content related to a subject or topic can be relatively easy, but you must use caution and rely on reputable sources. Relatively little of the material on the Web provides a way to ensure accuracy or balance.

Below are descriptions of common informational sites with varying degrees of reliability:

- Khan Academy (https://www.khanacademy.org) : This site is full of useful tutorials and videos on a wide range of subjects.
- Wikipedia (https://www.wikipedia.org) : Wikipedia is often frowned upon in some academic circles, because review of its content takes place *after* publication, potentially resulting in inaccurate or misleading information being available. But Wikipedia can provide a brief overview of a topic, and its lists of references is often quite extensive. You probably shouldn't rely Wikipedia as your only source, but it can be useful.
- Government website:. Most items that governments administer are referenced on informational websites. In the United States, these include educational statistics (https://nces.ed.gov) , economic

data (https://fred.stlouisfed.org) , health information (https://www.nih.gov) , and many other topics.

When choosing alternate content, it is imperative to compare it to the content that is being provided to you as a part of your course. If the alternate content does not line up, you should view it with a healthy skepticism. In those cases, it is always a good idea to share the content with your instructor and ask their opinion.

ACTIVITY

In this activity you will try an experiment by combining learning styles to see if it is something that works for you. The experiment will test the example of combining reading/writing and aural learning styles for better memorization.

To begin, you will start with a short segment of numbers. You will read the numbers only one time without saying them aloud. When you are finished, wait 10 seconds and try to remember the numbers in sequence by writing them down.

67914528

After you have finished you will repeat the experiment with a new set of numbers, but this time you will read them aloud, wait 10 seconds, and then see how easy they are to remember. During this part of the experiment you are free to say the numbers in any way you like. For example, the number 8734 could be read as eight-seven-three-four, eighty-seven thirty-four, or any combination you would like.

10387264

Did you find that there was a difference in your ability to memorize a short sequence of numbers for 10 seconds? Even if you were able to remember both, was the example that combined learning styles easier? What about if you had to wait for a full minute before attempting to rewrite the numbers? Would that make a difference?

What about Students with Disabilities?

Students with disabilities are sometimes the most informed when it comes to making decisions about their own learning. They should understand that it is in their best interest to take ownership of their own approach to education, especially when it comes to leveraging resources and opportunities. In this section, you will learn about the laws that regulate education for students with disabilities as well as look at some resources that are available to them.

Just like anyone else, under the law, qualified students with disabilities are entitled to the same education colleges and universities provide to students without disabilities. Even though a particular disability may make attending college more difficult, awareness on the part of the government, learning institutions, and the students themselves has brought about a great deal of change over the years. Now, students with disabilities find that they have available appropriate student services, campus accessibility, and academic resources that can make school attendance and academic success possible.

Due to this increased support and advocacy, colleges have seen an increase of students with disabilities.

According to the National Center for Education Statistics, in 2012, 11.1 percent of the total undergraduate population in the United States was made up of people with disabilities.[9]

The Legal Rights of Students with Disabilities

Section 504 of the Rehabilitation Act of 1973 protects students "with a physical or mental impairment which substantially limits one or more major life activities."[10] Learning definitely falls within the definition of major life activities.

In addition to Section 504, another set of laws that greatly help learners with disabilities is the Americans with Disabilities Act of 1990 (also known as ADA). Both of these acts have been driving forces in making certain that students with disabilities have equal access to higher education, and they have been instrumental in helping educators looking for new ways and resources to provide services that do just that.

What follows is a list of services that schools commonly provide to help students with disabilities. These are often referred to as *ADA accommodations* and are named after the American with Disabilities Act:

- Recordings of class lectures or lecture transcription by in-class note takers
- Text readers or other technologies that can deliver content in another format
- Test or assessment accommodations
- Interpreter services and Braille transcriptions
- Physical access accommodations
- Accommodations of time and due dates

Most colleges will have policies and staff that are designated to help arrange for these types of accommodations. They are often found within the Department of Student Services or in related departments within your college campus. If you are a student with disabilities protected under these acts, it is in your best interest to contact the person responsible for ADA accommodations at your school. Even if you decide that you do not need accommodations, it is a good idea to find out about any services and policies the school has in place.

Organizations

In addition to the accommodations that schools commonly provide, there are also a number of national and local organizations that can provide assistance and advice when it comes to being a student with a disability. If you fit into this category, it is recommended that you make contact with one or more of these organizations in order to find out how they can help. These can be tremendously beneficial resources that offer everything from information and support to simple social connections that can make pursuing a formal education easier.

2.5 Personality Types and Learning

Estimated completion time: 19 minutes.

Questions to consider:

- Is there any connection between personality types and learning?

---

9 U.S. Department of Education, National Center for Education Statistics. (2019). *Digest of Education Statistics, 2017* (2018-070), Chapter 3.
10 U.S. Department of Education. Protecting Students with Disabilities: Frequently Asked Questions. https://www2.ed.gov/about/offices/list/ocr/504faq.html

- Can the Myers-Briggs test be used to identify personality traits and learning styles?
- Is there a real correlation between personality styles and learning?
- What is the impact on learning with work that you enjoy?

Much like learning styles, there have been a number of theories surrounding the idea that different personality types may prefer different kinds of learning. Again, this builds on the original learning style concept that people may have a single preference toward how they learn, and then adds to it that certain personality traits may determine which learning style a person prefers.

Since it has already been determined that learning styles are more effective when selected for the subject being learned rather than the sensory preference of the learner, it might seem foolish to revisit another learning style theory. But, in this case, understanding how personality traits and learning styles are categorized can be useful in making decisions and choices for your own learning activities. In other words, we won't dismiss the theory out of hand without first seeing if there is anything useful in it.

One part of this theory that can be useful is the identification of personality traits that affect your motivation, emotions, and interests toward learning. You have already read a great deal about how these internal characteristics can influence your learning. What knowing about personality traits and learning can do for you is to help you be aware and informed about how these affect you so you can deal with them directly.

Myers-Briggs: Identifying Personality Traits and Styles

The Myers-Briggs system is one of the most popular personality tests, and it is relatively well known. It has seen a great deal of use in the business world with testing seminars and presentations on group dynamics. In fact, it is so popular that you may already be familiar with it and may have taken a test yourself to find out which of the 16 personality types you most favor.

The basic concept of Myers-Briggs is that there are four main traits. These traits are represented by two opposites, seen in the table below.

Extroverted (E)	vs.	Introverted (I)
Intuition (N)	vs.	Sensing (S)
Feeling (F)	vs.	Thinking (T)
Judging (J)	vs.	Perceiving (P)

Table 2.5

It is thought that people generally exhibit one trait or the other in each of these categories, or that they fall along a spectrum between the two opposites. For example, an individual might exhibit both Feeling and Thinking personality traits, but they will favor one more than the other.

Also note that with each of these traits there is a letter in parentheses. The letter is used to represent the specific traits when they are combined to define a personality type (e.g., Extrovert is E and Introvert is I, Intuition is N, etc.). To better understand these, each is briefly explained.

Extroverted (E) vs. Introverted (I): In the Myers-Briggs system, the traits of Extroverted and Introverted are somewhat different from the more common interpretations of the two words. The definition is more about an individual's attitude, interests, and motivation. The extrovert is primarily motivated by the outside world and social interaction, while the introvert is often more motivated by things that are internal to them—things like their own interests.

Intuition (N) vs. Sensing (S): This personality trait is classified as a preference toward one way of perceiving or another. It is concerned with how people tend to arrive at conclusions. A person on the intuitive end of the spectrum often perceives things in broader categories. A part of their process for "knowing things" is internal and is often described as *having a hunch* or *a gut feeling*. This is opposed to the preferred method of a sensing person, who often looks to direct observation as a means of perception. They prefer to arrive at a conclusion by details and facts, or by testing something with their senses.

Feeling (F) vs. Thinking (T): This trait is considered a decision-making process over the information gathered through the perception (N versus S). People that find themselves more on the Feeling end of the spectrum tend to respond based on their feelings and empathy. Examples of this would be conclusions about what is good versus bad or right versus wrong based on how they feel things should be. The Thinking person, on the other hand, arrives at opinions based on reason and logic. For them, feeling has little to do with it.

Judging (J) vs. Perceiving (P): This category can be thought of as a personal preference for using either the Feeling versus Thinking (decision-making) or the Intuition versus Sensing (perceiving) when forming opinions about the outside world. A person that leans toward the Judging side of the spectrum approaches things in a structured way—usually using Sensing and Thinking traits. The Perceiving person often thinks of structure as somewhat inhibiting. They tend to make more use of Intuition and Feeling in their approach to life.

The Impact of Personality Styles on Learning

To find out their own personality traits and learning styles, a person takes an approved Myers-Briggs test, which consists of a series of questions that help pinpoint their preferences. These preferences are then arranged in order to build a profile using each of the four categories.

For example, a person that answered questions in a way that favored Extroverted tendencies along with a preference toward Sensing, Thinking, and Judging would be designated as ESTJ personality type. Another person that tended more toward answers that aligned with Intuitive traits than Sensing traits would fall into the ENTJ category.

ESTJ	ISTJ	ENTJ	INTJ
ESTP	ISTP	ENTP	INTP
ESFJ	ISFJ	ENFJ	INFJ
ESFP	ISFP	ENFP	INFP

Table 2.6 Personality Types

As with other learning style models, Myers-Briggs has received a good deal of criticism based on the artificial restrictions and impairments it tends to suggest. Additionally, the claim that each person has a permanent and unwavering preference towards personality traits and learning styles has not turned out to be as concrete as it was once thought. This has been demonstrated by people taking tests like the Myers-Briggs a few weeks apart and getting different results based on their personal preferences at that time.

What this means is that, just as with the VAK and other learning style models, you should not constrain your own learning activities based on a predetermined model. Neither should you think of yourself as being limited to one set of preferences. Instead, different types of learning and different preferences can better fit your needs at different times. This and how to best apply the idea of personality types influencing learning styles is explained in the next section.

How to Use Personality Type Learning Styles

To recap, personality tests such as the Myers-Briggs can provide a great deal of insight into personal choices toward learning. Unfortunately, many people interpret them as being something that defines them as both a person and a learner. They tell themselves things like "I am an ESTJ, so I am only at my best when I learn a certain way" or "I rely on intuition, so a science course is not for me!" They limit themselves instead of understanding that while they may have particular preferences under a given situation, all of the different categories are open to them and can be put to good use.

What is important to know is that these sorts of models can serve you better as a way to think about learning. They can help you make decisions about how you will go about learning in a way that best suits your needs and goals for that particular task. As an example of how to do this, what follows are several different approaches to learning about the play *Julius Caesar* by William Shakespeare. In each case, Myers-Briggs categories are used to define what sort of activities would help you meet your desired learning goals.

- Your assignment is to read *Julius Caesar* as a work of English literature. Your learning goal is not just to read the play, but to be able to compare it to other, more modern works of literature. To do that, it would be beneficial to use a more *introverted* approach so that you can think about the influences that may have affected each author. You might also want to focus on a *thinking* learning style when examining and comparing the use of words and language in the 17th-century piece to more modern writing styles.
- Your use of learning style approaches would be very different if you were assigned to actually perform a scene from *Julius Caesar* as a part of a class. In this case, it would be better for you to rely on an *extroverted* attitude since you will be more concerned with audience reaction than your own inner thoughts about the work. And since one of your goals would be to create a believable character for the audience, you would want to base decisions on the gestures you might make during the performance through *feeling* so that you have empathy with the character and are convincing in your portrayal.
- A third, completely different assignment, such as examining the play *Julius Caesar* as a political commentary on English society during the reign of Queen Elizabeth, would have very different goals and therefore should be approached using different learning styles. In this example, you might want to begin by using a *sensing* approach to gather facts about what was happening politically in that time period and then switch to *intuition* for insight into the motivations of Shakespeare and the attitudes of his audience in England at that time.

As you can see in the examples above, the choices about each of the different approaches can be entirely dictated by what you will be doing with the learning. Because of this, being aware of the personality type learning styles you have available to you can make a tremendous difference in both how you go about it and your success.

> **ANALYSIS QUESTION**
>
> To find out more about personality types and learning styles, you can take an online personality test to experience it yourself. Several companies charge for this service, but there are a few that offer tests online for free. Click here for one such free online personality test. (https://openstax.org/l/jungtypology)
>
> Again, keep in mind that your results can change under different circumstances, but doing it for the first time will give you a place to start.
>
> Afterwards you can click here to read more about the connections between personality and learning styles. (https://openstax.org/l/learningstyles) There you can look up the results from your personality test and see how much you think it aligns with your learning style preferences. Again, this exercise is not to determine your ultimate learning style, but it is to give you a deeper understanding of what is behind the concept of connecting personality types to learning.

The Impact of Work You Enjoy

For a final word on personality types and learning styles, there is no denying that there are going to be different approaches you enjoy more than others. While you do have the ability to use each of the different approaches to meet the goals of your learning activities, some will come more easily for you in certain situations and some will be more pleasurable. As most people do, you will probably find that your work is actually better when you are doing things you like to do. Because of this, it is to your advantage to recognize your preferred methods of learning and to make use of them whenever possible. As discussed elsewhere in this book, in college you will often have opportunities to make decisions about the assignments you complete. In many instances, your instructor may allow for some creativity in what you do and in the finished product. When those opportunities arise, you have everything to gain by taking a path that will allow you to employ preferences you enjoy most. An example of this might be an assignment that requires you to give a presentation on a novel you read for class. In such a case, you might have the freedom to focus your presentation on something that interests you more and better aligns with how you like to learn. It might be more enjoyable for you to present a study on each of the characters in the book and how they relate to each other, or you might be more interested in doing a presentation on the historical accuracy of the book and the background research the author put into writing it.

Whatever the case, discuss your ideas with your instructor to make certain they will both meet the criteria of the assignment and fulfill the learning goals of the activity. There is a great potential for benefit in talking with your instructors when you have ideas about how you can personalize assignments or explore areas of the subject that interest you. In fact, it is a great practice to ask your instructors for guidance and recommendations and, above all, to demonstrate to them that you are taking a direct interest in your own learning. There is never any downside to talking with your instructors about your learning.

2.6 Applying What You Know about Learning

Estimated completion time: 17 minutes.

Questions to consider:

- How can I apply what I now know to learning?
- How can I make decisions about my own learning?
- Will doing so be different from what I have experienced before?

Another useful part of being an informed learner is recognizing that as a college student you will have many choices when it comes to learning. Looking back at the Uses and Gratification model, you'll discover that your motivations as well as your choices in how you interact with learning activities can make a significant difference in not only what you learn, but how you learn. By being aware of a few learning theories, students can take initiative and tailor their own learning so that it best benefits them and meets their main needs.

STUDENT PROFILE

"My seating choice significantly affects my learning. Sitting at a desk where the professor's voice can be heard clearly helps me better understand the subject; and ensuring I have a clear view helps me take notes. Therefore, sitting in the front of the classroom should be a "go to" strategy while attending college. It will keep you focused and attentive throughout the lecture. Also, sitting towards the front of the classroom limits the tendency to be on check my phone."

—**Luis Angel Ochoa**, Westchester Community College

Making Decisions about Your Own Learning

As a learner, the kinds of materials, study activities, and assignments that work best for you will derive from your own experiences and needs (needs that are both short-term as well as those that fulfill long-term goals). In order to make your learning better suited to meet these needs, you can use the knowledge you have gained about UGT and other learning theories to make decisions concerning your own learning. These decisions can include personal choices in learning materials, how and when you study, and most importantly, taking ownership of your learning activities as an active participant and decision maker. In fact, one of the main principles emphasized in this chapter is that students not only benefit from being involved in planning their instruction, but learners also gain by continually evaluating the actual success of that instruction. In other words: *Does this work for me? Am I learning what I need to by doing it this way?*

While it may not always be possible to control every component of your learning over an entire degree program, you can take every opportunity to influence learning activities so they work to your best advantage. What follows are several examples of how this can be done by making decisions about your learning activities based on what you have already learned in this chapter.

Make Mistakes Safe

Create an environment for yourself where mistakes are safe and mistakes are expected as just another part of learning. This practice ties back to the principles you learned in the section on grit and persistence. The key is to allow yourself the opportunity to make mistakes and learn from them *before* they become a part of your grades. You can do this by creating your own learning activities that you design to do just that. An example of this might be taking practice quizzes on your own, outside of the more formal course activities. The quizzes could be something you find in your textbook, something you find online, or something that you develop with a partner. In the latter case you would arrange with a classmate for each of you to produce a quiz and then exchange them. That particular exercise would serve double learning duty, since to create a good quiz you would need to learn the main concepts of the subject, and answering the questions on your partner's quiz might help you identify areas where you need more knowledge.

The main idea with this sort of practice is that you are creating a safe environment where you can make mistakes and learn from them before those mistakes can negatively impact your success in the course. Better to make mistakes on a practice run than on any kind of assignment or exam that can heavily influence your final grade in a course.

Make Everything Problem Centered

When working through a learning activity, the practical act of problem-solving is a good strategy. Problem-solving, as an approach, can give a learning activity more meaning and motivation for you, as a learner. Whenever possible it is to your advantage to turn an assignment or learning task into a problem you are trying to solve or something you are trying to accomplish.

In essence, you do this by deciding on some purpose for the assignment (other than just completing the assignment itself). An example of this would be taking the classic college term paper and writing it in a way that solves a problem you are already interested in.

Typically, many students treat a term paper as a collection of requirements that must be fulfilled—the paper must be on a certain topic; it should include an introduction section, a body, a closing, and a bibliography; it should be so many pages long, etc. With this approach, the student is simply completing a checklist of attributes and components dictated by the instructor, but other than that, there is no reason for the paper to exist.

Instead, writing it to solve a problem gives the paper purpose and meaning. For example, if you were to write a paper with the purpose of informing the reader about a topic they knew little about, that purpose would influence not only how you wrote the paper but would also help you make decisions on what information to include. It would also influence how you would structure information in the paper so that the reader might best learn what you were teaching them. Another example would be to write a paper to persuade the reader about a certain opinion or way of looking at things. In other words, your paper now has a purpose rather than just reporting facts on the subject. Obviously, you would still meet the format requirements of the paper, such as number of pages and inclusion of a bibliography, but now you do that in a way that helps to solve your problem.

Make It Occupation Related

Much like making assignments problem centered, you will also do well when your learning activities have meaning for your profession or major area of study. This can take the form of simply understanding how the things you are learning are important to your occupation, or it can include the decision to do assignments in a way that can be directly applied to your career. If an exercise seems pointless and possibly unrelated to your long-term goals, you will be much less motivated by the learning activity.

An example of understanding how a specific school topic impacts your occupation future would be that of a nursing student in an algebra course. At first, algebra might seem unrelated to the field of nursing, but if the nursing student recognizes that drug dosage calculations are critical to patient safety and that algebra can help them in that area, there is a much stronger motivation to learn the subject.

In the case of making a decision to apply assignments directly to your field, you can look for ways to use learning activities to build upon other areas or emulate tasks that would be required in your profession. Examples of this might be a communication student giving a presentation in a speech course on how the Internet has changed corporate advertising strategies, or an accounting student doing statistics research for an environmental studies course. Whenever possible, it is even better to use assignments to produce things that are much like what you will be doing in your chosen career. An example of this would be a graphic design student taking the opportunity to create an infographic or other supporting visual elements as a part of an assignment for another course. In cases where this is possible, it is always best to discuss your ideas with your instructor to make certain what you intend will still meet the requirements of the assignment.

Managing Your Time

One of the most common traits of college students is the constraint on their time. As adults, we do not always have the luxury of attending school without other demands on our time. Because of this, we must become efficient with our use of time, and it is important that we maximize our learning activities to be most effective. In fact, time management is so important that there is an entire chapter in this text dedicated to it. When you can, refer to that chapter to learn more about time management concepts and techniques that can be very useful.

Instructors as Learning Partners

In K-12 education, the instructor often has the dual role of both teacher and authority figure for students. Children come to expect their teachers to tell them what to do, how to do it, and when to do it. College learners, on the other hand, seem to work better when they begin to think of their instructors as respected experts that are partners in their education. The change in the relationship for you as a learner accomplishes several things: it gives you ownership and decision-making ability in your own learning, and it enables you to personalize your learning experience to best fit your own needs. For the instructor, it gives them the opportunity to help you meet your own needs and expectations in a rich experience, rather than focusing all of their time on trying to get information to you.

The way to develop learning partnerships is through direct communication with your instructors. If there is something you do not understand or need to know more about, go directly to them. When you have ideas about how you can personalize assignments or explore areas of the subject that interest you or better fit your needs, ask them about it. Ask your instructors for guidance and recommendations, and above all, demonstrate to them that you are taking a direct interest in your own learning. Most instructors are thrilled when they encounter students that want to take ownership of their own learning, and they will gladly become a resourceful guide for you.

APPLICATION

Applying What You Know about Learning to What You Are Doing: In this activity, you will work with an upcoming assignment from one of your courses—preferably something you might be dreading or are at least less than enthusiastic about working on. You will see if there is anything you can apply to the assignment from what you know about learning that might make it more interesting.

In the table below are several attributes that college students generally prefer in their learning activities, listed in the far left column. As you think about your assignment, consider whether or not it already possesses the attribute. If it does, go on to the next row. If it does not, see if there is some way you can approach the assignment so that it does follow preferred learning attributes; write that down in the last column, to the far right.

Does it ...?	Yes	No	What you can do to turn the assignment into something that is better suited to you as a learner?
Does it allow you to make decisions about your own learning?			In essence, you are doing this right now. You are making decisions on how you can make your assignment more effective for you.
Does it allow you to make mistakes without adversely affecting your grade?			Hints: *Are there ways for you to practice? Can you create a series of drafts for the assignment and get feedback?*
Is it centered on solving a problem?			Hint: *Can you turn the assignment into something that solves a problem? An example would be making a presentation that actually educated others rather than just covered what you may have learned.*
Is it related to your chosen occupation in any way?			Hint: *Can you turn the assignment into something you might actually do as a part of your profession or make it about your profession? Examples might be creating an informative poster for the workplace or writing a paper on new trends in your profession.*
Does it allow you to manage the time you work on it?			More than likely the answer here will be "yes," but you can plan how you will do it. For more information on this, see the chapter on time management.

Table 2.7

Does it ...?	Yes	No	What you can do to turn the assignment into something that is better suited to you as a learner?
Does it allow interaction with your instructor as a learning partner?			Hint: *Talking to your instructor about the ideas you have for making this assignment more personalized accomplishes this exact thing.*

Table 2.7

2.7 The Hidden Curriculum

Estimated completion time: 7 minutes.

Questions to consider:

- What is the hidden or invisible curriculum?
- How can I work within the hidden curriculum to prevent negative results?

The *hidden curriculum* is a phrase used to cover a wide variety of circumstances at school that can influence learning and affect your experience. Sometimes called the invisible curriculum, it varies by institution and can be thought of as a set of unwritten rules or expectations.

Situation: According to your syllabus, your history professor is lecturing on the chapter that covers the stock market crash of 1929 on Tuesday of next week.

Sounds pretty straightforward and common. Your professor lectures on a topic and you will be there to hear it. However, there are some unwritten rules, or hidden curriculum, that are not likely to be communicated. Can you guess what they may be?

- What is an unwritten rule about what you should be doing before attending class?
- What is an unwritten rule about what you should be doing in class?
- What is an unwritten rule about what you should be doing after class?
- What is an unwritten rule if you are not able to attend that class?

Some of your answers could have included the following:

Before class:	*read the assigned chapter, take notes, record any questions you have about the reading*
During class:	*take detailed notes, ask critical thinking or clarifying questions, avoid distractions, bring your book and your reading notes*

Table 2.8

After class:	*reorganize your notes in relation to your other notes, start the studying process by testing yourself on the material, make an appointment with your professor if you are not clear on a concept*
Absent:	*communicate with the professor, get notes from a classmate, make sure you did not miss anything important in your notes*

Table 2.8

The expectations before, during, and after class, as well as what you should do if you miss class, are often unspoken because many professors assume you already know and do these things or because they feel you should figure them out on your own. Nonetheless, some students struggle at first because they don't know about these habits, behaviors, and strategies. But once they learn them, they are able to meet them with ease.

While the previous example may seem obvious once they've been pointed out, most instances of the invisible curriculum are complex and require a bit of critical thinking to uncover. What follows are some common but often overlooked examples of this invisible curriculum.

One example of a hidden curriculum could be found in the beliefs of your professor. Some professors may refuse to reveal their personal beliefs to avoid your writing toward their bias rather than presenting a cogent argument of your own. Other professors may be outspoken about their beliefs to force you to consider and possibly defend your own position. As a result, you may be influenced by those opinions which can then influence your learning, but not as an official part of your study.

Other examples of how this hidden curriculum might not always be so easily identified can be found in classroom arrangements or even scheduling. To better understand this, imagine two different classes on the exact same subject and taught by the same instructor. One class is held in a large lecture hall and has over 100 students in it, while the other meets in a small classroom and has fewer than 20 students. In the smaller class, there is time for all of the students to participate in discussions as a learning activity, and they receive the benefit of being able to talk about their ideas and the lessons through direct interaction with each other and the professor. In the larger class, there is simply not enough time for all 100 students to each discuss their thoughts. On the flip side, most professors who teach lecture classes use technology to give them constant feedback on how well students understand a given subject. If the data suggests more time should be spent, these professors discover this in real time and can adapt the class accordingly.

Another instance where class circumstances might heavily influence student learning could be found in the class schedule. If the class was scheduled to meet on Mondays and Wednesdays and the due date for assignments was always on Monday, those students would benefit from having the weekend to finalize their work before handing it in. If the class met on a different day, students might not have as much free time just before handing in the assignment. The obvious solution would be better planning and time management to complete assignments in advance of due dates, but nonetheless, conditions caused by scheduling may still impact student learning.

Working Within the Hidden Curriculum

The first step in dealing with the hidden curriculum is to recognize it and understand how it can influence your learning. After any specific situation has been identified, the next step is to figure out how to work around the circumstances to either take advantage of any benefits or to remove any roadblocks.

To illustrate this, here are some possible solutions to the situations given as examples earlier in this section:

Prevailing Opinions—Simply put, you are going to encounter instructors and learning activities that you sometimes agree with and sometimes do not. The key is to learn from them regardless. In either case, take ownership of your learning and even make an effort to learn about other perspectives, even if it is only for your own education on the matter. There is no better time to expose yourself to other opinions and philosophies than in college. In fact, many would say that this is a significant part of the college experience. With a growth mindset, it is easy to view everything as a learning opportunity.

Classroom Circumstances—These kinds of circumstances often require a more structured approach to turn the situation to your advantage, but they also usually have the most obvious solutions. In the example of the large class, you might find yourself limited in the ability to participate in classroom discussions because of so many other students. The way around that would be to speak to several classmates and create your own discussion group. You could set up a time to meet, or you could take a different route by using technology such as an online discussion board, a Skype session, or even a group text. Several of the technologically based solutions might even be better than an in-class discussion since you do not all have to be present at the same time. The discussion can be something that occurs all week long, giving everyone the time to think through their ideas and responses.

Again, the main point is to first spot those things in the hidden curriculum that might put your learning at a disadvantage and devise a solution that either reduces the negative impact or even becomes a learning advantage.

 Summary

The purpose of this chapter is to help make you a motivated learner and empower you to make informed choices about your own learning. Throughout the chapter, you were introduced to ideas, research, and popular models on learning and given examples of how to use each of these as an effective part of your own learning experience.

Most importantly, you were able to explore how things like motivation, grit, and mindset are the most influential aspects of successful learning.

Career Connection

Watch this TEDx video (https://openstax.org/l/learningstyles_tedx) on learning styles and the importance of critical thinking. After you have watched the video, consider some of the reflective points below.

The concept of personalized learning styles has been popular for almost half a century. Given the information presented in this video, why do you think people are attracted to the idea of personal learning styles even though evidence shows they do not actually exist?

If you were going to devise an experiment to prove or disprove the idea of personalized learning styles, what would you do?

Rethinking

Recall the four statements that you evaluated at the beginning of this chapter (see below). Have you changed your mind about any of them, or do you intend to work on changing any of them? If you answered no to either or both, why do you feel no change is needed?

1. Learning for me is easy. I don't even have to think about it.
2. I have a preferred learning style.
3. If I can't learn something right away, I have difficulty staying with it.
4. I think my teachers are the most significant aspect of my learning.

Where do you go from here?

Learning about how we learn allows us to make informed decisions about our own learning activities. This chapter covered a number of concepts, and more than likely a few may have sparked a deeper interest in you. Hopefully these will be things you will choose to explore further. If you would like to learn more, choose from any of the topics covered in this chapter or from those in the list below.

1. More details about the growth mindset
2. Additional strategies for overcoming negative bias
3. The influence of grit as a personal trait
4. Uses and Gratification model as a structure for understanding our daily decisions

Figure 3.1 Our devices can be helpful tools for managing time, but they can also lead to distraction.

Chapter Outline

- **3.1** The Benefits of Time Management
- **3.2** Time Management in College
- **3.3** Procrastination: The Enemy Within
- **3.4** How to Manage Time
- **3.5** Prioritization: Self-Management of What You Do and When You Do It
- **3.6** Goal Setting and Motivation
- **3.7** Enhanced Strategies for Time and Task Management

Introduction

Student Survey

How do you feel about your time management abilities? Take this quick survey to figure it out, ranking questions on a scale of 1–4, 1 meaning "least like me" and 4 meaning "most like me." These questions will help you determine how the chapter concepts relate to you right now. As you are introduced to new concepts and practices, it can be informative to reflect on how your understanding changes over time. We'll revisit these questions at the end of the chapter to see whether your feelings have changed.

1. I regularly procrastinate completing tasks that don't interest me or seem challenging.
2. I use specific time management strategies to complete tasks.
3. I find it difficult to prioritize tasks because I am not sure what is really important.
4. I am pleased with my ability to manage my time.

You can also take the Chapter 3 survey (https://openstax.org/l/collegesurvey03) anonymously online.

STUDENT PROFILE

"Before I started college, I had heard that the amount of work would be overwhelming, and that it would be much harder than high school. That was true, but after being in college for a couple of weeks, I felt that people made it seem scarier than it actually was. I had some homework assignments here, some essays, some hard classes, but it wasn't that bad..until Midterms and Finals came knocking. I had so much to study and so little time. The pressure was unimaginable. And since there was so much material to learn, I kept procrastinating. The nights before the exams were a disaster.

"After the semester, I realized that I needed to do something differently. Instead of crashing before midterms and finals, I would study throughout the semester. I would review notes after class, do a few practice problems in the book even if homework wasn't assigned, and try to ask professors questions during their office hours if I was confused. This continual effort helped me do better on exams because I built up my understanding and was able to get a good night's sleep before the big test. I still studied hard, but the material was in reach and understanding it became a reasonable goal, not an impossibility. I also felt more confident going into the exams, because I knew that I had a deeper knowledge — I could recall things more easily. Most importantly, I now had peace of mind throughout the day and during the tests themselves, since I knew that I was better prepared."

—**Nachum Sash**, Actuarial Science Major, City University of New York

About This Chapter

In this chapter you will learn about two of the most valuable tools used for academic success: prioritizing and time management. By the time you complete this chapter, you should be able to do the following:

- Articulate the ways in which time management differs from high school to college.
- Outline reasons and effects of procrastination, and provide strategies to overcome it.
- Describe ways to evaluate your own time management skills.
- Discuss the importance and the process of prioritization.
- Articulate the importance of goal setting and motivation.
- Detail strategies and specific tactics for managing your time.

3.1 The Benefits of Time Management

Estimated completion time: 9 minutes.

"Poor time management can set into motion a series of events that can seriously jeopardize a student's success."

A very unfortunate but all-too-common situation in higher education is the danger students face from poor time management. Many college administrators that work directly with students are aware that a single mishap or a case of poor time management can set into motion a series of events that can seriously jeopardize a student's success. In some of the more extreme instances, the student may even fail to graduate because of it.

To better understand how one instance of poor time management can trigger a cascading situation with disastrous results, imagine that a student has an assignment due in a business class. She knows that she should be working on it, but she isn't quite in the mood. Instead she convinces herself that she should think a little more about what she needs to complete the assignment and decides to do so while looking at social media or maybe playing a couple more rounds of a game on her phone. In a little while, she suddenly realizes that she has become distracted and the evening has slipped away. She has little time left to work on her assignment. She stays up later than usual trying to complete the assignment but cannot finish it. Exhausted, she decides that she will work on it in the morning during the hour she had planned to study for her math quiz. She knows there will not be enough time in the morning to do a good job on the assignment, so she decides that she will put together what she has and hope she will at least receive a passing grade.

At this point in our story, an evening of procrastination has not only resulted in a poorly done business class assignment, but now she is going to take a math quiz that she has not studied for. She will take the quiz tired from staying up too late the night before. Her lack of time management has now raised potential issues in two courses. Imagine that each of these issues also causes additional problems, such as earning low scores on *both* the assignment and the quiz. She will now have to work harder in both courses to bring her grades up. Any other problems she has with future assignments in either course could cause a domino effect of circumstances that begins to overwhelm her.

In our imagined situation, you can see how events set into motion by a little procrastination can quickly spiral out of control. You can probably think of similar experiences in your own life, when one small bit of poor time management set off a chain of events that threatened to cause big problems.

The High Cost of Poor Time Management

It's not just your academic performance that can be affected by cascading events that have a domino effect on your college path. And dropping out of school is not your only danger. There are other consequences that affect the financial cost to you as a student if your lack of time management skills causes you to delay when you finish college.

Based on independent research, a *Washington Post* article details the financial impact delaying graduation by two semesters can have on a student.[1] (Spending a Few Extra Years in College May Cost You More Than You Think, Danielle Douglas-Gabriel, June 21, 2016)

According to the article, there is a significant cost associated with delaying graduation from college by only one year (by dropping and retaking courses, taking less than a full credit load, etc.). Not only will you pay for additional tuition, textbooks, and other fees associated with going to school, but if you are using student loans, you will also accumulate interest on those loans. On average this would come to an extra $12,557 in actual costs and $6,040 in interest at a public university, or $18,992 in tuition and fees and $7,823 in interest (over 10 years) at a private school. That's a lot of extra cost to you!

> **"In the long run, just two extra semesters of college can cost you almost $150,000."**

While a loss of $26,815 may seem like a lot of money, it pales in comparison to the other financial areas impacted by a single extra year in school. The *Washington Post* article estimates that one year's delay of graduation would cost you an additional $46,355 based on average lost earnings. To make matters worse, like the story of the student that procrastinates finishing her business assignment, there is a spiraling effect that takes place with loss of income when it comes to retirement investments. The figure cited by the *Washington*

---

1   https://wwww.washingtonpost.com/news/grade-point/wp/2016/06/21/spending-a-few-extra-years-in-college-may-cost-you-more-than-you-think/?noredirect=on&utm_term=.f06be365e5d6

Post as lost retirement earnings for taking five years instead of four years to graduate is $82,074. That brings the average total cost for only two extra semesters to over $150,000. Measured by the financial cost to you, even a slight delay of graduation can have a serious impact.

Average Cost of an Additional Year of College

Tuition, textbooks, and fees	$15,774
Interest on student loans	$6,932
Lost wages	$46,335
Lost retirement earnings	$82,074
Average total loss:	**$151,115**

Table 3.1 Credit: *Washington Post*. Note the numbers in the table above have been averaged between the two scenarios described.

It is worth noting that any situation that brings about a delay in graduation has the potential to increase the cost of college. This also includes attending school on a part-time basis. While in some instances responsibilities may make it impossible to go to school full-time, from a financial perspective you should do all you can to graduate as soon as you can.

While it may not be possible to prevent life challenges while you are in college, you can do a great deal to prevent the chaos and the chain reaction of unfortunate events that they can cause. This can be accomplished through thoughtful prioritization and time management efforts.

What follows in the rest of this chapter is a close look at the nature of time management and prioritization in ways that can help keep you on track to graduate college on time.

ANALYSIS QUESTION

Can you identify any areas in your life that might be a potential problem if there were a temporary setback (e.g., temporary loss of transportation, temporary loss of housing, an illness that lasted more than a week, etc.)? What could you do for a backup plan if something did happen?

3.2 Time Management in College

Estimated completion time: 11 minutes.

Questions to consider:

- Is time management different in college from what I am used to?
- How different is college schoolwork from high school work?

You may find that time management in college is very different from anything you have experienced previously. For the last 12 years, almost all your school time was managed by educators and your parents. What you did and when you did it was controlled by others. In many cases, even after-school time was set by scheduled activities (such as athletics) and by nightly homework that was due the next day.

In the workplace, the situation is not very different, with activities and time on task being monitored by the company and its management. This is so much a part of the working environment that many companies research how much time each task should take, and they hold employees accountable for the time spent on these job functions. In fact, having these skills will help you stand out on the job and in job interviews.

K–12	College
Many class activities are planned.	Class time is given to receiving information.
Homework is often similar for each student.	You may have freedom in homework choices.
Time is managed by others more often.	Time is managed by the student.

In college, there is a significant difference because a great deal of time management is left up to you. While it is true that there are assignment due dates and organized classroom activities, learning at the college level requires more than just the simple completion of work. It involves decision-making and the ability to evaluate information. This is best accomplished when you are an active partner in your own learning activities.

Figure 3.2 Students may set aside specific times and specific places to study.

As an example of how this works, think about a college assignment that involves giving a classroom presentation. To complete the assignment, you are given time to research and reflect on the information found. As a part of the assignment, you must reach your own conclusions and determine which information that you have found is best suited for the presentation. While the date of the actual presentation and how long it will last are usually determined by the instructor, how much time you spend gathering information, the sources you use, and how you use them are left to you.

WHAT STUDENTS SAY

1. How difficult is it for you to keep track of multiple tasks over the course of a term?
    a. Extremely easy
    b. Somewhat easy
    c. Somewhat difficult
    d. Extremely difficult
2. Do you use a particular app to help you manage your time?
    a. I use Google calendar
    b. I use the calendar on my phone
    c. I use a paper/notebook planner
    d. I use the calendar on my learning management system
    e. I use another app or system
    f. I don't use any type of planner or app
3. Rank the following in terms of what you would most like to improve regarding your time management skills.
    a. My ability to predict how much time my tasks will take.
    b. My ability to balance various obligations.
    c. My ability to avoid procrastination.
    d. My ability to limit distractions.

You can also take the anonymous What Students Say (https://openstax.org/l/collegesurvey1-5) surveys to add your voice to this textbook. Your responses will be included in updates.

Students offered their views on these questions, and the results are displayed in the graphs below.

How difficult is it for you to keep track of multiple tasks over the course of a term?

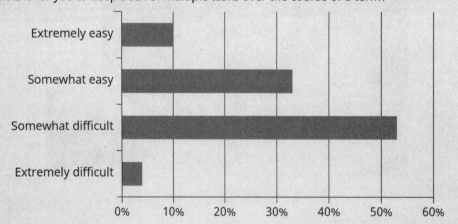

Figure 3.3

Do you use a particular app to help you manage your time?

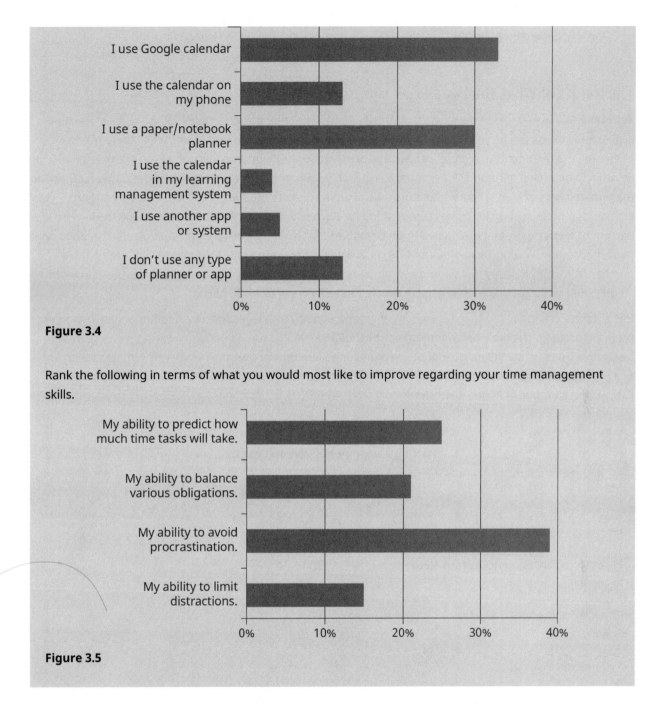

Figure 3.4

Rank the following in terms of what you would most like to improve regarding your time management skills.

Figure 3.5

You Have Lots of Time to Manage

For college-level learning, this approach is important enough that you can expect to spend much more time on learning activities outside the classroom than you will in the classroom. In fact, the estimated time you should spend will be at least two hours of outside learning for every one hour of lecture. Some weeks may be more intense, depending on the time of the semester and the courses you are taking. If those hours are multiplied over several courses in a given session, you can see how there is a significant amount of time to manage. Unfortunately, many students do not always take this into consideration, and they spend far less time than is needed to be successful. The results of poor time management are often a shock to them.

"In college, as an active participant in your own education, what you do and when you do it is

largely determined by you."

The Nature of What You Have to Do Has Changed

Returning to our example of the classroom-presentation assignment, you can see that the types of learning activities in college can be very different from what you have experienced previously. While there may have been similar assignments in high school, such as presentations or written papers, the level of expectation with length and depth is significantly different in college. This point is made very clear when comparing facts about the requirements of high school work to the type of work students produce in college. One very strong statistic that underscores this comes from a study conducted by the Pew Research Center. They found that 82 percent of teens report that their typical high school writing assignments were only a single paragraph to one page in length.[2] (Writing Technology and Teens, 2004, Pew Research Center) This is in stark contrast to a number of sources that say that writing assignments in lower-level college courses are usually 5–7 pages in length, while writing assignments in upper-level courses increase to 15–20 pages.

It is also interesting to note that the amount of writing done by a college student can differ depending on their program of study. The table below indicates the estimated average amount of writing assigned in several disciplines. To estimate the number of pages of assigned writing, the average number of writing assignments of a given page length was multiplied by an approximate number of pages for the assignment type (see **Estimating Number of Pages Written** for calculation details).

Writing Assignments Vary in Length

Discipline	Number of Pages Assigned in Introductory Course
Arts & Humanities	49
Biological Sciences, Agriculture, & Natural Resources	47
Physical Sciences, Mathematics, & Computer Science	44
Social Sciences	52
Business	48
Communications, Media, & Public Relations	50
Education	46
Engineering	46
Health Professions	43

Table 3.2 Credit: Updated NSSE (Since 2013)[3]

---

2   http://www.pewinternet.org/2008/04/24/writing-technology-and-teens/
3   http://nsse.indiana.edu/html/sample_analyses/amount_of_writing.cfm

Writing Assignments Vary in Length

Discipline	Number of Pages Assigned in Introductory Course
Social Service Professions	47

Table 3.2 Credit: Updated NSSE (Since 2013)

High school homework often consists of worksheets or tasks based on reading or classroom activities. In other words, all the students are doing the same tasks, at relatively the same time, with little autonomy over their own education.

Using the earlier example of the presentation assignment, not only will what you do be larger in scale, but the depth of understanding and knowledge you will put into it will be significantly more than you may have encountered in previous assignments. This is because there are greater expectations required of college graduates in the workplace. Nearly any profession that requires a college degree has with it a level of responsibility that demands higher-level thinking and therefore higher learning. An often-cited example of this is the healthcare professional. The learning requirements for that profession are strict because we depend on those graduates for our health and, in some cases, our lives. While not every profession may require the same level of study needed for healthcare, most do require that colleges maintain a certain level of academic rigor to produce graduates who are competent in their fields.

3.3 Procrastination: The Enemy Within

Estimated completion time: 13 minutes.

Questions to consider:

- Why do we procrastinate?
- What are the effects of procrastination?
- How can we avoid procrastination?

Figure 3.6 We can think of many creative ways to procrastinate, but the outcome is often detrimental. (Credit: University of the Fraser Valley / Flickr / Attribution 2.0 Generic (CC BY 2.0))

Simply put, procrastination is the act of delaying some task that needs to be completed. It is something we all do to greater and lesser degrees. For most people, a little minor procrastination is not a cause for great concern. But there are situations where procrastination can become a serious problem with a lot of risk. These include: when it becomes a chronic habit, when there are a number of tasks to complete and little time, or when the task being avoided is very important.

Because we all procrastinate from time to time, we usually do not give it much thought, let alone think about its causes or effects. Ironically, many of the psychological reasons for why we avoid a given task also keep us from using critical thinking to understand why procrastination can be extremely detrimental, and in some cases difficult to overcome.

To succeed at time management, you must understand some of the hurdles that may stand in your way. Procrastination is often one of the biggest. What follows is an overview of procrastination with a few suggestions on how to avoid it.

The Reasons behind Procrastination

There are several reasons we procrastinate, and a few of them may be surprising. On the surface we often tell ourselves it is because the task is something we do not want to do, or we make excuses that there are other things more important to do first. In some cases this may be true, but there can be other contributors to procrastination that have their roots in our physical well-being or our own psychological motivations.

Lack of Energy

Sometimes we just do not feel up to a certain task. It might be due to discomfort, an illness, or just a lack of energy. If this is the case, it is important to identify the cause and remedy the situation. It could be something as simple as a lack of sleep or improper diet. Regardless, if a lack of energy is continually causing you to procrastinate to the point where you are beginning to feel stress over not getting things done, you should definitely assess the situation and address it.

Lack of Focus

Much like having low physical energy, a lack of mental focus can be a cause of procrastination. This can be due to mental fatigue, being disorganized, or allowing yourself to be distracted by other things. Again, like low physical energy, this is something that may have farther-reaching effects in your life that go beyond the act of simply avoiding a task. If it is something that is recurring, you should properly assess the situation.

Fear of Failure

This cause of procrastination is not one that many people are aware of, especially if they are the person avoiding tasks because of it. To put it in simple words, it is a bit of trickery we play on ourselves by avoiding a situation that makes us psychologically uncomfortable. Even though they may not be consciously aware of it, the person facing the task is afraid that they cannot do it or will not be able to do it well. If they fail at the task, it will make them appear incompetent to others or even to themselves. Where the self-trickery comes in is by avoiding the task. In the person's mind, they can rationalize that the reason they failed at the task was because they ran out of time to complete it, not that they were incapable of doing it in the first place.

It is important to note that a fear of failure may not have anything to do with the actual ability of the person suffering from it. They could be quite capable of doing the task and performing well, but it is the fear that holds them back.

> **ANALYSIS QUESTION**
>
> Consider something right now that you may be procrastinating about. Are you able to identify the cause?

The Effects of Procrastination

In addition to the causes of procrastination, you must also consider what effects it can have. Again, many of these effects are obvious and commonly understood, but some may not be so obvious and may cause other issues.

Loss of Time

The loss of time as an effect of procrastination is the easiest to identify since the act of avoiding a task comes down to not using time wisely. Procrastination can be thought of as using the time you have to complete a task in ways that do not accomplish what needs to be done.

Loss of Goals

Another of the more obvious potentially adverse effects of procrastination is the loss of goals. Completing a task leads to achieving a goal. These can be large or small (e.g., from doing well on an assignment to being hired for a good job). Without goals you might do more than delay work on a task—you may not complete it at all. The risk for the loss of goals is something that is very impactful.

Loss of Self-Esteem

Often, when we procrastinate we become frustrated and disappointed in ourselves for not getting important tasks completed. If this continues to happen, we can begin to develop a low opinion of ourselves and our own abilities. We begin to suffer from low self-esteem and might even begin to feel like there is something wrong with us. This can lead to other increasingly negative mental factors such as anger and depression. As you can see, it is important for our own well-being to avoid this kind of procrastination effect.

Stress

Procrastination causes stress and anxiety, which may seem odd since the act of procrastination is often about avoiding a task we think will be stressful in itself! Anyone who has noticed that nagging feeling when they know there is something else they should be doing is familiar with this.

On the other hand, some students see that kind of stress as a boost of mental urgency. They put off a task until they feel that surge of motivation. While this may have worked in the past, they quickly learn that procrastinating when it comes to college work almost always includes an underestimation of the tasks to be completed— sometimes with disastrous results.

Strategies for Psyching Ourselves Out and Managing Procrastination

Now that you understand a few of the major problems procrastination can produce, let's look at methods to manage procrastination and get you on to completing the tasks, no matter how unpleasant you think they might be.

Get Organized

Much of this chapter is dedicated to defining and explaining the nature of time management. The most effective way to combat procrastination is to use time and project management strategies such as schedules, goal setting, and other techniques to get tasks accomplished in a timely manner.

Put Aside Distractions

Several of the methods discussed in this chapter deal specifically with distractions. Distractions are time-killers and are the primary way people procrastinate. It is too easy to just play a video game a little while longer, check out social media, or finish watching a movie when we are avoiding a task. Putting aside distractions is one of the primary functions of setting priorities.

Reward Yourself

Rewarding yourself for the completion of tasks or meeting goals is a good way to avoid procrastination. An example of this would be rewarding yourself with the time to watch a movie you would enjoy *after* you have finished the things you need to do, rather than using the movie to keep yourself from getting things done.

Be Accountable—Tell Someone Else

A strong motivational tool is to hold ourselves accountable by telling someone else we are going to do something and when we are going to do it. This may not seem like it would be very effective, but on a psychological level we feel more compelled to do something if we tell someone else. It may be related to our need for approval from others, or it might just serve to set a level of commitment. Either way, it can help us stay on task and avoid procrastination—especially if we take our accountability to another person seriously enough to warrant contacting that person and apologizing for not doing what we said we were going to do.

3.4 How to Manage Time

Estimated completion time: 25 minutes.

Questions to consider:

- How can I use time-on-task estimates to improve time management?
- What behaviors can help or hinder when it comes to managing time?

In this next section you will learn about managing time and prioritizing tasks. This is not only a valuable skill for pursuing an education, but it can become an ability that follows you through the rest of your life, especially if your career takes you into a leadership role.

Figure 3.7 An online calendar is a very useful tool for keeping track of classes, meetings, and other events. Most learning management systems contain these features, or you can use a calendar application.

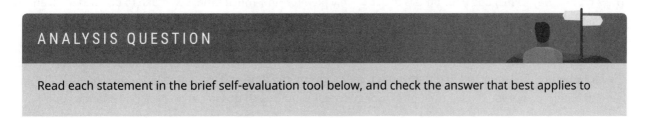

ANALYSIS QUESTION

Read each statement in the brief self-evaluation tool below, and check the answer that best applies to you. There are no right or wrong answers.

	Always	Usually	Sometimes	Rarely	Never
I like to be given strict deadlines for each task. It helps me stay organized and on track.					
I would rather be 15 minutes early than 1 minute late.					
I like to improvise instead of planning everything out ahead of time.					
I prefer to be able to manage when and how I do each task.					
I have a difficult time estimating how long a task will take.					
I have more motivation when there is an upcoming deadline. It helps me focus.					
I have difficulty keeping priorities in the most beneficial order.					

Table 3.3

This exercise is intended to help you recognize some things about your own time management style. The important part is for you to identify any areas where you might be able to improve and to find solutions for them. This chapter will provide some solutions, but there are many others that can be found by researching time management strategies.

After you have decided your best response to each statement, think about what they may mean in regard to potential strengths and/or challenges for you when it comes to time management in college. If you are a person that likes strict deadlines, what would you do if you took a course that only had one large paper due at the end? Would you set yourself a series of mini deadlines that made you more comfortable and that kept things moving along for you? Or, if you have difficulty prioritizing tasks, would it help you to make a list of the tasks to do and order them, so you know which ones must be finished first?

How to Manage Time

The simplest way to manage your time is to accurately plan for how much time it will take to do each task, and then set aside that amount of time. How you divide the time is up to you. If it is going to take you five hours to study for a final exam, you can plan to spread it over five days, with an hour each night, or you can plan on two hours one night and three hours the next. What you would not want to do is plan on studying only a few hours the night before the exam and find that you fell very short on the time you estimated you would need. If that were to happen, you would have run out of time before finishing, with no way to go back and change your decision. In this kind of situation, you might even be tempted to "pull an all-nighter," which is a phrase that has been used among college students for decades. In essence it means going without sleep for the entire night and using that time to finish an assignment. While this method of trying to make up for poor planning is common enough to have a name, rarely does it produce the best work.

ACTIVITY

Many people are not truly aware of how they actually spend their time. They make assumptions about how much time it takes to do certain things, but they never really take an accurate account.

In this activity, write down all the things you think you will do tomorrow, and estimate the time you will spend doing each. Then track each thing you have written down to see how accurate your estimates were.

Obviously, you will not want to get caught up in too much tedious detail, but you will want to cover the main activities of your day—for example, working, eating, driving, shopping, gaming, being engaged in entertainment, etc.

After you have completed this activity for a single day, you may consider doing it for an entire week so that you are certain to include all of your activities.

Many people that take this sort of personal assessment of their time are often surprised by the results. Some even make lifestyle changes based on it.

Activity	Estimated Time	Actual Time
Practice Quiz	5 minutes	15 minutes
Lab Conclusions	20 minutes	35 minutes
Food shopping	45 minutes	30 minutes
Drive to work	20 minutes	20 minutes
Physical Therapy	1 hour	50 minutes

Table 3.4 Sample Time Estimate Table

Of all the parts of time management, accurately predicting how long a task will take is usually the most difficult—and the most elusive. Part of the problem comes from the fact that most of us are not very accurate timekeepers, especially when we are busy applying ourselves to a task. The other issue that makes it so difficult to accurately estimate time on task is that our estimations must also account for things like interruptions or unforeseen problems that cause delays.?

When it comes to academic activities, many tasks can be dependent upon the completion of other things first, or the time a task takes can vary from one instance to another, both of which add to the complexity and difficulty of estimating how much time and effort are required.

For example, if an instructor assigned three chapters of reading, you would not really have any idea how long each chapter might take to read until you looked at them. The first chapter might be 30 pages long while the second is 45. The third chapter could be only 20 pages but made up mostly of charts and graphs for you to compare. By page count, it might seem that the third chapter would take the least amount of time, but actually studying charts and graphs to gather information can take longer than regular reading.?

To make matters even more difficult, when it comes to estimating time on task for something as common as reading, not all reading takes the same amount of time. Fiction, for example, is usually a faster read than a technical manual. But something like the novel *Finnegan's Wake* by James Joyce is considered so difficult that most readers never finish it.

ACTIVITY

To better understand how much time different kinds of material can take to read, try this experiment. You will use two examples of famous texts that are very close to being the same number of words: *The Gettysburg Address* and the opening paragraphs from *A Christmas Carol*. Before you begin, estimate how long it will take you to read each, and predict which you think will take longer. When you do the reading, use a stopwatch function on a device such as a phone or some other timer to see how long it actually takes.

Make certain that you are reading for understanding, not just skimming over words. If you must reread a section to better comprehend what is being said, that is appropriate. The goal here is to compare reading of different texts, not to see how fast you can sight-read the words on a page.

After you have finished *The Gettysburg Address*, read and time *A Christmas Carol* and compare both of your times.

The Gettysburg Address
Abraham Lincoln
Gettysburg, Pennsylvania November 19, 1863
Word count: 278

Four score and seven years ago our fathers brought forth on this continent, a new nation, conceived in Liberty, and dedicated to the proposition that all men are created equal.

Now we are engaged in a great civil war, testing whether that nation, or any nation so conceived and so dedicated, can long endure. We are met on a great battle-field of that war. We have come to dedicate a portion of that field, as a final resting place for those who here gave their lives that that nation might live. It is altogether fitting and proper that we should do this.

But, in a larger sense, we can not dedicate -- we can not consecrate -- we can not hallow -- this ground. The brave men, living and dead, who struggled here, have consecrated it, far above our poor power to add or detract. The world will little note, nor long remember what we say here, but it can never forget what they did here. It is for us the living, rather, to be dedicated here to the unfinished work which they who fought here have thus far so nobly advanced. It is rather for us to be here dedicated to the great task remaining before us -- that from these honored dead we take increased devotion to that cause for which they gave the last full measure of devotion -- that we here highly resolve that these dead shall not have died in vain -- that this nation, under God, shall have a new birth of freedom -- and that government of the people, by the people, for the people, shall not perish from the earth.

A Christmas Carol
Charles Dickens
Chapman & Hall, 1843
Word count: 260

Marley was dead: to begin with. There is no doubt whatever about that. The register of his burial was signed by the clergyman, the clerk, the undertaker, and the chief mourner. Scrooge signed it: and Scrooge's name was good upon 'Change, for anything he chose to put his hand to. Old Marley was as dead as a door-nail.

Mind! I don't mean to say that I know, of my own knowledge, what there is particularly dead about a door-nail. I might have been inclined, myself, to regard a coffin-nail as the deadest piece of ironmongery in the trade. But the wisdom of our ancestors is in the simile; and my unhallowed hands shall not disturb it, or the Country's done for. You will therefore permit me to repeat, emphatically, that Marley was as dead as a door-nail.

Scrooge knew he was dead? Of course he did. How could it be otherwise? Scrooge and he were partners for I don't know how many years. Scrooge was his sole executor, his sole administrator, his sole assign, his sole residuary legatee, his sole friend, and sole mourner. And even Scrooge was not so dreadfully cut up by the sad event, but that he was an excellent man of business on the very day of the funeral, and solemnised it with an undoubted bargain.

The mention of Marley's funeral brings me back to the point I started from. There is no doubt that Marley was dead. This must be distinctly understood, or nothing wonderful can come of the story I am going to relate.

In comparing the two, was one or the other easier to understand or faster to read? Was it the piece you predicted you would read faster?

It is important to note that in this case both readings were only three paragraphs long. While there may have only been half a minute or so between the reading of each, that amount of time would multiply greatly over an entire chapter.

Knowing Yourself

While you can find all sorts of estimates online as to how long a certain task may take, it is important to know these are only averages. People read at different speeds, people write at different speeds, and those numbers even change for each individual depending on the environment.

If you are trying to read in surroundings that have distractions (e.g., conversations, phone calls, etc.), reading 10 pages can take you a lot longer than if you are reading in a quiet area. By the same token, you may be reading in a quiet environment (e.g., in bed after everyone in the house has gone to sleep), but if you are tired, your attention and retention may not be what it would be if you were refreshed.

In essence, the only way you are going to be able to manage your time accurately is to know yourself and to know how long it takes you to do each task. But where to begin?

Below, you will find a table of common college academic activities. This list has been compiled from a large number of different sources, including colleges, publishers, and professional educators, to help students estimate their own time on tasks. The purpose of this table is to both give you a place to begin in your estimates and to illustrate how different factors can impact the actual time spent.

You will notice that beside each task there is a column for the *unit*, followed by the average *time on task*, and a column for notes. The *unit* is whatever is being measured (e.g., pages read, pages written, etc.), and the *time on task* is an average time it takes students to do these tasks. It is important to pay attention to the notes column, because there you will find factors that influence the time on task. These factors can dramatically change the amount of time the activity takes.

		Time on Task	
Activity	Unit	Time on task	Notes
General academic reading (textbook, professional journals)	1 page	5–7 minutes	Be aware that your personal reading speed may differ and may change over time.
Technical reading (math, charts and data)	1 page	10–15 minutes	Be aware that your personal reading speed may differ and may change over time.
Simple Quiz or homework question: short answer—oriented toward recall or identification type answers	Per question	1–2 minutes	Complexity of question will greatly influence the time required.
Complex Quiz or homework question: short answer—oriented toward application, evaluation, or synthesis of knowledge	Per question	2–3 minutes	Complexity of question will greatly influence the time required.
Math problem sets, complex	Per question	15 minutes	For example, algebra, complex equations, financial calculations
Writing: short, no research	Per page	60 minutes	Short essays, single-topic writing assignments, summaries, freewriting assignments, journaling—includes drafting, writing, proofing, and finalizing
Writing: research paper	Per page	105 minutes	Includes research time, drafting, editing, proofing, and finalizing (built into per-page calculation)
Study for quiz	Per chapter	60 minutes	45–90 minutes per chapter, depending upon complexity of material

Table 3.5 Time on task for common college activities.

Time on Task			
Activity	Unit	Time on task	Notes
Study for exam	Per exam	90 minutes	1–2 hours, depending upon complexity of material

Table 3.5 Time on task for common college activities.

Again, these are averages, and it does not mean anything if your times are a little slower or a little faster. There is no "right amount of time," only the time that it takes you to do something so you can accurately plan and manage your time.

There is also another element to look for in the table. These are differentiations in the similar activities that will also affect the time you spend. A good example of this can be found in the first four rows. Each of these activities involves reading, but you can see that depending on the material being read and its complexity, the time spent can vary greatly. Not only do these differences in time account for the different types of materials you might read (as you found in the comparative reading exercise earlier in this chapter), but also they also take into consideration the time needed to think about what you are reading to truly understand and comprehend what it is saying.

GET CONNECTED

Which apps help you best prepare for success when managing your time?

Do you have trouble keeping track of multiple tasks over the course of a term?

Trello (http://www.trello.com) lets you organize all your obligations in helpful boards. You can share them with others (project collaborators), set alerts as reminders, and mark tasks off as you complete them.

Do you use a particular app to help you manage your time?

Sticky note apps are available for PC, Mac, and mobile devices. They let you post quick reminders, reorganize them as needed, and view them separately or as a full to-do list.

What do you wish you could improve about your time management skills?

Toggl (https://toggl.com) helps you keep track of how and where you are spending your time so you can budget better and make time management changes that free you up for the really important stuff.

3.5 Prioritization: Self-Management of What You Do and When You Do It

Estimated completion time: 21 minutes.

Figure 3.8 Numbered lists are useful and easy tools to create.

Questions to consider:

- Why is prioritization important?
- What are the steps involved in prioritization?
- How do I deal with situation where others' priorities are not the same as my own?
- What do I do when priorities conflict?
- What are the best ways to make sure I complete tasks?

Prioritization: Self-Management of What You Do and When You Do It

Another key component in time management is that of prioritization. Prioritization can be thought of as ordering tasks and allotting time for them based on their identified needs or value.

This next section provides some insight into not only helping prioritize tasks and actions based on need and value, but also how to better understand the factors that contribute to prioritization.

How to Prioritize

The enemy of good prioritization is panic, or at least making decisions based on strictly emotional reactions. It can be all too easy to immediately respond to a problem as soon as it pops up without thinking of the consequences of your reaction and how it might impact other priorities. It is very natural for us to want to remove a stressful situation as soon as we can. We want the adverse emotions out of the way as quickly as possible. But when it comes to juggling multiple problems or tasks to complete, prioritizing them first may mean the difference between completing everything satisfactorily and completing nothing at all.

Make Certain You Understand the Requirements of Each Task

One of the best ways to make good decisions about the prioritization of tasks is to understand the requirements of each. If you have multiple assignments to complete and you assume one of those assignments will only take an hour, you may decide to put it off until the others are finished. Your assumption could be disastrous if you find, once you begin the assignment, that there are several extra components that you did not account for and the time to complete will be four times as long as you estimated. Or, one of the assignments may be dependent on the results of another—like participating in a study and then writing a report on the results. If you are not aware that one assignment depends upon the completion of the other before you begin, you could inadvertently do the assignments out of order and have to start over. Because of situations like this, it is critically important to understand exactly what needs to be done to complete a task before you determine its priority.

Make Decisions on Importance, Impact on Other Priorities, and Urgency

After you are aware of the requirements for each task, you can then decide your priorities based on the importance of the task and what things need to be finished in which order.

To summarize: *the key components to prioritization are making certain you understand each task and making decisions based on importance, impact, and urgency.*

ACTIVITY

To better see how things may need to be prioritized, some people make a list of the tasks they need to complete and then arrange them in a quadrant map based on importance and urgency. Traditionally this is called the Eisenhower Decision Matrix. Before becoming the 34th president of the United States, Dwight Eisenhower served as the Allied forces supreme commander during World War II and said he used this technique to better prioritize the things he needed to get done.

In this activity you will begin by making a list of things you need or want to do today and then draw your own version of the grid below. Write each item in one of the four squares; choose the square that best describes it based on its urgency and its importance. When you have completed writing each the tasks in its appropriate square, you will see a prioritization order of your tasks. Obviously, those listed in the Important and Urgent square will be the things you need to finish first. After that will come things that are "important but not urgent," followed by "not important, but urgent," and finally "not urgent and not important."

	Urgent	Not Urgent
Important	**Urgent and Important** • Paper due tomorrow • Apply for internship by deadline	**Not Urgent but Important** • Exam next week • Flu shot
Not Important	**Urgent but Not Important** • Amazon sale • Laundry	**Not Urgent and Not Important** • Check social • TV show

Figure 3.9 The Eisenhower Matrix can help organize priorities and ensure that you focus on the correct tasks.

Who Is Driving Your Tasks?

Another thing to keep in mind when approaching time management is that while you may have greater autonomy in managing your own time, many of your tasks are being driven by a number of different individuals. These individuals are not only unaware of the other things you need to do, but they often have goals that are in conflict with your other tasks. This means that different instructors, your manager at work, or even your friends may be trying to assert their needs into your priorities. An example of this might be a boss that would like for you to work a few hours of overtime, but you were planning on using that time to do research for a paper.

Just like assessing the requirements and needs for each priority, doing the same with how others may be influencing your available time can be an important part of time management. In some cases, keeping others informed about your priorities may help avert possible conflicts (e.g., letting your boss know you will need time on a certain evening to study, letting your friends know you plan to do a journal project on Saturday but can do something on Sunday, etc.).

It will be important to be aware of how others can drive your priorities and for you to listen to your own good judgment. In essence, time management in college is as much about managing all the elements of your life as it is about managing time for class and to complete assignments.

Making the Tough Decision When It Is Needed

Occasionally, regardless of how much you have planned or how well you have managed your time, events arise where it becomes almost impossible to accomplish everything you need to by the time required. While this is very unfortunate, it simply cannot be helped. As the saying goes, "things happen."

Finding yourself in this kind of situation is when prioritization becomes most important. You may find yourself in the uncomfortable position of only being able to complete one task or another in the time given. When this occurs with college assignments, the dilemma can be extremely stressful, but it is important to not feel overwhelmed by the anxiety of the situation so that you can make a carefully calculated decision based on the value and impact of your choice.

> **"What do you do when faced with priority conflicts?"**

As an illustration, imagine a situation where you think you can only complete one of two assignments that are both important and urgent, and you must make a choice of which one you will finish and which one you will not. This is when it becomes critical to understand all the factors involved. While it may seem that whichever assignment is worth the most points to your grade is how you make the choice, there are actually a number of other attributes that can influence your decision in order to make the most of a bad situation. For example, one of the assignments may only be worth a minimal number of points toward your total grade, but it may be foundational to the rest of the course. Not finishing it, or finishing it late, may put other future assignments in jeopardy as well. Or the instructor for one of the courses might have a "late assignment" policy that is more forgiving—something that would allow you to turn in the work a little late without too much of a penalty.

If you find yourself in a similar predicament, the first step is to try to find a way to get everything finished, regardless of the challenges. If that simply cannot happen, the next immediate step would be to communicate with your instructors to let them know about the situation. They may be able to help you decide on a course of action, or they may have options you had not thought of. Only then can you make the choices about prioritizing in a tough situation.

The key here is to make certain you are aware of and understand all the ramifications to help make the best decision when the situation dictates you make a hard choice among priorities.

Completing the Tasks

Another important part of time management is to develop approaches that will help you complete tasks in a manner that is efficient and works for you. Most of this comes down to a little planning and being as informed about the specifics of each task as you can be.

Knowing What You Need to Do

As discussed in previous parts of this chapter, many learning activities have multiple components, and sometimes they must occur in a specific order. Additionally, some elements may not only be dependent on the order they are completed, but can also be dependent on how they are completed. To illustrate this we will analyze a task that is usually considered to be a simple one: *attending a class session.* In this analysis we will look at not only what must be accomplished to get the most out of the experience, but also at how each element is dependent upon others and must be done in a specific order. The graphic below shows the interrelationship between the different activities, many of which might not initially seem significant enough to warrant mention, but it becomes obvious that other elements depend upon them when they are listed out this way.

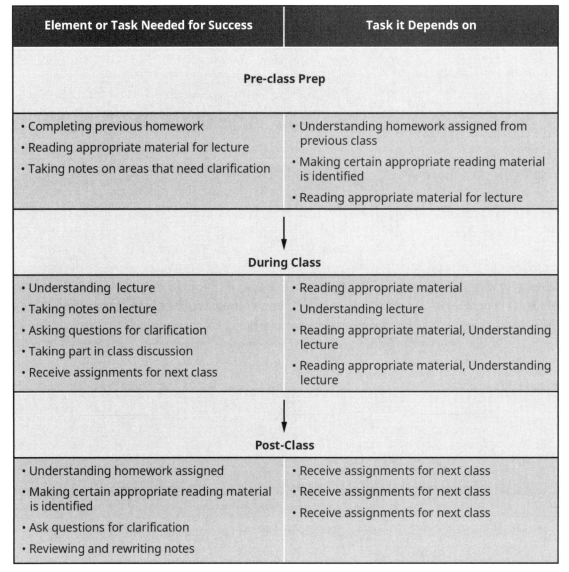

Figure 3.10 Many of your learning activities are dependent on others, and some are the gateways to other steps.

As you can see from the graphic above, even a task as simple as "going to class" can be broken down into a number of different elements that have a good deal of dependency on other tasks. One example of this is preparing for the class lecture by reading materials ahead of time in order to make the lecture and any complex concepts easier to follow. If you did it the other way around, you might miss opportunities to ask questions or receive clarification on the information presented during the lecture.

Understanding what you need to do and when you need to do it can be applied to any task, no matter how simple or how complex. Knowing what you need to do and planning for it can go a long way toward success and preventing unpleasant surprises.

Knowing How You Will Get It Done

After you have a clear understanding of what needs to be done to complete a task (or the component parts of a task), the next step is to create a plan for completing everything.

This may not be as easy or as simple as declaring that you will finish part one, then move on to part two, and so on. Each component may need different resources or skills to complete, and it is in your best interest to identify those ahead of time and include them as part of your plan.

A good analogy for this sort of planning is to think about it in much the same way you would preparing for a lengthy trip. With a long journey you probably would not walk out the front door and then decide how you were going to get where you were going. There are too many other decisions to be made and tasks to be completed around each choice. If you decided you were going by plane, you would need to purchase tickets, and you would have to schedule your trip around flight times. If you decided to go by car, you would need gas money and possibly a map or GPS device. What about clothes? The clothes you will need are dependent on how long will you be gone and what the climate will be like. If it far enough away that you will need to speak another language, you may need to either acquire that skill or at least come with something or someone to help you translate.

What follows is a planning list that can help you think about and prepare for the tasks you are about to begin.

What Resources Will You Need?

The first part of this list may appear to be so obvious that it should go without mention, but it is by far one of the most critical and one of the most overlooked. Have you ever planned a trip but forgotten your most comfortable pair of shoes or neglected to book a hotel room? If a missing resource is important, the entire project can come to a complete halt. Even if the missing resource is a minor component, it may still dramatically alter the end result.

Learning activities are much the same in this way, and it is also important to keep in mind that resources may not be limited to physical objects such as paper or ink. Information can be a critical resource as well. In fact, one of the most often overlooked aspects in planning by new college students is just how much research, reading, and information they will need to complete assignments.

Figure 3.11 Allowing time to think is an important part of learning. Credit: Juhan Sonin / Flickr / Attribution 2.0 Generic (CC BY 2.0))

For example, if you had an assignment in which you were supposed to compare and contrast a novel with a film adapted from that novel, it would be important to have access to both the movie and the book as resources. Your plans for completing the work could quickly fall apart if you learned that on the evening you planned to watch the film, it was no longer available.

What Skills Will You Need?

Poor planning or a bad assumption in this area can be disastrous, especially if some part of the task has a steep learning curve. No matter how well you planned the other parts of the project, if there is some skill needed that you do not have and you have no idea how long it will take to learn, it can be a bad situation.

Imagine a scenario where one of your class projects is to create a poster. It is your intent to use some kind of imaging software to produce professional-looking graphics and charts for the poster, but you have never used the software in that way before. It seems easy enough, but once you begin, you find the charts keep printing out in the wrong resolution. You search online for a solution, but the only thing you can find requires you to recreate them all over again in a different setting. Unfortunately, that part of the project will now take twice as long.

It can be extremely difficult to recover from a situation like that, and it could have been prevented by taking the time to learn how to do it correctly before you began or by at least including in your schedule some time to learn and practice.

Set Deadlines

Of course, the best way to approach time management is to set realistic deadlines that take into account which elements are dependent on which others and the order in which they should be completed. Giving yourself two days to write a 20- page work of fiction is not very realistic when even many professional authors average only 6 pages per day. Your intentions may be well founded, but your use of unrealistic deadlines will not be very successful.

Setting appropriate deadlines and sticking to them is very important—so much so that several sections in the rest of this chapter touch on effective deadline practices.

Be Flexible

It is ironic that the item on this list that comes just after a strong encouragement to make deadlines and stick to them is the suggestion to be flexible. The reason that *being flexible* has made this list is because even the best-laid plans and most accurate time management efforts can take an unexpected turn. The idea behind being flexible is to readjust your plans and deadlines when something does happen to throw things off. The worst thing you could do in such a situation is panic or just stop working because the next step in your careful planning has suddenly become a roadblock. The moment when you see that something in your plan may become an issue is when to begin readjusting your plan.

Adjusting a plan along the way is incredibly common. In fact, many professional project managers have learned that it seems something *always* happens or there is always some delay, and they have developed an approach to deal with the inevitable need for some flexibility. In essence, you could say that they are even planning for problems, mistakes, or delays from the very beginning, and they will often add a little extra time for each task to help ensure an issue does not derail the entire project or that the completion of the project does not miss the final due date.

"As you work through tasks, make certain you are always monitoring and adapting to ensure you complete them."

STUDENT PROFILE

"While in college, I recall an instance where I was awake for two nights in a row trying to cram for upcoming midterms. I quickly learned that trying to navigate through college while working full time posed a significant challenge. Because of inability to manage my responsibilities, my first year of college was quite miserable. I went through a lot of trial and error to find out that *time management* was the key. From my experiences, I have extrapolated three important components to this skill. First, knowing your *values* is imperative. Values will serve as a guide, which will help you to determine which actions bring you closer to your goals and those that don't. Second, know your *constraints*. Constraints (in form of time or other responsibilities) can help you set the parameter within which you can function efficiently. The last component is *action*. This component was the hardest for me to master, but it was the most fruitful. Because knowing values and limitations without engaging in appropriate actions does not serve any meaningful purpose. I strongly believe that learning time management can contribute greatly towards positive university experience."

—**Firdavs Khaydarov**, Psychology Major, Minnesota State University, Mankato

The Importance of Where You Do Your Work

Figure 3.12 Where you do work can be as important as when. (Credit: Mads Bodker / Flickr / Attribution 2.0 Generic (CC BY 2.0))

A large part of ensuring that you can complete tasks on time comes to setting up conditions that will allow you to do the work well. Much of this has to do with the environment where you will do your work. This not only includes physical space such as a work area, but other conditions like being free from distractions and your physical well-being and mental attitude.

The Right Space

Simple things, like where you are set up to do your work, can not only aid in your efficiency but also affect how well you can work or even if you can get the work completed at all. One example of this might be typing on a laptop. While it might seem more comfortable to lie back on a couch and type a long paper, sitting up at a desk or table actually increases your typing speed and reduces the number of mistakes. Even the kind of mouse you use can impact how you work, and using one you are comfortable with can make a big difference.

There are a host of other factors that can come into play as well. Do you have enough space? Is the space cluttered, or do you have the room to keep reference materials and other things you might need within arm's reach? Are there other ways you could work that might be even more efficient? For example, buying an inexpensive second monitor—even secondhand—might be the key to decreasing the amount of time you spend when you can have more than one document displayed at a time.

The key is to find what works for you and to treat your work space as another important resource needed to get the task finished.

Distraction Free

Few things are more frustrating than trying to do work while distractions are going on around you. If other people are continually interrupting you or there are things that keep pulling your attention from the task at hand, everything takes longer and you are more prone to mistakes.[4]

Many people say they work better with distractions—they prefer to leave the television or the radio on—but the truth is that an environment with too many interruptions is rarely helpful when focus is required. Before deciding that the television or talkative roommates do not bother you when you work, take an honest accounting of the work you produce with interruptions compared to work you do without.

If you find that your work is better without distractions, it is a good idea to create an environment that reduces interruptions. This may mean you have to go to a private room, use headphones, or go somewhere like a library to work. Regardless, the importance of a distraction-free environment cannot be emphasized enough.

Working at the Right Time

Most people are subject to their own rhythms, cycles, and preferences throughout their day. Some are alert and energetic in the mornings, while others are considered "night owls" and prefer to work after everyone else has gone to sleep. It can be important to be aware of your own cycles and to use them to your advantage. Rarely does anyone do their best work when they are exhausted, either physically or mentally. Just as it can be difficult to work when you are physically ill, it can also be a hindrance to try to learn or do mental work when you are tired or emotionally upset.

Your working environment definitely includes your own state of mind and physical well-being. Both have a significant influence on your learning and production ability. Because of this, it is not only important to be aware of your own condition and work preferences, but to actually try to create conditions that help you in these areas. One approach is to set aside a specific time to do certain kinds of work. You might find that you concentrate better after you have eaten a meal. If that is the case, make it a habit of doing homework every

---

4   https://en.calameo.com/read/00009178915b8f5b352ba

night after dinner. Or you might enjoy reading more after you are ready for bed, so you do your reading assignments just before you go to sleep at night. Some people find that they are more creative during a certain time of the day or that they are more comfortable writing with subtle lighting. It is worth taking the time to find the conditions that work best for you so that you can take advantage of them.

ANALYSIS QUESTION

Student Survey on Work Environment

Analysis: Take the time to think about where you will do your work and when. What can you do to help ensure your working environment will be helpful rather than harmful? What do you know doesn't work for you? What will you do to prevent those adverse conditions from creeping into your work environment?

Below is a quick survey to help you determine your own preferences in regard to your work space, the time you work, and distractions. Rank each option: 1–4, 1 meaning "least like me" and 4 meaning "most like me."

- I like my workspace to be organized and clean.
- There are certain places where I am more comfortable when I work.
- I prefer to be alone when I work on certain things.
- I find it difficult to read with other sounds or voices around me.
- There are certain times of the day when I can be more focused.
- My moods or emotions can interfere with my ability to concentrate

3.6 Goal Setting and Motivation

Estimated completion time: 11 minutes.

Questions to consider:

- How do I set motivational goals?
- What are SMART goals?
- What's the importance of an action plan?
- How do I keep to my plan?

Motivation often means the difference between success and failure. That applies to school, to specific tasks, and to life in general. One of the most effective ways to keep motivated is to set goals.

Goals can be big or small. A goal can range from *I am going to write one extra page tonight*, to *I am going to work to get an A in this course*, all the way to *I am going to graduate in the top of my class so I can start my career with a really good position*. The great thing about goals is that they can include and influence a number of other things that all work toward a much bigger picture. For example, if your goal is to get an A in a certain course, all the reading, studying, and every assignment you do for that course contributes to the larger goal. You have motivation to do each of those things and to do them well.

Setting goals is something that is frequently talked about, but it is often treated as something abstract. Like time management, goal setting is best done with careful thought and planning. This next section will explain how you can apply tested techniques to goal setting and what the benefits of each can be.

Set Goals That Motivate You

The first thing to know about goal setting is that a goal is a specific end result you desire. If the goal is not something you are really interested in, there is little motivational drive to achieve it. Think back to when you were much younger and some well-meaning adult set a goal for you—something that didn't really appeal to you at all. How motivated were you to achieve the goal? More than likely, if you were successful at all in meeting the goal, it was because you were motivated by earning the approval of someone or receiving a possible reward, or you were concerned with avoiding something adverse that might happen if you did not do what you were told. From an honest perspective in that situation, your real goal was based on something else, not the meeting of the goal set for you. To get the most from the goals you set, make sure they are things that you are interested in achieving.

That is not to say you shouldn't set goals that are supported by other motivations (e.g., If I finish studying by Friday, I can go out on Saturday), but the idea is to be intellectually honest with your goals.

Set SMART Goals

Goals should also be SMART. In this case, the word *smart* is not only a clever description of the type of goal, but it is also an acronym that stands for Specific, Measurable, Attainable, Relevant, and Time-bound. The reason these are all desirable traits for your goals is because they not only help you plan how to meet the goal, but they can also contribute to your decision-making processes during the planning stage.

What does it mean to create SMART goals?

- Specific—For a goal to be specific, it must be defined enough to actually determine the goal. A goal of *get a good job when I graduate* is too general. It doesn't define what a good job is. In fact, it doesn't even necessarily include a job in your chosen profession. A more specific goal would be something like *be hired as a nurse in a place of employment where it is enjoyable to work and that has room for promotion.*
- Measurable—The concept of *measurable* is one that is often overlooked when setting goals. What this means is that the goal should have clearly defined outcomes that are detailed enough to measure and can be used for planning of how you will achieve the goal. For example, setting a goal of *doing well in school* is a bit undefined, but making a goal of *graduating with a GPA above 3.0* is measurable and something you can work with. If your goal is measurable, you can know ahead of time how many points you will have to earn on a specific assignment to stay in that range or how many points you will need to make up in the next assignment if you do not do as well as you planned.
- Attainable—*Attainable* or *achievable* goals means they are reasonable and within your ability to accomplish. While a goal of *make an extra one million dollars by the end of the week* is something that would be nice to achieve, the odds that you could make that happen in a single week are not very realistic.
- Relevant—For goal setting, *relevant* means it applies to the situation. In relation to college, a goal of *getting a horse to ride* is not very relevant, but *getting dependable transportation* is something that would contribute to your success in school.
- Time-bound—Time-bound means you set a specific time frame to achieve the goal. *I will get my paper written by Wednesday* is time-bound. You know when you have to meet the goal. *I will get my paper written sometime soon* does not help you plan how and when you will accomplish the goal.

In the following table you can see some examples of goals that do and do not follow the SMART system. As you read each one, think about what elements make them SMART or how you might change those that are not.

Goal	Is it SMART?	
I am going to be rich someday.	No	There is nothing really specific, measurable, or time-bound in this goal.
I will graduate with my degree, on time.	Yes	The statement calls out specific, measureable, and time-bound details. The other attributes of attainable and relevant are implied.
I am going to save enough money to buy a newer car by June.	Yes	All SMART attributes are covered in this goal.
I would like to do well in all my courses next semester.	No	While this is clearly time-bound and meets most of the SMART goal attributes, it is not specific or measurable without defining what "do well" means.
I am going to start being a nicer person.	No	While most of the SMART attributes are implied, there is nothing really measurable in this goal.
I will earn at least a 3.0 GPA in all my courses next semester.	Yes	All of the SMART attributes are present in this goal.
I am going to start being more organized.	No	While most of the SMART attributes are implied, there is nothing really measurable in this goal.

Table 3.6

APPLICATION

Try writing two SMART goals—something with a one-week time frame and something that you will accomplish over the next year. Make certain that you include all the appropriate elements—Specific, Measurable, Attainable, Relevant, and Time-bound.

Make an Action Plan

Like anything else, making a step-by-step action plan of how you will attain your goals is the best way to make certain you achieve them. It doesn't matter if it is a smaller goal with immediate results (e.g., finish all your homework due by Friday) or something bigger that takes several years to accomplish (graduate with my degree in the proper amount of time).

The planning techniques you use for time management and achieving goals can be similar. In fact, accurate goal setting is very much a part of time management if you treat the completion of each task as a goal.

What follows is an example of a simple action plan that lists the steps for writing a short paper. You can use something like this or modify it in a way that would better suit your own preferences.

Action Plan

Task	Objective	When
Choose topic.	Select something interesting.	Needs to be done by Monday!
Write outline, look for references.	Create structure of paper and outline each part.	Monday, 6:00 p.m.
Research references to support outline, look for good quotes.	Strengthen paper and resources.	Tuesday, 6:00 p.m.
Write paper introduction and first page draft.	Get main ideas and thesis statement down.	Wednesday, 7:00 p.m.
Write second page and closing draft.	Finish main content and tie it all together.	Thursday, 6:00 p.m.
Rewrite and polish final draft.	Clean up for grammar, writing style, and effective communication.	Friday, 5:00 p.m.

Table 3.7

Another useful approach to goal setting is to create SMART goals and then write them down. For most people there is a higher level of commitment when we write something down. If you have your goals written out, you can refer to each component of the SMART acronym and make certain you are on track to achieve it.

Stick with It!

As with anything else, the key to reaching goals is to keep at it, keep yourself motivated, and overcome any obstacles along the way. In the following graphic you will find seven methods that highly successful people use to accomplish this.

Figure 3.13 These seven ways to stay motivated are good suggestions from highly successful people. What other strategies would you suggest?

3.7 Enhanced Strategies for Time and Task Management

Estimated completion time: 18 minutes.

Questions to consider:

- What strategy helps me prioritize my top tasks?
- How do I make the best use of my time when prioritizing?
- How do I make sure I tackle unpleasant tasks instead of putting them off?
- What's the best way to plan for long-term tasks?
- How do I find time in a busy schedule?

Over the years, people have developed a number of different strategies to manage time and tasks. Some of the strategies have proven to be effective and helpful, while others have been deemed not as useful.

The good news is that the approaches that do not work very well or do not really help in managing time do not get passed along very often. But others, those which people find of value, do. What follows here are three unique strategies that have become staples of time management. While not everyone will find that all three work for them in every situation, enough people have found them beneficial to pass them along with high recommendations.

Daily Top Three

The idea behind the *daily top three* approach is that you determine which three things are the most important to finish that day, and these become the tasks that you complete. It is a very simple technique that is effective because each day you are finishing tasks and removing them from your list. Even if you took one day off a week and completed no tasks on that particular day, a *daily top three* strategy would have you finishing 18 tasks in the course of a single week. That is a good amount of things crossed off your list.

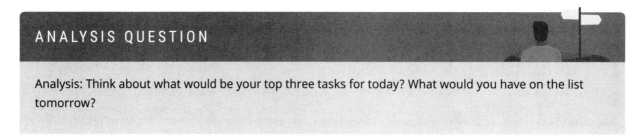

ANALYSIS QUESTION

Analysis: Think about what would be your top three tasks for today? What would you have on the list tomorrow?

Pomodoro Technique

Figure 3.14 The Pomodoro Technique is named after a type of kitchen timer, but you can use any clock or countdown timer. (Marco Verch /Flickr / Attribution 2.0 Generic (CC BY 2.0))

The Pomodoro Technique was developed by Francesco Cirillo. The basic concept is to use a timer to set work intervals that are followed by a short break. The intervals are usually about 25 minutes long and are called *pomodoros*, which comes from the Italian word for tomato because Cirillo used a tomato-shaped kitchen timer to keep track of the intervals.

In the original technique there are six steps:

1. Decide on the task to be done.
2. Set the timer to the desired interval.
3. Work on the task.
4. When the timer goes off, put a check mark on a piece of paper.
5. If you have fewer than four check marks, take a short break (3–5 minutes), then go to Step 1 or 2 (whichever is appropriate).
6. After four pomodoros, take a longer break (15–30 minutes), reset your check mark count to zero, and then go to Step 1 or 2.

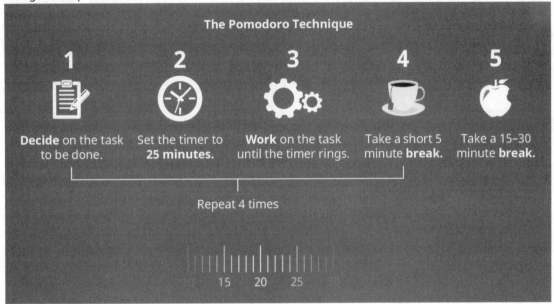

Figure 3.15 The Pomodoro Technique contains five defined steps.

There are several reasons this technique is deemed effective for many people. One is the benefit that is derived from quick cycles of work and short breaks. This helps reduce mental fatigue and the lack of productivity caused by it. Another is that it tends to encourage practitioners to break tasks down to things that can be completed in about 25 minutes, which is something that is usually manageable from the perspective of time available. It is much easier to squeeze in three 25-minute sessions of work time during the day than it is to set aside a 75- minute block of time.

Eat the Frog

Of our three quick strategies, *eat the frog* probably has the strangest name and may not sound the most inviting. The name comes from a famous quote, attributed to Mark Twain: "Eat a live frog first thing in the morning and nothing worse will happen to you the rest of the day." *Eat the Frog* is also the title of a best-selling book by Brian Tracy that deals with time management and avoiding procrastination.

How this applies to time and task management is based on the concept that if a person takes care of the biggest or most unpleasant task first, everything else will be easier after that.

Although stated in a humorous way, there is a good deal of truth in this. First, we greatly underestimate how much worry can impact our performance. If you are continually distracted by anxiety over a task you are dreading, it can affect the task you are working on at the time. Second, not only will you have a sense of accomplishment and relief when the task you are concerned with is finished and out of the way, but other tasks will seem lighter and not as difficult.

APPLICATION

Try Three Time Management Strategies

Over the next two weeks, try each of these three methods to see which ones might work for you. Is there one you favor over the others? Might each of these three approaches serve you better in different situations or with different tasks? Do you have a creative alternative or possibly a way to use some combination of these techniques?

In addition to these three strategies, you could also develop whole new approaches from suggestions found earlier in this chapter. For example, you could apply some of the strategies for avoiding procrastination or for setting appropriate priorities and see how they work in combination with these techniques or on their own.

The key is to find which system works best for you.

Breaking Down the Steps and Spreading Them over Shorter Work Periods

Above, you read about several different tried-and-tested strategies for effective time management—approaches that have become staples in the professional world. In this section you will read about two more creative techniques that combine elements from these other methods to handle tasks when time is scarce and long periods of time are a luxury you just do not have.

The concept behind this strategy is to break tasks into smaller, more manageable units that do not require as much time to complete. As an illustration of how this might work, imagine that you are assigned a two-page paper that is to include references. You estimate that to complete the paper—start to finish—would take you between four and a half and five hours. You look at your calendar over the next week and see that there simply are no open five-hour blocks (unless you decided to only get three hours of sleep one night). Rightly so, you decide that going without sleep is not a good option. While looking at your calendar, you do see that you can squeeze in an hour or so every night. Instead of trying to write the entire paper in one sitting, you break it up into much smaller components as shown in the table below:

Breaking Down Projects into Manageable-Sized Tasks

Day/Time	Task	Time
Monday, 6:00 p.m.	Write outline; look for references.	60 minutes
Tuesday, 6:00 p.m.	Research references to support outline; look for good quotes.	60 minutes
Wednesday, 7:00 p.m.	Write paper introduction and first page draft.	60 minutes
Thursday, 6:00 p.m.	Write second page and closing draft.	60 minutes
Friday, 5:00 p.m.	Rewrite and polish final draft.	60 minutes
Saturday, 10:00 a.m.	*Only if needed—finish or polish final draft.*	60 minutes?

Table 3.8

	Monday	Tuesday	Wednesday	Thursday	Friday	Saturday	Sunday
8:00–10:00		Work		Work			
10:00–12:00	Algebra	Work	Algebra	Work	Algebra	10 a.m.–11 a.m. *Only if needed*	Work
12:00–2:00	Lunch/study	1 p.m. English Comp	Lunch/study	1 p.m. English Comp	Lunch/study	Family picnic	Work
2:00–4:00	History	English Comp	History	English Comp	History	Family picnic	
4:00–6:00	Study for Algebra quiz.	Grocery	Study for History exam.	Study for History exam.	5 p.m.–6 p.m. Rewrite and polish final draft.	Family picnic	Laundry

Table 3.9

	Monday	Tuesday	Wednesday	Thursday	Friday	Saturday	Sunday
6:00–7:00	Write outline; look for references.	Research references to support outline; look for good quotes.	Research presentation project.	Write second page and closing draft	Create presentation.	Meet with Darcy.	Prepare school stuff for next week.
7:00–8:00	Free time	Free time	Write paper introduction and first page draft.	Research presentation project.	Create presentation.		Free time

Table 3.9

While this is a simple example, you can see how it would redistribute tasks to fit your available time in a way that would make completing the paper possible. In fact, if your time constraints were even more rigid, it would be possible to break these divided tasks down even further. You could use a variation of the Pomodoro Technique and write for three 20-minute segments each day at different times. The key is to look for ways to break down the entire task into smaller steps and spread them out to fit your schedule.

STUDENT PROFILE

"Time management is probably one of the hardest things I had to pick up when I got to college. For starters, I didn't have anyone to come wake me up if I forgot to set an alarm or to tell me to get out of bed so that I wouldn't be late. I had to start placing my phone far away from my bed; so that way, I would have to get out of bed in order to turn the alarm off. Accomplishing work on time can also be difficult. It's tough to find the fine balance between when you have to stay in and work on assignments and when is acceptable to go out and do leisure activities.

"I learned the 8-8-8 rule. Every day you spend eight hours working on school work or going to class, eight hours of free time to do what you want, and then eight hours to sleep at night so that you will get enough rest. Sleep is crucial for time management. I learned very quickly that you cannot focus or be productive if you are struggling to keep your head from falling over because you are so tired. Basically, I've learned that if you want to be successful in college, then you have to be on top of your game when it comes to time. It's something thing you cannot make up once it's gone."

—**Preston Allen**, University of Central Arkansas

Analyzing Your Schedule and Creating Time to Work

Of all the strategies covered in this chapter, this one may require the most discipline, but it can also be the most beneficial in time management. The fact is most of us waste time throughout the day. Some of it is due to a lack of awareness, but it can also be caused by the constraints of our current schedules. An example of this is when we have 15 to 20 minutes before we must leave to go somewhere. We don't do anything with that time because we are focused on leaving or where we are going, and we might not be organized enough to accomplish something in that short of a time period. In fact, a good deal of our 24- hour days are spent a few minutes at a time waiting for the next thing scheduled to occur. These small units of time add up to a fair amount each day.

The intent of this strategy is to recapture those lost moments and use them to your advantage. This may take careful observation and consideration on your part, but the results of using this as a method of time management are more than worth it.

The first step is to look for those periods of time that are wasted or that can be repurposed. In order to identify them, you will need to pay attention to what you do throughout the day and how much time you spend doing it. The example of waiting for the next thing in your schedule has already been given, but there are many others. How much time do you spend in activities after you have really finished doing them but are still lingering because you have not begun to do something else (e.g., letting the next episode play while binge-watching, reading social media posts or waiting for someone to reply, surfing the Internet, etc.)? You might be surprised to learn how much time you use up each day by just adding a few unproductive minutes here and there.

If you set a limit on how much time you spend on each activity, you might find that you can recapture time to do other things. An example of this would be limiting yourself to reading news for 30 minutes. Instead of reading the main things that interest you and then spending an additional amount of time just looking at things that you are only casually interested in because that is what you are doing at the moment, you could stop after a certain allotted period and use the extra time you have gained on something else.

After you identify periods of lost time, the next step will be to envision how you might restructure your activities to bring those extra minutes together into useful blocks of time. Using the following scenario as an illustration, we will see how this could be accomplished.

Figure 3.16 Sarah has to balance a lot of obligations.

On Tuesday nights, Sarah has a routine: After work, she does her shopping for the week (2 hours driving and shopping) and then prepares and eats dinner (1 hour). After dinner, she spends time on homework (1 hour) and catching up with friends, reading the news, and other Internet activities (1 hour), and then she watches television or reads before going to bed (1 hour). While it may seem that there is very little room for improvement in her schedule without cutting out something she enjoys, limiting the amount of time she spends on each activity and rethinking how she goes about each task can make a significant difference.

In this story, Sarah's Tuesday-night routine includes coming home from work, taking stock of which items in her home she might need to purchase, and then driving to the store. While at the store, she spends time picking out and selecting groceries as she plans for meals she will eat during the rest of the week. Then, after making her purchases, she drives home. Instead, if she took the time to make a list and plan for what she needed at the store before she arrived, she would not spend as much time looking for inspiration in each aisle. Also, if she had a prepared list, not only could she quickly pick up each item, but she could stop at the store on the way home from work, thus cutting out the extra travel time. If purchasing what she needed took 30 minutes less because she was more organized and she cut out an additional 20 minutes of travel time by saving the extra trip to the store from her house, she could recapture a significant amount of her Tuesday evening. If she then limited the time she spent catching up with friends and such to 30 minutes or maybe did some of that while she prepared dinner, she would find that she had added almost an extra hour and a half to the time available to her on that evening, without cutting out anything she needed to do or enjoys. If she decided to spend her time on study or homework, this would more than double the time she previously had available in her schedule for homework.

ANALYSIS QUESTION

Reflection

Analysis: Identify areas in the way you spend your day where you may be able to recapture and repurpose time. Are there things you can move around to gain more time? Are there ways you can combine tasks or reduce travel time?

Summary

This chapter began by pointing out the dangers of poor time management, both in cost and even the potential risk to graduation. After presenting why time management is important, sections of the text covered how time management for college can be different from what students may have experienced before. Following this, the chapter contained several sections on how to effectively manage time (including predicting time on task), how to use technology to your advantage, and how to prioritize tasks. Other topics included goal setting and motivation, some specific strategies for time and task management, and avoiding procrastination.

Career Connection

Rick says: I've wanted to work in radio since I was in high school and had great opportunities in college to learn at the campus station. I interned for a semester at a local Top 40 station and, after graduation, was offered a position as the producer of the station's morning show.

The only problem: I had to be at the radio station by 4:45 a.m. I couldn't do it. I tried everything—alarms on my phone, clock radio alarms, friends calling me. This is not a job you can be late for—dead air is a radio DJ's greatest nightmare. But no matter what I tried, I could not wake up on time. The third time I arrived late, the radio station let me go.

Reflection question: How might you have handled the situation differently? How might this aspiring radio DJ have managed his time differently to ensure he was not late for work?

For discussion: Is the Internet responsible for most of our wasted work time? Read through this article. What do you think?

https://openstax.org/l/whowastestime

Rethinking

Revisit the questions you answered at the beginning of the chapter, and consider one option you learned in this chapter that might change your answer to one of them.

1. I regularly procrastinate completing tasks that don't interest me or seem challenging.
2. I use specific time management strategies to complete tasks.
3. I find it difficult to prioritize tasks because I am not sure what is really important.

4. I am pleased with my ability to manage my time.

 Where do you go from here?

Refining your time management skills based on an honest assessment is something that should never stop. The benefits of good time management skills are something that will apply to the rest of your life. What would you like to learn more about? Choose a topic from the list below, and create an annotated bibliography that would direct further research.

- Psychological reasons for procrastinating
- Technology and social media as distractions
- Additional time management strategies
- Time management strategies that successful people use

Figure 4.1 Credit: University of the Fraser Valley / Flickr / Attribution 2.0 Generic (CC-BY 2.0)

Chapter Outline

- **4.1** Defining Values and Setting Goals
- **4.2** Planning Your Degree Path
- **4.3** Making a Plan
- **4.4** Managing Change and the Unexpected

Introduction

Student Survey

How do you feel about your readiness to create an academic and life plan? These questions will help you determine how the chapter concepts relate to you right now. As you are introduced to new concepts and practices, it can be informative to reflect on how your understanding changes over time. We'll revisit these questions at the end of the chapter to see whether your feelings have changed. Take this quick survey to figure it out, ranking questions on a scale of 1–4, 1 meaning "least like me" and 4 meaning "most like me."

1. I have reflected on and can identify my personal values.
2. I have set both short- and long-term academic goals.
3. I am familiar with the requirements I must complete and options I must select to obtain a college degree.
4. I am familiar with the resources, tools, and individuals who can assist me in developing an effective plan for success.

You can also take the Chapter 4 survey (https://openstax.org/l/collegesurvey04) anonymously online.

STUDENT PROFILE

"I came into my university with little to no knowledge about how to decide a college major. I can now say with confidence that I have found the major for me! This was not an easy process though. It takes a lot of reflection to decide where you will focus your time and energy for your college career. The most important thing I had to consider was what major would provide me with learning outcomes that matter the most to me? I switched my major three or four times and each time I weighed the pros and cons of the major I was exiting and the one I was transitioning into. I decided to major in sociology and it has been the best decision of my academic career! I value social awareness and deep understandings of social phenomenon and sociology provided the course material necessary to place me on a path to begin learning about those topics. As a first-generation and low-income student navigating college pathways can be difficult. That is why it is so important to be open to change and set on learning what you want to learn how to get yourself to the next step!"

—**Drew Carter**, Rice University

About This Chapter

Among the most celebrated differences between high school and college is the freedom that students look forward to when they complete their mandatory high school education and take up the voluntary pursuit of a college degree. Though not every college freshman comes fresh from high school, those who do might be looking forward to the freedom of moving away from home onto a campus or into an apartment. Others might be excited about the potential to sleep in on a Monday morning and take their classes in the afternoon. For others, balancing a class schedule with an already-busy life filled with work and other responsibilities may make college seem less like freedom and more like obligation. In either case, and however they might imagine their next experience to be, students can anticipate increased freedom of choice in college and the ability to begin to piece together how their values, interests, and developing knowledge and skills will unfold into a career that meets their goals and dreams.

In Chapter 3, Managing Your Time and Priorities, we cover how goal setting and prioritizing help you plan and manage your time effectively. This chapter extends that discussion by recognizing that it can be challenging to stay on task and motivated if you don't see how those tasks fit into a larger plan. Even the freedom to choose can become overwhelming without a plan to guide those choices. The goal of this chapter is to help you develop the personal skills and identify the resources, tools, and support people to help you make sense of your choices and formulate a personal academic and career plan. We will also consider how to take those first steps toward making your plan a reality and what to do if or when you realize you're off track from where you had hoped to be.

By the time you complete this chapter, you should be able to do the following:

- Use your personal values to guide your decision-making, set short-term goals that build toward a long-term goal, and plan how you will track progress toward your goals.
- List the types of college certificates, degrees, special programs, and majors you can pursue, as well as general details about their related opportunities and requirements.
- Take advantage of resources to draft and track an academic plan.
- Recognize decision-making and planning as continuous processes, especially in response to unexpected change.

4.1 Defining Values and Setting Goals

Estimated completion time: 24 minutes.

Questions to consider:

- What beliefs help shape your decision-making and goals?
- How do you set manageable goals that will help you stay on track?

Figure 4.2 Figuring out the best major and your academic pathway can be confusing and challenging. (Credit: Bruce Mars / Pexels)

> **"In every single thing you do, you are choosing a direction. Your life is a product of choices."**
>
> — Dr. Kathleen Hall, CEO of the Stress Institute and Mindful Living Network[1]

A recent high school graduate, Mateo was considering his options for the future. He knew he wanted to go to college, but he wasn't quite sure what he would study. At a family picnic to celebrate his graduation, he talked about his indecision with his two uncles. One uncle, his Uncle Nico, told him that his best bet was to find out what types of jobs would be hiring in a couple years at high enough salary for Mateo to afford to live however he desired. His other uncle, who rarely agreed with Uncle Nico, nodded and said, "Hey, that's one way to look at it, but don't you want to enjoy what you do every day regardless of how much money you make? You should do whatever interests you. After all, don't they say that if you love what you do, you'll never work a day in your life?"

Mateo appreciated the advice of his uncles and realized that they might both be right. He wanted to do something that interested him, but he also wanted to be employable and to make money. Clarifying his interests and recognizing his values would be key to helping Mateo decide his path.

Values

Values are the basic beliefs that guide our thinking and actions. Whether we are consciously aware of them or not, values influence both our attitudes and our actions. They help us determine what is important and what

---

1 Hall, Kathleen. *Alter Your Life: Overbooked, Overworked, Overwhelmed?* Oak Haven Press. Georgia. 2005.

makes us happy. It is important to think about and reflect on your values, especially as you make decisions.

ACTIVITY

Determining Your Values

To begin to identify some of your personal values, consider the examples listed below. As a first step, select the five that you find most important, that bring you the greatest happiness, or that make you feel the most proud. Then, rank those five values in order of importance. Feel encouraged to write in other options that are relevant to you.

Achievement	Efficiency	Hard Work	Positivity
Adventure	Empathy	Health	Security
Ambition	Equality	Honesty	Selflessness
Balance	Excellence	Honor	Service
Belonging	Exploration	Humility	Simplicity
Calm	Fairness	Independence	Spontaneity
Challenge	Faith	Intelligence	Stability
Commitment	Family	Joy	Strength
Community	Fitness	Justice	Success
Competition	Flexibility	Love	Trustworthiness
Contribution	Freedom	Loyalty	Understanding
Control	Friends	Making a Difference	Uniqueness
Creativity	Fun	Merit	
Curiosity	Generosity	Openness	
Dependability	Growth	Originality	
Diversity	Happiness	Perfection	

Table 4.1

Another way to recognize the important influence of values is to consider if you have ever made a decision that you later regretted. Did you reflect on your values prior to making that choice? Sometimes others ask us to do things that are inconsistent with our values. Knowing what you value and making plans accordingly is an important effort to help you stay on track toward your goals.

> ### ANALYSIS QUESTION
>
> Recall a decision that you have recently made (for example, a smaller decision about how to spend your Saturday, or maybe a larger decision about where to apply for part-time work). Did the values you identified through this exercise influence that decision? If so, how?

Figure 4.3 Credit: Curt Smith / Flickr / Attribution 2.0 Generic (CC-BY 2.0)

Goals and Planning

Have you ever put together a jigsaw puzzle? Many people start by looking for the edge and corner pieces to assemble the border. Some will then group pieces with similar colors, while others just try to fit in new pieces as they pick them up. Regardless of strategy, a jigsaw puzzle is most easily solved when people have a picture to reference. When you know what the picture should look like, you can gauge your progress and avoid making mistakes. If you were to put a puzzle together facedown (cardboard side up, rather than picture side up), you could still connect the pieces, but it would take you much longer to understand how it should fit together. Your attempts, beyond the border, would be mostly by trial and error. Pursuing anything without goals and a plan is like putting together an upside-down puzzle. You can still finish, or get to where you're meant to be, but it will take you much longer to determine your steps along the way.

In Chapter 3, you learned about the SMART goal method for setting actionable goals, or goals that are planned and stated with enough clarity for the goal-setter to take realistic action toward meeting those goals. SMART goals help you focus on your priorities and manage your time while also providing a means of organizing your thinking and actions into manageable steps. Long- and short-term goals help to connect the action steps.

Long-Term Goals

Long-term goals are future goals that often take years to complete. An example of a long-term goal might be to complete a bachelor of arts degree within four years. Another example might be purchasing a home or running a marathon. While this chapter focuses on academic and career planning, long-term goals are not exclusive to these areas of your life. You might set long-term goals related to fitness, wellness, spirituality, and relationships, among many others. When you set a long-term goal in any aspect of your life, you are demonstrating a commitment to dedicate time and effort toward making progress in that area. Because of this commitment, it is important that your long-term goals are aligned with your values.

Short-Term Goals

Setting short-term goals helps you consider the necessary steps you'll need to take, but it also helps to chunk a larger effort into smaller, more manageable tasks. Even when your long-term goals are SMART, it's easier to stay focused and you'll become less overwhelmed in the process of completing short-term goals.

You might assume that short-term and long-term goals are different goals that vary in the length of time they take to complete. Given this assumption, you might give the example of a long-term goal of learning how to create an app and a short-term goal of remembering to pay your cell phone bill this weekend. These are valid goals, but they don't exactly demonstrate the intention of short- and long-term goals for the purposes of effective planning.

Instead of just being bound by the difference of time, short-term goals are the action steps that take less time to complete than a long-term goal, but that help you work toward your long-term goals. To determine your best degree option, it might make sense to do some research to determine what kind of career you're most interested in pursuing. Or, if you recall that short-term goal of paying your cell phone bill this weekend, perhaps this short-term goal is related to a longer-term goal of learning how to better manage your budgeting and finances.

Setting Long- and Short-Term Goals

Sunil's story provides an example of effective goal setting. While meeting with an academic advisor at his college to discuss his change of major, Sunil was tasked with setting long- and short-term goals aligned with that major. He selected a degree plan in business administration, sharing with his advisor his intention to work in business and hopefully human relations in particular. His advisor discussed with him how he could set short-term goals that would help his progress on that plan. Sunil wondered if he should be as specific as setting short-term goals week by week or for the successful completion of every homework assignment or exam. His advisor shared that he could certainly break his goals down into that level of specificity if it helped him to stay focused, but recommended that he start by outlining how many credits or courses he would hope to complete. Sunil drafted his goals and planned to meet again with his advisor in another week to discuss.

	My Goals – Sunil Shah
Long-term	My goal is to graduate from my college in a total of 4 years with a degree in business administration, concentrating in human relations.
Short-term	• Finish the 12 credits I am taking in my first semester with at least a 3.0 GPA • Take 15 credits in the spring semester while maintaining my GPA • Take a 3 credit class online in the summer • Take 15 credits in my third semester • Apply for study abroad program in my third semester • Take 18 credits in my fourth semester • Complete study abroad program for business during my fifth semester (12 credits) • Apply for summer internship program during fifth semester • Take 15 credits in my sixth semester • Complete summer internship program • Take 15 credits in my seventh semester • Take 15 credits in my eighth semester • Graduate in four years and take my parents out for an awesome dinner to thank them for their support!

Figure 4.4 Sunil drafted his goals before meeting with his advisor to discuss them.

Sunil worried that his list of short-term goals looked more like a checklist of tasks than anything. His advisor reassured him, sharing that short-term goals can absolutely look like a checklist of tasks because their purpose is to break the long-term goal down into manageable chunks that are easier to focus on and complete. His advisor then recommended that Sunil add to his plan an additional note at the end of every other semester to "check in" with his advisor to make certain that he was on track.

Planning for Adjustments

You will recall from the SMART goals goal-setting model that goals should be both measurable and attainable. Far too often, however, we set goals with the best of intentions but then fail to keep track of our progress or adjust our short-term goals if they're not helping us to progress as quickly as we'd like. When setting goals, the most successful planners also consider when they will evaluate their progress. At that time, perhaps after each short-term goal should have been met, they may reflect on the following:

1. **Am I meeting my short-term goals as planned?**
    - If so, celebrate!
    - If not, you may want to additionally consider:
2. **Are my short-term goals still planned across time in a way where they will meet my long-term goals?**
    - If so, continue on your path.
    - If not, reconsider the steps you need to take to meet your long-term goal. If you've gotten off track or if you've learned that other steps must be taken, set new short-term goals with timelines appropriate to each step. You may also want to seek some additional advice from others who have successfully met long-term goals that are similar to your own.

3. **Are my long-term goals still relevant, or have my values changed since I set my goals?**
    - If your goals are still relevant to your interests and values, then continue on your path, seeking advice and support as needed to stay on track.
    - If your goals are no longer relevant or aligned with your values, give careful consideration to setting new goals.

While departing from your original goals may seem like a failure, taking the time to reflect on goals before you set them aside to develop new ones is a success. Pivoting from a goal to new, better-fitting goal involves increased self-awareness and increased knowledge about the processes surrounding your specific goal (such as the details of a college transfer, for example). With careful reflection and information seeking, your change in plans may even demonstrate learning and increased maturity!

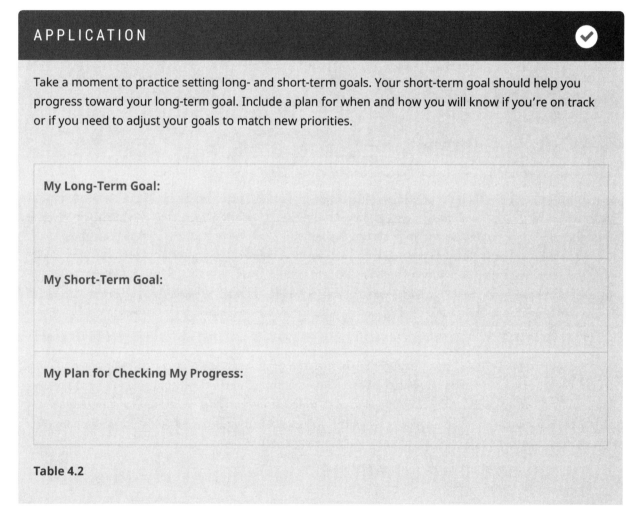

APPLICATION

Take a moment to practice setting long- and short-term goals. Your short-term goal should help you progress toward your long-term goal. Include a plan for when and how you will know if you're on track or if you need to adjust your goals to match new priorities.

My Long-Term Goal:

My Short-Term Goal:

My Plan for Checking My Progress:

Table 4.2

Keep in mind that values and goals may change over time as you meet new people, your life circumstances change, and you gain more wisdom or self-awareness. In addition to setting goals and tracking your progress, you should also periodically reflect on your goals to ensure their consistency with your values.

ANALYSIS QUESTION

Now that you've set some goals, what is your plan to track your progress on those goals? Can you identify a time you will set aside to intentionally reflect on your progress and whether you need to set any new short-term goals or perhaps adjust your larger plans?

4.2 Planning Your Degree Path

Estimated completion time: 32 minutes.

Questions to consider:

- What types of college degrees or certifications can I pursue?
- What is the difference between majors and minors?
- How do preprofessional programs differ from other majors?
- Do some majors have special requirements beyond regular coursework?

To set goals for your academic and career path, you must first have an understanding of the options available for you to pursue and the requirements you will need to meet. The next section provides an overview of academic programs and college degrees that are common among many colleges and universities in the United States. Please note that each institution will have its own specific options and requirements, so the intention of this section is both to help you understand your opportunities and to familiarize you with language that colleges typically use to describe these opportunities. After reviewing this section, you should be better able to formulate specific questions to ask at your school or be better prepared to navigate and search your own college's website.

Types of Degrees

Whereas in most states high school attendance through the 12th grade is mandatory, or *compulsory*, a college degree may be pursued voluntarily. There are fields that do not require a degree. Bookkeeping, computer repair, massage therapy, and childcare are all fields where certification programs—tracks to study a specific subject or career without need of a complete degree—may be enough.

However, many individuals will find that an associate's or bachelor's degree is a requirement to enter their desired career field. According to United States Census data published in 2017, more than one-third of the adult population in the country has completed at least a bachelor's degree, so this may be the degree that is most familiar to you.

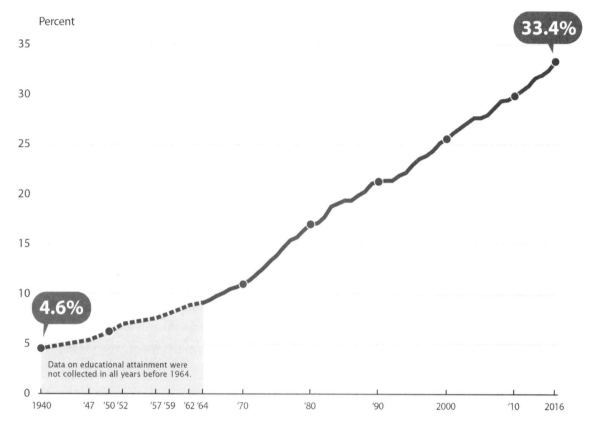

Figure 4.5 The number of American's receiving Bachelor's degrees has increased significantly. While not every job requires one, the level of overall education required for most careers continues to go up. (Credit: US Department of Commerce / Public Domain)

Not every job requires a bachelor's degree, and some require even higher degrees or additional specialized certifications. As you develop your academic plan, it is important to research your field of interest to see what requirements might be necessary or most desirable.

Require Associate's Degrees	Require Bachelor's Degrees	Require Additional Certifications	Require Graduate Degrees
Radiology Technician	Nurse	Public School Teacher	Lawyer
Dental Hygienist	Computer/Information Systems Manager	Accountant	College or University Professor
Web Developer	Airline Pilot	Financial Advisor	Pharmacist
Graphic Designer	Electrical Engineer		Marriage and Family Therapist
Automotive Technician	Construction Manager		Occupational Therapist

Table 4.3 Example Jobs by Minimum Degree Qualification[2]

To distinguish between the types of degrees, it is useful to understand that courses are often assigned a number of credits, sometimes called *semester hours* as well. Credits relate to the calculated hours during a course that a student spends interacting with the instructor and/or the course material through class time, laboratory time, online discussions, homework, etc. Courses at all degree levels are typically assigned a value of one to six credits, although students often need to complete a developmental education course or two, often in English or math. These requirements, which cost as much as typical college courses but do not grant college credit, are meant to provide some basic information students may have missed in high school but that will be necessary to keep up in college-level coursework.

The minimum or maximum number of credits required to graduate with different degrees varies by state or institution, but approximate minimum numbers of credits are explained below. Keep in mind that although a minimum number of credits must be completed to get a certain degree, total credits completed is not the only consideration for graduation—you must take your credits or courses in particular subjects indicated by your college.

To determine your best degree option, it might make sense to do some research to determine what kind of career you're most interested in pursuing. Visit your campus career center to meet with a counselor to guide you through this process. These services are free to students—similar services can be pricey once you've graduated, so take advantage. There are other tools online you can investigate.

GET CONNECTED

These free, online self-assessments help you narrow down your choices.

---

2 Minimum degree qualifications may vary by state.

> - MyPlan (https://openstax.org/l/valuesassessment) identifies your motivations by having you rank different aspects of work, then creating a ranked list of different possible jobs.
> - MAPP Test (https://openstax.org/l/MAPPassessment) helps you determine what you love to do and what you don't love to do and then creates a list of jobs that might be a good fit for you.
> - The Career Cluster Interest Survey (https://openstax.org/l/clustersurvey) is a quick tool to let you create career clusters based on personal qualities and school subjects and activities you especially enjoy.

Associate's Degrees

To enter an associate's degree program, students must have a high school diploma or its equivalent. Associate's degree programs may be intended to help students enter a technical career field, such as automotive technology, graphic design, or entry-level nursing in some states. Such technical programs may be considered an Associate of Applied Arts (AAA) or Associate of Applied Science (AAS) degrees, though there are other titles as well.

Other associate's degree programs are intended to prepare a student with the necessary coursework to transfer into a bachelor's degree program upon graduation. These transfer-focused programs usually require similar general education and foundational courses that a student would need in the first half of a bachelor's degree program. Transfer-focused associate's degrees may be called Associate of Arts (AA) or Associate of Science (AS), or other titles, depending on the focus of study.

Figure 4.6 Air traffic controllers are extremely important and well-paid jobs that typically require an associates degree. (Credit: Expert Infantry / Flickr / Attribution 2.0 Generic (CC-BY 2.0))

An associate's degree is typically awarded when a student has completed a minimum of 60 credits, approximately 20 courses, meeting the requirements of a specific degree. Some technical associate's degrees, such as nursing, may require additional credits in order to meet requirements for special certifications. You may find that your college or university does not offer associate's degrees. Most associate's degrees are offered by community or junior colleges, or by career and technical colleges.

ACTIVITY

What to Ask

If you're planning your associate's degree, here are some specific questions you may want to research.

If you intend to enter a technical career that requires special certification:

- Does your college prepare you to take a certification exam, or will you be meeting those requirements through your courses?
- Does your college have any special internship or employment placement arrangements with employers to help you gain experience or get started in the field?

If you intend to transfer upon graduation:

- Is your college regionally accredited?
- Does your college have any special transfer agreements for guaranteed transfer of credits or perhaps for discounted tuition?
- Does your state have special transfer agreements or requirements that make it easier to transfer to colleges or universities within the same state?

Bachelor's Degrees

When someone generally mentions "a college degree," they are often referring to the bachelor's degree, or baccalaureate degree. Because it takes four years of full-time attendance to complete a bachelor's degree, this degree is also referred to as a "four-year degree." Similar to an associate's degree, to enter a bachelor's degree program a student must have completed a high school diploma or its equivalent. Both associate's degrees and bachelor's degrees are considered *undergraduate degrees*, thus students working toward these degrees are often called *undergraduates*. A student with an associate's degree may transfer that degree to meet some (usually half) of the requirements of a bachelor's degree; however, completion of an associate's degree is not necessary for entry into a bachelor's degree program.

A bachelor's degree is usually completed with a minimum of 120 credits, or approximately 40 courses. Some specialized degree programs may require more credits. (If an associate's degree has been transferred, the number of credits from that degree usually counts toward the 120 credits. For example, if an associate's degree was 60 credits, then a student must take 60 additional credits to achieve their bachelor's degree.)

Bachelor of Arts (BA), Bachelor of Science (BS), Bachelor of Science in Nursing (BSN), and Bachelor of Fine Arts (BFA) are the most popular degree titles at this level and differ primarily in their focus on exploring a broader range of subject areas, as with a BA, versus focusing in more depth on a particular subject, as with a BS, BSN, or BFA. Regardless of whether a student is pursuing a BA, BS, BSN, or BFA, each of these programs requires a balance of credits or courses in different subject areas. In the United States, a bachelor's degree comprises courses from three categories: *general education* courses, *major* courses, and *electives*. A fourth category of courses would be those required for a minor, which we will discuss in more detail in the section on majors and minors.

General Education

General education, also called *core curriculum*, is a group of courses that are often set as requirements by your state or by your individual college. These courses provide you with a foundation of knowledge across a breadth of fields and are also intended to help you further develop college-level critical-thinking and problem-solving abilities. You may be able to select courses from a general education menu of courses available at your institution. More than half of your bachelor's degree program is likely made up of general education courses.

English composition
Humanities courses that study our beliefs and the expression of our beliefs such as literature, philosophy, politics, art, or religious studies
Social science courses that study our behavior such as psychology, sociology, anthropology, or economics
Laboratory science courses such as biology, chemistry, physics, and environmental science
Mathematics
Technology or computer skills
Foreign language, diversity, or global studies courses that provide introduction to different cultures or global social issues and promote cultural awareness
College success or first-year experience courses that provide introduction to your specific institution, discuss college-level expectations and skills, and/or provide assistance with academic and career planning

Table 4.4 General Education Categories. While your college may use different labels, general education courses often include a selection of courses from these categories.

Major Courses

Major courses are courses in your field of interest and provide you with the foundational knowledge required for further study in that field or with the skills necessary to enter your career. Some schools may refer to these as *career studies* courses. Major courses often have a series of *prerequisites*, or courses that must be taken in sequence prior to other courses, starting with an introductory course and progressing into more depth. Major courses usually make up about a fourth or more of a bachelor's degree (30 credits, or approximately 10 courses). A BS or BFA degree may require more major courses than a BA degree. Colleges and universities usually require students to select a major by the time they've completed 30 total credits.

Electives

Electives are free-choice courses. Though you may have a choice to select from a menu of options to meet general education and major requirements, electives are even less restricted. Some students may be able to take more electives than others due to their choice of major or if they are able to take courses that meet more than one requirement (for example, a sociology course may be both a major requirement and a general education social science course). Some colleges intentionally allow room for electives in a program to ensure that students, particularly those students who are undecided about their major, are able to explore different programs without exceeding the total number of credits required to graduate with a bachelor's degree. In other cases, students may have taken all of their major courses and fulfilled their general education requirements but still need additional credits to fulfill the minimum to graduate. The additional courses taken to meet the total credit requirement (if necessary) are considered electives.

Graduate Degrees

According to United States Census data published in 2018, 13.1 percent of the U.S. adult population have completed advanced degrees.[3] Whereas associate's and bachelor's degrees are considered undergraduate degrees and require high school graduation for entry, advanced degrees called graduate degrees require prior completion of a bachelor's degree. Some professions require graduate degrees as a minimum job qualification, such as pharmacists, lawyers, physical therapists, psychologists, and college professors. In other cases, students may be motivated to pursue a graduate degree to obtain a higher-level job or higher salary, or to be more competitive in their field. Some students are also interested in learning about some subject in greater depth than they did at the undergraduate level. Because graduate degrees do not include general education or free elective courses, they are very focused on career-specific knowledge and skills. Graduate degrees include master's, doctoral, and professional degrees. *Master's degrees* often require 30–60 credits and take one to two years of full-time attendance to complete. Some master's degrees, like those for counselors, require supervised job experience as a component of the degree and therefore require more credits.

Figure 4.7 Pharmacists and related scientific or medical careers require master's degrees. (Credit: US Department of Agriculture / Flickr / Public Domain)

Doctorate and professional degrees are the highest level of advanced degrees. Approximately 3.5% of the U.S. adult population has completed a doctorate or professional degree. Very few careers require this level of education for entry, so fewer individuals pursue these degrees. Doctorates are offered in many subjects and primarily prepare students to become researchers in their field of study. This in-depth level of education often

---

3 United States Census Bureau. (2019, February 21). Number of People with Master's and Doctoral Degrees Doubles Since 2000. Retrieved from: https://www.census.gov/library/stories/2019/02/number-of-people-with-masters-and-phd-degrees-double-since-2000.html

requires an additional 90–120 credits beyond the bachelor's degree, and may or may not require a master's degree prior to entry. (A master's degree as an entry requirement may reduce the number of credits required to complete the doctoral degree.)

Professional degrees are a specific type of doctorate-level degree that focus on skills to be applied in a *practical*, or hands-on, career rather than as a researcher. The most common professional degrees are Doctor of Medicine (MD) for aspiring medical doctors, Juris Doctor (JD) for aspiring lawyers, Doctor of Pharmacy (PharmD) for aspiring pharmacists, and Doctor of Education (EdD) for aspiring school and college or university administrators. If the career you are pursuing requires a graduate degree, you should keep this end goal in mind as you plan for the timeline and finances required to meet your goals. You may also want to inquire about special agreements that your college or university may have to expedite admission into or completion of graduate degrees. For example, some universities offer *4+1 master's programs*, wherein students take both bachelor's and master's level courses during their last year as an undergraduate to accelerate the completion of both degrees.

Other Post-Baccalaureate Credentials

Post-baccalaureate refers to structured learning experiences pursued after a bachelor's degree is achieved. While some such activities are structured into graduate degrees as described in the sections above, other fields value continuing education credits, competency badges, and additional certifications. These post-baccalaureate credentials may need to be completed prior to entering a career field, may be obtained as an option to gain competitive advantage for hiring, or may be achieved during the course of an individual's career to stay current, maintain qualification, or be promoted. To determine if your field requires post-baccalaureate credentials, you may want to speak with an established professional in that career, review the qualifications section of related job descriptions, or visit with a career counselor on your campus. In a world that changes as rapidly as ours, engaging in lifelong learning is advisable regardless of the specific requirements of any particular career choice.

Figure 4.8 Some computing, networking, and database careers require post-baccalaureate certificates. (Credit: WOCinTechChat / Flickr / Attribution 2.0 Generic (CC-BY 2.0))

ACTIVITY

Draft an Education Timeline

Use the Bureau of Labor Statistics online Occupational Outlook Handbook (https://www.openstax.org/l/OOH) to search for occupations that interest you, and note the level of education that these jobs require. Refer to your college's academic catalog (frequently located on the college's website) or curriculum maps to see the suggested sequence of courses for majors that relate to your career or careers of interest.

Select three interesting jobs and sketch a timeline for each, starting with your first semester of undergraduate study (whether you're getting an associate's or a bachelor's) and ending with the point when you will meet the minimum requirements to be qualified for that job. Keep in mind that the timeline of students attending full-time may differ from those who are attending part-time.

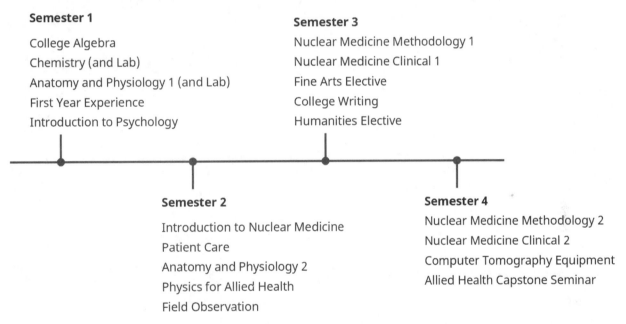

Figure 4.9 This example timeline for a nuclear medicine technician spaces different types of courses across four semesters. Note that some courses may be prerequisites for other courses and experiences. For example, Introduction to Nuclear Medicine, Patient Care, and a Field Observation may be required before students engage in the formal Clinical in Semester 3. When planning, look at each course description in the college catalog to understand its prerequisites.

Majors and Minors

One of the most common questions an undergraduate college student will be asked is "What's your major?" As we already noted, your major is only one part of your undergraduate (associate's or bachelor's) degree, but it is the part that most demonstrates your interests and possible future goals. At some point during your studies you will be asked to decide on, or *declare*, a major. You may also be able to select a *minor* or additional concentration. Whereas a major comprises approximately 10–12 courses of a bachelor's degree program and is required, a minor is usually 5–8 courses, is often optional, and may count toward or contribute to exceeding the total number of credits required for graduation. Rather than take elective courses, some students will select courses that meet the requirements for a minor. When selecting a major and possibly a minor, you'll want to consider how the knowledge and skills you gain through those fields of study prepare you for a particular career. Majors and minors can be complementary. For example, a major in business might be well-matched with a minor in a foreign language, thus allowing the student to pursue a career in business with a company that hires bilingual employees. It is important to research careers of interest to you when selecting your major and/or minor to determine what will best help you to meet your goals.

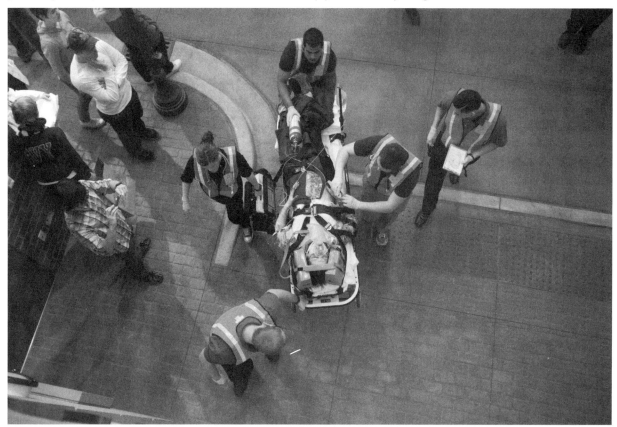

Figure 4.10 Many majors, such nursing, allied health, and emergency medical technician, may include simulations and other activities to expose students to the real-world activities of their field. (Credit: COD Newsroom / Flickr / Attribution 2.0 Generic (CC-BY 2.0))

Preprofessional Programs

Some undergraduate degrees are specifically designed to prepare students to later pursue professional degrees (such as the MD or PharmD) at the graduate level. Such programs are called *preprofessional programs, preprofessional majors,* or *preprofessional tracks.* The most common preprofessional programs are premed, prelaw, and prepharmacy, but you may see other offerings. Although some preprofessional programs are structured as majors that you can declare, many preprofessional programs are a sequence of recommended courses and activities that a student can follow alongside a related major. While following a preprofessional program may not guarantee your admittance to a professional program, it does increase the likelihood of acceptance to and preparation for a graduate professional program.

Consider Loretta's story as an example of how a student might be on a preprofessional track. Loretta has decided that she would like to become a medical doctor. She has declared biology as her major and is taking the courses required to graduate with a bachelor of science degree in biology. Her university does not have a premed major, but it does have a premed track. She informs her academic advisor of her career goals, and her advisor provides her information about the premed track. The premed track includes a list of courses that students should take to prepare for the medical school entrance exams, called MCATs. Some of these courses are biology courses that overlap with Loretta's biology major, while others are higher-level chemistry courses that are not required for her major. She can take these chemistry courses, and any other premed-track courses, as her elective courses. The premed track at Loretta's university includes opportunities to attend MCAT study workshops and premed student club meetings. It also provides recommendations for summer volunteering and internships that will strengthen Loretta's resume and application to medical school following the completion of her bachelor's degree.

Special Requirements of Majors

While preprofessional programs prepare students for entrance into graduate professional degree programs, some undergraduate majors involve special requirements beyond the usual courses and classroom experience to prepare students for entrance to their career. Such requirements provide students practical experience or prerequisites for licensure necessary for a particular job. When requirements are major-specific, it is often because the requirement is state-mandated for that job. Majors that often include state-mandated special requirements are education, social work, and nursing. Some colleges and universities may require all students to participate in additional experiences beyond their regular coursework. You will want to ask your college about details specific to your major or institution. In this section we will generally discuss four such special requirements and experiences: fieldwork and internships, clinicals, student teaching, and service learning.

Fieldwork and Internships

Fieldwork and internships may also be referred to as *practicums* and field experience. These requirements provide hands-on work experience in a career, or *field*. When fieldwork or internships are required for your major, such as with a social work major, it is often listed as a course requirement among your major requirements. In other words, you usually receive credits for your fieldwork as you would for a lab or lecture course. Your fieldwork instructor will likely ask you to reflect on and report on your experiences. They will likely confer with a supervisor at your *fieldwork site*, the place where you are working, to help assess your hands-on learning. Fieldwork and internships provide students with opportunities to practice the skills they've learned in the classroom while also introducing them to the values and culture of the organizations and communities in which they hope to be employed. It is important to note that fieldwork and internship experiences are often available to students even if they are not required for their major. You may want to inquire with your academic advisors, faculty, or career services office to determine what opportunities might be available for you to gain this type of experience in your field of interest.

Clinicals

Clinicals are a type of fieldwork specifically required of nursing students. Clinicals may take place in hospitals, nursing homes, or mental health facilities. They provide nursing students who are nearing the end of their degree programs with the opportunity to practice nursing skills that cannot be learned in a regular classroom. During clinicals, students will interact with real patients to conduct physical examinations, draw blood, administer medicine, and provide other care as necessary. Because of the risk to patients, students participating in clinicals are more closely supervised by experienced professionals than those in other types of fieldwork experiences. Thus, clinicals function very much like a real-world classroom and progress to more independent work through the semester. Before undertaking clinicals, nursing students will need to complete certain coursework and pass a physical examination and background check. Because clinicals are often much longer than a class meeting, students will need to work with staff from the program to plan their schedule. It may not be feasible to work at another job while completing clinicals, so if you must work while you're in college, it's important to discuss this with nursing staff or academic advisors and to plan ahead.

Student Teaching

Student teaching is a specific type of fieldwork undertaken by students who plan to teach at the preschool, elementary, or middle and high school levels. Education students are often required to complete a student teaching experience in order to obtain a teaching license in their state. Students must often complete core education coursework prior to student teaching and must complete a background check prior to placement in a school setting. During their student teaching experience, students are usually paired one-on-one with an experienced teacher and have the opportunity to observe that teacher, get to know the students, understand the classroom culture, and participate in lessons as a teaching assistant as needed or appropriate. Much like nursing clinicals, this highly supervised fieldwork experience usually progresses to more independent work when the student teacher is asked to deliver and reflect on a lesson plan of their own design. Keep in mind as you plan for student teaching that unlike other fieldwork experiences, student teaching is limited to fall or spring semesters and cannot be completed in the summer because most schools are closed during the summer terms. Also, it may not be feasible to work at another job while completing your student teaching experience, so if you must work while you're in college, it's important to discuss this with your program staff or academic advisors and to plan ahead.

Figure 4.11 Student teaching is an extremely important aspect of becoming a K-12 educator. The experience helps future teachers practice their skills and understand the complexity of working in the classroom. (Credit: seansinnit / Flickr / Attribution 2.0 Generic (CC-BY 2.0))

Service Learning

While service learning may not be required of a specific major, you may see this special requirement for a course or as a general graduation requirement for your college or university. It's also an excellent opportunity to try out something that interests you, something that could lead to or be part of your eventual career.

Service learning is very much like volunteering or community service. The purpose of service learning is to interact with and meet the needs of your local community. Service learning does differ from volunteering in that it is more structured to meet specific learning goals. For example, if you were engaging in service learning for an environmental science course, your activities would likely be focused on local environmental issues. Or, if you were engaging in service learning for a sociology course, you would likely be working with local community groups or organizations not only to assist these organizations, but also to observe how groups interact. Like fieldwork, service learning provides you an opportunity to observe and apply concepts learned in the classroom in a real-world setting. Students are often asked to reflect on their service learning activities in the context of what they've been learning in class, so if you're engaged in service learning, be thinking about how the activities you do relate to what you've learned and know.

WHAT STUDENTS SAY

1. Does your major have any special requirements that must be completed outside of the classroom?
   a. Fieldwork, internships, and/or student teaching
   b. Clinicals
   c. Other (write in)
   d. None
2. While in college, which of the following do you think you are most likely to do?
   a. Internship
   b. Part-time job
   c. Full-time job
   d. Study Abroad
3. What has influenced your academic and career plan the most? (rank order)
   a. The advice of friends and/or family
   b. The practical, hands-on experiences I've had outside of the classroom
   c. The knowledge and skills I've learned in class
   d. The advice I've gotten from mentors, advisors, or college faculty

You can also take the anonymous What Students Say (https://openstax.org/l/collegesurvey1-5) surveys to add your voice to this textbook. Your responses will be included in updates.

Students offered their views on these questions, and the results are displayed in the graphs below.

Does your major have any special requirements that must be completed outside of the classroom?

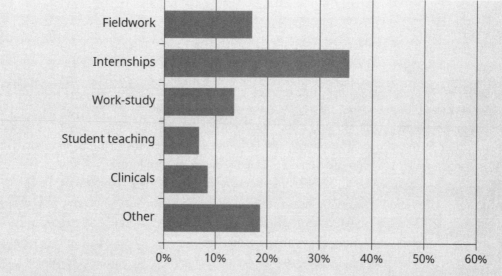

Figure 4.12

While in college, which of the following do you think you are most likely to do?

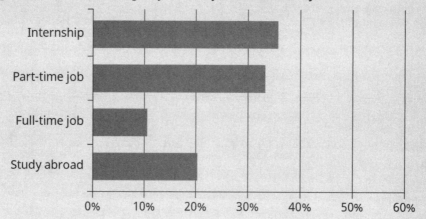

Figure 4.13

What has influenced your academic and career plan the most?

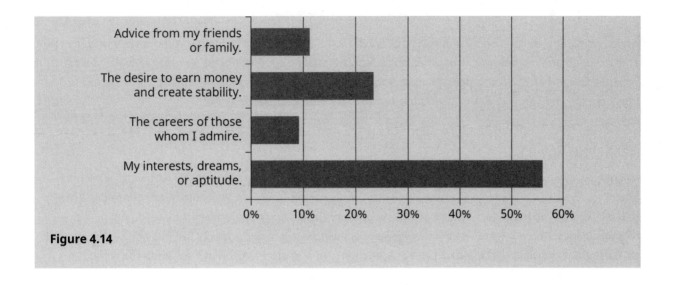

Figure 4.14

4.3 Making a Plan

Estimated completion time: 28 minutes.

Questions to consider:

- What resources are available to help me understand my degree program requirements?
- Who can assist me in making a plan?
- What tools are available to help me develop and track the progress of my plan?
- Is there anything else I can do now to plan for after I graduate?

As previously noted, most associate's degrees require a minimum of 60 credit hours for completion, and bachelor's degrees minimally require a total of 120 credits. Some individuals refer to these degrees as "two-year" and "four-year" degrees, respectively. To complete a 60-credit associate's degree in two years, you would need to take 15 credits (about five classes) in the fall and spring semesters during both years of your attendance. To complete a 120-credit bachelor's degree in four years, you would need to take 15 credits in the fall and spring semesters each of your four years. It is therefore entirely possible to complete these degrees in two and four years, particularly if you use the three primary resources that colleges provide to help you with your planning: curriculum maps, academic advisors, and interactive planning technology.

Curriculum Maps

Many colleges and universities will provide *curriculum maps*, or course checklists to illustrate the sequence of courses necessary to follow this timeline. These timelines often assume that you are ready to take college-level math and English courses and that you will be attending college as a full-time student. If placement tests demonstrate a need for prerequisite math and English coursework to get you up to speed, your timeline will likely be longer.

Many students attend college part-time, often because of family or work responsibilities. This will obviously have an impact on your completion timeline as well. Programs that have special requirements may also require that you plan for additional time. For example, it may be the case that you cannot take other courses while completing clinicals or student teaching, so you will need to plan accordingly. Alternatively, you may be able to speed up, or *accelerate*, your timeline to degree by taking courses during summer or winter terms. Or if you take fewer than 15 credits per semester, you can take courses during the summer terms to "make up" those credits and stay on track toward those two- or four-year graduation goals.[4]

Academic Advisors

All colleges and universities provide resources such as a curriculum map to assist you with your academic planning. Academic advisors may also be called success coaches, mentors, preceptors, or counselors. They may be staff members, or faculty may provide advisement as an additional role to their teaching responsibilities. Regardless of what your college calls this role, academic advisors are individuals who are able to assist you in navigating the puzzle of your academic plan and piecing your courses and requirements together with your other life obligations to help you meet your goals.

An advisor is an expert on college and major requirements and policies, while you are the expert on your life circumstances and your ability to manage your study time and workload. It is also an advisor's responsibility to understand the details of your degree requirements. This person can teach you how to best utilize college resources to make decisions about your academic and career path. An advisor can help you connect with other college staff and faculty who might be integral to supporting your success. Together with your advisor, you can create a semester-by-semester plan for the courses you will take and the special requirements you will meet. Refer to the end of this section for a detailed planning template that you could use in this process. Even if your college does not require advising, it is wise to meet with your advisor every semester to both check your progress and learn about new opportunities that might lend you competitive advantage in entering your career.

Common Functions of Academic Advisors

Academic advisors can help you:

- Set educational and career goals
- Select a major and/or minor
- Understand the requirements of your degree
- Navigate the online tools that track the progress of your degree
- Calculate your GPA and understand how certain choices may impact your GPA
- Discuss your academic progress from semester to semester
- Assist with time management strategies
- Connect with other support and resources at the college such as counseling, tutoring, and career services
- Navigate institutional policies such as grade appeals, admission to special programs, and other concerns
- Strategize how to make important contacts with faculty or other college administrators and staff as necessary (such as discussing how to construct professional emails)
- Discuss transfer options, if applicable
- Prepare for graduate school applications

---

4 Brookdale Community College Office of Career and Leadership Development. (2016). *Your Career Checklist*. Retrieved from: http://www.brookdalecc.edu/career

Interactive Planning Technology

In addition to a curriculum map and an advisor, colleges and universities usually have technological tools that can assist you in your academic planning. Degree audit reporting systems, for example, are programmed to align with degree requirements and can track individual student progress toward completion. They function like an interactive checklist of courses and special requirements. Student planning systems often allow students to plan multiple semesters online, to register for planned courses, and to track the progress of their plan. Though friends and family are well-intentioned in providing students with planning advice and can provide important points for students to consider, sometimes new students make the mistake of following advice without consulting their college's planning resources. It's important to bring all of these resources together as you craft your individual plan.

Despite all of the resources and planning assistance that is available to you, creating an individual plan can still be a daunting task. Making decisions about which major to pursue, when to take certain courses, and whether to work while attending school may all have an impact on your success, and it is tough to anticipate what to expect when you're new to college. Taking the time to create a plan and to revise it when necessary is essential to making well-informed, mindful decisions. Spur-of-the-moment decisions that are not well-informed can have lasting consequences to your progress.

The key to making a mindful decision is to first be as informed as possible about your options. Make certain that you have read the relevant resources and discussed the possibilities with experts at your college. Then you'll want to weigh your options against your values and goals. You might ask: Which option best fits my values and priorities? What path will help me meet my goals in the timeframe I desire? What will be the impact of my decision on myself or on others? Being well-informed, having a clear sense of purpose, and taking the necessary time to make a thoughtful decision will help to remove the anxiety associated with making the "right" decision, and help you make the best decision for you.

APPLICATION

Academic Planning Readiness Checklist: Review the checklist below and mark each item if you agree. For those you cannot yet answer, consult your instructor, academic advisor, or college website to locate these important details.

1. I know the total number of credits required to graduate from my program.
2. I know the difference between general education, major, and elective classes.
3. I know whether I am required to take preparatory or developmental courses in math and English, and whether these courses will count among my total credits toward my degree.
4. I am aware of the special requirements of my major (if any) and the prerequisites I must complete.
5. I am aware of the minimum entry requirements for my desired career field and know whether I should be preparing to plan for a graduate degree as well.

ACTIVITY

Draft an Academic Plan

With the assistance of your instructor or academic advisor, find the curriculum map for your major or for an example major that you might be considering if you're still exploring. Use the information in the curriculum map to draft an academic plan for your undergraduate degree. This plan should include both a semester-by-semester sequence of courses and a list of related activities to help you progress toward your career or graduate school goals. Keep in mind any personal circumstances that may impact your plan (such as whether you'll need to attend part-time or full-time). You may use the grid provided or utilize your college's student planning software if available. For your reference, you will find the start of an example grid from a dedicated environmental science student below.

Note: If your college offers courses using the quarter system rather than semesters, you may need to draft your own grid. You can find example planning grids for quarter systems online.

Example Semester # 1: Fall 20___	**Example Semester # 2:** Spring 20___
List your planned courses here:	**List your planned courses here:**
English Composition 1 (3 credits)	English Composition 2 (3 credits)
General Biology 1 + lab (4 credits)	General Biology 2 + lab (4 credits)
Environmental Science (4 credits)	Principles of Sustainability (3 credits)
History of Western Civilization (3 credits)	Pre-Calculus Mathematics (4 credits)
First Year Success Seminar (2 credits)	Total semester credits – 14
Total semester credits – 16	Total first year credits planned – 30
List your planned activities here:	**List your planned activities here:**
• Meet with my advisor to review my plan.	• Visit with Career Services Office early to ask about summer volunteering related to my major
• Attend an environmental science student club meeting.	

Example Summer Plans:

List your planned courses here: None this summer

List your planned activities here: Volunteer for local road or park clean-up days or start one if none exist in my area, follow and read that blog I found about becoming an environmental policy advocate, and research possible internships for my 2nd or 3rd year.

Figure 4.15 This sample of an academic plan was completed with the help of a college advisor. Below you'll find a blank template that you can use (or adapt) for your own plan.

Example Semester # 1:	Example Semester # 2:
List your planned courses here:	List your planned courses here:
List your planned activities here:	List your planned activities here:

Example Summer Plans:

List your planned courses here:

List your planned activities here:

Example Semester # 1:	Example Semester # 2:
List your planned courses here:	List your planned courses here:
List your planned activities here:	List your planned activities here:

Example Summer Plans:

List your planned courses here:

List your planned activities here:

Figure 4.16 This two-year version of the planning document may need to be adopted for colleges operating on a quarter, trimester, or other schedule. (Downloadable versions are available at OpenStax.org.)

Planning for After Graduation

Students usually pursue a college degree with some additional end goal in mind, whether that goal is further study as a graduate student or entry into a desired career. As you develop a plan for your undergraduate studies, you can also plan pursuits outside of the classroom to prepare for these future goals. To begin planning for life after graduation, consider the experiences that would best complement your coursework. If you are not required to participate in fieldwork or internships, perhaps you could plan a summer internship to help you gain workplace experience and learn more about what you do and do not want to do. It is also valuable to gain leadership experience through participation in student clubs and organizations. Plan to find a club that matches your interests. Set a goal to attend regularly your first year and then run for a club leadership role in your second or third year.

Figure 4.17 Graduation is a significant milestone, both for students and often for their families, friends, and support networks. A good academic plan will help you reach this important step, and then go far beyond it. (Credit: COD Newsroom / Flickr / Attribution 2.0 Generic (CC-BY 2.0))

Even before you begin an internship or career search in earnest, sites like Internships.com (https://www.internships.com) can be helpful simply to explore the possibilities and get ideas. Often, a dedicated career-oriented website will provide more filtered and specific information than a general search engine.

Consult with services or offices at your college that can assist with you with making your future plans and incorporating experiences into your academic plan that will prepare you to enter your career. These services are often accessible both to current students as well as to graduates, providing assistance with résumé writing and job searches. Chapter 12: Planning for Your Future provides further insight into career planning and college career services.

Alumni associations help graduates connect with other former students of all ages so that they can begin to build and strengthen their professional networks, leading to further job opportunities. And don't discount the role of your professors in helping you build your network as well! In addition to providing valuable letters of recommendation for both graduate school and job applications, professors often have well-established professional networks and may be willing to help connect dedicated students with additional opportunities. You can plan these experiences to be distributed across your academic semesters and during the summer.

Exploring Options

- Locate and visit your career services office on campus to discover what services are available.
- Take a career assessment that matches your values, interests, and skills to career options.
- Join a student organization.
- Seek volunteer opportunities to gain additional skills.
- Research trends and salary expectations for careers of interest.

Gain Experience

- Develop relationships with faculty by visiting during office hours and speaking to them after class.
- Network with employers by attending career fairs.
- Pursue an internship or part-time employment that is relevant to your field of interest.
- Take a leadership role on campus or in a student organization.
- Practice for interviews with friends or career counselors.

Document Experiences

- Begin your resume and continuously update it to include new experiences.
- Create a LinkedIn profile.
- Review and monitor your social media accounts through the lens of a potential employer.
- Solidify relationships with faculty and ask about letters of recommendation.
- Draft additional job application materials, such as cover letters.
- Seek assistance from career counselors on campus in reviewing your resumes/cover letters/portfolios.

Table 4.5 Prepare for Your Career While in College

This Draft an Academic Plan activity provides you an opportunity to consider and plan experiences alongside your coursework that could help you better prepare to meet your career goals. Also, the chapter on Planning Your Career goes into these topics in more depth.

Managing Change and the Unexpected

Estimated completion time: 18 minutes.

Questions to consider:

- What happens if things don't go according to plan?
- How can I make adjustments to my plan if things change?
- Is it OK to ask for planning help, and from whom?

Though we've discussed planning in a great degree of detail, the good news is that you don't have to have it all figured out in order to be successful. Recall the upside-down puzzle analogy from earlier in this chapter. You can still put a puzzle together picture-side down by fitting together the pieces with trial and error. Similarly, you can absolutely be successful in your academic and career life even if you don't have it all figured out. It will be especially important to keep this in mind as circumstances change or things don't go according to your original plan.

Consider Elena's and Ray's stories as examples.

Elena had always intended to go to college. It was her goal to become a nurse like her grandmother. She decided that the best path would be to complete her BSN degree at a state university nearby. She researched the program, planned her bachelor's degree semester by semester, and was very excited to work with real patients while completing her clinicals! During her second year, Elena's grandmother fell ill and needed more regular care. Elena made the difficult decision to stop-out of her program to help care for her grandmother. She spoke with her academic advisor, who told her about the policies for readmission. Because the nursing program was limited to a certain number of students, it would be challenging to reenter her program whenever she was ready to return.

At first Elena felt discouraged, but then her advisor assisted her in mapping a plan to take some prerequisite courses part-time at a community college near her home while she cared for her grandmother. She could then transfer those credits back to the university so they would count toward her degree there, or she could finish an associate's degree and then return to a bachelor's degree program whenever she was able. Although things weren't following her original plans, she would be able to continue working toward her goals while also tending to one of her greatest values—her family. Elena's plans changed, but her values and long-term goals didn't have to change.

Ray's parents wanted him to go to college to increase his chances of getting a good job. He wasn't really sure what he wanted to study, so his dad suggested he choose business. During Ray's first semester he took an introduction to business course that was required of all business majors in their first semester. He did well in the course, but it wasn't his favorite topic. Conversely, he loved the history course on early Western civilization that he was taking to meet a general education requirement. He wasn't necessarily ready to change his major from business to history, so he met with an academic advisor to see if there were any classes he could take during his second semester that would count toward either major. Ray was still exploring and had yet to set specific goals. But Ray did know that he wanted to finish college within a reasonable amount of time, so he made flexible plans that would allow him to change his mind and change his major if necessary.

Expecting Change

After you've devoted time to planning, it can be frustrating when circumstances unexpectedly change. Change can be the result of internal or external factors. Internal factors are those that you have control over. They may include indecision, or changing your mind about a situation after receiving new information or recognizing that something is not a good fit for your values and goals. Though change resulting from internal factors can be stressful, it is often easier to accept and to navigate because you know why the change must occur. You can plan for a change and make even better decisions for your path when the reason for change is, simply put—you! Ray's story demonstrates how internal factors contribute to his need or desire to change plans.

External factors that necessitate change are often harder to plan for and accept. Some external factors are very personal. These may include financial concerns, your health or the health of a loved one, or other family circumstances, such as in Elena's example. Other external factors may be more related to the requirements of a major or college. For example, perhaps you are not accepted into the college or degree program that you had always hoped to attend or study. Or you may not perform well enough in a class to continue your studies without repeating that course during a semester when you had originally planned to move on to other courses. Change caused by external factors can be frustrating. Because external factors are often unexpected, when you encounter them you'll often have to spend more time changing your plans or even revising your goals before you'll feel as though you're back on track.

Managing Change

It is important to recognize that change, whether internal or external, is inevitable. You can probably think of an example of a time when you had to change your plans due to unforeseen circumstances. Perhaps it's a situation as simple as canceling a date with friends because of an obligation to babysit a sibling. Even though this simple example would not have had long-term consequences, you can probably recall a feeling of disappointment. It's okay to feel disappointed; however, you'll also want to recognize that you can manage your response to changing circumstances. You can ask yourself the following questions:

- What can I control in this situation?
- Do I need to reconsider my values?
- Do I need to reconsider my goals?
- Do I need to change my plans as a result of this new information or these new circumstances?
- What resources, tools, or people are available to assist me in revising my plans?

When encountering change, it helps to remember that decision-making and planning are continuous processes. In other words, active individuals are always engaged in decision-making, setting new plans, and revising old plans. This continuous process is not always the result of major life-changing circumstances either. Oftentimes, we need to make changes simply because we've learned some new information that causes a shift in our plans. Planning, like learning, is an ongoing lifetime process.

Asking for Help

> "Be strong enough to stand alone, be yourself enough to stand apart, but be wise enough to stand together when the time comes."
>
> — Mark Amend, American Author

Figure 4.18 Your instructors are an important not only in your courses, but as potential advisors and mentors. (Credit: Rural Institute / Flickr / Public Domain)

Throughout this chapter we have made mention of individuals who can help you plan your path, but noted that your path is ultimately your own. Some students make the mistake of taking too much advice when planning and making decisions. They may forgo their values and goals for others' values and goals for them.

Or they may mistakenly trust advice that comes from well-meaning but ill-informed sources.

In other cases, students grapple with unfamiliar college paperwork and technology with little assistance as they proudly tackle perhaps newfound roles as adult decision makers. It's important to know that seeking help is a strength, not a weakness, particularly when that help comes from well-informed individuals who have your best interests in mind. When you share your goals and include others in your planning, you develop both a support network and a system of personal accountability. Being held *accountable* for your goals means that others are also tracking your progress and are interested in seeing you succeed. When you are working toward a goal and sticking to a plan, it's important to have unconditional cheerleaders in your life as well as folks who keep pushing you to stay on track, especially if they see you stray. It's important to know who in your life can play these roles.

For those facing personal and emotional challenges including depression and anxiety, specific guidance is covered in Chapter 11.

Asking for Help: Anton's Story

Anton is in his first semester at State University. His high school guidance counselor, who he was required to meet with in his junior and senior years, was very helpful in preparing his college applications and in discussing what he could expect through the admissions process. When he was accepted to State University, she celebrated with him as well! Now that he's arrived at college, though, he's found it to be different from his high school. There are so many more options available to him and more freedom to plan his own time. About halfway through the semester, Anton falls behind in his information technology course, the introductory class for his major. He had been so excited to study more about computers and systems networking, but he's finding it harder and harder to understand the content and he feels discouraged.

After learning that he's headed for a D grade in the course, Anton is not certain what to do both about the class and about his major. In high school he would have spoken with his guidance counselor, who he knew by name and ran into in the hallway frequently. But he's not yet well-connected to resources at his college. When his mom texts him from back home to share a story about his younger sister, he considers confiding in her about the course but doesn't want her to worry about his focus or dedication. Anton is the first person from his family to attend college, so he feels a particular pressure to succeed and isn't even certain if his mom would know how to help. He ends the text thread with a generic thumbs-up emoji and heads to the college fitness center to let off some steam.

At the fitness center he sees another student from his class, Noura, who mentions that she just came from meeting with an academic advisor. After talking a bit more about Noura's interaction with her advisor, Anton learns that advising is both free and available on a walk-in basis. In fact, he finds out that at State University he even has an advisor who is assigned to him, similar to his high school counselor. Anton heads over to the advising center after class the next morning. He's a bit hesitant to share about his concerns about his grade, but he feels more confident after speaking with Noura about her experiences. When he meets his advisor, Anton also finds out that the information he shares is confidential to his personal academic records. After introductions and sharing this privacy information, Anton's advisor starts by asking him how everything is going this term. The casual conversation develops from there into a detailed plan for how Anton can seek some additional help in his course, including language he can use in an email to his instructor, the hours and location of the computer science tutoring lab, and "intel" on where the computer science students hang out so he can drop by to discuss their experiences in classes further along in the major. When Anton leaves his advisor's office, he's still considering a change to his major but decides to focus on improving his grade first and then making more decisions from there. Anton makes arrangements to meet with his advisor again before registering for the next semester and plans to follow up with him about his course via email after he speaks with his instructor. The whole experience was more casual and friendly than he could have imagined. He looks forward to running into Noura again to thank her (after he texts his mom back, of course!).

Mentors

When making academic decisions and career plans, it is also useful to have a mentor who has had similar goals. A *mentor* is an experienced individual who helps to guide a *mentee*, the less experienced person seeking advice. A good mentor for a student who is engaged in academic and career planning is someone who is knowledgeable about the student's desired career field and is perhaps more advanced in their career than an entry-level position. This is a person who can model the type of values and behaviors that are essential to a successful career. Your college or university may be able to connect you with a mentor through an organized mentorship program or through the alumni association. If your college does not have an organized mentor program, you may be able to find your own by reaching out to family friends who work in your field of interest, searching online for a local professional association or organization related to your field (as some associations have mentorship programs as well), or speaking to the professors who teach the courses in your major.

ACTIVITY

Your Support Call List

When you start a new job, go to a new school, or even fill out paperwork at a new doctor's office, you're often asked to provide contact information for someone who can assist in making decisions and look out for your best interests in the event of an emergency. Academic decision-making and planning doesn't involve the same level of urgency, but it's useful to have in mind the people in your life or the offices and individuals available to you at your college who motivate and support your plans, or can assist you in setting them. Prepare your support call (or text, email, or DM) list now so that all you have to do is pick up your phone to get the support you need. Keep in mind that one person can fulfill more than one role.

Who knows your interests? Knows what you love or what you hate to do sometimes even before you do? Who can list your strengths and weaknesses without bias? This is the person who can support you when you are deciding on a degree program or major:	Name of individual(s) or office:
Who knows the college or university degree and program details, policies, procedures, and technological systems? This is the person who can support you when you are drafting your plan:	Name of individual(s) or office:

Table 4.6

Who knows the career and graduate school opportunities available to someone in your major or program? This is the person who can support you in planning for activities beyond your courses:	Name of individual(s) or office:
Who is your biggest cheerleader who you can contact when you're feeling discouraged or unmotivated? This is the person who can support you when plans need to change:	Name of individual(s) or office:
Who has successfully navigated all of this college planning in the past and is now working in a career that interests you as well? This is the person who can become your mentor:	Name of individual or office:

Table 4.6

ANALYSIS QUESTION

Consider, are you someone who panics if there is a change in plans, or are you relatively flexible? What techniques will you employ to help you manage change if you encounter it?

This chapter focuses on the importance of decision-making and planning, stressors that can sometimes feel overwhelming. If you are feeling less excited about the possibilities of planning and more overwhelmed, it's important that you take a break from this process. If you talk to others who are already working in their career fields, even those who work at your college, you'll probably find many individuals who were undecided in their path. Take some comfort in their stories and in knowing that you can absolutely find success even if you don't yet have a plan. Take a break and engage in those self-care activities that bring you some peace of mind. You can also reference Chapter 11: Health and Wellness, which provides further details regarding these concerns. If you are ever feeling anxious, stressed, depressed, or overwhelmed, please find the resources available at your college to assist you.

STUDENT PROFILE

"I graduated with my bachelor's degree in elementary education about 10 years ago and was lucky to get a job at the same school where I completed my student teaching requirement. I absolutely love my students and am very happy as a teacher. Recently, though, I've had the opportunity to mentor some new teachers at my school. After I got over the shock of not being the new teacher myself anymore (am I that old?!), I realized how much I enjoyed helping new teachers get established in their classroom as well. I've been thinking about maybe going to back school to get a master's degree in education so that I can someday become an administrator or maybe a principal at a school. I guess I should start researching programs that will help me meet my goal, because I know I won't get started until I have a plan in place. I'll need a program that can allow me to continue working full-time while going back to school. It's totally exciting, but I'm also overwhelmed."

—**Amara**, Brookdale Community College

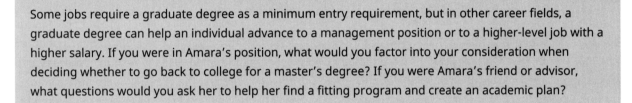

ANALYSIS QUESTION

Some jobs require a graduate degree as a minimum entry requirement, but in other career fields, a graduate degree can help an individual advance to a management position or to a higher-level job with a higher salary. If you were in Amara's position, what would you factor into your consideration when deciding whether to go back to college for a master's degree? If you were Amara's friend or advisor, what questions would you ask her to help her find a fitting program and create an academic plan?

Summary

This chapter began by describing the personal guideposts for our planning: our values and our goals. After a discussion of the relationship between short- and long-term goals and the importance of tracking the progress of our goals, the chapter dove into the specifics of academic plans. Sections on degree types and the special considerations and requirements of certain programs should help you understand the type of opportunities that may be available to you and the types of questions you should research and ask. The section on planning your semesters provides you with the types of resources, people, and tools that you should look for when developing your academic plan. It also provides you an example planning grid to begin to draft a plan for your undergraduate studies. Keep in mind that you may need to make changes to your plan as you follow it. You can refer back to the section on managing change to consider how you might respond. Finally, the chapter concludes with a section on asking for help. Recall that others can both help you plan and hold you accountable to your plan, but only you set your values, so stick to them!

Career Connection

This article (https://openstax.org/l/makingharddecisions) discusses the challenges that business leaders face in making decisions under pressure and the impact of stress in making poorer decisions. Read the article and consider times when you've had to make consequential decisions. Can you relate to the pitfalls of making decisions under stress rather than taking the time to think things through and develop a plan?

Rethinking

Revisit the questions you answered at the beginning of the chapter. After reviewing this chapter, were you as ready to plan as you thought you were? Are you more prepared now? Rate your readiness again, ranking questions on a scale of 1–4, 1 meaning "least like me" and 4 meaning "most like me."

1. I have reflected on and can identify my personal values.
2. I have set both short- and long-term academic goals.
3. I am familiar with the requirements I must complete and options I must select to obtain a college degree.
4. I am familiar with the resources, tools, and individuals who can assist me in developing an effective plan for success.

Where do you go from here?

Planning and decision-making are continuous processes, but if you're reading this text you presumably have a specific educational end goal in mind—you want to graduate with a degree! After you've decided on a degree and major path, you're already well-prepared to begin your academic planning. Use the resources discussed in this chapter and available at your college or university to draft your plan, and then review it with others who can provide feedback. If you're undecided about your degree and major, you will still have some work ahead of you before you can craft a more detailed academic plan. Here are some steps you can take to help you find a major that's right for you:

- Consider your interests and skills. Your academic advisor and/or your college's career services office can connect you with an academic and career path through discussion about your interests and skills. These offices and individuals often provide interest and skills tests that offer a starting point for your discussion. There are also free assessments available on the internet, such as the this one (https://openstax.org/l/interestprofiler) , that can help identify your interests and skills and match them with careers and related majors. (Refer to the Get Connected section earlier in this chapter for additional online resources.)
- Consider the future. Imagine yourself in job. What types of tasks or work environments are attractive to you? Is there anything you would absolutely hate to do that you can already rule out? Also consider the future of work. The Bureau of Labor Statistics' Occupational Outlook Handbook identifies some career fields as having a bright outlook with expected job growth in the future. Ideally, you'll want to study for a career that's growing, not declining.
- Consider your preferred lifestyle. Although we all like to have a balanced life, perhaps it's less important to you to follow your interests and more important to follow the bottom line. If your preferred lifestyle will require that you make a high salary, you'll want to research those jobs that are highest paying and take note of the degrees and majors that prepare you for those fields.

Figure 5.1 Each of us reads and records information in our own way.

Chapter Outline

- **5.1** The Nature and Types of Reading
- **5.2** Effective Reading Strategies
- **5.3** Taking Notes

Introduction

Student Survey

These questions will help you determine how the chapter concepts relate to you right now. As we are introduced to new concepts and practices, it can be informative to reflect on how your understanding changes over time. We'll revisit these questions at the end of the chapter to see whether your feelings have changed.

On a scale of 1 (I need significant improvement) to 4 (I'm doing great), reflect on how you're doing right now on these statements:

1. I am reading on a college level.
2. I take good notes that help me study for exams.
3. I understand how to manage all the reading I need to do for college.
4. I recognize the need for different notetaking strategies for different college subjects.

You can also take the Chapter 5 survey (https://openstax.org/l/collegesurvey05) anonymously online.

STUDENT PROFILE

"Before I came to college, I always loathed reading from the textbook, taking notes during class, and even listening to lectures. I've since learned that in most cases I should do what my teacher suggests. I have a course that requires me to read two textbook chapters each week. Taking notes on the chapters is optional, making it easy to brush off these assignments. But there are reasons that professors tell students to read and do other classwork. They believe it is valuable information for a student to learn. Note taking in class may become tedious and, in some cases, feel redundant. But you can't recall a whole class from memory. There is not much time to learn the contents of a class in one semester, and it can feel overwhelming. It's important to take notes because writing them helps you remember."

—**Christopher Naldini**, Westchester Community College

About this Chapter

In this chapter we will explore two skills you probably think you already understand—reading and notetaking. But the goal is to make sure you've honed these skills well enough to lead you to success in college. By the time you finish this chapter, you should be able to do the following:

- Discuss the way reading differs in college and how to successfully adapt to that change.
- Demonstrate the usefulness of strong notetaking for college students.

Reading and consuming information are increasingly important today because of the amount of information we encounter. Not only do we need to read critically and carefully, but we also need to read with an eye to distinguishing fact from opinion and identifying solid sources. Reading helps us make sense of the world—from simple reminders to pick up milk to complex treatises on global concerns, we read to comprehend, and in so doing, our brains expand. An interesting study from Emory University in Atlanta, Georgia, used MRI scans to track the brain conductivity while participants were reading. The researchers assert that a biological change to your brain actually happens when you read, and it lingers. If you want to read the study, published in the journal *Brain Connectivity,* you can find it online at https://openstax.org/l/brainconnectivity (https://openstax.org/l/brainconnectivity) .

In academic settings, as we deliberately work to become stronger readers and better notetakers, we are both helping our current situation and enhancing our abilities to be successful in the future. Seems like a win-win. Take advantage of all the study aids you have at hand, including human, electronic, and physical resources, to increase your performance in these crucial skill sets.

Why? You need to read. It improves your thinking, your vocabulary, and your ability to make connections between disparate parts, which are all parts of critical thinking. Educational researchers Anne Cunningham and Keith Stanovich discovered after extensive study with college students that "reading volume [how much you read] made a significant contribution to multiple measures of vocabulary, general knowledge, spelling, and verbal fluency."

Research continues to assess and support the fact that one of the most significant learning skills necessary for success in any field is reading. You may have performed this skill for decades already, but learning to do it more effectively and practicing the skill consistently is critical to how well you do in all subjects. If reading *isn't your thing,* strive to make that your challenge. Your academic journey, your personal well-being, and your professional endeavors will all benefit from your reading. Put forth the effort and make it your thing. The long-term benefits will far outweigh the sacrifices you make now.

5.1 The Nature and Types of Reading

Estimated completion time: 16 minutes.

Questions to consider:

- What are the pros and cons of online reading?
- How can distinguishing between reading types help you academically and personally?
- How can you best prepare to read for college?

Research supports the idea that reading is good for you. Students who read at or above reading level throughout elementary and secondary school have a higher chance of starting—and more importantly, finishing—college. Educational researchers convincingly claim that reading improves everything from grades to vocabulary (Cunningham 2).

If you don't particularly enjoy reading, don't despair. We read for a variety of reasons, and you may just have to step back and take a bigger picture of your reading habits to understand why you avoid engaging in this important skill. The myriad distractions we now face as well as the intense information overload we can suffer on a daily basis in all aspects of our lives can combine to make it difficult to slow down to read, an activity that demands at least a modicum of attention in a way that most television and music do not. You may need to adjust your schedule for more reading time, especially in college, because every class you take will expect you to read more pages than you probably have in the past.

Types of Reading

We may read small items purely for immediate information, such as notes, e-mails, or directions to an unfamiliar location. You can find all sorts of information online about how to fix a faucet or tie a secure knot. You won't have to spend too much time reading these sorts of texts because you have a specific goal in mind for them, and once you have accomplished that goal, you do not need to prolong the reading experience. These encounters with texts may not be memorable or stunning, but they don't need to be. When we consider why we read longer pieces—outside of reading for pleasure—we can usually categorize the reasons into about two categories: 1) reading to introduce ourselves to new content, and 2) reading to more fully comprehend familiar content.

Figure 5.2 A bookstore or library can be a great place to explore. Aside from books and resources you need, you may find something that interests you or helps with your course work.

Reading to Introduce New Content

Glenn felt uncomfortable talking with his new roommates because he realized very quickly that he didn't know anything about their major—architecture. Of course he knew that it had something to do with buildings and construction sites, but the field was so different from his discipline of biology that he decided he needed to find out more so he could at least engage in friendly conversation with his roommates. Since he would likely not go into their field, he didn't need to go into full research mode. When we read to introduce new content, we can start off small and increase to better and more sophisticated sources. Much of our further study and reading depends on the sources we originally read, our purpose for finding out about this new topic, and our interest level.

Chances are, you have done this sort of exploratory reading before. You may read reviews of a new restaurant or look at what people say about a movie you aren't sure you want to spend the money to see at the theater. This reading helps you decide. In academic settings, much of what you read in your courses may be relatively new content to you. You may have heard the word *volcano* and have a general notion of what it means, but until you study geology and other sciences in depth, you may not have a full understanding of the environmental origins, ecological impacts, and societal and historic responses to volcanoes. These perspectives will come from reading and digesting various material. When you are working with new content, you may need to schedule more time for reading and comprehending the information because you may need to look up unfamiliar terminology and you may have to stop more frequently to make sure you are truly grasping what the material means. When you have few ways to connect new material to your own prior knowledge, you have to work more diligently to comprehend it.

APPLICATION

Try an experiment with a group of classmates. Without looking on the Internet, try to brainstorm a list of 10 topics about which all of you may be interested but for which you know very little or nothing at all. Try to make the topics somewhat obscure rather than ordinary—for example, the possibility of the non-planet Pluto being reclassified again as opposed to something like why we need to drink water.

After you have this random list, think of ways you could find information to read about these weird topics. Our short answer is always: Google. But think of other ways as well. How else could you read about these topics if you don't know anything about them? You may well be in a similar circumstance in some of your college classes, so you should listen carefully to your classmates on this one. Think beyond pat answers such as "I'd go to the library," and press for what that researcher would do once at the library. What types of articles or books would you try to find? One reason that you should not always ignore the idea of doing research at the physical library is because once you are there and looking for information, you have a vast number of other sources readily available to you in a highly organized location. You also can tap into the human resources represented by the research librarians who likely can redirect you if you cannot find appropriate sources.

Reading to Comprehend Familiar Content

Reading about unfamiliar content is one thing, but what if you do know something about a topic already? Do you really still need to keep reading about it? Probably. For example, what if during the brainstorming activity in the previous section, you secretly felt rather smug because you know about the demotion of the one-time planet Pluto and that there is currently quite the scientific debate going on about that whole de-planet-ation thing. Of course, you didn't say anything during the study session, mostly to spare your classmates any embarrassment, but you are pretty familiar with Pluto-gate. So now what? Can you learn anything new?

Again—probably. When did Pluto's qualifications to be considered a planet come into question? What are the qualifications for being considered a planet? Why? Who even gets to decide these things? Why was it called *Pluto* in the first place? On Amazon alone, you can find hundreds of books about the once-planet Pluto (not to be confused with the Disney dog also named Pluto). A Google search brings up over 34 million options for your reading pleasure. You'll have plenty to read, even if you do know something or quite a bit about a topic, but you'll approach reading about a familiar topic and an unfamiliar one differently.

With familiar content, you can do some initial skimming to determine what you already know in the book or article, and mark what may be new information or a different perspective. You may not have to give your full attention to the information you know, but you will spend more time on the new viewpoints so you can determine how this new data meshes with what you already know. Is this writer claiming a radical new definition for the topic or an entirely opposite way to consider the subject matter, connecting it to other topics or disciplines in ways you have never considered?

When college students encounter material in a discipline-specific context and have some familiarity with the topic, they sometimes can allow themselves to become a bit overconfident about their knowledge level. Just because a student may have read an article or two or may have seen a TV documentary on a subject such as the criminal mind, that does not make them an expert. What makes an expert is a person who thoroughly studies a subject, usually for years, and understands all the possible perspectives of a subject as well as the potential for misunderstanding due to personal biases and the availability of false information about the topic.

5.2 Effective Reading Strategies

Estimated completion time: 25 minutes.

Questions to consider:

- What methods can you incorporate into your routine to allow adequate time for reading?
- What are the benefits and approaches to active reading?
- Do your courses or major have specific reading requirements?

Allowing Adequate Time for Reading

You should determine the reading requirements and expectations for every class very early in the semester. You also need to understand why you are reading the particular text you are assigned. Do you need to read closely for minute details that determine cause and effect? Or is your instructor asking you to skim several sources so you become more familiar with the topic? Knowing this reasoning will help you decide your timing, what notes to take, and how best to undertake the reading assignment.

Figure 5.3 If you plan to make time for reading while you commute, remember that unexpected events like delays and cancellations could impact your concentration.

Depending on the makeup of your schedule, you may end up reading both primary sources—such as legal documents, historic letters, or diaries—as well as textbooks, articles, and secondary sources, such as summaries or argumentative essays that use primary sources to stake a claim. You may also need to read current journalistic texts to stay current in local or global affairs. A realistic approach to scheduling your time to allow you to read and review all the reading you have for the semester will help you accomplish what can sometimes seem like an overwhelming task.

When you allow adequate time in your hectic schedule for reading, you are investing in your own success. Reading isn't a magic pill, but it may seem like it when you consider all the benefits people reap from this ordinary practice. Famous successful people throughout history have been voracious readers. In fact, former U.S. president Harry Truman once said, "Not all readers are leaders, but all leaders are readers." Writer of the U.S. Declaration of Independence, inventor, and also former U.S. president Thomas Jefferson claimed "I cannot live without books" at a time when keeping and reading books was an expensive pastime. Knowing what it meant to be kept from the joys of reading, 19th-century abolitionist Frederick Douglass said, "Once you learn to read, you will be forever free." And finally, George R. R. Martin, the prolific author of the wildly successful *Game of Thrones* empire, declared, "A reader lives a thousand lives before he dies . . . The man who never reads lives only one."

You can make time for reading in a number of ways that include determining your usual reading pace and speed, scheduling active reading sessions, and practicing recursive reading strategies.

Determining Reading Speed and Pacing

To determine your reading speed, select a section of text—passages in a textbook or pages in a novel. Time yourself reading that material for exactly 5 minutes, and note how much reading you accomplished in those 5 minutes. Multiply the amount of reading you accomplished in 5 minutes by 12 to determine your average reading pace (5 times 12 equals the 60 minutes of an hour). Of course, your reading pace will be different and take longer if you are taking notes while you read, but this calculation of reading pace gives you a good way to estimate your reading speed that you can adapt to other forms of reading.

Example Reading Times

Reader	Pages Read in 5 Minutes	Pages per Hour	Approximate Hours to Read 500 Pages
Marta	4	48	10 hours, 30 minutes
Jordi	3	36	13 hours
Estevan	5	60	8 hours, 20 minutes

So, for instance, if Marta was able to read 4 pages of a dense novel for her English class in 5 minutes, she should be able to read about 48 pages in one hour. Knowing this, Marta can accurately determine how much time she needs to devote to finishing the novel within a set amount of time, instead of just guessing. If the novel Marta is reading is 497 pages, then Marta would take the total page count (497) and divide that by her hourly reading rate (48 pages/hour) to determine that she needs about 10 to 11 hours overall. To finish the novel spread out over two weeks, Marta needs to read a little under an hour a day to accomplish this goal.

Calculating your reading rate in this manner does not take into account days where you're too distracted and you have to reread passages or days when you just aren't in the mood to read. And your reading rate will likely vary depending on how dense the content you're reading is (e.g., a complex textbook vs. a comic book). Your pace may slow down somewhat if you are not very interested in what the text is about. What this method *will* help you do is be realistic about your reading time as opposed to waging a guess based on nothing and then becoming worried when you have far more reading to finish than the time available.

Chapter 3, "Time Management and Prioritization," offers more detail on how best to determine your speed from one type of reading to the next so you are better able to schedule your reading.

Scheduling Set Times for Active Reading

Active reading takes longer than reading through passages without stopping. You may not need to read your latest sci-fi series actively while you're lounging on the beach, but many other reading situations demand more attention from you. Active reading is particularly important for college courses. You are a scholar actively engaging with the text by posing questions, seeking answers, and clarifying any confusing elements. Plan to spend at least twice as long to read actively than to read passages without taking notes or otherwise marking select elements of the text.

To determine the time you need for active reading, use the same calculations you use to determine your traditional reading speed and double it. Remember that you need to determine your reading pace for all the classes you have in a particular semester and multiply your speed by the number of classes you have that require different types of reading.

Example Active Reading Times

Reader	Pages Read in 5 Minutes	Pages per Hour	Approximate Hours to Read 500 Pages	Approximate Hours to Actively Read 500 Pages
Marta	4	48	10 hours, 30 minutes	21 hours
Jordi	3	36	13 hours	26 hours
Estevan	5	60	8 hours, 20 minutes	16 hours, 40 minutes

Practicing Recursive Reading Strategies

One fact about reading for college courses that may become frustrating is that, in a way, it never ends. For all the reading you do, you end up doing even more rereading. It may be the same content, but you may be reading the passage more than once to detect the emphasis the writer places on one aspect of the topic or how frequently the writer dismisses a significant counterargument. This rereading is called recursive reading.

For most of what you read at the college level, you are trying to make sense of the text for a specific purpose—not just because the topic interests or entertains you. You need your full attention to decipher everything that's going on in complex reading material—and you even need to be considering what the writer of the piece may *not* be including and why. This is why reading for comprehension is recursive.

Specifically, this boils down to seeing reading not as a formula but as a process that is far more circular than linear. You may read a selection from beginning to end, which is an excellent starting point, but for comprehension, you'll need to go back and reread passages to determine meaning and make connections between the reading and the bigger learning environment that led you to the selection—that may be a single course or a program in your college, or it may be the larger discipline, such as all biologists or the community of scholars studying beach erosion.

People often say writing is rewriting. For college courses, reading is rereading.

Strong readers engage in numerous steps, sometimes combining more than one step simultaneously, but knowing the steps nonetheless. They include, not always in this order:

- bringing any prior knowledge about the topic to the reading session,
- asking yourself pertinent questions, both orally and in writing, about the content you are reading,
- inferring and/or implying information from what you read,
- learning unfamiliar discipline-specific terms,
- evaluating what you are reading, and eventually,
- applying what you're reading to other learning and life situations you encounter.

Let's break these steps into manageable chunks, because you are actually doing quite a lot when you read.

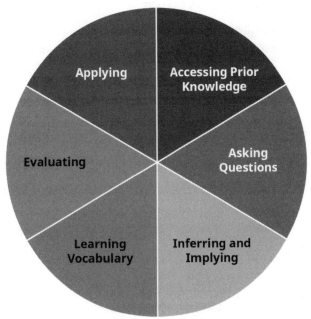

Figure 5.4 The six elements of recursive reading should be considered as a circular, not linear, process.

Accessing Prior Knowledge

When you read, you naturally think of anything else you may know about the topic, but when you read deliberately and actively, you make yourself more aware of accessing this prior knowledge. Have you ever watched a documentary about this topic? Did you study some aspect of it in another class? Do you have a hobby that is somehow connected to this material? All of this thinking will help you make sense of what you are reading.

> **APPLICATION**
>
> Imagining that you were given a chapter to read in your American history class about the Gettysburg Address, write down what you already know about this historic document. How might thinking through this prior knowledge help you better understand the text?

Asking Questions

Humans are naturally curious beings. As you read actively, you should be asking questions about the topic you are reading. Don't just say the questions in your mind; write them down. You may ask: Why is this topic important? What is the relevance of this topic currently? Was this topic important a long time ago but irrelevant now? Why did my professor assign this reading?

You need a place where you can actually write down these questions; a separate page in your notes is a good place to begin. If you are taking notes on your computer, start a new document and write down the questions. Leave some room to answer the questions when you begin and again after you read.

Inferring and Implying

When you read, you can take the information on the page and *infer*, or conclude responses to related challenges from evidence or from your own reasoning. A student will likely be able to infer what material the professor will include on an exam by taking good notes throughout the classes leading up to the test.

Writers may *imply* information without directly stating a fact for a variety of reasons. Sometimes a writer may not want to come out explicitly and state a bias, but may imply or hint at his or her preference for one political party or another. You have to read carefully to find implications because they are indirect, but watching for them will help you comprehend the whole meaning of a passage.

Learning Vocabulary

Vocabulary specific to certain disciplines helps practitioners in that field engage and communicate with each other. Few people beyond undertakers and archeologists likely use the term *sarcophagus* in everyday communications, but for those disciplines, it is a meaningful distinction. Looking at the example, you can use context clues to figure out the meaning of the term *sarcophagus* because it is something undertakers and/or archeologists would recognize. At the very least, you can guess that it has something to do with death. As a potential professional in the field you're studying, you need to know the lingo. You may already have a system in place to learn discipline-specific vocabulary, so use what you know works for you. Two strong strategies are to look up words in a dictionary (online or hard copy) to ensure you have the exact meaning for your discipline and to keep a dedicated list of words you see often in your reading. You can list the words with a short definition so you have a quick reference guide to help you learn the vocabulary.

Evaluating

Intelligent people always question and evaluate. This doesn't mean they don't trust others; they just need verification of facts to understand a topic well. It doesn't make sense to learn incomplete or incorrect information about a subject just because you didn't take the time to evaluate all the sources at your disposal. When early explorers were afraid to sail the world for fear of falling off the edge, they weren't stupid; they just didn't have all the necessary data to evaluate the situation.

When you evaluate a text, you are seeking to understand the presented topic. Depending on how long the text is, you will perform a number of steps and repeat many of these steps to evaluate all the elements the author presents. When you evaluate a text, you need to do the following:

- Scan the title and all headings.
- Read through the entire passage fully.
- Question what main point the author is making.
- Decide who the audience is.
- Identify what evidence/support the author uses.
- Consider if the author presents a balanced perspective on the main point.
- Recognize if the author introduced any biases in the text.

When you go through a text looking for each of these elements, you need to go beyond just answering the surface question; for instance, the audience may be a specific field of scientists, but could anyone else understand the text with some explanation? Why would that be important?

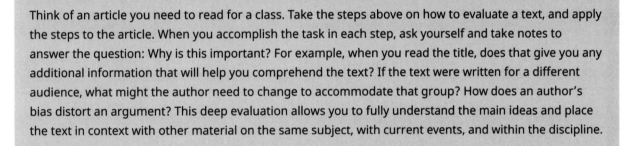

ANALYSIS QUESTION

Think of an article you need to read for a class. Take the steps above on how to evaluate a text, and apply the steps to the article. When you accomplish the task in each step, ask yourself and take notes to answer the question: Why is this important? For example, when you read the title, does that give you any additional information that will help you comprehend the text? If the text were written for a different audience, what might the author need to change to accommodate that group? How does an author's bias distort an argument? This deep evaluation allows you to fully understand the main ideas and place the text in context with other material on the same subject, with current events, and within the discipline.

Applying

When you learn something new, it always connects to other knowledge you already have. One challenge we have is applying new information. It may be interesting to know the distance to the moon, but how do we apply it to something we need to do? If your biology instructor asked you to list several challenges of colonizing Mars and you do not know much about that planet's exploration, you may be able to use your knowledge of how far Earth is from the moon to apply it to the new task. You may have to read several other texts in addition to reading graphs and charts to find this information.

That was the challenge the early space explorers faced along with myriad unknowns before space travel was a more regular occurrence. They had to take what they already knew and could study and read about and apply it to an unknown situation. These explorers wrote down their challenges, failures, and successes, and now scientists read those texts as a part of the ever-growing body of text about space travel. Application is a sophisticated level of thinking that helps turn theory into practice and challenges into successes.

Preparing to Read for Specific Disciplines in College

Different disciplines in college may have specific expectations, but you can depend on all subjects asking you to read to some degree. In this college reading requirement, you can succeed by learning to read actively, researching the topic and author, and recognizing how your own preconceived notions affect your reading. Reading for college isn't the same as reading for pleasure or even just reading to learn something on your own because you are casually interested.

In college courses, your instructor may ask you to read articles, chapters, books, or *primary sources* (those original documents about which we write and study, such as letters between historic figures or the Declaration of Independence). Your instructor may want you to have a general background on a topic before you dive into that subject in class, so that you know the history of a topic, can start thinking about it, and can engage in a class discussion with more than a passing knowledge of the issue.

If you are about to participate in an in-depth six-week consideration of the U.S. Constitution but have never read it or anything written about it, you will have a hard time looking at anything in detail or understanding how and why it is significant. As you can imagine, a great deal has been written about the Constitution by scholars and citizens since the late 1700s when it was first put to paper (that's how they did it then). While the actual document isn't that long (about 12–15 pages depending on how it is presented), learning the details on how it came about, who was involved, and why it was and still is a significant document would take a considerable amount of time to read and digest. So, how do you do it all? Especially when you may have an instructor who drops hints that you may also *love* to read a historic novel covering the same time period . . . in your *spare time*, not required, of course! It can be daunting, especially if you are taking more than one course that has time-consuming reading lists. With a few strategic techniques, you can manage it all, but know that you must have a plan and schedule your required reading so you *are* also able to pick up that recommended historic novel—it may give you an entirely new perspective on the issue.

Strategies for Reading in College Disciplines

No universal law exists for how much reading instructors and institutions expect college students to undertake for various disciplines. Suffice it to say, it's a LOT.

For most students, it is the volume of reading that catches them most off guard when they begin their college careers. A full course load might require 10–15 hours of reading per week, some of that covering content that will be more difficult than the reading for other courses.

You cannot possibly read word-for-word every single document you need to read for all your classes. That doesn't mean you give up or decide to only read for your favorite classes or concoct a scheme to read 17 percent for each class and see how that works for you. You need to learn to skim, annotate, and take notes. All of these techniques will help you comprehend more of what you read, which is why we read in the first place. We'll talk more later about annotating and notetaking, but for now consider what you know about skimming as opposed to active reading.

Skimming

Skimming is not just glancing over the words on a page (or screen) to see if any of it sticks. Effective skimming allows you to take in the major points of a passage without the need for a time-consuming reading session that involves your active use of notations and annotations. Often you will need to engage in that painstaking level of active reading, but skimming is the first step—not an alternative to deep reading. The fact remains that neither do you need to read everything nor could you possibly accomplish that given your limited time. So learn this valuable skill of skimming as an accompaniment to your overall study tool kit, and with practice and experience, you will fully understand how valuable it is.

When you skim, look for guides to your understanding: headings, definitions, pull quotes, tables, and context clues. Textbooks are often helpful for skimming—they may already have made some of these skimming guides in bold or a different color, and chapters often follow a predictable outline. Some even provide an overview and summary for sections or chapters. Use whatever you can get, but don't stop there. In textbooks that have some reading guides, or especially in text that does not, look for introductory words such as *First* or *The purpose of this article* . . . or summary words such as *In conclusion* . . . or *Finally*. These guides will help you read only those sentences or paragraphs that will give you the overall meaning or gist of a passage or book.

Now move to the meat of the passage. You want to take in the reading as a whole. For a book, look at the titles of each chapter if available. Read each chapter's introductory paragraph and determine why the writer chose this particular order. Depending on what you're reading, the chapters may be only informational, but often you're looking for a specific argument. What position is the writer claiming? What support, counterarguments, and conclusions is the writer presenting?

Don't think of skimming as a way to buzz through a boring reading assignment. It is a skill you should master so you can engage, at various levels, with all the reading you need to accomplish in college. End your skimming session with a few notes—terms to look up, questions you still have, and an overall summary. And recognize that you likely will return to that book or article for a more thorough reading if the material is useful.

Active Reading Strategies

Active reading differs significantly from skimming or reading for pleasure. You can think of active reading as a sort of conversation between you and the text (maybe between you and the author, but you don't want to get the author's personality too involved in this metaphor because that may skew your engagement with the text).

When you sit down to determine what your different classes expect you to read and you create a reading schedule to ensure you complete all the reading, think about when you should read the material strategically, not just how to *get it all done*. You should read textbook chapters and other reading assignments *before* you go into a lecture about that information. Don't wait to see how the lecture goes before you read the material, or you may not understand the information in the lecture. Reading before class helps you put ideas together between your reading and the information you hear and discuss in class.

Different disciplines naturally have different types of texts, and you need to take this into account when you schedule your time for reading class material. For example, you may look at a poem for your world literature class and assume that it will not take you long to read because it is relatively short compared to the dense textbook you have for your economics class. But reading and understanding a poem can take a considerable amount of time when you realize you may need to stop numerous times to review the separate word meanings and how the words form images and connections throughout the poem.

The SQ3R Reading Strategy

You may have heard of the **SQ3R** method for active reading in your early education. This valuable technique is perfect for college reading. The title stands for **S**urvey, **Q**uestion, **R**ead, **R**ecite, **R**eview, and you can use the steps on virtually any assigned passage. Designed by Francis Pleasant Robinson in his 1961 book *Effective Study,* the active reading strategy gives readers a systematic way to work through any reading material.

Survey is similar to skimming. You look for clues to meaning by reading the titles, headings, introductions, summary, captions for graphics, and keywords. You can survey almost anything connected to the reading selection, including the copyright information, the date of the journal article, or the names and qualifications of the author(s). In this step, you decide what the general meaning is for the reading selection.

Question is your creation of questions to seek the main ideas, support, examples, and conclusions of the reading selection. Ask yourself these questions separately. Try to create valid questions about what you are about to read that have come into your mind as you engaged in the Survey step. Try turning the headings of the sections in the chapter into questions. Next, how does what you're reading relate to you, your school, your community, and the world?

Read is when you actually read the passage. Try to find the answers to questions you developed in the previous step. Decide how much you are reading in chunks, either by paragraph for more complex readings or by section or even by an entire chapter. When you finish reading the selection, stop to make notes. Answer the questions by writing a note in the margin or other white space of the text.

You may also carefully underline or highlight text in addition to your notes. Use caution here that you don't try to rush this step by haphazardly circling terms or the other extreme of underlining huge chunks of text. Don't over-mark. You aren't likely to remember what these cryptic marks mean later when you come back to use this active reading session to study. The text is the source of information—your marks and notes are just a way to organize and make sense of that information.

Recite means to speak out loud. By reciting, you are engaging other senses to remember the material—you read it (visual) and you said it (auditory). Stop reading momentarily in the step to answer your questions or clarify confusing sentences or paragraphs. You can recite a summary of what the text means to you. If you are not in a place where you can verbalize, such as a library or classroom, you can accomplish this step adequately by *saying* it in your head; however, to get the biggest bang for your buck, try to find a place where you can speak aloud. You may even want to try explaining the content to a friend.

Review is a recap. Go back over what you read and add more notes, ensuring you have captured the main points of the passage, identified the supporting evidence and examples, and understood the overall meaning. You may need to repeat some or all of the SQR3 steps during your review depending on the length and complexity of the material. Before you end your active reading session, write a short (no more than one page is optimal) summary of the text you read.

Reading Primary and Secondary Sources

Primary sources are original documents we study and from which we glean information; primary sources include letters, first editions of books, legal documents, and a variety of other texts. When scholars look at these documents to understand a period in history or a scientific challenge and then write about their findings, the scholar's article is considered a secondary source. Readers have to keep several factors in mind when reading both primary and secondary sources.

Primary sources may contain dated material we now know is inaccurate. It may contain personal beliefs and biases the original writer didn't intent to be openly published, and it may even present fanciful or creative ideas that do not support current knowledge. Readers can still gain great insight from primary sources, but readers need to understand the context from which the writer of the primary source wrote the text.

Likewise, secondary sources are inevitably another person's perspective on the primary source, so a reader of secondary sources must also be aware of potential biases or preferences the secondary source writer inserts in the writing that may persuade an incautious reader to interpret the primary source in a particular manner.

For example, if you were to read a secondary source that is examining the U.S. Declaration of Independence (the primary source), you would have a much clearer idea of how the secondary source scholar presented the information from the primary source if you also read the Declaration for yourself instead of trusting the other writer's interpretation. Most scholars are honest in writing secondary sources, but you as a reader of the source are trusting the writer to present a balanced perspective of the primary source. When possible, you should attempt to read a primary source in conjunction with the secondary source. The Internet helps immensely with this practice.

WHAT STUDENTS SAY

1. What is the most influential factor in how thoroughly you read the material for a given course?
    a. How engaging the material is or how much I enjoy reading it.
    b. Whether or not the course is part of my major.
    c. Whether or not the instructor assesses knowledge from the reading (through quizzes, for example), or requires assignments based on the reading.
    d. Whether or not knowledge or information from the reading is required to participate in lecture.
2. What best describes your reading approach for required texts/materials for your classes?
    a. I read all of the assigned material.
    b. I read most of the assigned material.
    c. I skim the text and read the captions, examples, or summaries.
3. What best describes your notetaking style?
    a. I use a systematic method such as the Cornell method or something similar.
    b. I highlight or underline all the important information.
    c. I create outlines and/or note-cards.
    d. I use an app or program.
    e. I write notes in my text (print or digital).
    f. I don't have a style. I just write down what seems important.
    g. I don't take many notes.

You can also take the anonymous What Students Say (https://openstax.org/l/collegesurvey1-5) surveys to add your voice to this textbook. Your responses will be included in updates.

Students offered their views on these questions, and the results are displayed in the graphs below.

What is the most influential factor in how thoroughly you read the material for a given course?

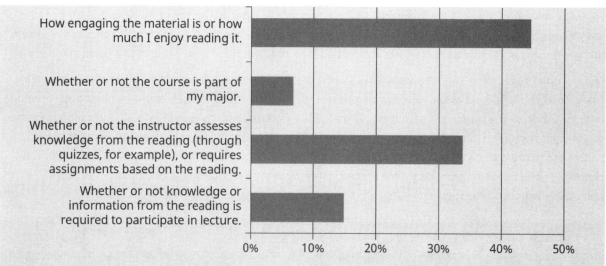

Figure 5.5

What best describes your reading approach for required texts/materials for your classes?

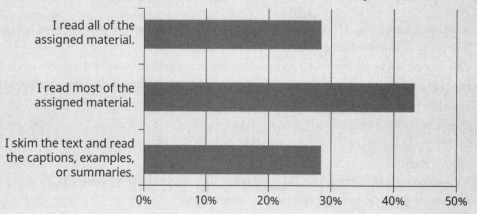

Figure 5.6

What best describes your notetaking style?

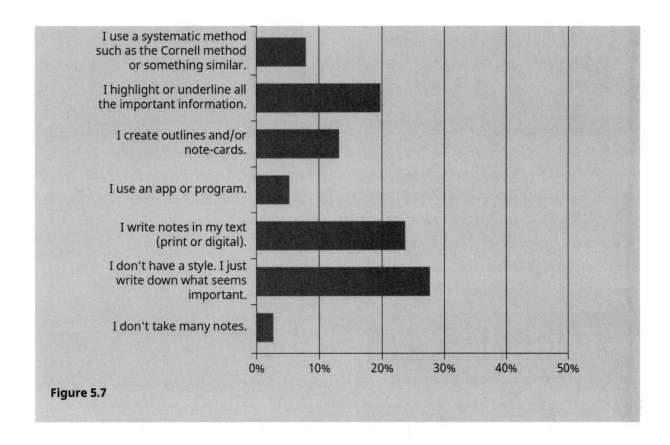

Figure 5.7

Researching Topic and Author

During your preview stage, sometimes called pre-reading, you can easily pick up on information from various sources that may help you understand the material you're reading more fully or place it in context with other important works in the discipline. If your selection is a book, flip it over or turn to the back pages and look for an author's biography or note from the author. See if the book itself contains any other information about the author or the subject matter.

The main things you need to recall from your reading in college are the topics covered and how the information fits into the discipline. You can find these parts throughout the textbook chapter in the form of headings in larger and bold font, summary lists, and important quotations pulled out of the narrative. Use these features as you read to help you determine what the most important ideas are.

Figure 5.8 Learning about the book you're reading can provide good context and information. Look for an author's biography and forward on the back cover or in the first few pages. (Credit: Mark Hillary / Flickr / Attribution 2.0 Generic (CC-BY 2.0))

Remember, many books use quotations about the book or author as testimonials in a marketing approach to sell more books, so these may not be the most reliable sources of unbiased opinions, but it's a start. Sometimes you can find a list of other books the author has written near the front of a book. Do you recognize any of the other titles? Can you do an Internet search for the name of the book or author? Go beyond the search results that want you to buy the book and see if you can glean any other relevant information about the author or the reading selection. Beyond a standard Internet search, try the library article database. These are more relevant to academic disciplines and contain resources you typically will not find in a standard search engine. If you are unfamiliar with how to use the library database, ask a reference librarian on campus. They are often underused resources that can point you in the right direction.

Understanding Your Own Preset Ideas on a Topic

Laura really enjoys learning about environmental issues. She has read many books and watched numerous televised documentaries on this topic and actively seeks out additional information on the environment. While Laura's interest can help her understand a new reading encounter about the environment, Laura also has to be aware that with this interest, she also brings forward her preset ideas and biases about the topic. Sometimes these prejudices against other ideas relate to religion or nationality or even just tradition. Without evidence, thinking the way we always have is not a good enough reason; evidence can change, and at the very least it needs honest review and assessment to determine its validity. Ironically, we may not want to learn new ideas because that may mean we would have to give up old ideas we have already mastered, which can be a daunting prospect.

With every reading situation about the environment, Laura needs to remain open-minded about what she is about to read and pay careful attention if she begins to ignore certain parts of the text because of her preconceived notions. Learning new information can be very difficult if you balk at ideas that are different from what you've always thought. You may have to force yourself to listen to a different viewpoint multiple times to make sure you are not closing your mind to a viable solution your mindset does not currently allow.

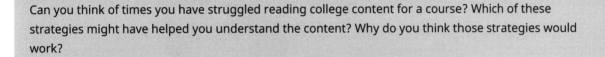

ANALYSIS QUESTION

Can you think of times you have struggled reading college content for a course? Which of these strategies might have helped you understand the content? Why do you think those strategies would work?

5.3 Taking Notes

Estimated completion time: 21 minutes.

Questions to consider:

- How can you prepare to take notes to maximize the effectiveness of the experience?
- What are some specific strategies you can employ for better notetaking?
- Why is annotating your notes after the notetaking session a critical step to follow?

Beyond providing a record of the information you are reading or hearing, notes help you organize the ideas and help you make meaning out of something about which you may not be familiar, so notetaking and reading are two compatible skill sets. Taking notes also helps you stay focused on the question at hand. Nanami often takes notes during presentations or class lectures so she can follow the speaker's main points and condense the material into a more readily usable format. Strong notes build on your prior knowledge of a subject, help you discuss trends or patterns present in the information, and direct you toward areas needing further research or reading.

Figure 5.9 Strong notes build on your prior knowledge of a subject, help you discuss trends or patterns present in the information, and direct you toward areas needing further research or reading.

It is not a good habit to transcribe every single word a speaker utters—even if you have an amazing ability to do that. Most of us don't have that court-reporter-esque skill level anyway, and if we try, we would end up missing valuable information. Learn to listen for main ideas and distinguish between these main ideas and details that typically support the ideas. Include examples that explain the main ideas, but do so using understandable abbreviations.

Think of all notes as potential study guides. In fact, if you only take notes without actively working on them after the initial notetaking session, the likelihood of the notes helping you is slim. Research on this topic concludes that without active engagement after taking notes, most students forget 60–75 percent of material over which they took the notes—within two days! That sort of defeats the purpose, don't you think? This information about memory loss was first brought to light by 19th-century German psychologist Hermann Ebbinghaus. Fortunately, you do have the power to thwart what is sometimes called the Ebbinghaus Forgetting Curve by reinforcing what you learned through review at intervals shortly after you take in the material and frequently thereafter.

If you are a musician, you'll understand this phenomenon well. When you first attempt a difficult piece of music, you may not remember the chords and notes well at all, but after frequent practice and review, you generate a certain muscle memory and cognitive recall that allows you to play the music more easily.

Notetaking may not be the most glamorous aspect of your higher-education journey, but it is a study practice you will carry throughout college and into your professional life. Setting yourself up for successful notetaking is almost as important as the actual taking of notes, and what you do after your notetaking session is equally significant. Well-written notes help you organize your thoughts, enhance your memory, and participate in class discussion, and they prepare you to respond successfully on exams. With all that riding on your notes, it would behoove you to learn how to take notes properly and continue to improve your notetaking skills.

> **ANALYSIS QUESTION**
>
> Do you currently have a preferred way to take notes? When did you start using it? Has it been effective? What other strategy might work for you?

Preparing to Take Notes

Preparing to take notes means more than just getting out your laptop or making sure you bring pen and paper to class. You'll do a much better job with your notes if you understand why we take notes, have a strong grasp on your preferred notetaking system, determine your specific priorities depending on your situation, and engage in some version of efficient shorthand.

Like handwriting and fingerprints, we all have unique and fiercely independent notetaking habits. These understandably and reasonably vary from one situation to the next, but you can only improve your skills by learning more about ways to take effective notes and trying different methods to find a good fit.

The very best notes are the ones you take in an organized manner that encourages frequent review and use as you progress through a topic or course of study. For this reason, you need to develop a way to organize all your notes for each class so they remain together and organized. As old-fashioned as it sounds, a clunky three-ring binder is an excellent organizational container for class notes. You can easily add to previous notes, insert handouts you may receive in class, and maintain a running collection of materials for each separate course. If the idea of carrying around a heavy binder has you rolling your eyes, then transfer that same structure into your computer files. If you don't organize your many documents into some semblance of order on your computer, you will waste significant time searching for improperly named or saved files.

You may be interested in relatively new research on what is the more effective notetaking strategy: handwriting versus typing directly into a computer. While individuals have strong personal opinions on this subject, most researchers agree that the format of student notes is less important than what students do with the notes they take afterwards. Both handwriting notes and using a computer for notetaking have pros and cons.

Figure 5.10 The best notes are the ones you take in an organized manner. Frequent review and further annotation are important to build a deep and useful understanding of the material. (Credit: English106 / Flickr / Attribution 2.0 Generic (CC-BY 2.0))

Managing Notetaking Systems (Computer, Paper/Pen, Note Cards, Textbook)

Whichever of the many notetaking systems you choose (and new ones seem to come out almost daily), the very best one is the one that you will use consistently. The skill and art of notetaking is not automatic for anyone; it takes a great deal of practice, patience, and continuous attention to detail. Add to that the fact that you may need to master multiple notetaking techniques for different classes, and you have some work to do. Unless you are specifically directed by your instructor, you are free to combine the best parts of different systems if you are most comfortable with that hybrid system.

Just to keep yourself organized, all your notes should start off with an identifier, including at the very least the date, the course name, the topic of the lecture/presentation, and any other information you think will help you when you return to use the notes for further study, test preparation, or assignment completion. Additional, optional information may be the number of notetaking sessions about this topic or reminders to cross-reference class handouts, textbook pages, or other course materials. It's also always a good idea to leave some blank space in your notes so you can insert additions and questions you may have as you review the material later.

Notetaking Strategies

You may have a standard way you take all your notes for all your classes. When you were in high school, this one-size-fits-all approach may have worked. Now that you're in college, reading and studying more advanced topics, your general method may still work some of the time, but you should have some different strategies in place if you find that your method isn't working as well with college content. You probably will need to adopt different notetaking strategies for different subjects. The strategies in this section represent various ways to take notes in such a way that you are able to study after the initial notetaking session.

Cornell Method

One of the most recognizable notetaking systems is called the *Cornell Method*, a relatively simple way to take effective notes devised by Cornell University education professor Dr. Walter Pauk in the 1940s. In this system, you take a standard piece of note paper and divide it into three sections by drawing a horizontal line across your paper about one to two inches from the bottom of the page (the summary area) and then drawing a vertical line to separate the rest of the page above this bottom area, making the left side about two inches (the recall column) and leaving the biggest area to the right of your vertical line (the notes column). You may want to make one page and then copy as many pages as you think you'll need for any particular class, but one advantage of this system is that you can generate the sections quickly. Because you have divided up your page, you may end up using more paper than you would if you were writing on the entire page, but the point is not to keep your notes to as few pages as possible. The Cornell Method provides you with a well-organized set of notes that will help you study and review your notes as you move through the course. If you are taking notes on your computer, you can still use the Cornell Method in Word or Excel on your own or by using a template someone else created.

Topic/Objective:		Name:
		Class/Period:
		Date:
Essential Question:		

Questions:	Notes:

Summary:

Figure 5.11 The Cornell Method provides a straightforward, organized, and flexible approach

Now that you have the notetaking format generated, the beauty of the Cornell Method is its organized simplicity. Just write on one side of the page (the right-hand notes column)—this will help later when you are reviewing and revising your notes. During your notetaking session, use the notes column to record information over the main points and concepts of the lecture; try to put the ideas into your own words, which will help you not transcribe the speaker's words verbatim. Skip lines between each idea in this column.

Practice the shortcut abbreviations covered in the next section and avoid writing in complete sentences. Don't make your notes too cryptic, but you can use bullet points or phrases equally well to convey meaning—we do it all the time in conversation. If you know you will need to expand the notes you are taking in class but don't have time, you can put reminders directly in the notes by adding and underlining the word *expand* by the ideas you need to develop more fully.

As soon as possible after your notetaking session, preferably within eight hours but no more than twenty-four hours, read over your notes column and fill in any details you missed in class, including the places where you indicated you wanted to expand your notes. Then in the recall column, write any key ideas from the corresponding notes column—you can't stuff this smaller recall column as if you're explaining or defining key ideas. Just add the one- or two-word main ideas; these words in the recall column serve as cues to help you remember the detailed information you recorded in the notes column.

Once you are satisfied with your notes and recall columns, summarize this page of notes in two or three sentences using the summary area at the bottom of the sheet. This is an excellent time to get with another classmate or a group of students who all heard the same lecture to make sure you all understood the key points. Now, before you move onto something else, cover the large notes column, and quiz yourself over the key ideas you recorded in the recall column. Repeat this step often as you go along, not just immediately before an exam, and you will help your memory make the connections between your notes, your textbook reading, your in-class work, and assignments that you need to succeed on any quizzes and exams.

Academic Essay Elements	
Topic	Topic – Establishes context – Limits scope of essay – Introduces Issue/Problem
Thesis	Thesis – Central argument or point of paper – Arrives early in paper—usually toward end of first paragraph (maybe a bit later in longer papers) – Focused, clear, and specific – Reflects writer's position on the topic/issue
Supporting Details	Supporting Detail Paragraphs – Each paragraph has a specific topic – Clarify, explain, illustrate, expand on topic – Provide EVIDENCE—quotes, data, references <u>Cite everything properly!</u>
Conclusion	Conclusion – Tie back to intro/thesis – Show how details supported the argument – Why is it important? – Point to implications/outcomes, but don't introduce entirely new ideas

Use the structure, but don't follow it too rigidly. The most important pieces are a strong thesis and good evidence to back it up. The conclusion should not just summarize—take it a little further.

Figure 5.12 This sample set of notes in the Cornell Method is designed to make sense of a large amount of information. The process of organizing the notes can help you retain the information more effectively than less consistent methods.

The main advantage of the Cornell Method is that you are setting yourself up to have organized, workable notes. The neat format helps you move into study-mode without needing to re-copy less organized notes or making sense of a large mass of information you aren't sure how to process because you can't remember key ideas or what you meant. If you write notes in your classes without any sort of system and later come across something like "Napoleon—short" in the middle of a glob of notes, what can you do at this point? Is that important? Did it connect with something relevant from the lecture? How would you possibly know? You are your best advocate for setting yourself up for success in college.

Outlining

Other note organizing systems may help you in different disciplines. You can take notes in a formal outline if you prefer, using Roman numerals for each new topic, moving down a line to capital letters indented a few spaces to the right for concepts related to the previous topic, then adding details to support the concepts indented a few more spaces over and denoted by an Arabic numeral. You can continue to add to a formal outline by following these rules.

You don't absolutely have to use the formal numerals and letter, but you have to then be careful to indent so you can tell when you move from a higher level topic to the related concepts and then to the supporting information. The main benefit of an outline is how organized it is. You have to be on your toes when you are taking notes in class to ensure you keep up the organizational format of the outline, which can be tricky if the lecture or presentation is moving quickly or covering many diverse topics.

The following formal outline example shows the basic pattern:

I. Dogs *(main topic–usually general)*
    A. German Shepherd *(concept related to main topic)*
        1. Protection *(supporting info about the concept)*
        2. Assertive
        3. Loyal
    B. Weimaraner *(concept related to main topic)*
        1. Family-friendly *(supporting info about the concept)*
        2. Active
        3. Healthy
II. Cats *(main topic)*
    Siamese

You would just continue on with this sort of numbering and indenting format to show the connections between main ideas, concepts, and supporting details. Whatever details you do not capture in your notetaking session, you can add after the lecture as you review your outline.

Chart or table

Similar to creating an outline, you can develop a chart to compare and contrast main ideas in a notetaking session. Divide your paper into four or five columns with headings that include either the main topics covered in the lecture or categories such as How?, What?, When used?, Advantages/Pros, Disadvantages/Cons, or other divisions of the information. You write your notes into the appropriate columns as that information comes to light in the presentation.

Example of a Chart to Organize Ideas and Categories

	Structure	Types	Functions in Body	Additional Notes
Carbohydrates				
Lipids				
Proteins				
Nucleic Acid				

This format helps you pull out the salient ideas and establishes an organized set of notes to study later. (If you haven't noticed that this *reviewing later* idea is a constant across all notetaking systems, you should...take note of that.) Notes by themselves that you never reference again are little more than scribblings. That would be a bit like compiling an extensive grocery list so you stay on budget when you shop, work all week on it, and then just throw it away before you get to the store. You may be able to recall a few items, but likely won't be as efficient as you could be if you had the notes to reference. Just as you cannot read all the many books, articles, and documents you need to peruse for your college classes, you cannot remember the most important ideas of all the notes you will take as part of your courses, so you must review.

Concept Mapping and Visual Notetaking

One final notetaking method that appeals to learners who prefer a visual representation of notes is called *mapping* or sometimes *mind mapping* or *concept mapping,* although each of these names can have slightly different uses. Variations of this method abound, so you may want to look for more versions online, but the basic principles are that you are making connections between main ideas through a graphic depiction; some can get rather elaborate with colors and shapes, but a simple version may be more useful at least to begin. Main ideas can be circled or placed in a box with supporting concepts radiating off these ideas shown with a connecting line and possibly details of the support further radiating off the concepts. You can present your main ideas vertically or horizontally, but turning your paper long-ways, or in landscape mode, may prove helpful as you add more main ideas.

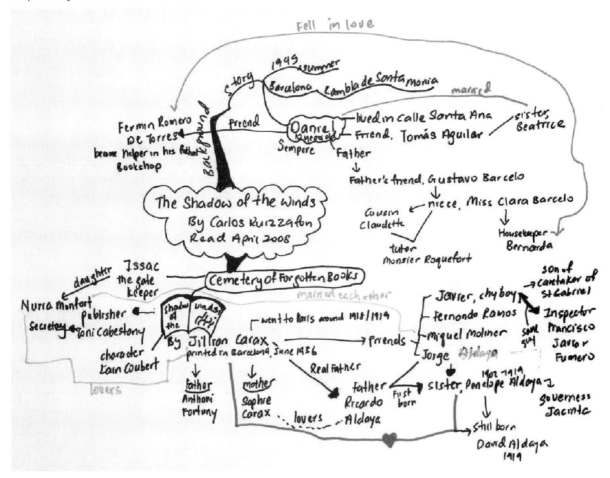

Figure 5.13 Concept mapping, sometimes referred to as mind mapping, can be an effective and very personalized approach to capturing information. (Credit: ArtistIvanChew / Flickr / Attribution 2.0 Generic (CC-BY 2.0))

You may be interested in trying visual notetaking or adding pictures to your notes for clarity. Sometimes when you can't come up with the exact wording to explain something or you're trying to add information for complex ideas in your notes, sketching a rough image of the idea can help you remember. According to educator Sherrill Knezel in an article entitled "The Power of Visual Notetaking," this strategy is effective because "When students use images and text in notetaking, it gives them two different ways to pull up the information, doubling their chances of recall." Don't shy away from this creative approach to notetaking just because you believe you aren't an artist; the images don't need to be perfect. You may want to watch Rachel Smith's TEDx Talk called "Drawing in Class" (https://openstax.org/l/drawinginclass) to learn more about visual notetaking.

You can play with different types of notetaking suggestions and find the method(s) you like best, but once you find what works for you, stick with it. You will become more efficient with the method the more you use it, and your notetaking, review, and test prep will become, if not easier, certainly more organized, which can delete decrease your anxiety.

Practicing Decipherable Shorthand

Most college students don't take a class in shorthand, once the domain of secretaries and executive assistants, but maybe they should. That almost-lost art in the age of computers could come in very handy during intense notetaking sessions. Elaborate shorthand systems do exist, but you would be better served in your college notetaking adventures to hone a more familiar, personalized form of shorthand to help you write more in a shorter amount of time. Seemingly insignificant shortcuts can add up to ease the stress notetaking can induce—especially if you ever encounter an "I'm not going to repeat this" kind of presenter! Become familiar with these useful abbreviations:

Shortcut symbol	Meaning
w/, w/o, w/in	with, without, within
&	and
#	number
b/c	because
X, √	incorrect, correct
Diff	different, difference
etc.	and so on
ASAP	as soon as possible
US, UK	United States, United Kingdom
info	information
Measurements: ft, in, k, m	foot, inch, thousand, million
¶	paragraph or new paragraph

Shortcut symbol	Meaning
Math symbols: =, +, >, <, ÷	equal, plus, greater, less, divided by
WWI, WWII	World Wars I and II
impt	important
?, !, **	denote something is very significant; don't over use

Do you have any other shortcuts or symbols that you use in your notes? Ask your parents if they remember any that you may be able to learn.

Annotating Notes After Initial Notetaking Session

Annotating notes after the initial notetaking session may be one of the most valuable study skills you can master. Whether you are highlighting, underlining, or adding additional notes, you are reinforcing the material in your mind and memory.

Admit it—who can resist highlighting markers? Gone are the days when yellow was the star of the show, and you had to be very careful not to press too firmly for fear of obliterating the words you were attempting to emphasize. Students now have a veritable rainbow of highlighting options and can color-code notes and text passages to their hearts' content. Technological advances may be important, but highlighter color choice is monumental! Maybe.

The only reason to highlight anything is to draw attention to it, so you can easily pick out that ever-so-important information later for further study or reflection. One problem many students have is not knowing when to stop. If what you need to recall from the passage is a particularly apt and succinct definition of the term important to your discipline, highlighting the entire paragraph is less effective than highlighting just the actual term. And if you don't rein in this tendency to color long passages (possibly in multiple colors) you can end up with a whole page of highlighted text. Ironically, that is no different from a page that is not highlighted at all, so you have wasted your time. Your mantra for highlighting text should be *less is more*. Always read your text selection first before you start highlighting anything. You need to know what the overall message is before you start placing emphasis in the text with highlighting.

Another way to annotate notes after initial notetaking is underlying significant words or passages. Albeit not quite as much fun as its colorful cousin highlighting, underlining provides precision to your emphasis.

Some people think of annotations as only using a colored highlighter to mark certain words or phrases for emphasis. Actually, annotations can refer to anything you do with a text to enhance it for your particular use (either a printed text, handwritten notes, or other sort of document you are using to learn concepts). The annotations may include highlighting passages or vocabulary, defining those unfamiliar terms once you look them up, writing questions in the margin of a book, underlining or circling key terms, or otherwise marking a text for future reference. You can also annotate some electronic texts.

Realistically, you may end up doing all of these types of annotations at different times. We know that repetition in studying and reviewing is critical to learning, so you may come back to the same passage and annotate it separately. These various markings can be invaluable to you as a study guide and as a way to see the evolution of your learning about a topic. If you regularly begin a reading session writing down any questions you may have about the topic of that chapter or section and also write out answers to those questions at the end of the reading selection, you will have a good start to what that chapter covered when you eventually need to study for an exam. At that point, you likely will not have time to reread the entire selection especially if it is a long reading selection, but with strong annotations in conjunction with your class notes, you won't need to do that. With experience in reading discipline-specific texts and writing essays or taking exams in that field, you will know better what sort of questions to ask in your annotations.

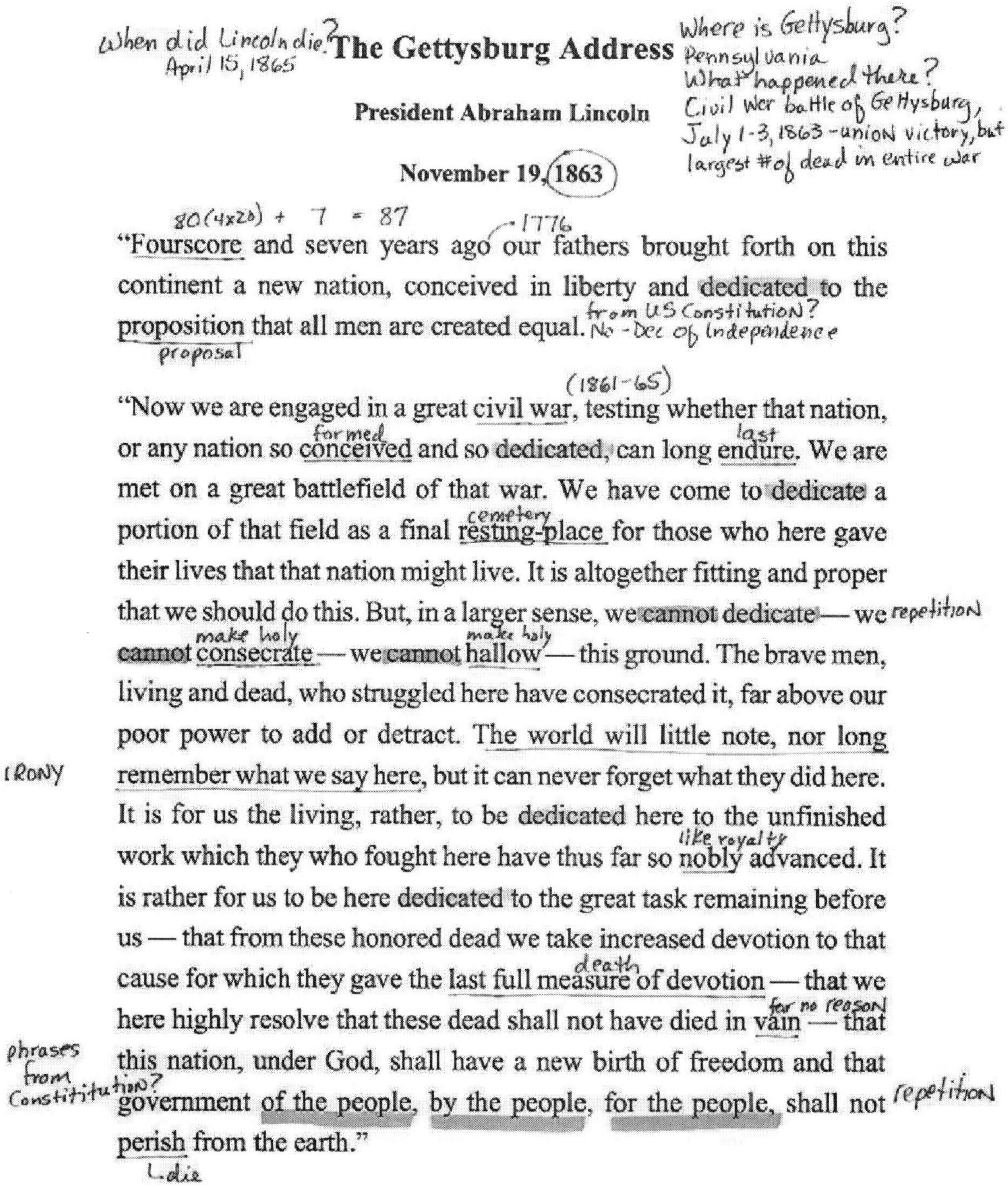

When did Lincoln die?
April 15, 1865

The Gettysburg Address

Where is Gettysburg? Pennsylvania
What happened there? Civil war battle of Gettysburg, July 1-3, 1863 – union victory, but largest # of dead in entire war

President Abraham Lincoln

November 19, (1863)

80(4x20) + 7 = 87   *– 1776*

"**Fourscore** and seven years ago our fathers brought forth on this continent a new nation, conceived in liberty and **dedicated** to the proposition that all men are created equal. *from US Constitution? No – Dec of Independence proposal*

"Now we are engaged in a great civil war, *(1861-65)* testing whether that nation, or any nation so conceived *(formed)* and so dedicated, can long endure *(last)*. We are met on a great battlefield of that war. We have come to **dedicate** a portion of that field as a final resting-place *(cemetery)* for those who here gave their lives that that nation might live. It is altogether fitting and proper that we should do this. But, in a larger sense, we **cannot dedicate** — we cannot consecrate *(make holy)* — we cannot hallow *(make holy)* — this ground. The brave men, living and dead, who struggled here have consecrated it, far above our poor power to add or detract. The world will little note, nor long remember what we say here, but it can never forget what they did here. *IRONY* It is for us the living, rather, to be **dedicated** here to the unfinished work which they who fought here have thus far so nobly *(like royalty)* advanced. It is rather for us to be here **dedicated** to the great task remaining before us — that from these honored dead we take increased devotion to that cause for which they gave the last full measure *(death)* of devotion — that we here highly resolve that these dead shall not have died in vain *(for no reason)* — that *phrases from Constitution?* this nation, under God, shall have a new birth of freedom and that government of the people, by the people, for the people, shall not *repetition* perish from the earth."
L. die

Figure 5.14 Annotations may include highlighting important topics, defining unfamiliar terms, writing questions in, underlining or circling key terms, or otherwise marking a text for future reference. Whichever approach you choose, try not to overdo it; neat, organized, and efficient notes are more effective than crowded or overdone notes.

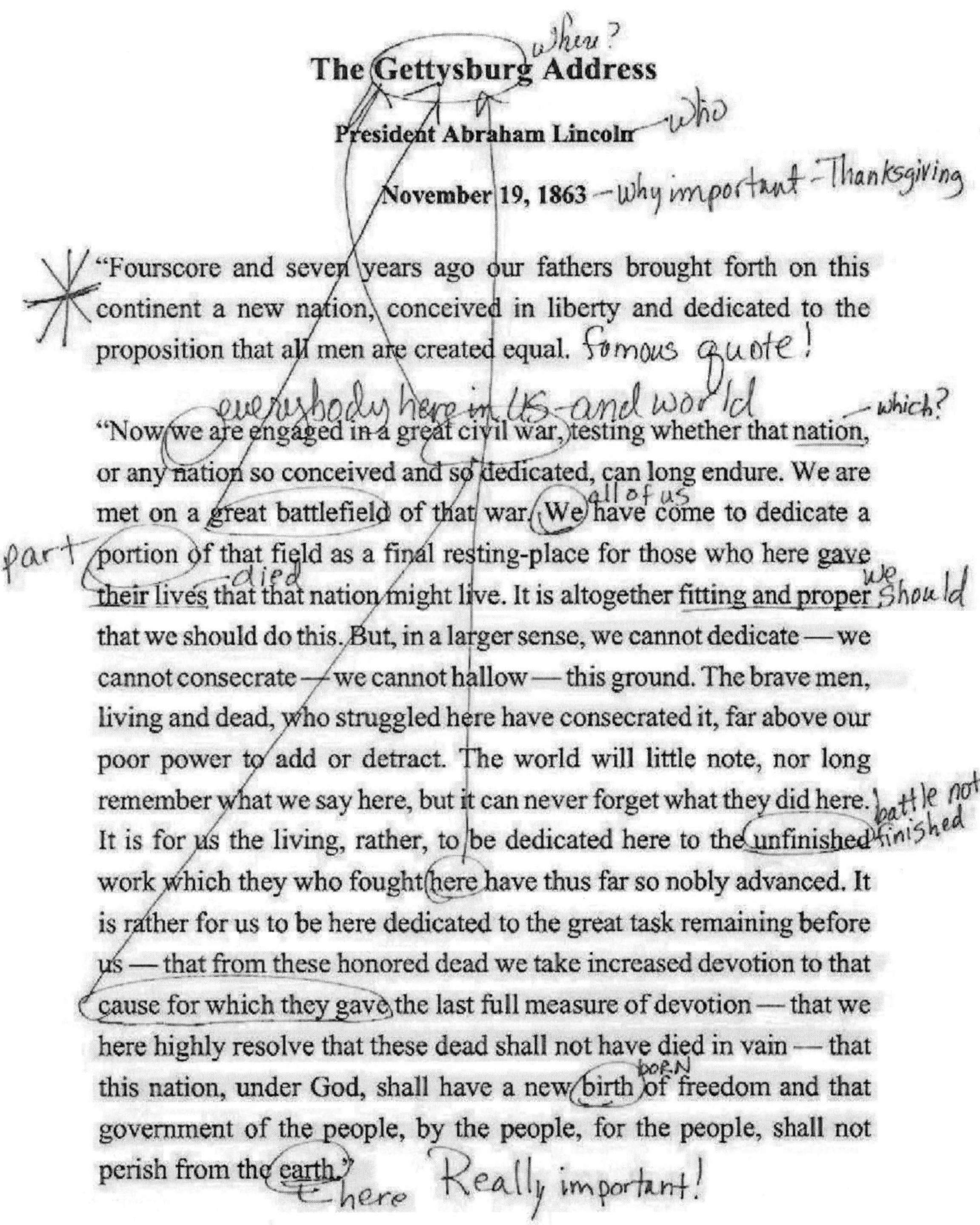

The Gettysburg Address

President Abraham Lincoln

November 19, 1863

[Handwritten annotations: "when?" pointing to Gettysburg; "who" pointing to Lincoln; "why important – Thanksgiving" next to the date]

"Fourscore and seven years ago our fathers brought forth on this continent a new nation, conceived in liberty and dedicated to the proposition that all men are created equal. *[famous quote!]*

"Now we are engaged in a great civil war, testing whether that nation, or any nation so conceived and so dedicated, can long endure. We are met on a great battlefield of that war. We have come to dedicate a portion of that field as a final resting-place for those who here gave their lives that that nation might live. It is altogether fitting and proper that we should do this. But, in a larger sense, we cannot dedicate — we cannot consecrate — we cannot hallow — this ground. The brave men, living and dead, who struggled here have consecrated it, far above our poor power to add or detract. The world will little note, nor long remember what we say here, but it can never forget what they did here. It is for us the living, rather, to be dedicated here to the unfinished work which they who fought here have thus far so nobly advanced. It is rather for us to be here dedicated to the great task remaining before us — that from these honored dead we take increased devotion to that cause for which they gave the last full measure of devotion — that we here highly resolve that these dead shall not have died in vain — that this nation, under God, shall have a new birth of freedom and that government of the people, by the people, for the people, shall not perish from the earth." *[Really important!]*

[Additional handwritten annotations throughout: "everybody here in US – and world"; "which?"; "all of us"; "part"; "died"; "we should"; "battle not finished"; "born"; "here"]

Figure 5.15 While these notes may be meaningful to the person who took them, they are neither organized nor consistent. For example, note that some of the more commonly used terms, like "we" and "unfinished," are defined, but less common ones -- "consecrate" and "hallow" -- are not.

What you have to keep in the front of your mind while you are annotating, especially if you are going to conduct multiple annotation sessions, is to not overdo whatever method you use. Be judicious about what you annotate and how you do it on the page, which means you must be neat about it. Otherwise, you end up with a mess of either color or symbols combined with some cryptic notes that probably took you quite a long time to create, but won't be worth as much to you as a study aid as they could be. This is simply a waste of time and effort.

You cannot eat up every smidgen of white space on the page writing out questions or summaries and still have a way to read the original text. If you are lucky enough to have a blank page next to the beginning of the chapter or section you are annotating, use this, but keep in mind that when you start writing notes, you aren't exactly sure how much space you'll need. Use a decipherable shorthand and write only what you need to convey the meaning in very small print. If you are annotating your own notes, you can make a habit of using only one side of the paper in class, so that if you need to add more notes later, you could use the other side. You can also add a blank page to your notes before beginning the next class date in your notebook so you'll end up with extra paper for annotations when you study.

Professional resources may come with annotations that can be helpful to you as you work through the various documentation requirements you'll encounter in college as well. Purdue University's Online Writing Lab (OWL (https://openstax.org/l/mlaformatting)) provides an annotated sample for how to format a college paper according to guidelines in the Modern Language Association (MLA) manual that you can see, along with other annotations.

Adding Needed Additional Explanations to Notes

Marlon was totally organized and ready to take notes in a designated course notebook at the beginning of every philosophy class session. He always dated his page and indicated what the topic of discussion was. He had various colored highlighters ready to denote the different note purposes he had defined: vocabulary in pink, confusing concepts in green, and note sections that would need additional explanations later in yellow. He also used his own shorthand and an impressive array of symbols to indicate questions (red question mark), highly probable test material (he used a tiny bomb exploding here), additional reading suggestions, and specific topics he would ask his instructor before the next class. Doing everything so precisely, Marlon's methods seemed like a perfect example of how to take notes for success. Inevitably though, by the end of the hour-and-a-half class session, Marlon was frantically switching between writing tools, near to tears, and scouring his notes as waves of yellow teased him with uncertainty. What went wrong?

As with many of us who try diligently to do everything we know how to do for success or what we think we know because we read books and articles on success in between our course work, Marlon is suffering from trying to do too much simultaneously. It's an honest mistake we can make when we are trying to save a little time or think we can multitask and kill two birds with one stone.

Unfortunately, this particular error in judgement can add to your stress level exponentially if you don't step back and see it for what it is. Marlon attempted to take notes in class as well as annotate his notes to get them ready for his test preparation. It was too much to do at one time, but even if he could have done all those things during class, he's missing one critical point about notetaking.

As much as we may want to hurry and get it over with, notetaking in class is just the beginning. Your instructor likely gave you a pre-class assignment to read or complete before coming to that session. The intention of that preparatory lesson is for you to come in with some level of familiarity for the topic under consideration and questions of your own. Once you're in class, you may also need to participate in a group discussion, work with your classmates, or perform some other sort of lesson-directed activity that would necessarily take you away from taking notes. Does that mean you should ignore taking notes for that day? Most likely not. You may just need to indicate in your notes that you worked on a project or whatever other in-class event you experienced that date.

Very rarely in a college classroom will you engage in an activity that is not directly related to what you are studying in that course. Even if you enjoyed every minute of the class session and it was an unusual format for that course, you still need to take some notes. Maybe your first note could be to ask yourself why you think the instructor used that unique teaching strategy for the class that day. Was it effective? Was it worth using the whole class time? How will that experience enhance what you are learning in that course?

If you use an ereader or ebooks to read texts for class or read articles from the Internet on your laptop or tablet, you can still take effective notes. Depending on the features of your device, you have many choices. Almost all electronic reading platforms allow readers to highlight and underline text. Some devices allow you to add a written text in addition to marking a word or passage that you can collect at the end of your notetaking session. Look into the specific tools for your device and learn how to use the features that allow you to take notes electronically. You can also find apps on devices to help with taking notes, some of which you may automatically have installed when you buy the product. Microsoft's OneNote, Google Keep, and the Notes feature on phones are relatively easy to use, and you may already have free access to those.

Taking Notes on Non-Text Items (i.e., Tables, Maps, Figures, etc.)

You may also encounter situations as you study and read textbooks, primary sources, and other resources for your classes that are not actually texts. You can still take notes on maps, charts, graphs, images, and tables, and your approach to these non-text features is similar to when you prepare to take notes over a passage of text. For example, if you are looking at the following map, you may immediately come up with several questions. Or it may initially appear overwhelming. Start by asking yourself these questions:

What is the main point of this map?

- Who is the intended audience?
- Where is it?
- What time period does it depict?
- What does the map's legend (the explanation of symbols) include?
- What other information do I need to make sense of this map?

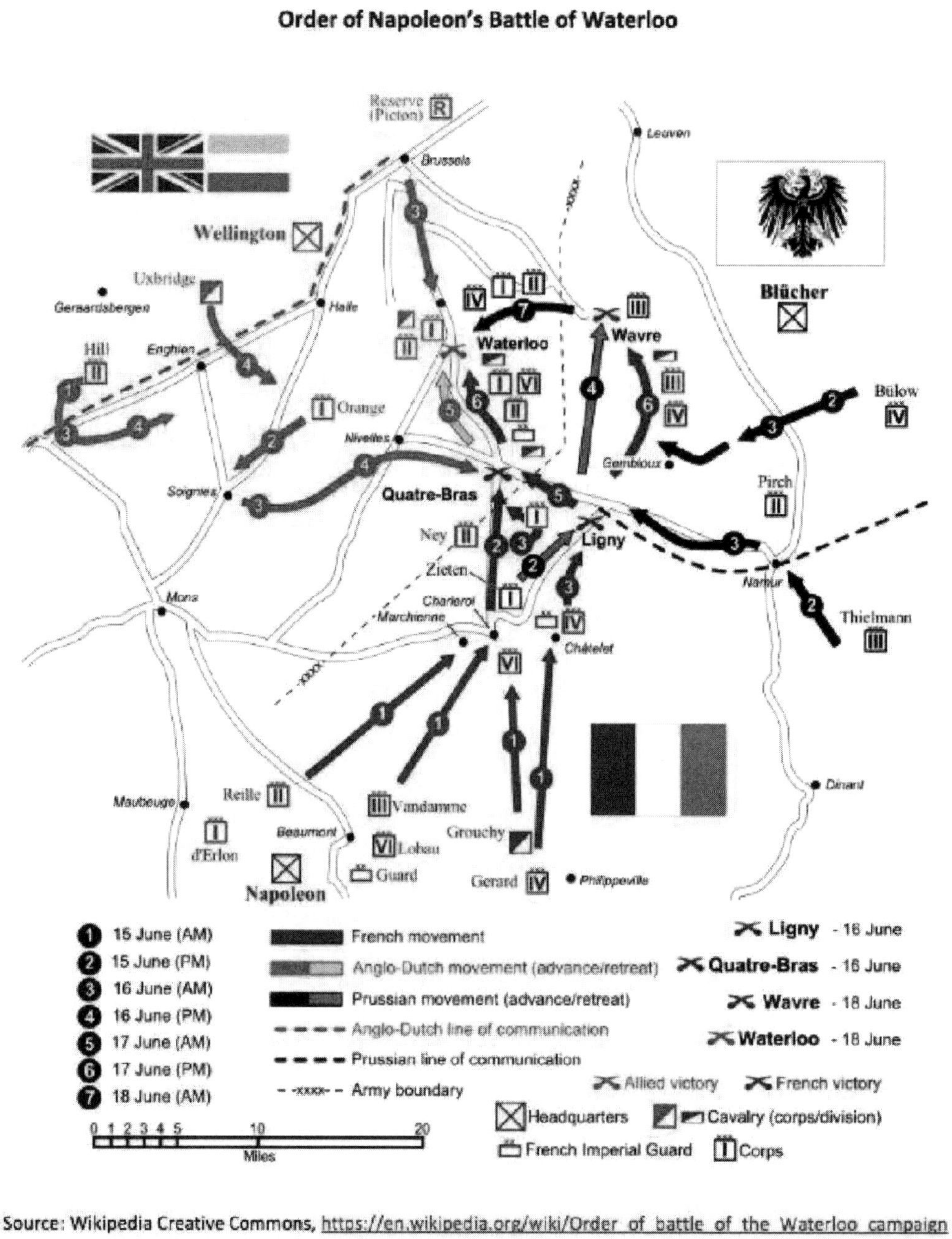

Figure 5.16 Graphics, charts, graphs, and other visual items are also important to annotate. Not only do they often convey important information, but they may appear on exams or in other situations where you'll need to use or demonstrate knowledge. Credit: "Lpankonin" / Wikipedia Commons / Attribution 3.0 Generic (CC BY 3.0)

You may want to make an extra copy of a graphic or table before you add annotations if you are dealing with a lot of information. Making sense of all the elements will take time, and you don't want to add to the confusion.

Returning to Your Notes

Later, as soon as possible after the class, you can go back to your notes and add in missing parts. Just as you may generate questions as you're reading new material, you may leave a class session or lecture or activities with many questions. Write those down in a place where they won't get lost in all your other notes.

The exact timing of when you get back to the notes you take in class or while you are reading an assignment will vary depending on how many other classes you have or what other obligations you have in your daily schedule. A good starting place that is also easy to remember is to make every effort to review your notes within 24 hours of first taking them. Longer than that and you are likely to have forgotten some key features you need to include; must less time than that, and you may not think you need to review the information you so recently wrote down, and you may postpone the task too long.

Use your phone or computer to set reminders for all your note review sessions so that it becomes a habit and you keep on top of the schedule.

Your personal notes play a significant role in your test preparation. They should enhance how you understand the lessons, textbooks, lab sessions, and assignments. All the time and effort you put into first taking the notes and then annotating and organizing the notes will be for naught if you do not formulate an effective and efficient way to use them before sectional exams or comprehensive tests.

The whole cycle of reading, notetaking in class, reviewing and enhancing your notes, and preparing for exams is part of a continuum you ideally will carry into your professional life. Don't try to take short cuts; recognize each step in the cycle as a building block. Learning doesn't end, which shouldn't fill you with dread; it should help you recognize that all this work you're doing in the classroom and during your own study and review sessions is ongoing and cumulative. Practicing effective strategies now will help you be a stronger professional.

ACTIVITY

What resources can you find about reading and notetaking that will actually help you with these crucial skills? How do you go about deciding what resources are valuable for improving your reading and notetaking skills?

The selection and relative value of study guides and books about notetaking vary dramatically. Ask your instructors for recommendations and see what the library has available on this topic. The following list is not comprehensive, but will give you a starting point for books and articles on notetaking in college.

- *College Rules!: How to Study, Survive, and Succeed in College,* by Sherri Nist-Olejnik and Jodi Patrick Holschuh. More than just notetaking, this book covers many aspects of transitioning into the rigors of college life and studying.
- *Effective Notetaking,* by Fiona McPherson. This small volume has suggestions for using your limited time wisely before, during, and after notetaking sessions.
- *How to Study in College,* by Walter Pauk. This is the book that introduced Pauk's notetaking suggestions we now call the Cornell Method. It is a bit dated (from the 1940s), but still contains some valuable information.

- *Learn to Listen, Listen to Learn 2: Academic Listening and Note-taking,* by Roni S. Lebauer. The main point of this book is to help students get the most from college lectures by watching for clues to lecture organization and adapting this information into strong notes.
- *Study Skills: Do I Really Need this Stuff?,* by Steve Piscitelli. Written in a consistently down-to-earth manner, this book will help you with the foundations of strong study skills, including time management, effective notetaking, and seeing the big picture.
- "What Reading Does for the Mind," by Anne Cunningham and Keith Stanovich, 1998, https://www.aft.org/sites/default/files/periodicals/cunningham.pdf (https://www.aft.org/sites/default/files/periodicals/cunningham.pdf)
- Adler, Mortimer J. and Charles Van Doren. *How to Read a Book: The Classic Guide to Intelligent Reading. NY: Simon & Schuster, 1940.*
- Berns, Gregory S., Kristina Blaine, Michael J. Prietula, and Brandon E. Pye. *Brain Connectivity.* Dec 2013.ahead of print http://doi.org/10.1089/brain.2013.0166 (http://doi.org/10.1089/brain.2013.0166)

Summary

Reading and notetaking are major elements of college studying and learning. The expectations in college is that you read considerable amounts of text for each subject. You may encounter reading situations, such as professional journal articles and long textbook chapters, that are more difficult to understand than texts you have read previously. As you progress through your college courses, you can employ reading strategies to help you complete your college reading assignments. Likewise, you will take notes in college that need to be complete so you can study and recall the information you learn in lectures and lab sessions. With so much significant information that you need to collect, study, and recall for your college courses, you need to be deliberate in your reading and notetaking.

Career Connection

Sanvi is a pre-nursing student who is having trouble between all the reading she is expected to complete, her general dislike of reading, and her need to comprehend both her reading assignments and her own notes to be successful in nursing school. She has spoken with several of her instructors and a tutor at the Student Success Center on campus, and their advice centers around Sanvi's reluctance to read in general. She is working on how to manage her time so she has more dedicated time to read her assignments in between her classes and her work schedule.

That is helping some, but Sanvi is still worried because she knows one problem is that she doesn't exactly know what types of reading or notetaking she would need to know how to do as a professional nurse. This confusion makes her doubt that the extra reading she is doing now is really beneficial. After some reflection on what was holding her back, Sanvi mentioned this aspect of her studying to one of her instructors who had been a hospital RN for years before coming to the college to teach. She recalled that the first time she read a patient chart in the hospital, she had to think quickly about how to get all the meaning out of the chart in the same way she would have read a complex textbook chapter.

Sanvi's nursing instructor reminded her that all professions need their personnel to read. They may not all need to read books or articles, but all jobs involve reading to some extent. For example, consider this list of disciplines and the typical types of reading they do. You may be surprised that not all reading is in text form.

Nurses/doctors	Patient charts, prescription side effects, medical articles
Teachers	Student work, lesson plans, educational best practices
Architects	Blueprints, construction contracts, permit manuals
Accountants	Financial spreadsheets, tax guidelines, invoices, trend diagrams
Beauticians	Client hair and facial features, best practices articles, product information
Civil engineers	Work site maps, government regulations, financial spreadsheets
Auto mechanics	Car engines, auto manuals, government regulations

As this incomplete list shows, not every job you pursue will require you to read text-based documents, but all jobs require some reading.

- How could Sanvi and her instructor use this list to make more sense of how college reading will prepare Sanvi to be a stronger nurse?
- How would understanding the types of professional reading help you complete your reading assignments?
- If your chosen field of study is not listed above, can you think of what sort of reading those professionals would need to do?

Think about the questions that opened this chapter and what you have read. How do you feel about your reading and notetaking skills now that you have some more strategies?

 ## Rethinking

Revisit the questions you answered at the beginning of the chapter, and consider one option you learned in this chapter that might change your answer to one of them.

1. I am reading on a college level
2. I take good notes that help me study for exams
3. I understand how to manage all the reading I need to do for college
4. I recognize the need for different notetaking strategies for different college subjects

 ## Where do you go from here?

Reading is such a part of our everyday lives that we sometimes take it for granted. And even we don't formally write down our thoughts, we take notes in our heads far more often than we use our notetaking skills to make sense of a textbook passage or a graphic. Honing these fundamental skills can only help you succeed in college and beyond. What else about reading and note taking would you like to learn more about? Choose topics form the list below to research more.

- How to maximize e-readers to comprehend texts.
- How professional use reading and note taking in their careers.
- Is speed-reading a myth or a viable strategy?
- Compare reading and notetaking strategies from different countries to those you use

Figure 6.1 How we study is as important as what we study. The environment is a critical element of success.

Chapter Outline

- **6.1** Memory
- **6.2** Studying
- **6.3** Test Taking

Introduction

Student Survey

How confident are you in preparing for and taking tests? Take this quick survey to figure it out, ranking questions on a scale of 1–4, 1 meaning "least like me" and 4 meaning "most like me." These questions will help you determine how the chapter concepts relate to you right now. As you are introduced to new concepts and practices, it can be informative to reflect on how your understanding changes over time. We'll revisit these questions at the end of the chapter to see whether your feelings have changed.

1. I set aside enough time to prepare for tests.
2. If I don't set aside enough time, or if life gets in the way, I can usually cram and get positive results.
3. I prefer to pull all-nighters. The adrenaline and urgency help me remember what I need come test time.
4. I study my notes, highlight book passages, and use flash cards, but I still don't feel like I'm as successful as I should be on tests.

You can also take the Chapter 6 Survey (https://openstax.org/l/collegesurvey06) anonymously online.

STUDENT PROFILE

"I didn't have to study much for tests in high school, but I learned really quick that you have to for college. One of the best strategies is to test yourself over the material. This will help you improve your retrieval strength and help you remember more when it comes to the test. I also learned about reviewing your graded tests. This will help you see where you went wrong and why. Being able to see your mistakes and correct them helps the storage and retrieval strength as well as building those dendrites. Getting a question wrong will only improve those things helping you remember the next time it comes up."

—**Lilli Branstetter**, University of Central Arkansas

About this Chapter

By the time you finish this chapter, you should be able to do the following:

- Outline the importance of memory when studying, and note some opportunities to strengthen memory.
- Discuss specific ways to increase the effectiveness of studying.
- Articulate test-taking strategies that minimize anxiety and maximize results.

Kerri didn't need to study in high school. She made good grades, and her friends considered her lucky because she never seemed to sweat exams or cram. In reality, Kerri did her studying during school hours, took excellent notes in class, asked great questions, and read the material before class meetings—all of these are excellent strategies. Kerri just seemed to do them without much fuss.

Then when she got to college, those same skills weren't always working as well. Sound familiar? She discovered that, for many classes, she needed to read paragraphs and textbook passages more than once for comprehension. Her notes from class sessions were longer and more involved—the subject material was more complicated and the problems more complex than she had ever encountered. College isn't high school, as most students realize shortly after enrolling in a higher ed program. Some old study habits and test-taking strategies may serve as a good foundation, but others may need major modification.

It makes sense that, the better you are at studying and test taking, the better results you'll see in the form of high grades and long-term learning and knowledge acquisition. And the more experience you have using your study and memorization skills and employing success strategies during exams, the better you'll get at it. But you have to keep it up—maintaining these skills and learning better strategies as the content you study becomes increasingly complex is crucial to your success. Once you transition into a work environment, you will be able to use these same skills that helped you be successful in college as you face the problem-solving demands and expectations of your job. Earning high grades is one goal, and certainly a good one when you're in college, but true learning means committing content to long-term memory.

6.1 Memory

Estimated completion time: 32 minutes.

Questions to consider:

- How does working memory work, exactly?

- What's the difference between working and short-term memory?
- How does long-term memory function?
- What obstacles exist to remembering?
- When and how should you memorize things?

In what situations is it best to memorize, and what do you memorize?

What can you do consistently to improve both your short- and long-term memory?

Memory is one of those cherished but mysterious elements in life. Everyone has memories, and some people are very good at rapid recall, which is an enviable skill for test takers. We know that we seem to lose the capacity to remember things as we age, and scientists continue to study how we remember some things but not others and what memory means, but we don't know that much about memory, really.

Nelson Cowan is one researcher who is working to explain what we do know about memory. His article "What Are the Differences between Long-Term, Short-Term, and Working Memory?" breaks down the different types of memory and what happens when we recall thoughts and ideas. When we remember something, we actually do quite a lot of thinking.[1]

We go through three basic steps when we remember ideas or images: we encode, store, and retrieve that information. Encoding is how we first perceive information through our senses, such as when we smell a lovely flower or a putrid trash bin. Both make an impression on our minds through our sense of smell and probably our vision. Our brains encode, or label, this content in short-term memory in case we want to think about it again.

If the information is important and we have frequent exposure to it, the brain will store it for us in case we need to use it in the future in our aptly named long-term memory. Later, the brain will allow us to recall or retrieve that image, feeling, or information so we can do something with it. This is what we call remembering.

Figure 6.2

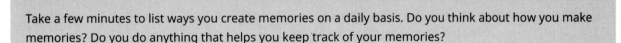

ANALYSIS QUESTION

Take a few minutes to list ways you create memories on a daily basis. Do you think about how you make memories? Do you do anything that helps you keep track of your memories?

Foundations of Memory

William Sumrall et al. in the *International Journal of Humanities and Social Science* explain the foundation of memory by noting: "Memory is a term applied to numerous biological devices by which living organisms acquire, retain, and make use of skills and knowledge. It is present in all forms of higher order animals. The most evolutionary forms of memory have taken place in human beings. Despite much research and exploration, a complete understanding of human memory does not exist."[2]

---

1   NCBI. "What are the differences between long-term, short-term, and working memory?" **https://www.ncbi.nlm.nih.gov/pmc/articles/PMC2657600/**
2   Sumrall, William, et. al. "A Review of Memory Theory." International Journal of Humanities and Social Science, 2016. Vol. 6. No. 5.

Working Memory

Working memory is a type of short-term memory, but we use it when we are actively performing a task. For example, nursing student Marilyn needs to use her knowledge of chemical reactions to suggest appropriate prescriptions in various medical case studies. She does not have to recall every single fact she learned in years of chemistry classes, but she does need to have a working memory of certain chemicals and how they work with others. To ensure she can make these connections, Marilyn will have to review and study the relevant chemical details for the types of drug interactions she will recommend in the case studies.

In working memory, you have access to whatever information you have stored in your memory that helps you complete the task you are performing. For instance, when you begin to study an assignment, you certainly need to read the directions, but you must also remember that in class your professor reduced the number of problem sets the written instructions indicated you needed to finish. This was an oral addition to the written assignment. The change to the instructions is what you bring up in working memory when you complete the assignment.

Short-Term Memory

Short-term memory is a very handy thing. It helps us remember where we set our keys or where we left off on a project the day before. Think about all the aids we employ to help us with short-term memory: you may hang your keys in a particular place each evening so you know exactly where they are supposed to be. When you go grocery shopping, do you ever choose a product because you recall an advertising jingle? You see the box of cereal and you remember the song on the TV commercial. If that memory causes you to buy that product, the advertising worked. We help our memory along all the time, which is perfectly fine. In fact, we can modify these everyday examples of memory assistance for purposes of studying and test taking. The key is deliberate use of strategies that are not so elaborate that they are too difficult to remember in our short-term memory.

ACTIVITY

Consider this list of items. Look at the list for no more than 30 seconds. Then, cover up the list and use the spaces below to complete an activity.

Baseball	Picture frame	Tissue	Paper clip
Bread	Pair of dice	Fingernail polish	Spoon
Marble	Leaf	Doll	Scissors
Cup	Jar of sand	Deck of cards	Ring
Blanket	Ice	Marker	String

Without looking at the list, write down as many items as you can remember.

Now, look back at your list and make sure that you give yourself credit for any that you got right. Any items that you misremembered, meaning they were not in the original list, you won't count in your total.
TOTAL ITEMS REMEMBERED _____.

There were 20 total items. Did you remember between 5 and 9 items? If you did, then you have a typical short-term memory and you just participated in an experiment, of sorts, to prove it.

Harvard psychology professor George A. Miller in 1956 claimed humans can recall about five to nine bits of information in our short-term memory at any given time. Other research has come after this claim, but this concept is a popular one. Miller's article is entitled "The Magical Number Seven, Plus or Minus Two" and is easily accessible online if you're interested in learning more about this seminar report.[3]

Considering the vast amount of knowledge available to us, five to nine bits isn't very much to work with. To combat this limitation, we clump information together, making connections to help us stretch our capacity to remember. Many factors play into how much we can remember and how we do it, including the subject matter, how familiar we are with the ideas, and how interested we are in the topic, but we certainly cannot remember absolutely everything, for a test or any other task we face. As such, we have to use effective strategies, like those we cover later in this chapter, to get the most out of our memories.

ACTIVITY

Now, let's revisit the items above. Go back to them and see if you can organize them in a way that you would have about five groups of items. See below for an example of how to group them.

Row 1: Items found in a kitchen

Row 2: Items that a child would play with

Row 3: Items of nature

Row 4: Items in a desk drawer/school supplies

Row 5: Items found in a bedroom

Cup	Spoon	Ice	Bread	
Baseball	Marble	Pair of dice	Doll	Deck of cards
Jar of sand	Leaf			
Marker	String	Scissors	Paper clip	
Ring	Picture frame	Fingernail polish	Tissue	Blanket

---

3   Miller, George A. "The Magical Number Seven, Plus or Minus Two: Some Limits on Our capacity for Processing Information." Psychological Review, 1956.

> Now that you have grouped items into categories, also known as chunking, you can work on remembering the categories and the items that fit into those categories, which will result in remembering more items. Check it out below by covering up the list of items again and writing down what you can remember.
>
> Now, look back at your list and make sure that you give yourself credit for any that you got right. Any items that you misremembered, meaning they were not in the original list, you won't count in your total. TOTAL ITEMS REMEMBERED _____. Did you increase how many items you could remember?

Long-Term Memory

Long-term memory is exactly what it sounds like. These are things you recall from the past, such as the smell of your elementary school cafeteria or how to pop a wheelie on a bicycle. Our brain keeps a vast array of information, images, and sensory experiences in long-term memory. Whatever it is we are trying to keep in our memories, whether a beautiful song or a list of chemistry vocabulary terms, must first come into our brains in short-term memory. If we want these fleeting ideas to transfer into long-term memory, we have to do some work, such as causing frequent exposure to the information over time (such as studying the terms every day for a period of time or the repetition you performed to memorize multiplication tables or spelling rules) and some relevant manipulation for the information.

According to Alison Preston of the University of Texas at Austin's Center for Learning and Memory, "A short-term memory's conversion to a long-term memory requires changes within the brain . . . and result[s] in changes to neurons (nerve cells) or sets of neurons. . . . For example, new synapses—the connections between neurons through which they exchange information—can form to allow for communication between new networks of neurons. Alternatively, existing synapses can be strengthened to allow for increased sensitivity in the communication between two neurons."[4]

When you work to convert your thoughts into memories, you are literally *changing your mind.* Much of this brain work begins in the part of the brain called the *hippocampus*. Preston continues, "Initially, the hippocampus works in concert with sensory-processing regions distributed in the neocortex (the outermost layer of the brain) to form the new memories. Within the neocortex, representations of the elements that constitute an event in our life are distributed across multiple brain regions according to their content. . . . When a memory is first formed, the hippocampus rapidly combines this distributed information into a single memory, thus acting as an index of representations in the sensory-processing regions. As time passes, cellular and molecular changes allow for the strengthening of direct connections among the neocortical regions, enabling access to the memory independent of the hippocampus."

We learn the lyrics of a favorite song by singing and/or playing the song over and over. That alone may not be enough to get that song into the coveted long-term memory area of our brain, but if we have an emotional connection to the song, such as a painful breakup or a life-changing proposal that occurred while we were listening to the song, this may help. Think of ways to make your study session memorable and create connections with the information you need to study. That way, you have a better chance of keeping your study material in your memory so you can access it whenever you need it.

---

4   Preston, Alison. "Ask the Experts: How do short-term memories become long-term memories?" Scientific American, Dec. 2017. https://www.scientificamerican.com/article/how-do-short-term-memories-become-l/

ANALYSIS QUESTION

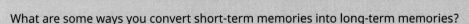

What are some ways you convert short-term memories into long-term memories?

Do your memorization strategies differ for specific courses (e.g., how you remember for math or history)?

Obstacles to Remembering

If remembering things we need to know for exams or for learning new disciplines were easy, no one would have problems with it, but students face several significant obstacles to remembering, including a persistent lack of sleep and an unrealistic reliance on cramming. Life is busy and stressful for all students, so you have to keep practicing strategies to help you study and remember successfully, but you also must be mindful of obstacles to remembering.

Lack of Sleep

Let's face it, sleep and college don't always go well together. You have so much to do! All that reading, all those papers, all those extra hours in the science lab or tutoring center or library! And then we have the social and emotional aspects of going to school, which may not be the most critical aspect of your life as you pursue more education but are a significant part of who you are. When you consider everything you need to attend to in college, you probably won't be surprised that sleep is often the first thing we give up as we search for more time to accomplish everything we're trying to do. That seems reasonable—just wake up an hour earlier or stay up a little later. But you may want to reconsider picking away at your precious sleep time.

Sleep benefits all of your bodily functions, and your brain needs sleep time to dream and rest through the night. You probably can recall times when you had to do something without adequate sleep. We say things like "I just can't wake up" and "I'm walking around half asleep."

In fact, you may actually be doing just that. Lack of sleep impairs judgment, focus, and our overall mood. Do you know anyone who is always grumpy in the morning? A fascinating medical study from the University of California Los Angeles (UCLA) claims that sleep deprivation is as dangerous as being drunk, both in what it does to our bodies and in the harm we may cause to ourselves and others in driving and performing various daily tasks.[5][6]

If you can't focus well because you didn't get enough sleep, then you likely won't be able to remember whatever it is you need to recall for any sort of studying or test-taking situation. Most exams in a college setting go beyond simple memorization, but you still have a lot to remember for exams. For example, when Saanvi sits down to take an exam on introductory biology, she needs to recall all the subject-specific vocabulary she read in the textbook's opening chapters, the general connections she made between biological studies and other scientific fields, and any biology details introduced in the unit for which she is taking the exam.

---

5   Nir, Yuval, et. al. "Selective neuronal lapses precede human cognitive lapses following sleep deprivation," Nature Medicine volume23, pages 1474–1480 (2017).

6   UCLA Health. "Drowsy Driving." https://www.uclahealth.org/sleepcenter/drowsy-driving

Trying to make these mental connections on too little sleep will take a large mental toll because Saanvi has to concentrate even harder than she would with adequate sleep. She isn't merely tired; her brain is not refreshed and primed to conduct difficult tasks. Although not an exact comparison, think about when you overtax a computer by opening too many programs simultaneously. Sometimes the programs are sluggish or slow to respond, making it difficult to work efficiently; sometimes the computer shuts down completely and you have to reboot the entire system. Your body is a bit like that on too little sleep.

On the flip side, though, your brain on adequate sleep is amazing, and sleep can actually assist you in making connections, remembering difficult concepts, and studying for exams. The exact reasons for this is still a serious research project for scientists, but the results all point to a solid connection between sleep and cognitive performance.

If you're interested in learning more about this research, the American Academy of Sleep Medicine (AASM) is a good place to start. One article is entitled "College Students: Getting Enough Sleep Is Vital to Academic Success."

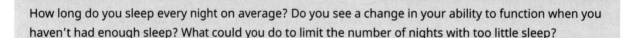

ANALYSIS QUESTION

How long do you sleep every night on average? Do you see a change in your ability to function when you haven't had enough sleep? What could you do to limit the number of nights with too little sleep?

Downside of Cramming

At least once in their college careers, most students will experience the well-known pastime called *cramming*. See if any of this is familiar: Shelley has lots of classes, works part-time at a popular restaurant, and is just amazingly busy, so she puts off serious study sessions day after day. She isn't worried because she has set aside time she would have spent sleeping to cram just before the exam. That's the idea anyway. Originally, she planned to stay up a little late and study for four hours from 10 p.m. to 2 a.m. and still get several hours of refreshing sleep. But it's Dolphin Week or Beat State Day or whatever else comes up, and her study session doesn't start until midnight—she'll pull an *all-nighter* (to be more precise, this is actually an *all-really-early-morning-er,* but it doesn't quite have the same ring to it). So, two hours after her original start time, she tries to *cram* all the lessons, problems, and information from the last two weeks of lessons into this one session. Shelley falls asleep around 3 a.m. with her notes and books still on her bed. After her late night, she doesn't sleep well and goes into the morning exam tired.

Shelley does OK but not great on the exam, and she is not pleased with her results. More and more research is showing that the stress Shelley has put on her body doing this, combined with the way our brains work, makes cramming a seriously poor choice for learning.

One sleep researcher, Dr. Susan Redline from Boston, says, "Sleep deficiency can affect mood and the ability to make memories and learn, but it also affects metabolism, appetite, blood pressure, levels of inflammation in the body and perhaps even the immune response."[7]

Your brain simply refuses to cooperate with cramming—it sounds like a good idea, but it doesn't work.

---

7   Redline, Susan https://abcnews.go.com/Health/Sleep/health-hazards-linked-lack-sleep/story?id=16524313

Cramming causes stress, which can lead to paralyzing test anxiety; it erroneously supposes you can remember and understand something fully after only minimal exposure; and it overloads your brain, which, however amazing it is, can only focus on one concept at a time and a limited number of concepts all together for learning and retention.

Leading neuroscientist John Medina claims that the brain begins to wander at about 10 minutes, at which point you need a new stimulus to spark interest.[8] That doesn't mean you can't focus for longer than 10 minutes; you just have to switch gears a lot to keep your brain engaged. Have you ever heard a speaker drone on about one concept for, say, 30 minutes without somehow changing pace to engage the listeners? It doesn't take much to re-engage—pausing to ask the listeners questions or moving to a different location in the room will do it—but without these subtle attention markers, listeners start thinking of something else. The same thing happens to you if you try to cram all reading, problem-solving, and note reviewing into one long session; your brain will wander.

WHAT STUDENTS SAY

1. Which of the following is your most common method of studying?
    a. Reading or rereading the text or my class notes.
    b. Watching videos of my instructor's lecture or other people discussing the topics.
    c. Taking practice quizzes/tests.
    d. Creating/using study tools (flashcards, mnemonic devices, etc.)
    e. Working with a study group, tutor, or academic support.
2. Which of the following do you have the most difficulty remembering?
    a. Vocabulary and facts (such as Biology vocab, Historical facts.)
    b. Problem-solving methods (such as in Math)
    c. Details from text and literature
    d. Skills and processes (such as a lab technique or a building process)
    e. Computer functions/locations/processes
    f. Which formulas, processes, or categories to apply in situations (such as in Physics or Accounting)
3. How much anxiety do you feel when an exam or other major course evaluation is approaching?
    a. A great deal
    b. A lot
    c. A moderate amount
    d. A little
    e. None at all

You can also take the anonymous What Students Say (https://openstax.org/l/collegesurvey6-12) **surveys to add your voice to this textbook. Your responses will be included in updates.**

Students offered their views on these questions, and the results are displayed in the graphs below.

Which of the following is your most common method of studying?

---

8 Medina, John. Brain Rules. 2018, Pear Press.

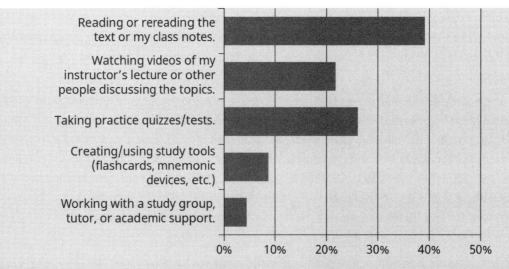

Figure 6.3

Which of the following do you have the most difficulty remembering?

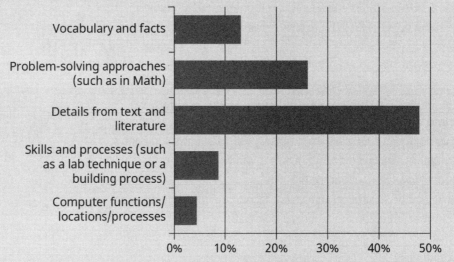

Figure 6.4

How much anxiety do you feel when an exam or other major course evaluation is approaching?

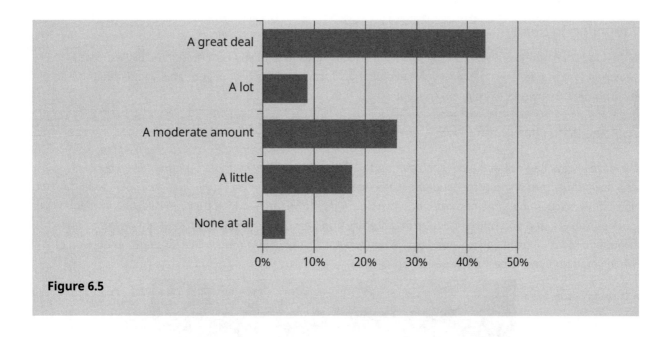

Figure 6.5

Determining When/What to Memorize

In the realm of learning and studying, some conditions warrant memorization as the most effective way to work with information. For instance, if you are expected to have a working knowledge of conversational French or Spanish, you will have to memorize some words. Simply knowing a long list of terms isn't going to help you order food in a café or ask for directions in a foreign country because you also need to understand the other language's grammar and have some sort of context for what needs to be said from your vocabulary list. But you cannot say the words in a different language if you cannot remember your vocabulary. From this scenario, you can assume that memorization is a good fit for some parts of language acquisition.

A worthwhile book on memory, thinking, and learning is a short study called *Make It Stick: The Science of Successful Learning* by Peter Brown, Henry Roediger, and Mark McDaniel. The authors conclude, after extensive research, that our attempts to speed up learning and make studying easier are not good ideas. Studying is hard work, and it should be. For learning to *stick*, we need to work hard to pull the information out of our memory and use it by continually pushing ourselves to accomplish increasingly difficult tasks.[9]

6.2 Studying

Estimated completion time: 27 minutes.

Questions to consider:

- How do you prepare yourself and your environment for successful studying?
- What study strategies will be most beneficial to you?
- What are learning preferences and strategies, and how can you leverage those to your advantage?

---

9 Brown, Peter, et. al. Make It Stick: The Science of Successful Learning. Brown, Roediger, Daniel, 2014.

Preparing to Study

Studying is hard work, but you can still learn some techniques to help you be a more effective learner. Two major and interrelated techniques involve avoiding distractions to the best of your ability and creating a study environment that works to help you concentrate.

Avoiding Distractions

We have always had distractions—video games, television shows, movies, music, friends—even housecleaning can distract us from doing something else we need to do, like study for an exam. That may seem extreme, but sometimes vacuuming is the preferred activity to buckling down and working through calculus problems! Cell phones, tablets, and portable computers that literally bring a world of possibilities to us anywhere have brought *distraction* to an entirely new level. When was the last time you were with a large group of people when you didn't see at least a few people on devices?

Figure 6.6 Video games are a common distraction, but we need to be aware that even tedious activities like cleaning can be a distraction from studying.

When you study, your biggest challenge may be to block out all the competing noise. And letting go of that connection to our friends and the larger world, even for a short amount of time, can be difficult. Perhaps the least stressful way to allow yourself a distraction-free environment is to make the study session a definite amount of time: long enough to get a significant amount of studying accomplished but short enough to hold your attention.

You can increase that attention time with practice and focus. Pretend it is a professional appointment or meeting during which you cannot check e-mail or texts or otherwise engage with your portable devices. We have all become very attached to the ability to check in—anonymously on social media or with family and friends via text, chat, and calls. If you set a specific amount of time to study without interruptions, you can convince your wandering mind that you will soon be able to return to your link to the outside world. Start small and set an alarm—a 30-minute period to review notes, then a brief break, then another 45-minute study session to quiz yourself on the material, and so on.

When you prepare for your optimal study session, remember to do these things:

- Put your phone out of sight—in another room or at least some place where you will not see or hear it

vibrate or ring. Just flipping it over is not enough.
- Turn off the television or music (more on that in the next section).
- Unless you are deliberately working with a study group, study somewhere alone if possible or at least away from others enough to not hear them talking.

If you live with lots of other people or don't have access to much privacy, see if you can negotiate some space alone to study. Ask others to leave one part of the house or an area in one room as a quiet zone during certain hours. Ask politely for a specific block of time; most people will respect your educational goals and be willing to accommodate you. If you're trying to work out quiet zones with small children in the house, the bathtub with a pillow can make a fine study oasis.

Study Environment

You may not always be in the mood or inspired to study. And if you have a long deadline, maybe you can blow off a study session on occasion, but you shouldn't get into the habit of ignoring a strong study routine. Jane Austen once wrote in a letter, "I am not at all in a humor for writing; I must write on till I am." Sometimes just starting is the hard part; go ahead and begin. Don't wait around for your study muse; start working, and she'll show up.

Sometimes you just need to plop down and study whenever and wherever you can manage—in the car waiting for someone, on the bus, at the Little League field as you cheer on your shortstop. And that's OK if this is the exception. For long-term success in studying, though, you need a better study setting that will help you get the most out of your limited study time. Whatever your space limitations, carve out a place that you can dedicate to reading, writing, note taking, and reviewing. This doesn't need to be elaborate and expensive—all you truly need is a flat surface large enough to hold either your computer or writing paper, book or notes, pens/pencils/markers, and subject-specific materials you may need (e.g., stand-alone calculators, drawing tools, and notepads). Your space should be cool or warm enough for you to be comfortable as you study. What do you have now that you consider your study space? Is it set up for your optimal success?

Figure 6.7 Which is before, and which is after? (Credit: Ali West / Flickr / Attribution 2.0 Generic (CC-BY 2.0))

If it is at all possible, try to make this area exclusive to your study sessions and something you can leave set up all the time and a place out of the way of family or roommate traffic. For example, Martina thought setting up her study station on the dining room table was a good idea at first. The view was calming, and the table was big enough to spread out and could even hold all her materials to study architectural drawings, her favorite subject. But then she needed the table for a small family dinner party, so she had to find a cubbyhole to hide away her supplies with some needing to go into a closet in the next room. Now she was spread out over multiple study spaces. And the family TV was in an adjacent room, not visible from the table but certainly an auditory distraction. Martina ultimately decided to forgo her view and create a smaller station in an unused bedroom so she could leave her supplies out and have a quieter area. You may have to try out numerous places to determine what works best for you.

Wherever you study, try to make it a welcoming place you want to be in—not an uncomfortable environment that makes you want to just do the minimum you must complete and leave. You should include the basics: a good chair, a work surface, and whatever materials, books, notes, and other supplies you need for the subject you are studying. If you want to make it even more of a productive place, you can look in magazines for ideas or search the web to see how others have set up simple areas or more elaborate arrangements. Don't let decorating your workspace be an excuse to get out of studying!

You don't need an elaborate setting, but you may want to consider including a few effective additions if you have the space:

- small bulletin board for often-used formulas
- encouraging quotes or pictures of your goal
- whiteboard for brainstorming
- sticky notes for reminders in texts and notes
- file holder for most-used documents
- bookshelf for reference books

ACTIVITY

Describe every element in your ideal study environment and explain why it's there as well as how it will make more efficient use of your time, limit distractions, or in some other way strengthen your ability to study.

After you have described your ideal study environment, think about how you can adapt that environment if you cannot be in your favorite place to study. How do you *make your own space* in the library, a student lounge, or a dedicated space on campus for student studying?

Debunking Study Myths

MYTH #1: You can multitask while studying.

How many times do you eat in the car? Watch TV while you write out a grocery list? Listen to music while you cook dinner? What about type an e-mail while you're on the phone with someone else and jot down notes about the call? The common term for this attempt to do more than one thing at a time is multitasking, and almost everyone does it at some point. On some days, you simply cannot accomplish all that you want to get done, so you double up. The problem is, multitasking doesn't really work. Of course, it exists, and we do it. For instance, we walk and chew gum or drive and talk, but we are not really thinking about two or more distinct things or doing multiple processes simultaneously.

MYTH #2: Highlighting main points of a text is useful.

Another myth of studying that seems to have a firm hold is that the idea of highlighting text—in and of itself—is the best way to review study material. It is one way, and you can get some benefit from it, but don't trick yourself into spending too much time on this surface activity and consider your study session complete.

Annotating texts or notes is a first-step type of study practice. If you allow it to take up all your time, you may want to think you are fully prepared for an exam because you put in the time. Actually, you need much more time reviewing and retrieving your lessons and ideas from the text or class lecture as well as quizzing yourself to accomplish your goal of learning so you can perform well on the exam. Highlighting is a task you can do rather easily, and it makes you feel good because you are actively engaging with your text, but true learning needs more steps.

MYTH #3: Studying effectively is effortless.

There is nothing effortless, or even pleasant at times, about studying. This is why so many students don't put in the time necessary to learn complex material: it takes time, effort, and, in some cases, a little drudgery. This is not to say that the outcome, learning—and maybe making an A—is not pleasant and rewarding. It is just that when done right, learning takes focus, deliberate strategies, and time. Think about a superstar athlete who puts in countless hours of drills and conditioning so that she makes her work on the field look easy. If you can also *enjoy* the studying, the skill development, and the knowledge building, then you will most likely be more motivated to do the work.

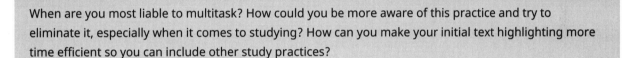

ANALYSIS QUESTION

When are you most liable to multitask? How could you be more aware of this practice and try to eliminate it, especially when it comes to studying? How can you make your initial text highlighting more time efficient so you can include other study practices?

Study Strategies

Everyone wishes they had a better memory or a stronger way to use memorization. You can make the most of the memory you have by making some conscious decisions about how you study and prepare for exams. Incorporate these ideas into your study sessions:

Practicing effective memorization is when you use a trick, technique, or strategy to recall something—for another class, an exam, or even to bring up an acquaintance's name in a social situation. Really whatever works for you to recall information is a good tool to have. You can create your own quizzes and tests to go over material from class. You can use mnemonics to jog your memory. You can work in groups to develop unique ways to remember complex information. Whatever methods you choose to enhance your memory, keep in mind that repetition is one of the most effective tools in any memory strategy. Do whatever you do over and over for the best results.

Using Mnemonics

Mnemonics (pronounced new-monics) are a way to remember things using reminders. Did you learn the points of the compass by remembering NEWS (north, east, west, and south)? Or the notes on the music staff as FACE or EGBDF (every good boy does fine)? These are mnemonics. When you're first learning something and you aren't familiar with the foundational concepts, these help you bring up the information quickly, especially for multistep processes or lists. After you've worked in that discipline for a while, you likely don't need the mnemonics, but you probably won't forget them either.

Here are some familiar mnemonics you may find useful:

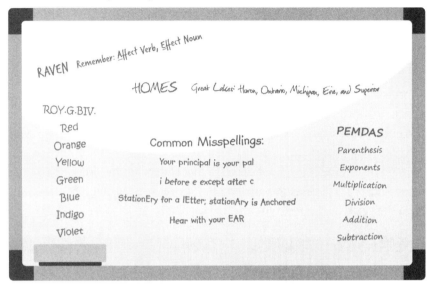

Figure 6.8

You can certainly make up your own mnemonics, but be careful that your reminder isn't so complex and convoluted that it is more difficult to remember than the information you were relating it to!

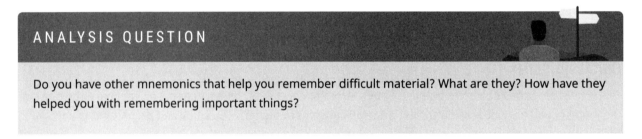

Do you have other mnemonics that help you remember difficult material? What are they? How have they helped you with remembering important things?

Practicing Concept Association

When you study, you're going to make connections to other things—that's a good thing. It shows a highly intelligent ability to make sense of the world when you can associate like and even somewhat unlike components. If, for instance, you were reading Martin Luther King Jr.'s "Letter from a Birmingham Jail," and you read the line that he had been in Birmingham, you may remember a trip you took with your family last summer through Alabama and that you passed by and visited the civil rights museum in Birmingham. This may remind you of the different displays you saw and the discussions you had with your family about what had happened concerning civil rights in the 1950s, '60s, and '70s in the United States.

This is a good connection to make, but if your assignment is to critique the literary aspects of King's long epistle, you need to be able to come back to the actual words of the letter and see what trends you can see in his writing and why he may have used his actual words to convey the powerful message. The connection is fine, but you can't get lost in going down rabbit holes that may or may not be what you're supposed to be doing at the time. Make a folder for this assignment where you can put things such as a short summary of your trip to Alabama. You may eventually include notes from this summary in your analysis. You may include something from a website that shows you information about that time period. Additionally, you could include items about Martin Luther King Jr.'s life and death and his work for civil rights. All of these elements may help you understand the significance of this one letter, but you need to be cognizant of what you're doing at the time and remember it is not usually a good idea to just try to keep it all in your head. The best idea is to have a way to access this information easily, either electronically or in hard copy, so that if you are able to use it, you can find it easily and quickly.

Generating Idea Clusters

Like mnemonics, idea clusters are nothing more than ways to help your brain come up with ways to recall specific information by connecting it to other knowledge you already have. For example, Andrea is an avid knitter and remembers how to create complicated stitches by associating them with nursery rhymes she read as a child. A delicate stitch that requires concentration because it makes the yarn look like part of it is hiding brings to mind Red Riding Hood, and connecting it to that character helps Andrea recall the exact order of steps necessary to execute the design. You can do the same thing with song lyrics, lines from movies, or favorite stories where you draw a connection to the well-known phrase or song and the task you need to complete.

APPLICATION

Choose one of the following, and create an idea cluster to group and organize:

- Example A: aviation jobs in North America
- Example B: the use of analytics in sports to determine team rosters
- Example C: how social media affects political campaigns

Start the idea cluster with the topic circled in the middle of the page. For Example A, you might make one cluster off the main circle for specific positions; you could add another cluster for salary ranges and another for geographic regions.

Three Effective Study Strategies

There are more than three study strategies, but focusing on the most effective strategies will make an enormous difference in how well you will be able to demonstrate learning (also known as "acing your tests"). Here is a brief overview of each of the three strategies:

- Spacing—This has to do with *when* you study. Hint: Don't cram; study over a period of days, preferably with "breaks" in between.
- Interleaving—This has to do with *what* you study. Hint: Don't study just one type of content, topic, chapter, or unit at a time; instead, mix up the content when you study.
- Practice testing—This has to do with *how* you study. Hint: Don't just reread content. You must quiz or test your ability to retrieve the information from your brain.

Spacing

We all know that cramming is not an effective study strategy, but do we know why? Research on memory suggests that giving yourself time in between study sessions actually helps you forget the information. And forgetting, which sounds like it would be something you *don't* want to do, is actually good for your ability to remember information long-term. That's because every time you forget something, you need to relearn it, leading to gains in your overall understanding and "storage" of the material. The table below demonstrates how spacing works. Assume you are going to spend about four hours studying for a Sociology exam. Cramming would have you spending most of those four hours the night before the exam. With spacing, on the other hand, you would study a little bit each day.

Spacing

	Sunday	Monday	Tuesday	Wednesday	Thursday	Friday	Saturday
Cramming				Study for 1 hour	Study for 3 hours	**Sociology Test**	
Spacing	Study for 1 hour		Study for 30 minutes	Study for 1 hour	Study for 90 minutes	**Sociology Test**	

Table 6.1

Interleaving

One particular studying technique is called interleaving, which calls for students to mix up the content that is being studied. This means not just spending the entire study session on one sort of problem and then moving on to a different sort of problem at a later time.

If you take the schedule we used for the spacing example above, we can add the interleaving concepts to it. Notice that interleaving includes revisiting material from a previous chapter or unit or revisiting different types of problems or question sets. The benefit is that your brain is "mixing up" the information, which can sometimes lead to short-term forgetting but can lead to long-term memory and learning.

Interleaving

Sunday	Monday	Tuesday	Wednesday	Thursday	Friday
Reread Sociology, Chapter 1. Reorganize notes		Reread Sociology, Chapter 1 and 2. Take Ch 1 online quiz. Create Chapter 2 concept map	Reread Sociology, Chapters 1-3. Take online quizzes for chapters 2 and 3. Reorganize notes. Create practice test	Reread notes. Review items missed on online quizzes. Take practice test and review challenge areas.	**TEST in sociology, Chapters 1-3**

Table 6.2

Practice Testing

You can do a practice "test" in two ways. One is to test yourself as you are reading or taking in information. This is a great way to add a little variety to your studying. You can ask yourself what a paragraph or text section means as you read. To do this, read a passage in a text, cover up the material, and ask yourself, "What was the main idea of this section?" Recite aloud or write down your answer, and then check it against the original information.

Another, more involved, way to practice test is to create flashcards or an actual test by writing a test. This takes more time, but there are online programs such as Quizlet that make it a little easier. Practice testing is an effective study strategy because it helps you practice *retrieving* information, which is what you want to be able to do when you are taking the real test.

One of the best ways to learn something is to teach it to someone else, so ask a friend or family member if you can explain something to them, and *teach* them the lesson. You may find you know more about the subject than you thought . . . or you may realize quickly that you need to do more studying. Why does teaching someone else rank as one of the most effective ways to learn something? It is a form of practice testing that requires you to demonstrate you know something in front of someone else! No one wants to look like they don't know what they are talking about, even if it your audience is another classmate.

Recognizing Strengths/Weaknesses of Preferred Study Approaches

Most children don't learn to ride a bicycle by reading a manual; they learn by watching other kids, listening to instructions, and getting up on the seat and learning to balance—sometimes with training wheels or a proud parent holding on, but ultimately without any other support. They may fall over and feel insecure, but usually, they learn to make the machine go. Most of us employ multiple methods of study all the time. You usually only run into trouble if you stubbornly rely on just one way to learn or study and the material you're studying or the task you want to accomplish doesn't lend itself to that preference. You can practice specific strategies to help you learn in your preferred learning approach. Can you think of a time when the way you usually study a situation didn't work?

When deciding on a study approach, consider what you know about the material and the type of knowledge it involves. Is it a group of concepts related to problem-solving methods, such as those you'd find in a physics class? Or is it a literary analysis of a novel? Consider as many elements as possible about the material -- and the way the material will be assessed -- to help choose a study approach.

You should also consider your instructor's preferred method of teaching and learning. Watching the way they teach lessons or convey necessary course information to the class. Do they almost always augment lessons with video clips to provide examples or create a memorable narrative? Do they like to show you how something works by demonstrating and working with their hands—for instance, assembling a piece of equipment by taking it apart and putting it back together again? Echoing their teaching approach may help your study. That doesn't mean you have to change your entire learning approach to match your instructors' methods. Many instructors understand that their students will have different ways of learning and try to present information in multiple ways.

Practicing Active Continuous Improvement for All Preferences

You can certainly learn through specific approaches or according to specific preferences, but you will also need to adapt to different situations, skills, and subject areas. Don't limit yourself to thinking you can *only* learn one way or another. That mindset induces anxiety when you encounter a learning situation that doesn't match your preference. What if your instructor *only* uses a spoken lecture to teach concepts in your chemistry class, and you consider yourself a visual learner? Or what if the only method presented to you for learning mathematical computations is to see videos of others working problems, and you're more hands-on? You may have to concentrate in a different way or devise other strategies to learn, but you can do it. In fact, you should sometimes work on the styles/preferences that you feel are your least favorite; it will actually strengthen your overall ability to learn and retain information.[10]

Dr. Stephen Covey, famous leadership coach and businessman, called this attention to knowing and honing all your skill sets, not just your favorites, *sharpening the saw.* He advised that people should be aware of their strengths but should always hone their weaknesses by saying, "We must never become too busy sawing to take time to sharpen the saw."[11] For instance, in the chemistry lecture example, you may need to take good notes from the spoken lecture and then review those notes as you sketch out any complex ideas or formulas. If the math videos are not enough for you to grasp difficult problems, you may ask for or find your own problems for additional practice covering that particular mathematical concept to solve on your own.

6.3 Test Taking

Estimated completion time: 23 minutes.

Questions to consider:

- What are the differences between test prep and taking the actual test?
- How can you take a *whole person* approach to test taking?
- What can you do on test day to increase your confidence and success?
- What should you know about test anxiety?

---

10   Newton, Phillip M., & Miah, Mahallad. "Evidence-Based Higher Education—Is the Learning Style 'Myth' Important?" *Frontiers in Psychology* 8:444 (2017) DOI: 10. 3389/FPSYG. 2017.00444.
11   Covey, Stephen. The 7 Habits of Highly Effective People ® https://www.franklincovey.com/the-7-habits.html

Once you are practicing good study habits, you'll be better prepared for actual test taking. Since studying and test taking are both part of learning, honing your skills in one will help you in the other.

Probably the most obvious differences between your preparation for an exam and the actual test itself is your level of urgency and the time constraints. A slight elevation in your stress level can actually be OK for testing—it keeps you focused and *on your game* when you need to bring up all the information, thinking, and studying to show what you've learned. Properly executed, test preparation mixed in with a bit of stress can significantly improve your actual test-taking experience.

Preparation vs. Actual Test

You can replicate the effective sense of urgency an actual test produces by including timed writing into your study sessions. You don't need all of your study time to exactly replicate the test, but you would be well served to find out the format of the exam in advance and practice the skills you'll need to use for the various test components. On one early exam in history, Stuart learned the prof was going to include several short-answer essay questions—one for each year of the time period covered. Stuart set up practice times to write for about 15 to 20 minutes on significant events from his notes because he estimated that would be about how much time he could devote out of the hour-long testing session to write one or two required short-answer questions. He would write a prompt from his notes, set a timer, and start writing. If you're ready and you have practiced and know the material, 20 minutes is adequate to prepare, draft, and revise a short response, but you don't have a lot of extra time.

Likewise, in a math exam, you will need to know what kinds of problems you will have to solve and to what extent you'll need to show your computational work on the exam. If you are able to incorporate this sort of timed problem-solving into your study time, you'll be more prepared and confident when you actually come to the exam. Making yourself adhere to a timed session during your study can only help. It puts a sense of urgency on you, and it will help you to find out what types of problems you need to practice more than ones that perhaps you're more comfortable solving.

Leveraging Study Habits for Test Prep

In your mind, you probably know what you need to do to be prepared for tests. Occasionally, something may surprise you—emphasis on a concept you considered unimportant or a different presentation of a familiar problem. But those should be exceptions. You can take all your well-honed study habits to get ready for exams. Here's a checklist for study and test success for your consideration:

Figure 6.9

Read this list with each separate class in mind, and check off the items you already do. Give yourself one point for every item you checked. If you always take the success steps—congratulations! They are not a guarantee, but doing the steps mindfully will give you a nice head start. If you do fewer than five of the steps—you have some work to do. But recognition is a good place to start, and you can incorporate these steps starting now.

As strange as this may sound, you can find some interesting research articles online about using the taste or smell of peppermint to increase memory, recall, and focus. Read more at: http://naturalsociety.com/mint-scent-improve-brain-cognition-memory. While sucking on a peppermint disk won't replace studying, why not experiment with this relatively easy idea that seems to be gaining some scientific traction?

Whole Person Approach to Testing

Just because you are facing a major exam in your engineering class (or math or science or English class) doesn't mean everything else in your life comes to a stop. Perhaps that's somewhat annoying, but that's reality. Allergies still flare up, children still need to eat, and you still need to sleep. You must see your academic life as one segment of who you are—it's an important segment, but just one aspect of who you are as a whole person. Neela tries to turn off everything else when she has exams coming up in her nursing program, which is pretty often. She ignores her health, puts off her family, tries to reschedule competing work tasks, and focuses all her energy on the pending exam. On the surface, that sounds like a reasonable approach, but if she becomes really sick by ignoring a minor head cold, or if she misses an important school deadline for one of her children, Neela risks making matters worse by attempting to compartmentalize so strictly. Taking care of her own health by eating and sleeping properly; asking for help in other aspects of her busy life, such as attending to the needs of her children; and seeing the big picture of how it all fits together would be a better approach. Pretending otherwise may work sporadically, but it is not sustainable for the long run.

A whole person approach to testing takes a lot of organization, scheduling, and attention to detail, but the life-long benefits make the effort worthwhile.

Establishing Realistic Expectations for Test Situations

Would you expect to make a perfect pastry if you've never learned how to bake? Or paint a masterpiece if you've never tried to work with paints and brushes? Probably not. But often we expect ourselves to perform at much higher levels of achievement than that for which we've actually prepared. If you become very upset and stressed if you make any score lower than the highest, you probably need to reevaluate your own expectations for test situations. Striving to always do your best is an admirable goal. Realistically knowing that your current *best* may not achieve the highest academic ratings can help you plot your progress.

Realistic continuous improvement is a better plan, because people who repeatedly attempt challenges for which they have not adequately prepared and understandably fail (or at least do not achieve the desired highest ranking) often start moving toward the goal in frustration. They simply quit. This doesn't mean you settle for mediocre grades or refrain from your challenges. It means you become increasingly aware of yourself and your current state and potential future. Know yourself, know your strengths and weaknesses, and be honest with yourself about your expectations.

Understanding Accommodations and Responsibilities

As with so many parts of life, some people take exams in stride and do just fine. Others may need more time or change of location or format to succeed in test-taking situations. With adequate notice, most faculty will provide students with reasonable accommodations to assist students in succeeding in test situations. If you feel that you would benefit from receiving these sorts of accommodations, first speak with your instructor. You may also need to talk to a student services advisor for specific requirements for accommodations at your institution.

If you need accommodations, you are responsible for understanding what your specific needs are and communicating your needs with your instructors. Before exams in class, you may be allowed to have someone else take notes for you, receive your books in audio form, engage an interpreter, or have adaptive devices in the classroom to help you participate. Testing accommodations may allow for additional time on the test, the use of a scribe to record exam answers, the use of a computer instead of handwriting answers, as well as other means to make the test situation successful. Talk to your instructors if you have questions about testing accommodations.

Prioritizing Time Surrounding Test Situations

Keep in mind that you don't have any more or less time than anyone else, so you can't *make time* for an activity. You can only use the time everyone gets wisely and realistically. Exams in college classes are important, but they are not the only significant events you have in your classes. In fact, everything leading up to the exam, the exam itself, and the post-exam activities are all one large continuum. Think of the exam as an event with multiple phases, more like a long-distance run instead of a 50-yard dash. Step back and look at the big picture of this timeline. Draw it out on paper. What needs to happen between now and the exam so you feel comfortable, confident, and ready?

If your instructor conducts some sort of pre-exam summary or prep session, make sure to attend. These can be invaluable. If this instructor does not provide that sort of formal exam prep, create your own with a group of classmates or on your own. Consider everything you know about the exam, from written instructions to notes you took in class, including any experiential notes you may have from previous exams, such as the possibility of bonus points for answering an extra question that requires some time management on your part. You can read more about time management in Chapter 3.

GET CONNECTED

Which apps can help you study for a test, increase your memory, and even help you overcome test anxiety?

Personal (https://personalzen.com/) Zen is a free online gaming app clinically proven to reduce stress and anxiety. The games retrain your brain to think more positively, reducing stress to help you focus on the experiences around you.

Games like solitaire, hangman, and Simon Says all build on your memory, keeping it sharp and active. There are loads of fun, free online memory games you can use to make time wasting a little less wasteful. For more than 250 options, visit the Memory Improvement Tips (https://www.memory-improvement-tips.com/free-online-memory-games.html) website.

iTunes University (https://apps.apple.com/us/app/itunes-u/id490217893) might be able to help you dig into a research topic or find additional content to help you if you're struggling with a course. Their library of free lectures and content comes from some of the most highly respected universities around the world.

Chegg Prep (https://www.chegg.com/flashcards) is a flashcard-based self-quizzing resource. It provides millions of pre-made flashcards and decks organized by course and topic, which you can search, sort,

> bookmark, and use in a variety of ways. The service is free and does not require a login unless you'd like to save or create your own cards.

Test Day

Once you get to the exam session, try your best to focus on nothing but the exam. This can be very difficult with all the distractions in our lives. But if you have done all the groundwork to attend the classes, completed the assignments, and scheduled your exam prep time, you are ready to focus intently for the comparatively short time most exams last.

Arriving to class:

Don't let yourself be sidetracked right at the end. Beyond the preparation we've discussed, give yourself some more advantages on the actual test day:

- Get to the testing location a few minutes early so you can settle into your place and take a few relaxing breaths.
- Don't let other classmates interrupt your calmness at this point.
- Just get to your designated place, take out whatever supplies and materials you are allowed to have, and calm your mind.

Taking the test:

Once the instructor begins the test:

- Listen carefully for any last-minute oral directions that may have changed some detail on the exam, such as the timing or the content of the questions.
- As soon as you receive the exam sheet or packet, make a quick scan over the entire test.
- Don't spend a lot of time on this initial glance, but make sure you are familiar with the layout and what you need to do.
- Using this first review, decide how you will allocate your available time for each section.
- You can even jot down how many minutes you can allow for the different sections or questions.

Then for each section, if the exam is divided this way, be sure you **read the section directions** very carefully so you don't miss an important detail. For example, instructors often offer options—so you may have four short-answer questions from which to choose, but you only need to answer two of them. If you had not read the directions for that section, you may have thought you needed to provide answers to all four prompts. Working on extra questions for which you likely will receive no credit would be a waste of your limited exam time. The extra time you spend at the beginning is like an investment in your overall results.

Answer every required question on the exam. Even if you don't complete each one, you may receive some credit for partial answers. Whether or not you can receive partial credit would be an excellent question to ask before the exam during the preparation time. If you are taking an exam that contains multiple-choice questions, go through and answer the questions about which you are the most confident first.

Read the entire question carefully even if you think you know what the stem (the introduction of the choices) says, and read all the choices. Skip really difficult questions or ones where your brain goes blank. Then you can go back and concentrate on those skipped ones later after you have answered the majority of the questions confidently. Sometimes a later question will trigger an idea in your mind that will help you answer the skipped questions.

And, in a similar fashion to spending a few minutes right at the beginning of the test time to read the directions carefully and identify the test elements, **allow yourself a few minutes at the end of the exam session to review your answers.** Depending on what sort of exam it is, you can use this time to check your math computations, review an essay for grammatical and content errors, or answer the difficult multiple-choice questions you skipped earlier. Finally, **make sure you have completed the entire test:** check the backs of pages, and verify that you have a corresponding answer section for every question section on the exam. It can be easy to skip a section with the idea you will come back to it but then forget to return there, which can have a significant impact on your test results.

After the Test

As you leave the exam room, the last thing you may want to think about is that particular test. You probably have numerous other assignments, projects, and life obligations to attend to, especially if you pushed some of those off to study for this completed exam. Give yourself some space from this exam, but only for the duration of the time when your instructor is grading your exam. Once you have your results, study them—whether you did really well (Go, you!) or not as well as you had hoped (Keep your spirits up!). Both scenarios hold valuable information if you will use it.

Thandie had a habit of going all-out for exams before she took them, and she did pretty well usually, but once the instructor passed back the graded tests, she would look at the letter grade, glance half-heartedly at the instructor's comments, and toss the exam away, ready to move on to the next chapter, section, or concept. A better plan would be to learn from her exam results and analyze both what she did well and where she struggled. After a particularly unimpressive exam outing in her statistics class, Thandie took her crumpled-up exam to the campus tutoring center, where the tutor reviewed the test with her section by section. Together they discovered that Thandie did particularly well on the computational sections, which she admitted were her favorites, and not well at all on the short-answer essay questions that she did not expect to find in a stats class, which in her experience had been more geared toward the mathematical side of solving statistical problems.

Going forward in this class, Thandie should practice writing out her explanations of how to compute the problems and talk to her instructor about ways to hone this skill. This tutoring session also proved to Thandie the benefit of holding on to important class papers—either electronically or in hard copy, depending on the class setup—for future reference. For some classes, you probably don't need to keep every scrap of paper (or file) associated with your notes, exams, assignments, and projects, but for others, especially for those in your major, those early class materials may come in very handy in your more difficult later undergraduate courses or even in grad school when you need a quick refresher on the basic concepts.

Test Anxiety

Figure 6.10 Text anxiety can be a common occurrence, but you can use strategies to manage it.

Test anxiety is very real. You may know this firsthand. Almost everyone gets a little nervous before a major exam, in the same way most people get slightly anxious meeting a new potential date or undertaking an unfamiliar activity. We second-guess whether we're ready for this leap, if we prepared adequately, or if we should postpone this potentially awkward situation. And in most situations, testing included, that reasonable level of nervous anticipation can be a good thing—enhancing your focus and providing you with a bit of bravado to get you through a difficult time.

Test anxiety, however, can cause us to doubt ourselves so severely that we underperform or overcompensate to the point that we do not do well on the exam. Don't despair; you can still succeed if you suffer from test anxiety. The first step is to understand what it is and what it is not, and then to practice some simple strategies to cope with your anxious feelings relative to test taking. Whatever you do, don't use the label *test anxiety* to keep you from your dreams of completing your education and pursuing whatever career you have your eyes on. You are bigger than any anxiety.

Understanding Test Anxiety

If someone tries to tell you that test anxiety is *all in your head*, they're sort of right. Our thinking is a key element of anxiety of any sort. On the other hand, test anxiety can manifest itself in other parts of our bodies as well. You may feel queasy or light-headed if you are experiencing test anxiety. Your palms may sweat, or you may become suddenly very hot or very cold for no apparent reason. At its worst, test anxiety can cause its sufferers to experience several unpleasant conditions including nausea, diarrhea, and shortness of breath. Some people may feel as though they may throw up, faint, or have a heart attack, none of which would make going into a testing situation a pleasant idea. You can learn more about symptoms of test anxiety from the Anxiety and Depression Association of America that conducts research on this topic.[12]

Back to our minds for a minute. We think constantly, and if we have important events coming up, such as

---

12 Reteguiz, Jo-Ann. "Relationship between anxiety and standardized patient test performance in the medicine clerkship." Journal of general internal medicine vol. 21,5 (2006): 415-8. doi:10.1111/j.1525-1497.2006.00419.

exams, but other significant events as well, we tend to think about them seemingly all the time. Almost as if we have a movie reel looping in our heads, we can anticipate everything that may happen during these events—both sensational results and catastrophic endings. What if you oversleep on the test day? What if you're hit by a bus on the way to campus? What if you get stung by a mysterious insect and have to save the world on the very day of your exam?

How about the other way? You win the lottery! Your screenplay is accepted by a major publisher! You get a multimillion-dollar record deal! It could happen. Typically, though, life falls somewhere in between those two extremes, unless you live in an action movie. Our minds, however, (perhaps influenced by some of those action movies or spy novels we've seen and read) often gravitate to those black-and-white, all-or-nothing results. Hence, we can become very nervous when we think about taking an exam because if we do really poorly, we think, we may have to face consequences as dire as dropping out of school or never graduating. Usually, this isn't going to happen, but we can literally make ourselves sick with anxiety if we dwell on those slight possibilities. You actually may encounter a few tests in your academic careers that are so important that you have to alter your other life plans temporarily, but truly, this is the exception, not the rule. Don't let the most extreme and severe result take over your thoughts. Prepare well and do your best, see where you land, and then go from there.

Using Strategies to Manage Test Anxiety

You have to work hard to control test anxiety so it does not take an unhealthy hold on you every time you face a test situation, which for many of you will last well into your careers. One of the best ways to control test anxiety is to be prepared for the exam. You can control that part. You can also learn effective relaxation techniques including controlled breathing, visualization, and meditation. Some of these practices work well even in the moment: at your test site, take a deep breath, close your eyes, and smile—just bringing positive thoughts into your mind can help you meet the challenges of taking an exam without anxiety taking over.

The tests in the corporate world or in other career fields may not look exactly like the ones you encounter in college, but professionals of all sorts take tests routinely. Again, being prepared helps reduce or eliminate this anxiety in all these situations. Think of a presentation or an explanation you have provided well numerous times—you likely are not going to feel anxious about this same presentation if asked to provide it again. That's because you are prepared and know what to expect. Try to replicate this feeling of preparation and confidence in your test-taking situations.

Many professions require participants to take frequent licensing exams to prove they are staying current in their rapidly changing work environments, including nursing, engineering, education, and architecture, as well as many other occupations. You have tools to take control of your thinking about tests. Better to face it head-on and let test anxiety know who's in charge!

Summary

Studying and taking tests will always be a large part of college, so learning now to do these well can only help you be more successful. Experts provide us with many tools, techniques, and ideas to use when we determine how best to study, use our memories effectively, and prepare to take exams. You can help yourself by taking these guidelines seriously and tracking your progress. If one strategy works better for you in some classes and another is more suited to a different course, keep that in mind when you begin to study. Use all the resources available to you, and you'll be well on your way to success in college.

 ## Career Connection

Studies have shown that parents contribute to test anxiety in children by drawing students' attention to the test day and increasing pressure to perform well. Do you think that worrying about an upcoming test is as harmful as anxiety while taking the test? What do you think can be done to minimize worry?

This article (https://openstax.org/l/testanxiety) discusses how to help with test anxiety.

 ## Rethinking

Revisit the questions you answered at the beginning of the chapter, and consider one option you learned in this chapter that might change your answer to one of them.

How confident are you in your skills at preparing for and taking tests? Take this quick survey to figure it out, ranking questions on a scale of 1–4, 1 meaning "least like me" and 4 meaning "most like me."

1. I believe I set aside enough time to prepare for tests.
2. If I don't set aside enough time, or if life gets in the way, I can usually cram and get similar results.
3. I prefer to pull all-nighters. The adrenaline and urgency help me remember what I need come test time.
4. I study my notes, highlight book passages, and use flash cards, but I still don't feel like I'm as successful as I should be on tests.

 ## Where do you go from here?

Studying and test taking skills often need to evolve to meet the needs of college responsibilities. What would you like to learn more about? Choose a topic from the list below and create an annotated bibliography that would direct further research.

- the importance of memory in learning new material
- strategies to increase memory
- strategies to increase the effectiveness of studying
- test anxiety

7 Thinking

Figure 7.1 Games like basketball require many types and levels of thinking. Players and coaches must analyze their opponents' offense and defense, solve problems related to opposing players' skills and their own team's weaknesses, and constantly create through split-second decision making. (Credit: San Francisco Foghorn / Flickr / Attribution 2.0 Generic (CC BY 2.0))

Chapter Outline

7.1 What Thinking Means
7.2 Creative Thinking
7.3 Analytical Thinking
7.4 Critical Thinking
7.5 Problem-Solving
7.6 Metacognition
7.7 Information Literacy

Introduction

Student Survey

How do you feel about the ways you think? Take this quick survey to figure it out, ranking questions on a scale of 1–4, 1 meaning "least like me" and 4 meaning "most like me." These questions will help you determine how the chapter concepts relate to you right now. As you are introduced to new concepts and practices, it can be informative to reflect on how your understanding changes over time. We'll revisit these questions at the end of the chapter to see whether your feelings have changed.

1. I understand how to approach problem-solving.
2. I have creative potential.
3. I often think about how I'm learning
4. I know how to find and evaluate valid information.

You can also take the Chapter 7 Survey (https://openstax.org/l/collegesurvey07) anonymously online.

STUDENT PROFILE

"I never considered myself a problem solver. I was more creative. I wrote music and fiction, and saw myself in a musical theater career. Two years of college and two majors later, I had moved into a related pathway: entertainment management. I was thrilled to find something that suited my passions and gave me a great shot at a number of jobs. But I hadn't counted on the business and math courses I needed to take. Solving these types of problems wasn't in my skill set. I didn't have the background, and kept missing half the ideas. I started going to the academic success center and office hours, and managed to keep my grades in the passing range. But I wasn't excelling and couldn't stay ahead. It was a struggle.

"During a study session, a success counselor noticed that I was approaching a problem all wrong. She helped me for the next hour -- not working on the problem itself, but on how I was thinking about it and others like it. She asked me about the information I knew, how I put it together, and so on. She taught me a progression of steps to analyze the components, get the data I needed, ignore the unimportant information, and run the numbers. Then she had me watch a TED talk (https://openstax.org/l/criticalthinking) with some more information.

"I realized that it wasn't my prior knowledge that was holding me back. It was the way I was thinking about the work. I started asking my professors more about how to approach the courses -- how to think about them. I didn't start getting A's right away, but I did get better results, and even felt more creative as I started to try new things."

About This Chapter

In this chapter, you'll be introduced to different ways of thinking about the way you think. By the time you complete this chapter, you should be able to do the following:

- Describe *thinking* as a process and the reasons it is important.
- Discuss the importance of *creative thinking* and ways of generating original ideas.
- Define *analytical thinking*, its component parts, and outcomes.
- Articulate the process and importance of *critical thinking*.
- Describe the best approaches to *problem-solving*.
- Define *metacognition* and describe ways to become thoughtful about your thinking.
- Define *information literacy* for college students.

Whether we admit it or not or even consider it or not, we cannot stop thinking. We think during intense work situations, while we're playing games, when we eat, as we watch a movie, even during meditation that purports to empty the mind of all thought. Skilled and practiced yogis may be able to get into a state that resembles non-thinking, but most of us keep thinking all the time. Perhaps as you read these lines, you doubt their accuracy suggesting that you don't really think when you're just relaxing with friends. But you do. You may think about the other people in the group and what you do or do not know about them. You may wonder what you'll eat for your next meal. Your mind may flit to question whether you locked the door on the way out. Or you may debate internally whether you'll finish on time the assignment due for one of your classes. Now, you may not act on any of those random thoughts during this relaxing time, but you *are* nonetheless thinking. As you begin this exploration of thinking, consider all the ways we turn to technology to assist with our thinking and how thinking impacts and defines various careers.

When you consider the word *thinking,* does your mind drift toward:

a. School
b. Work
c. Relationships
d. Free time

Reflect on your answer, and write one or two sentences on why you associate this idea with thinking.

In this chapter, we'll look more closely at several distinct types of thinking including creative, analytical, and critical thinking, all of which come into play for problem-solving. We'll also explore the multitude of resources available relative to understanding and enhancing your thinking skills, all of which constitutes metacognition, the practice of thinking about your thinking.

7.1 What Thinking Means

Estimated completion time: 8 minutes.

Thinking is one of those hard-to-pinpoint aspects of life we typically don't analyze much—like breathing or walking or sleeping. We constantly think, and becoming more attuned to how we think and what we do when we encounter new ideas is an excellent habit to pursue.

> **"If you're going to do anything as much as you think, you might just as well learn about it and hone this skill."**

You may have read quotes or inspirational slogans that claim *you are what you think.* What does that mean? Can you *think* yourself into a good mood? Can you *think* you have a million dollars in your pocket? Does that mean you are the next music sensation if you often sing at parties? Not necessarily, but consider Jose, for instance. He isn't a rock and roll star, but Jose spends a lot of his leisure time thinking about music, analyzing performances, memorizing his favorite musicians' characteristics, buying fan clothing, and even designing a creative means to explain his excitement for music to his friends through a homemade video. Jose certainly could allow his fascination to seep into other aspects of his life. Do you have a hobby or interest you spend a lot of time thinking about?

Many people go to great lengths to attend a concert by a favorite music star. They think creatively about how to save enough money for tickets; they think analytically about scheduling their other obligations to have time off work to attend or how to make up work in their college classes. This much planning involves a great deal of thinking, and not all about music. In the example about Jose, thinking directs the actions of the person doing the thinking. So, in fact, what we think *does* influence who we are and how we act. We have many resources available to be more effective thinkers, and learning about these resources gives us options.

GET CONNECTED

Apps and search engines literally bring thinking to our fingertips. Consider how often you visit Google. The use of this familiar site has become so commonplace as to render the proper name of the company into a verb—*to google* a topic. Basic calculators or word-processing software programs are other simple examples of technology we often use without recognizing them as thinking aids.

While apps, software programs, thinking games, and thought exercises may help you stretch your brain, don't let their simplicity fool you into thinking that cultivating an inquisitive, thoughtful mind is easy or automatic. Thinking is as complex as it is necessary for our success in life. Some tools you may find useful are applications that provide challenges using mind puzzles are Peak (https://www.peak.net/) and Elevate (https://www.elevateapp.com/) . These training apps offer brain training that varies from quick matching memory games to more sophisticated thought-processing speed scenarios. You can even use a straightforward tool like a flashcard app, such as Chegg Prep (https://www.chegg.com/flashcards) , to create your own thinking games -- using word associations or pictures to help you connect topics and build your skills.

A familiar element of the thinking apps is a progression tracker to help thinkers improve their focus and memory as well as to learn and practice math and verbal skills over time. Researchers are still investigating the correlation between thought-invoking game playing and the decrease in mental agility, memory, and cognitive vitality. Early studies have produced numerous findings, including a long-term investigation of the onset of Alzheimer's disease conducted with nuns; you can look up the *Nun Study* to learn more, or go to this article (https://openstax.org/l/nunstudy) .

7.2 Creative Thinking

Estimated completion time: 28 minutes.

Questions to consider:

- How can you go about generating original ideas?
- What is the best way to approach working with unconventional ideas?

Has anyone ever told you that you have a flair for the creative? If so, celebrate! That's a good personality trait to nurture. Creativity is needed in all occupations and during all stages of life. Learning to be more in tune with your own version of creativity can help you think more clearly, resolve problems, and appreciate setbacks. You're creative if you repurpose old furniture into a new function. You're also creative if you invent a new cookie recipe for a friend who has a nut allergy. And you're using creativity if you can explain complex biological concepts to your classmates in your lab class. Creativity pops up everywhere. When creative thinking comes into play, you'll be looking for both original and unconventional ideas, and learning to recognize those ideas improves your thinking skills all around.

Would you learn more about the French Revolution by eating foods popular in that era? What if you were to stop using your phone for all non-emergency communication to understand how news flowed in the early 20th century? These examples present creative ways to approach learning the experiences of a specific time in history. When actors want to learn about a character they'll be playing, they often engage in method acting to immerse themselves in the role. They may maintain a different accent or wear only clothes their character would wear even when they are not at rehearsals, all so they can feel what it was like for their character. Think of ways you may be able to apply method acting to your learning experiences.

WHAT STUDENTS SAY

1. Which type of thinking do you think is most important for your academic studies?
   a. Creative thinking
   b. Analytical thinking
   c. Critical thinking
2. In which area do you have the most difficulty being creative?
   a. Writing
   b. In-class discussions/activities
   c. Personal life
   d. Problem-solving
   e. Finding resources/help
3. In which course areas or activities do you make the most use of problem-solving skills?
   a. Math or quantitative classes
   b. Computer or technical classes
   c. Social science classes
   d. Real-life situations

You can also take the anonymous What Students Say (https://openstax.org/l/collegesurvey6-12) surveys to add your voice to this textbook. Your responses will be included in updates.

Students offered their views on these questions, and the results are displayed in the graphs below.

Which type of thinking do you think is most important for your academic studies?

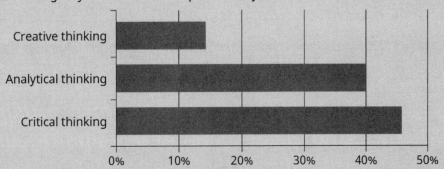

Figure 7.2

In which area do you have the most difficulty being creative?

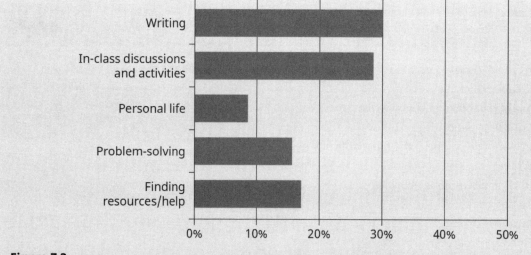

Figure 7.3

In which course areas or activities do you make the most use of problem-solving skills?

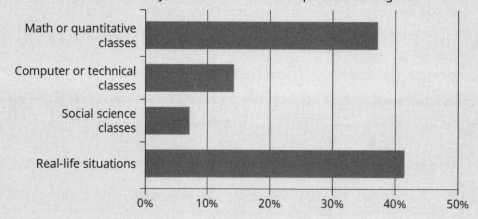

Figure 7.4

ANALYSIS QUESTION

In what ways could thinking creatively help you be a better student? Write a one-paragraph reflection on that aspect and how you could realistically go about being more creative.

ANALYSIS QUESTION

Some people say creativity is the realm of children. Can you think of how a child's curiosity and willingness to explore may help you understand a college discipline that is unfamiliar to you now? Write a one-paragraph reflection on how you could use curiosity toward one of your most difficult courses in college.

Creativity doesn't always present itself in the guise of a chart-topping musical hit or other artistic expression. We need creative solutions throughout the workplace—whether board room, emergency room, or classroom. It was no fluke that the 2001 revised Bloom's cognitive taxonomy, originally developed in 1948, placed a new word at the apex—*create*. That is the highest level of thinking skills. As noted in previous chapters, we do all need to use and develop the lower thinking skills that include remembering, applying, and analyzing, but true intelligence and successful thinking move beyond these levels to invention.

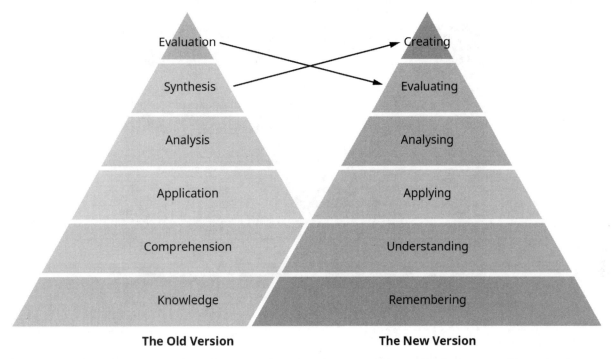

Figure 7.5 Bloom's Taxonomy is an important learning theory used by psychologists, cognitive scientists, and educators to demonstrate levels of thinking. Many assessments and lessons you've seen during your schooling have likely been arranged with Bloom's in mind. Researchers recently revised it to place creativity -- invention -- as the highest level.

Regurgitating the minute details of *Goldilocks* or *Beowulf* demonstrates far less comprehension than fashioning an original ending that turns the tables or developing a board game from the story. Author Gregory Maguire used the base plot of L. Frank Baum's 1900 book *The Wonderful Wizard of Oz* and the 1939 movie *The Wizard of Oz* to create the smash-hit 2003 Broadway musical *Wicked* that tells the story from the perspective of the Wicked Witch of the West, making her a sympathetic character. This creative approach calls for far more critical and creative thinking than memorizing facts.

> **"Creating new out of old or new out of nothing is how we ended up with manned space flight, cell phones, the Constitution, and rap music."**

Continuing to support creativity in whatever form it takes will be how we cure cancer, establish peace, and manipulate the time-space continuum. Don't shortchange your own creativity.

Generating Original Ideas

Nineteenth-century American writer and humorist Mark Twain may have been partially correct when he said:

There is no such thing as a new idea. It is impossible. We simply take a lot of old ideas and put them into a sort of mental kaleidoscope. We give them a turn and they make new and curious combinations. We keep on turning and making new combinations indefinitely; but they are the same old pieces of colored glass that have been in use through all the ages.

(*Mark Twain's Own Autobiography* by Mark Twain)

Figure 7.6 You may feel like you cannot come up with new ideas, but even the process of combining and recombining familiar concepts and approaches is a creative act. A kaleidoscope creates a nearly infinite number of new images by repositioning the same pieces of glass.

It is certainly a pretty metaphor of idea generation, but even if old ideas are reworked to create new solutions to existing problems or we embellish a current thought to include new ways of living or working, that renewal is the epitome of the creative process.

It's common to think of creativity as something used mostly by traditional artists—people who paint, draw, or sculpt. Indeed, artists are creative, but think of other fields in which people think just a little differently to approach situations in their discipline. The famous heart surgeon Dr. Denton Cooley didn't have an exact model when he first implanted an artificial heart. Chemist Stephanie Kwoleck discovered life-saving Kevlar when she continued work on a substance that would usually be thrown away. Early US astronauts owed their ability to orbit and return to Earth based on creative uses of mathematics by people like Karen Johnson. Inventor and actress Hedy Lamarr used diagrams of fish and birds to help aviation pioneer Howard Hughes produce faster airplanes. Indeed, biomimicry, an approach to innovation that seeks sustainable solutions to human challenges by emulating nature's time-tested patterns and strategies, is now a huge field of study. This list could go on and on.

Figure 7.7 Denton Cooley (Credit: Texas Children's Hospital / Public Domain), Stephanie Kwolek (Credit: Chemical Heritage Foundation / Attribution 3.0), Karen Johnson (Credit: NASA / Public Domain), and Hedy Lamarr (Credit: MGM / Public Domain). These individuals employed extensive creativity in the fields of science and math, leading to significant discoveries and accomplishments.

ACTIVITY

Work with two or three classmates to determine a product or service you could develop. Think of a situation in your life where a new way of doing something or a not-yet-invented process or device would make your life easier, more convenient, or more purposeful. And this is not limited to the creation of something big. Just looking at something you see all the time with a different lens/perspective is also creative, and we can all do that. What adaptation would you need to make? Let your imagination go wild—driverless cars, wireless communication . . . oh wait, already here. Keep thinking! Each member of your group should write a paragraph that describes the product/service, what you would need to create it, and how it will be received by others. Read each other's paragraphs and discuss the merits of the ideas.

You may actually be very good at coming up with original creative ideas. Some people naturally seem to think more creatively than others, but we all have the capacity to create and devise. Do you enjoy rearranging furniture or organizing your closet? If you already think "I could make that so much better!" as you walk through shops or events, you're on the right track. Do you tinker with wood, paper, yarn, or dirt? Are you a doodler? One way to enhance your creativity is to track your ideas. You can keep a running list on your phone, jot down ideas on index cards you can later sort into categories, or keep ideas flowing in a paper journal. Some creative people design storyboards to visualize goals or projects using pictures from magazines or online for creative inspiration. Play around with ways to keep up with ideas you may be able to incorporate in some various aspects of your life.

Since the 1980s, Roger von Oech, the president of Creative Think, a California consulting firm, has been encouraging employees in corporations, educational institutions, and government agencies to think more creatively. His pithy stories, examples, scenarios, and challenges present either a barrier to creative thinking that needs to be overcome or an example of how to harness seemingly unproductive ideas. Sometimes creative ideas do not initially seem viable or productive compared to a known process or product, but talking out ideas with others and considering new approaches without fear of ridicule or censure can help individuals and groups think beyond the status quo. Von Oech's discussion starters recommend that thinkers *Avoid Arrogance, Fight for It, Get Rid of Excuses,* and *Listen to That Hunch.* You may be interested in looking these up on the Creative Think website (http://creativethink.com) . If you do, you may find some of von Oech's ideas a little out of the ordinary, but great ideas sometimes are, and thinking about them in a different way may be the spark you need to come up with your own version of an idea that will prove effective for you. Stay open to different approaches even if you aren't immediately comfortable with the ideas.

Another creative thinking group you may be interested in investigating is koozai.com, a digital marketing consulting firm based in the United Kingdom with clients worldwide. You may not be in need of help with digital marketing, but the koozai.com website is worth a look to see how creativity can highlight excellent customer service, detail award-winning services, and inject a sense of fun and vitality into a service that may not seem very exciting on the surface, namely helping companies optimize their web presence for increased exposure and profits. The team is a creative mix of engineers, designers, and analysts who use data-based evidence to find the right fit for their clients in a relaxed and productive environment. The actual nuts-and-bolts work involved in web marketing involves a great deal of tedious coding and specialized web design often performed by software engineers working alone, but you don't get a sense of bored, isolated office workers when you peruse the koozai.com site.

Working with Unconventional Ideas

Working with unconventional ideas can produce anxiety because the ideas are unfamiliar and the results of implementing these ideas could be unpredictable. People may not immediately accept your nontraditional ideas. Some may never accept them. If your original creation were to require individuals to give up their current cell phones, you can imagine the resistance. Even if the new idea is an improvement in communication, some people would hesitate.

To work in this possibly uncomfortable realm, you have to remain open-minded, focus on your organizational skills, and learn to communicate your ideas well. If a coworker at a café where you work suggests serving breakfast in addition to the already-served lunch and dinner, keeping an open mind means thinking through the benefits of this new plan (e.g., potential new customers, increased profits) instead of merely focusing on the possible drawbacks (e.g., possible scheduling problems, added start-up costs, loss of lunch business). Implementing this plan would mean a new structure for buying, workers' schedules and pay, and advertising, so you would have to organize all of these component areas. And finally, you would need to communicate your ideas on how to make this new plan work not only to the staff who will work the new shift, but also to the public who frequent your café and the others you want to encourage to try your new hours.

"Because we've always done it that way" is not a valid reason to not try a new approach. It may very well be that the old process is a very good way to do things, but it also may just be that the old, comfortable routine is not as effective and efficient as a new process could be.

Can you think of any routine task you do now that you've never questioned, such as doing laundry, studying for exams, spending downtime, or preparing food? Consider how you came to learn this routine. Are you following a pattern your parents set for you growing up? Do you ask friends how they perform these tasks and follow their example? How well do these routines work for you? Think of at least one different way you could approach one of these tasks. Would it be a good idea to change the way you do it? How would that benefit you? If not, why is the best approach to keep doing this thing the way you have always done it? Reflect on your thinking behind this routine. How could creative thinking help you identify and assess all of your options?

Another element of working with unconventional ideas is to pay attention to how you organize your thoughts. Organizing includes establishing a clear goal to accomplish, outlining the steps toward that goal, and monitoring progress with specific deadlines. You may be able to add flexibility to this plan since creativity deals in the unknown and that may take longer than you initially expected, but an organized map of your thinking and where you hope to take it can move creative projects forward.

For example, what if you were asked to build a shed for a project or as part of your job? You would need a plan of some sort. It wouldn't be prudent to run to the hardware store and just buy various supplies you see on the spur of the moment. Rather, you would organize your thoughts around this project and determine some specific goals about the size of the shed, its ultimate location and use, the type of materials that would best serve your purposes, and how long the project will take so you can budget time and money toward the accomplishment of the goal. Do you need a building permit in your area for this sort of home improvement project? Will you or others need to sacrifice something (yard space, time, money, a special view) for you to build this shed? Do you have time to complete all the steps? Do you have the skills to put the shed together, or can you learn how to do it? How much are you willing to spend on this? Without an organized plan, you may end up with a good idea, some random supplies, and an incomplete building project that wastes both time and money and does not meet your initial expectations.

Figure 7.8 Thinking through a plan isn't just for school. Household activities and projects require forethought and strategic thinking. (Credit: TWP, Inc. / Flickr / Attribution 2.0 Generic (CC BY 2.0))

In addition to the need to remain open-minded and organized, creative thinking calls for a dissemination plan. Unconventional ideas typically don't get off the ground without the creator of the ideas communicating those thoughts to others. Do you set yourself up to be in the company of other creative thinkers? It's not a bad idea. Creativity is somewhat contagious. You may not think you have a creative way to approach a situation, but if you were to bounce ideas off like-minded friends and also friends who would offer a completely different way of looking at something, you may discover that indeed you do have some good ideas ready to come to fruition. This creative brainstorming doesn't just happen though. You need to set aside specific times to work with others to flesh out ideas and think through obstacles. And then you'll need some more time alone for the ideas to gel. Sometimes the creative answers to problems come to you at odd moments once you have laid the groundwork—be ready to capture the ideas in some form of note when your lightbulb goes off.

Creative thinking isn't just helpful in solving problems. You may want to enhance an otherwise good plan to make it fantastic and memorable, which is when you can bring in creative thinking. If you want to surprise your best friend with a special birthday celebration but are low on funds, you could think of creative ways to make this event one to remember. You could take in a free museum night or window shop at the mall or make a photo collage from pictures on your phone that bring back great memories.

ACTIVITY

What is one of your favorite creative projects that you've recently accomplished? What made it creative? Ask at least one other person that same question and see if his or her answer inspires your own creative thinking on how to handle these situations:

- living with roommates who have different priorities or interests
- breaking away from family and old friends without severing ties all together
- determining if the major you initially chose really fits your personality
- scheduling your time for study, campus activities, work, and personal interests
- ensuring your assignments, presentations, or class artifacts show your best work

Think of ways you may approach these situations.

Creative Process Applied to a Sample Campus Activity

Creative Process Step	Description and Notes
Problem to Solve or Item/Work to Create	**Create a new logo for our Commuter Student Association**
Requirements and Needs	• Will be used on Insta/Twitter, merch, print • Must incorporate school colors but be readable in grayscale • Must be understandable at large and small sizes (computer/phone)
Parameters and Limitations	• Cannot look like other logos on campus • Cannot use photos-illustration only • Timeline: 7 weeks (in time for next year's college catalog) • Budget: $450
Inspiration and Ideas	• Look at Commuter Association logos from other colleges. • Look at city and state transit logos. • Go to library to look at our school's old yearbooks.

Table 7.1 Creative processes should include a plan that considers the goals of the project and provides opportunities for brainstorming and feedback. The steps in this table may not work for everyone, but you can use them to think about what is needed in a process of your own. See the student resources for a blank version you can adapt.

Creative Process Applied to a Sample Campus Activity

Creative Process Step	Description and Notes
Resources/Knowledge	• Graphic design • Copyright info (consult student govt) • Market research
Dissemination and Brainstorming	• Create a survey for all our commuters • Launch a contest for ideas and submissions? • Share drafts with advisor for approval. • Talk to graphic design club?
Implementation Plan	• Samples needed in 3 weeks. From there: • 1 week for survey feedback • 1 week for improvement • 1 week for additional feedback on final candidates • 1 week for finalization and approval
Reflection and Revision	• Ask all new club members in Fall for feedback. • Consider improving logo during Spring semester next year.

Table 7.1 Creative processes should include a plan that considers the goals of the project and provides opportunities for brainstorming and feedback. The steps in this table may not work for everyone, but you can use them to think about what is needed in a process of your own. See the student resources for a blank version you can adapt.

7.3 Analytical Thinking

Estimated completion time: 18 minutes.

Questions to consider:

- How can you best establish component parts in thinking?
- How can you use analysis to improve efficiency?

Thinking helps in many situations, as we've discussed throughout this chapter. When we work out a problem or situation systematically, breaking the whole into its component parts for separate analysis, to come to a solution or a variety of possible solutions, we call that *analytical thinking*. Characteristics of analytical thinking include setting up the parts, using information literacy, and verifying the validity of any sources you reference. While the phrase *analytical thinking* may sound daunting, we actually do this sort of thinking in our everyday lives when we brainstorm, budget, detect patterns, plan, compare, work puzzles, and make decisions based on multiple sources of information. Think of all the thinking that goes into the logistics of a dinner-and-a-movie date—where to eat, what to watch, who to invite, what to wear, popcorn or candy—when choices and decisions are rapid-fire, but we do it relatively successfully all the time.

Employers specifically look for candidates with analytical skills because they need to know employees can use clear and logical thinking to resolve conflicts that cause work to slow down or may even put the company in jeopardy of not complying with state or national requirements. If everything always went smoothly on the shop floor or in the office, we wouldn't need front-line managers, but everything doesn't always go according to plan or company policy. Your ability to think analytically could be the difference between getting a good job and being passed over by others who prove they are stronger thinkers. A mechanic who takes each car apart piece by piece to see what might be wrong instead of investigating the entire car, gathering customer information, assessing the symptoms, and focusing on a narrow set of possible problems is not an effective member of the team. Some career fields even have set, formulaic analyses that professionals in those fields need to know how to conduct and understand, such as a cost analysis, a statistical analysis, or a return on investment (ROI) analysis. You can learn more about these in Chapters 4 and 12.

ACTIVITY

Generate a list of at least two courses you are taking now that you think would routinely practice analytical thinking. Now, think of the profession you are interested in joining. How could the deliberate use of analytical thinking processes be beneficial for that career field? What are you currently learning about in your courses that apply directly to your chosen career path? Think of at least two ways analytical thinking would be used in the career field you are pursuing.

Establishing Component Parts

Component parts refer to the separate elements of a situation or problem. It might include the people involved, the locations of the people, the weather, market fluctuations, or any number of other characteristics of the situation you're examining. If you don't identify all parts of a problem, you run the risk of ignoring a critical element when you offer the solution. For example, if you have a scheduling problem at home and seem to never see your loved ones, the first step in thinking through this problem analytically would be to decide what is contributing to this unfavorable result. To begin, you may examine the family members' individual work, school, and personal schedules, and then create a group calendar to determine if pockets of time exist that are not taken by outside commitments. Perhaps rather than reading your homework assignments at the college library, you could plan to one day a week read with other members of your family who are doing quiet work. You may also need to determine how time is spent to better understand the family's use of time, perhaps using categories such as work/school, recreation, exercise, sleep, and meals. Once you sort the categories for all the family members, you may see blocks of time spent that would lend themselves to combining with other categories—if you and your significant other both exercise three times a week for an hour each time but at separate locations, one possible solution may be to work out together. You could alternate locations if both people have favorite places to run, or you could compromise and decide on one location for both of you—one week at the park, one week at the campus rec center. This may not ultimately be the solution, but after establishing the component parts and thinking analytically, you have provided at least one viable solution.

What if you look at the situation and decide you have too many component parts? Consider, for instance, how Amazon delivers packages every day. That's a lot of items going to and from seemingly countless locations within a relatively short time—sometimes within just one day. An organization such as Amazon must use a great deal of thinking and organizing to deliver goods and services.

Figure 7.9 Warehouse designers must think through complex problems and allow for a range of package sizes and shapes -- even ones they haven't yet seen -- to work within their systems. (Credit: Scott Lewis / Flickr / Attribution 2.0 Generic (CC-BY 2.0))

One way to maintain clear thinking with so many parts is hyper organization. Proper labeling (for Amazon to ship it uses the foundation of our mailing system, unique ZIP codes that each address must contain to be delivered) as well as a strong sense of categorization (fulfillment warehouses, customer return warehouses, grocery item warehouses, etc.) are necessary for Amazon to do business. If you were faced with a major research paper your freshman composition professor expects to be polished by the end of the semester, where do you start? What are the component parts of a high-quality research paper? What tasks do you need to finish and how quickly to accomplish the overall goals? A partial list might include generating ideas, selecting a topic, researching, reviewing the available literature, outlining, drafting, and reviewing. What if you encounter setbacks in any of the steps? Do you have a contingency plan? In the construction industry, engineers called this *float,* and they deliberately build in extra time and money in case problems arise on the project. This allows them to avoid getting off schedule, for instance if a severe storm makes access to the worksite impossible.

Figure 7.10 Construction planners and engineers allow for a range of contingencies and conditions they cannot control, such as weather, supply problems, safety adjustments, and so on. (Credit: Metropolitan Transportation Authority of New York / Flickr / Attribution Generic 2.0 (CC-BY 2.0))

Forging a Revolution

While most problems require a variety of thinking types, analytical thinking is arguably required in solving all.

There was a time when manufacturing was completed by a few people who moved around a workspace to complete their projects. As companies grew, this became more and more inefficient, leading to the need for automation. Henry Ford, the early-20th-century American auto inventor, used analytical thinking to revolutionize the way companies increase production by inventing the assembly line. He perceived the problem in his own factory. When the demand for cars increased but his workers continued their work at the same pace, he analyzed their process to create something more efficient in the assembly line. This invention allowed one person to perform the same role over and over before sending the car chassis to another person who also performed the same role over and over as the evolving car moved down a sort of conveyor-belt system. The workers on Ford's assembly lines still had to think and make sure that the task for which they were responsible was properly constructed, free of defects, and ready to move to the next station; they just did this thinking about their one area of expertise. Instead of various skilled workers wasting time and energy moving themselves and their tools around the factory from one incomplete car to the next, possibly getting in the way of each other's work, the cars came to the workers. Ford vastly improved production rates and decreased manufacturing time by thinking about this then-new way of doing things.

In the 1960s, companies did not have a fast, reliable, and cost-effective way to deliver urgent documents or packages to each other. The standard mail system was slow but inexpensive, and the only alternative was a private courier, which, while faster, was prohibitively expensive. That's when Frederick W. Smith came up with the idea of a national, overnight delivery service as a part of an assignment in his undergraduate economics class at Yale University. As the story goes, Smith received only an average grade because evidently his professor wasn't all that impressed with the concept, but after analyzing the problems with the current system, thinking through his original ideas more fully, and refining his business plan, Smith launched FedEx, the largest, now global, overnight delivery service in the world.[1] This isn't a parable about ignoring your professors, but a testimony to thinking through ideas others may not initially support or even understand; thinking can create change and always has. As with Ford's assembly line and Smith's overnight delivery service, any service we now use and any problem we may still face provides thinkers with opportunities to generate solutions and viable options for improvement. Your thinking may result in a new personal service, a cure for cancer, or a revolutionary way to deliver water to developing countries.

7.4 Critical Thinking

Estimated completion time: 18 minutes.

Questions to consider:

- How can determining the situation help you think critically?
- How do you present informed, unbiased thinking?
- What is the difference between factual arguments and opinions?

Critical thinking has become a buzz phrase in education and corporate environments in recent years. The definitions vary slightly, but most agree that thinking critically includes some form of judgement that thinkers generate after careful analysis of the perspectives, opinions, or experimental results present for a particular problem or situation. Before you wonder if you're even capable of critical thinking, consider that you think critically every day. When you grab an unwashed T-shirt off the top of the pile on the floor of your bedroom to wear into class but then suddenly remember that you may see the person of your dreams on that route, you may change into something a bit less disheveled. That's thinking critically—you used data (the memory that

---

1 "Online Extra: Fred Smith on the Birth of FedEx." Bloomberg Business Week. 2004. Retrieved 1/28/20. https://www.bloomberg.com/news/articles/2004-09-19/online-extra-fred-smith-on-the-birth-of-fedex

your potential soul mate walks the same route you use on that day on campus) to change a sartorial decision (dirty shirt for clean shirt), and you will validate your thinking if and when you do have a successful encounter with said soul mate.

Likewise, when you decide to make your lunch rather than just grabbing a bag of chips, you're thinking critically. You have to plan ahead, buy the food, possibly prepare it, arrange to and carry the lunch with you, and you may have various reasons for doing that—making healthier eating choices, saving money for an upcoming trip, or wanting more quiet time to unwind instead of waiting in a crowded lunch line. You are constantly weighing options, consulting data, gathering opinions, making choices, and then evaluating those decisions, which is a general definition of critical thinking.

Consider the following situations and how each one demands your thinking attention. Which do you find most demanding of critical thinking? Why?

1. Participating in competitive athletic events
2. Watching competitive athletic events
3. Reading a novel for pleasure
4. Reading a textbook passage in science

Critical thinking forces you to determine the actual situation under question and to determine your thoughts and actions around that situation.

Determining the Problem

One component to keep in mind to guide your critical thinking is to determine the situation. What problem are you solving? When problems become complex and multifaceted, it is easy to be distracted by the simple parts that may not need as much thinking to resolve but also may not contribute as much to the ultimate problem resolution. What aspect of the situation truly needs your attention and your critical thinking?

Imagine you're planning a fantasy vacation as a group assignment in a class you're taking where each person is allowed only $200. The group doles out specific preliminary tasks to each member to decide where to go, what sort of trip to take, and how to keep costs low, all in the name of a fun fantasy vacation. In this scenario, whose plan demonstrates the most effective critical thinking?

a. DeRhonda creates an elaborate invitation for a dinner party she'll coordinate at an exclusive mountain cabin.
b. Patrick researches cruises, cabin rentals, and staycation options, considering costs for various trip lengths.
c. Rodrigio puts down a deposit for a private dining room for 25 at an expensive local restaurant for a date six weeks from the end of the semester.

Write out what each person's thinking reflects about their expectations for this trip and why their actions may or may not help the group at this stage of the planning.

Critical thinking differs according to the subject you're thinking about, and as such it can be difficult to pin down any sort of formula to make sure you are doing a good job of thinking critically in all situations. While you may need to adapt this list of critical thinking components, you can get started if you do the following:

- Question everything
- Conduct legitimate research
- Limit your assumptions
- Recognize your own biases

- Gather and weigh all options

Additionally, you must recognize that changes will occur and may alter your conclusions now and in the future. You may eventually have to revisit an issue you effectively resolved previously and adapt to changing conditions. Knowing when to do that is another example of critical thinking. Informed flexibility, or knowing that parts of the plan may need to change and how those changes can work into the overall goal, is also a recognized element of thinking critically.

For example, early in the 20th century, many people considered cigarette smoking a relaxing social pastime that didn't have many negative consequences. Some people may still consider smoking a way to relax; however, years of medical research have proven with mounting evidence that smoking causes cancer and exacerbates numerous other medical conditions. Researchers asked questions about the impact of smoking on people's overall health, conducted regulated experiments, tracked smokers' reactions, and concluded that smoking did impact health. Over time, attitudes, evidence, and opinions change, and as a critical thinker, you must continue to research, synthesize newly discovered evidence, and adapt to that new information.

Figure 7.11 Information, attitudes, laws, and acceptance of smoking changed dramatically over time. More recently, vaping and related practices have rekindled debates and launched new research into safety. (Credit: Satish Krishnamurthy / Flickr / Attribution 2.0 Generic (CC-BY 2.0))

Defending against Bias

Once you have all your information gathered and you have checked your sources for currency and validity, you need to direct your attention to how you're going to present your now well-informed analysis. Be careful on this step to recognize your own possible biases. Facts are verifiable; opinions are beliefs without supporting evidence. Stating an opinion is just that. You could say "Blue is the best color," and that's your opinion. If you were to conduct research and find evidence to support this claim, you could say, "Researchers at Oxford University recognize that the use of blue paint in mental hospitals reduces heart rates by 25% and contributes to fewer angry outbursts from patients." This would be an informed analysis with credible evidence to support the claim.

Not everyone will accept your analysis, which can be frustrating. Most people resist change and have firm beliefs on both important issues and less significant preferences. With all the competing information surfacing online, on the news, and in general conversation, you can understand how confusing it can be to make any decisions. Look at all the reliable, valid sources that claim different approaches to be the *best* diet for healthy living: ketogenic, low-carb, vegan, vegetarian, high fat, raw foods, paleo, Mediterranean, etc. All you can do in this sort of situation is conduct your own serious research, check your sources, and write clearly and concisely to provide your analysis of the information for consideration. You cannot force others to accept your stance, but you can show your evidence in support of your thinking, being as persuasive as possible without lapsing into your own personal biases. Then the rest is up to the person reading or viewing your analysis.

Factual Arguments vs. Opinions

Thinking and constructing analyses based on your thinking will bring you in contact with a great deal of information. Some of that information will be factual, and some will not be. You need to be able to distinguish between facts and opinions so you know how to support your arguments. Begin with basic definitions:

- **Fact:** a statement that is true and backed up with evidence; facts can be verified through observation or research
- **Opinion:** a statement someone holds to be true without supporting evidence; opinions express beliefs, assumptions, perceptions, or judgements

Of course, the tricky part is that most people do not label statements as fact and opinion, so you need to be aware and recognize the difference as you go about honing your critical thinking skills.

You probably have heard the old saying "Everyone is entitled to their own opinions," which may be true, but conversely, not everyone is entitled to their own facts. Facts are true for everyone, not just those who want to believe in them. For example, *mice are animals* is a fact; *mice make the best pets* is an opinion.

ACTIVITY

Determine if the following statements are facts or opinions based on just the information provided here, referring to the basic definitions above. Some people consider scientific findings to be opinions even when they are convincingly backed by reputable evidence and experimentation. However, remember the definition of *fact*—verifiable by research or observation. Think about what other research you may have to conduct to make an informed decision.

- Oregon is a state in the United States. (How would this be proven?)
- Beef is made from cattle. (See current legislation concerning vegetarian "burgers.")
- Increased street lighting decreases criminal behavior. (What information would you need to validate this claim?)
- In 1952, Elizabeth became Queen of England. (What documents could validate this?)
- Oatmeal tastes plain. (What factors might play into this claim?)
- Acne is an embarrassing skin condition. (Who might verify this claim?)
- Kindergarten decreases student dropout rates. (Think of different interest groups that may take sides on this issue.)
- Carbohydrates promote weight gain. (Can you determine if this is a valid statement?)
- Cell phones cause brain tumors. (What research considers this claim?)

> • Immigration is good for the US economy. (What research would help you make an informed decision on this topic?)

Many people become very attached to their opinions, even stating them as facts despite the lack of verifiable evidence. Think about political campaigns, sporting rivalries, musical preferences, and religious or philosophical beliefs. When you are reading, writing, and thinking critically, you must be on the lookout for sophisticated opinions others may present as factual information. While it's possible to be polite when questioning another person's opinions when engaging in intellectual debate, thinking critically requires that you do conduct this questioning.

For instance, someone may say or write that a particular political party should move its offices to different cities every year—that's an opinion regardless of whether you side with one party or the other. If, on the other hand, the same person said that one political party is headquartered in a specific city, that is a fact you can verify. You could find sources that can validate or discredit the statement. Even if the city the person lists as the party headquarters is incorrect, the statement itself is still a fact—just an erroneous one. If you use biased and opinionated information or even incorrect facts as your evidence to support your factual arguments, then you have not validated your sources or checked your facts well enough. At this point, you would need to keep researching.

7.5 Problem-Solving

Estimated completion time: 12 minutes.

Questions to consider:

- How can determining the best approach to solve a problem help you generate solutions?
- Why do thinkers create multiple solutions to problems?

When we're solving a problem, whether at work, school, or home, we are being asked to perform multiple, often complex, tasks. The most effective problem-solving approach includes some variation of the following steps:

- Determine the issue(s)
- Recognize other perspectives
- Think of multiple possible results
- Research and evaluate the possibilities
- Select the best result(s)
- Communicate your findings
- Establish logical action items based on your analysis

Determining the best approach to any given problem and generating more than one possible solution to the problem constitutes the complicated process of problem-solving. People who are good at these skills are highly marketable because many jobs consist of a series of problems that need to be solved for production, services, goods, and sales to continue smoothly. Think about what happens when a worker at your favorite coffee shop slips on a wet spot behind the counter, dropping several drinks she just prepared. One problem is the employee may be hurt, in need of attention, and probably embarrassed; another problem is that several customers do not have the drinks they were waiting for; and another problem is that stopping production of drinks (to care for the hurt worker, to clean up her spilled drinks, to make new drinks) causes the line at the cash register to back up. A good manager has to juggle all of these elements to resolve the situation as quickly and efficiently as possible. That resolution and return to standard operations doesn't happen without a great deal of thinking: prioritizing needs, shifting other workers off one station onto another temporarily, and dealing with all the people involved, from the injured worker to the impatient patrons.

Determining the Best Approach

Faced with a problem-solving opportunity, you must assess the skills you will need to create solutions. Problem-solving can involve many different types of thinking. You may have to call on your creative, analytical, or critical thinking skills—or more frequently, a combination of several different types of thinking—to solve a problem satisfactorily. When you approach a situation, how can you decide what is the best type of thinking to employ? Sometimes the answer is obvious; if you are working a scientific challenge, you likely will use analytical thinking; if you are a design student considering the atmosphere of a home, you may need to tap into creative thinking skills; and if you are an early childhood education major outlining the logistics involved in establishing a summer day camp for children, you may need a combination of critical, analytical, and creative thinking to solve this challenge.

ACTIVITY

What sort of thinking do you imagine initially helped in the following scenarios? How would the other types of thinking come into resolving these problems?

1. Mission Control reacting to the Apollo 13 emergency
   a. Analytical thinking
   b. Creative thinking
   c. Critical thinking
2. Automakers coordinating the switch from fuel-based to electric cars
   a. Analytical thinking
   b. Creative thinking
   c. Critical thinking
3. The construction of the New York subway system
   a. Analytical thinking
   b. Creative thinking
   c. Critical thinking

Write a one- to two-sentence rationale for why you chose the answers you did on the above survey.

Generating Multiple Solutions

Why do you think it is important to provide multiple solutions when you're going through the steps to solve problems? Typically, you'll end up only using one solution at a time, so why expend the extra energy to create alternatives? If you planned a wonderful trip to Europe and had all the sites you want to see planned out and reservations made, you would think that your problem-solving and organizational skills had quite a workout. But what if when you arrived, the country you're visiting is enmeshed in a public transportation strike experts predict will last several weeks if not longer? A back-up plan would have helped you contemplate alternatives you could substitute for the original plans. You certainly cannot predict every possible contingency—sick children, weather delays, economic downfalls—but you can be prepared for unexpected issues to come up and adapt more easily if you plan for multiple solutions.

Write out at least two possible solutions to these dilemmas:

- Your significant other wants a birthday present—you have no cash.
- You have three exams scheduled on a day when you also need to work.
- Your car needs new tires, an oil change, and gas—you have no cash. (Is there a trend here?)
- You have to pass a running test for your physical education class, but you're out of shape.

Providing more than one solution to a problem gives people options. You may not need several options, but having more than one solution will allow you to feel more in control and part of the problem-solving process.

7.6 Metacognition

Estimated completion time: 19 minutes.

Questions to consider:

- How can you become more aware of your own thinking?
- What is the benefit of thinkers using their thoughts deliberately?

For many of us, it was in kindergarten or first grade when our teacher asked our class to "put on our thinking caps." That may partially have been a clever way for a harried teacher to get young scholars to calm down and focus, but the idea is an apt depiction of how we think. Depending on the situation, we may have to don several very different caps to do our best thinking. Knowing which cap to wear in which situation so we are most prepared, effective, and efficient becomes the work of a lifetime. When you can handle more than one complex thought at a time or when you need to direct all your focus on one crucial task is highly individual. Some people study well with music on in the background while others need absolute silence and see any noise as a distraction. Many chefs delight in creating dinners for hundreds of people in a chaotic kitchen but don't care for making a meal for two at home.

When an individual thinks about how he or she thinks, this practice is called *metacognition*. Developmental psychiatrist John Flavell coined the term metacognition and divided the theory into three processes of planning, tracking, and assessing your own understanding.[2]

> **"Becoming aware of your thought processes and using this awareness deliberately is a sign of mature thinking."**

For example, you may be reading a difficult passage in a textbook on chemistry and recognize that you are not fully understanding the meaning of the section you just read or its connection to the rest of the chapter. Students use metacognition when they practice self-awareness and self-assessment. You are the best judge of how well you know a topic or a skill. In college especially, thinking about your thinking is crucial so you know what you don't know and how to fix this problem, i.e., what you need to study, how you need to organize your calendar, and so on.

If you stop and recognize this challenge with the aim of improving your comprehension, you are practicing

---

2 Flavell, J. H. (1976). Metacognitive aspects of problem solving. In L. B. Resnick (Ed.), The nature of intelligence (pp. 231–236). Hillsdale, NJ: Erlbaum

metacognition. You may decide to highlight difficult terms to look up, write a summary of each paragraph in as few sentences as you can, or join a peer study group to work on your comprehension. If you know you retain material better if you hear it, you may read out loud or watch video tutorials covering the material. These are all examples of thinking about how you think and adapting your behavior based on this metacognition. Likewise, if you periodically assess your progress toward a goal, such as when you check your grades in a course every few weeks during a long semester so you know how well you are doing, this too is metacognition.

Beyond just being a good idea, thinking about your own thinking process allows you to reap great benefits from becoming more aware of and deliberate with your thoughts. If you know how you react in a specific thinking or learning situation, you have a better chance to improve how well you think or to change your thoughts altogether by tuning into your reaction and your thinking. You can plan how to move forward because you recognize that the way you think about a task or idea makes a difference in what you do with that thought. The famous Greek philosopher Socrates allegedly said, "The unexamined life isn't worth living." Examine your thoughts and be aware of them.

Becoming Aware of Your Thinking

Just as elite athletes watch game footage and work with coaches to improve specific aspects of their athletic performance, students can improve their mindset and performance reliant upon their thinking by starting to be aware of what they think. If a baseball pitcher recognizes that the curveball that once was so successful in producing strikeouts has not worked as well recently, the pitcher may break down every step of the physical movement required for the once-successful pitch. He and his coaches may notice a slight difference they can remedy during practice to improve the pitche

Figure 7.12 Baseball pitchers and coaches analyze every component of their motion using video and other technology. (Credit: West Point, The US Military Academy / Flickr / Attribution 2.0 Generic (CC-BY 2.0))

Likewise, if Shamika, for instance, wants to be more generally optimistic and not dwell on negative thoughts, she may ask her friends to mention every time she adds a negative post on social media. Shamika may go even further by stopping herself when she says something that is not in line with her new, optimistic mindset. She could jot down the instance in a journal and capture her feelings at the time so that later she could analyze or think through why she was negative at that time. If you procrastinate on assignments, you may ask a friend to be your accountability buddy to help keep you on track. Thinking about how to focus on the positive, in Shamika's case, or avoid procrastination doesn't magically change the situation. It does, however, allow the owner of the thought to contemplate alternatives instead of becoming frustrated or mindlessly continuing to sabotage sincere goals. Think now of a personal example of a habit you may want to change, such as smoking, or an attribute such as patience or perseverance you may want to improve in yourself. Can you determine what steps you may need to undertake to change this habit or to develop a stronger awareness of the need to change?

Using Thought Deliberately

If you need to plan, track, and assess your understanding to engage in metacognition, what strategies do you need to employ? Students can use metacognition strategies before, during, and after reading, lectures, assignments, and group work.

Planning

Students can plan and get ready to learn by asking questions such as:

- What am I supposed to learn in this situation?
- What do I already know that might help me learn this information?
- How should I start to get the most out of this situation?
- What should I be looking for and anticipating as I read or study or listen?

As part of this planning stage, students may want to jot down the answers to some of the questions they considered while preparing to study. If the task is a writing assignment, prewriting is particularly helpful just to get your ideas down on paper. You may want to start an outline of ideas you think you may encounter in the upcoming session; it probably won't be complete until you learn more, but it can be a place to start.

Tracking

Students can keep up with their learning or track their progress by asking themselves:

- How am I doing so far?
- What information is important in each section?
- Should I slow down my pace to understand the difficult parts more fully?
- What information should I review now or mark for later review?

In this part of metacognition, students may want to step away from a reading selection and write a summary paragraph on what the passage was about without looking at the text. Another way to track your learning progress is to review lecture or lab notes within a few hours of the initial note-taking session. This allows you to have a fresh memory of the information and fill in gaps you may need to research more fully.

Assessing

Students can assess their learning by asking themselves:

- How well do I understand this material?
- What else can I do to understand the information better?
- Is there any element of the task I don't get yet?
- What do I need to do now to understand the information more fully?
- How can I adjust how I study (or read or listen or perform) to get better results moving forward?

Looking back at how you did on assignments, tests, and reading selections isn't just a means to getting a better grade the next time, even if that does sometimes happen as a result of this sort of reflection. If you rework the math problems you missed on a quiz and figure out what went wrong the first time, you will understand that mathematical concept better than if you ignore the opportunity to learn from your errors. Learning is not a linear process; you will bring knowledge from other parts of your life and from your reading to understand something new in your academic or personal learning for the rest of your life. Using these planning, tracking, and assessing strategies will help you progress as a learner in all subjects.

Have you ever been in a situation where a series of events transpired that on reflection you wish you had handled differently? For instance, what if you were tired after a long day at work or school and snapped at your roommates over an insignificant problem and that heated exchange ruined your weekend plans? You'd been anticipating a fun outing with a large group, but now several people don't want to go because of the increased tension. Afterwards, you come up with several other ways you wish you had acted—you might have explained how tired you were, ignored the irritation, or even asked if you could continue your discussion of the problem at another time when you were less tired. You could call that wish metacognition after the fact. How much more effective could you be in general if instead of *reacting* to events and then contemplating better alternatives later, you were able to do the thinking *proactively* before the situation arises? Just the act of pausing to think through the potential consequences is a good first step to accomplishing the goal of using metacognition to reduce negative results. Can you think of a situation in which you reacted to events around you with less than ideal results? How about a time when you thought through a situation beforehand and reaped the benefits of this proactive approach?

Let's look at two seemingly ordinary examples of this concept. Think about your reaction and the eventual long- and short-term results of you walking into your math class on Tuesday afternoon to recall only then that you have a major closed-book exam that class session. You look around to see nervous classmates reading notecards or working practice problems. You choose to stay and take the exam wholly unprepared. You end up with a low D on the exam and now must contemplate the consequences of that result.

Figure 7.13 Self-awareness and self-assessment are critical in preparing for tests. (Credit: Magharebia / Flickr / Attribution 2.0 Generic (CC-BY 2.0))

Scoring such a low exam grade may not be the end of the world, certainly, but you may not maintain the GPA you had hoped to post, you may need to repeat the course, or you may get further behind in this subject because you didn't master the skills on this test. This is quite a bit of awareness about your thinking. Now you need to decide what actions to take as a result of your self-awareness thinking. Contemplating this negative consequence may lead you to make an appointment with your instructor to discuss your situation, which is always a good idea. Could you take an alternate exam to replace this atypical low score? Even if the answer is no, you have still made a connection and shown your instructor that you are seriously thinking about your coursework.

Now consider the opposite scenario. What if you had entered your exam schedule onto your calendar beforehand and devised a viable plan to be prepared? You likely would have prepared in advance of exam days, studied the required materials, worked through similar problems, and come to the exam session more prepared than you did in the first example. Because you know you need a set amount of time to prepare for exams, you would have blocked that time on your calendar, possibly changing your work schedule for the week, declining social invitations, and otherwise altering your daily routine to accommodate this significant event. Consider how much better your results would be with this amount of preparation and how this would improve your overall performance in the course. You can take advantage of thinking about consequences before they happen so you can employ specific strategies to improve your learning.

7.7 Information Literacy

Estimated completion time: 23 minutes.

Questions to consider:

- How do you go about verifying source validity, and why is this important?
- How do you use resources to improve your thinking?
- Where do you go to find print and online resources?

What type of system best helps you to manage your resources?

When conducting any type of thinking, you need to have a firm grasp on *information literacy*, or knowing how to access the sources you may need. Practicing good information literacy skills involves more than simply using a search engine such as Google, although that could be a starting point. You also engage in creative thinking (i.e., generating topics to research), analytical thinking (i.e., reading and examining the parts of sources), and critical thinking (i.e., evaluating sources for accuracy, authority, etc.). Then there is synthesis that is used when incorporating multiple sources into a research project. Information literacy utilizes all of the necessary thinking skills. If you saw the name of a person on the cover of a magazine, for instance, you might assume the person did something important to merit the attention. If you were to google the person's name, you would instantly need to use context clues to determine if the information your search produced is actually about your person and not someone else with the same or a similar name, whether the information is accurate, and if it is current. If it is not, you would need to continue your research with other sources.

Verifying Source Validity

The American Library Association defines information literacy as a set of skills that allow you to "recognize when information is needed and have the ability to locate, evaluate, and use effectively the needed information."[3] We need information almost all the time, and with practice, you'll become more and more

---

3 "Information Literacy." American Library Association. Accessed February 1, 2020. https://literacy.ala.org/information-literacy/

efficient at knowing where to look for answers on certain topics. As information is increasingly available in multiple formats, not only in print and online versions but also through audio and visual means, users of this information must employ critical thinking skills to sift through it all.

In today's information environment, what would be the best way to find valid information about climate change? Would it be Wikipedia, NASA, a printed encyclopedia from 1985, or a report from a political campaign?

If you chose any answer except the NASA website, can you see how the other answers may have a vested interest in encouraging readers to believe a particular theory? The encyclopedia may not intentionally attempt to mislead readers; however, the write-up is not current. And Wikipedia, being an open-source site where anyone may upload information, is not reliable enough to lend full credence to the articles. A professional, government organization that does not sell items related to the topic and provides its ethics policy for review is worthy of more consideration and research. This level of critical thinking and examined consideration is the only way to ensure you have all the information you need to make decisions.

You likely know how to find some sources when you conduct research. And remember—we think and research all the time, not just in school or on the job. If you're out with friends and someone asks where to find the best Italian food, someone will probably consult a phone app to present choices. This quick phone search may suffice to provide an address, hours, and possibly even menu choices, but you'll have to dig more deeply if you want to evaluate the restaurant by finding reviews, negative press, or personal testimonies.

Why is it important to verify sources? The words we write (or speak) and the sources we use to back up our ideas need to be true and honest, or we would not have any basis for distinguishing facts from opinions that may be, at the least damaging level, only uninformed musings but, at the worst level, intentionally misleading and distorted versions of the truth. Maintaining a strict adherence to verifiable facts is a hallmark of a strong thinker.

You probably see information presented as fact on social media daily, but as a critical thinker, you must practice validating facts, especially if something you see or read in a post conveniently fits your perception. You may be familiar with the Facebook and Instagram hoaxes requiring users to copy and paste a statement that they will not grant permission for these social media sites to make public the content from their private pages. Maybe you've seen any number of posts and memes that inaccurately associate famous people with memorable quotations. We may even allow ourselves to believe inaccurate claims as truth when we experience different emotions including anger, fear, or loneliness; we want to believe a claim is true because it aligns with how we are feeling, regardless of any verifiable source. Be diligent in your critical thinking to avoid misinformation!

Determining how valid a source is typically includes looking into the author's credentials, experience, and status in the discipline; the actual content of the source material; any evidence the source presents as support; and whether any biases exist that may make the source questionable. Once you know who controls the content of the source you've chosen, you need to determine what biases or special interests the site or article may exhibit.

ACTIVITY

Reflect on what bias the following sites may have. Without consulting the Internet, write one to two

> sentences on what ideas the following organizations may present. After you consider these on your own, conduct a search and see if you were accurate in your assumptions about the entities.
>
> a. National Dairy Council
> b. Yoga Society
> c. People for the Ethical Treatment of Animals (PETA)
> d. The American Medical Association

Whatever you write or declare based on sources should be correct and truthful. Reliable sources present current and honest information backed up with evidence you can check. Any source that essentially says you should believe this "because I said so" isn't a valid source for critically thinking, information-literate individuals.

Evaluating books, articles, and websites for validity presents different challenges. For books and scholarly articles, in print or online, you can typically establish if the source is current and from a reputable publisher or organization with information on the copyright page or journal publication information.

> | About | Articles | Submission Guidelines |
>
> Original research | Open Access | Published: 09 December 2019
>
> # Fuel dynamics and reburn severity following high-severity fire in a Sierra Nevada, USA, mixed-conifer forest
>
> Jamie M. Lydersen ✉, Brandon M. Collins, Michelle Coppoletta, Melissa R. Jaffe, Hudson Northrop & Scott L. Stephens
>
> *Fire Ecology* **15**, Article number: 43 (2019) | Cite this article
> **551** Accesses | **9** Altmetric | Metrics
>
> ## Abstract
>
> **Background**
> High-severity fire in forested landscapes often produces a post-fire condition of high shrub cover and large loads of dead wood. Given the increasing patch size of high-severity fire and the tendency for these areas to reburn at high severity in subsequent wildfires, post-fire management often targets restoration of these areas. However, these areas are challenging to manage, in part due to limited knowledge of post-fire fuel dynamics over space and time and

Figure 7.14 The most reliable sources of online information may be journals or related research-oriented websites, which include the author names, their credentials, and other data. However, unless they are "peer-reviewed," meaning independent experts have read and verified the quality of the information, even credible-looking sites may be more opinion- than fact-oriented. (Credit: Springer Open. https://fireecology.springeropen.com)

For a website, you should determine who owns this site. Is it a professional organization such as the American Medical Association? You can usually find this info in the *About* section of the site or in a copyright designation near the end of the landing page. Domain names can help you determine the purpose of the site, but you shouldn't rely solely on this website marker.

Domain	User
.edu	Used by **edu**cational institutions (i.e., colleges, universities, school districts); usually reliable sources of information, but individual members of these institutions may be able to create web pages on the site under the official domain that do not reflect the values of the school
.com/.biz	Used by **com**mercial or business groups; may be valid, but also may be used to sell products, services, or ideas

Domain	User
.gov	Used by **gov**ernment agencies; typically valid
.org	Used by **org**anizations, such as nonprofit groups or religious entities; may present information slanted toward a specific denomination or cause. You'll need to conduct additional research to verify validity.
.net	Originally created for networks or groups of people working on the same problem, .net is still a viable option for noncommercial sites such as personal blogs or family websites. You'll need to conduct additional research to verify validity.
Many other domains exist	Research the validity of domain names outside these most common ones.

Resources for Thinking

When you look into books, articles, and documentaries on thinking, you will find plenty of choices. Some books or articles on thinking may seem to apply only to a narrow group of readers, such as entrepreneurs or artists. For example, the audiences for these two books about thinking seem highly selective: Carl Sagan's *The Demon-Haunted World: Science as a Candle in the Dark* may be mostly directed to the science community, and James Lohan's *Lies My Teacher Told Me: Everything Your American History Textbook Taught Wrong* is likely of interest primarily to historians. And some chapters may focus specifically on those groups; however, most texts on thinking are also applicable to other disciplines. You may have to work a bit harder to find a common ground or generate your own examples that explain the concepts from the book, but you can still reap benefits from understanding different perspectives. Don't immediately disregard a book or article just because it doesn't seem to fit your thinking perspective on the surface; dig a bit more deeply to see what you can learn. Remember, being open-minded and considering as many alternate approaches as possible are two hallmarks of critical thinking.

Finding Print and Online Resources

When you need to research a topic, you probably start with a search engine. That can be helpful, but can easily lead you down incorrect paths and waste time. Use advanced searches, filters, and other means to target your results more specifically. However, don't limit yourself to just Internet sources; print journals, books, and articles are still significant sources of information.

Your college may have access to extensive stores of subscription-based site content, photos, videos, and other media through its library, providing more than enough information to start researching and analyzing any topic. Depending on the specific database and school, you may be able to access some of these resources remotely; others may require you to visit the library in person. Remember, when you are gathering and arranging pieces of information, keep track of the source and the URL so that you can both cite it correctly and return to learn more if needed.

Some other more general places to explore educational, inspirational, and thought-provoking material follow:

- Exploring the TED website (http://www.ted.com) is worth a few minutes of time. There you'll find short videos (limited to 18 minutes) of speaking demonstrations by diverse experts in fields covering all disciplines. If you are in an exploratory phase of your thinking and researching, you can scan the TED Talk topics related to your interest area.
- You may be familiar with the Khan Academy, created in 2008 by Salman Khan, as an online learning resource for students and teachers containing tutorials, videos, and practice sets in a variety of subjects from science and mathematics to grammar lessons.
- Massive Open Online Courses (MOOCs) provided by Coursera, Udemy, and Udacity, provide learners and thinkers the chance to take courses, attend webinars and discussions, and learn about a large number of subjects, often free of charge. Much of the content is provided by major universities, and the courses are often facilitated by faculty.
- For-profit companies and nonprofit groups such as the Foundation for Critical Thinking (FCT) can also help you hone your thinking. The FCT presents materials, seminars, and conferences to help people think with "clarity, relevance, logic, accuracy, depth, significance, precision, breadth, and fairness."

Creating a System for Managing Resources

You could have all the money (or time or cars or great ideas) in the world, but that won't do you any good if you haven't also created a system for managing all your resources. In the same way you might feel overwhelmed with all the choices when a waiter gives you a book-sized menu with hundreds of options, you can stall your thinking if you don't have an effective and efficient way to access all the great articles, websites, books, podcasts, webinars, and other idea resources you can amass for the life of a project or during a college course or for a life event.

Systems to manage your ideas and thoughts don't need to be elaborate. The best idea-management system is the one that gets used, so you need to be comfortable with what all is involved in managing these thoughts. Keep in mind, once you get into the swing of researching for and keeping good ideas, you're going to end up with resources in many different formats. Gone are the days when one shelf of an oak bookcase near your desk could contain all your thinking resources on a topic. You may still find books, so you don't need to discard the bookcase just yet, but very likely, you'll also have online resources including search results, document files, websites, blogs, audio files, videos, and more. You can use filing folders, binders, online folders, boxes, or computer systems to organize your ideas.

A word about stacking papers and clutter: don't. Clutter impedes creativity, steals focus, and represents procrastination. Fight the temptation to allow clutter to overwhelm your projects and workspace. File or trash anything you are not using right at the moment; this daily practice will save you a tremendous amount of time that you could waste looking for papers or articles you saved for later review.

Like physical clutter, a messy online environment can stall productivity and clear thinking. One key to effective information and idea management is a simple, consistent labeling system. Some companies call this a *naming protocol or naming convention,* a standard way all online files, folders, and drives are labeled for easier retrieval and long-term storage. If you don't think through a file name with this forward-looking approach and then you don't access that file for several months, you aren't likely to remember which file is which, and you may end up wasting valuable time opening random files in an attempt to find the one you need. This isn't a very efficient way to operate, and in some work environments would not be acceptable on large-scale and important projects. For example, if you were taking an upper-level literature course studying poetry, and remember you filed an excellent summary of one of the poems a few years earlier in your freshman composition class, you won't be too happy when you have 78 documents called *Notes.* Great idea—lousy document/idea management system.

If your searches will take place on multiple devices--a laptop and a smartphone, for example, you could use a notetaking app such as Evernote, which contains a wealth of organizational tools and has various levels of access. You can access the same note regardless of where you're searching. In the same way, you could even use a series of Google Docs or Sheets, as long as you consider the file naming and organizational conventions mentioned above. For example, if you needed to put together a research paper requiring 20 data sources, you could use a spreadsheet to keep track of the source article name, author, topics, potential data points you plan to use, the source, and the URL. Even if you didn't incorporate everything into the final paper, such a method would save you a lot of time trying to track down small pieces of information. (The sheet would also be a great reference when you write your bibliography.)

Finding print and online sources demands a great deal of time and effort. Understanding how different approaches to thinking are appropriate for various situations as you research will help you be more creative and critical as you identify and verify your sources.

ACTIVITY

Quite literally, all careers need thinkers. Many jobs today expect employees to come up with original ways of doing routine tasks. Nurses may consider a more effective way to convey necessary information about patient care to other members of the medical team. Teachers must reconcile individual student learning needs with the reality of large classrooms. Attorneys think about all the consequences of presenting a client's case in a certain manner. And chefs balance the cost of using the finest ingredients with customer preferences and profit margins.

Any career you can imagine has some amount of thinking involved. The most successful workers in any industry are the ones who think beyond the ordinary limits or expectations established in that profession and create new and improved ways to do ordinary jobs.

Consider the types of thinking required for the jobs in the table below.

Industry	Job Title	Job Descriptions	Thinking type Required
Transportation	Air traffic controller	Regulates air traffic for outgoing and incoming aircraft; responds to emergencies; schedules planes to specific gates to minimize delays	

Industry	Job Title	Job Descriptions	Thinking type Required
Healthcare	Pediatric oncology nurse	Cares for critically ill children; assists doctors in diagnoses, treatment, and examinations; communicates with patients and care providers	
Internet technology	Computer analyst	Maintains computer hardware and software systems; troubleshoots user problems; suggests modifications for improved productivity	
Education	College professor	Teaches, evaluates, and guides post-secondary students through various academic subjects working toward various degrees and certificates	

Career Connection

All professions need thinkers to take good ideas and make them better and to tackle problems that seem unresolvable and make sense of them. No job or career area is exempt from this crucial human resource. Your critical thinking in college will help you succeed in the work you do after your academic journey. Make a list of your top three ideal careers. What types of thinking are required of each? How will your time in college better prepare you for this type of work?

Rethinking

Revisit the questions you answered at the beginning of the chapter, and consider one option you learned in this chapter that might change your answer to one of them.

How do you feel about the ways you think? Take this quick survey to figure it out, ranking questions on a scale of 1–4, 1 meaning "least like me" and 4 meaning "most like me."

a. I understand how to approach problem-solving.
b. I have creative potential.
c. I often think about how I'm learning
d. I know how to find and evaluate valid information.

Where do you go from here?

Thinking isn't something we can turn on and off when we enter or leave a classroom—we think about everything. We may have different strategies and processes for thinking in different environments, but all thinking starts with our own ideas coming into contact with new information and experiences. What would you like to learn more about? Choose topics from the list below, or create your own ideas relative to thinking and research them.

- learning to be a creative thinker
- technological advances in the study of the brain
- thinking and brain trauma
- thinking in leadership roles
- theories of nontraditional learning methods

8 Communicating

Figure 8.1 With so many individuals, subgroups, sections, soloists, sounds, variables, and technologies, an orchestra would be chaotic without someone directing: the conductor. Communication has a similar range of inputs and influences, and can become just as chaotic without direction. You need to be your own conductor and establish control in order to communicate effectively and productively. (Credit: Rob Swyston / Flickr / Attribution 2.0 Generic (CC-BY 2.0))

Chapter Outline

8.1 An Overview of Communication
8.2 Purpose of Communication
8.3 Communication and Technology
8.4 The Context of Communication
8.5 Barriers to Effective Communication

Introduction

Student Survey

How do you communicate? Take this quick survey to figure it out, ranking questions on a scale of 1–4, 1 meaning "least like me" and 4 meaning "most like me." These questions will help you determine how the chapter concepts relate to you right now. As we are introduced to new concepts and practices, it can be informative to reflect on how your understanding changes over time. We'll revisit these questions at the end of the chapter to see whether your feelings have changed.

1. I think my mobile device is effective and appropriate for most communication.
2. I have a good sense of how to communicate in different environments/situations.
3. I listen more than I talk.
4. I have a lot of experience with research projects and essays.

You can also take the Chapter 8 Survey (https://openstax.org/l/collegesurvey08) anonymously online.

STUDENT PROFILE

"My preferred communication methods are face-to-face and email. But no matter the method, clear goals are essential. I have had in-person meetings go terribly wrong and others be wildly successful. The difference: preparation! Have an agenda, possibly sending questions ahead of the meeting so that others have time to think about them or find answers. If you go to a meeting prepared like it is a court case, the victories will come far more than the failures. Have evidence to support your needs and positions.

"Be confident, but also be ready to learn. Communication is speaking *and* listening. Before you enter a conversation, consider the questions you need to ask to reach your goal. Asking what you need to know may open doors to understanding the issue better and finding the best avenue to finding solutions.

"I like emailing because it has the advantage to retain the communication, while allowing time to ponder and proofread a clear and concise response. It is essential to watch the tone of the email (never aggressive, always assertive). Use complete sentences, college-level grammar, a subject heading, and the correct greeting (Dr., Professor, Ms., Mr., Full Name) and closing salutations. Save important emails for your records to remember what was said or decided."

— **Barbara Gooch**, Volunteer State Community College

About This Chapter

> **"The single biggest problem in communication is the illusion that it has taken place."**
>
> — *William H. Whyte*[1]

Communication has always been a complex life skill for everyone. How we pass information to others and how we understand what is being conveyed to us can often be complicated. And today, with the ever-increasing number of communication tools at our fingertips, our need to understand how, when, and what we communicate is even more crucial. Well-honed communication skills can improve all aspects of your life. This is true regarding relationships with friends, significant others, family, acquaintances, people with whom you work, colleagues in your classes, and professors. In other words, everyone! Communication is probably the most important skill you can develop in your life.

By the time you complete this chapter, you should be able to do the following:

- Articulate the variables to communication.
- Define the forms and purpose of communication.
- Understand how technology has changed communication.
- Discuss various contexts of communication.
- Describe barriers to effective communication.

8.1 An Overview of Communication

Estimated completion time: 18 minutes.

---

1 "Is Anybody Listening?" William H. Whyte and the editors of Fortune Magazine. Simon And Schuster. 1952. (Note: Often misattributed.)

Chapter 8 Communicating

Questions to consider:

- Do I think about the ways in which I communicate?
- Do I consider the variables present in every communication method and situation?

> **"We take communication for granted because we do it so frequently, but it's actually a complex process."**
>
> — *Joseph Sommerville*[2]

To begin with, let's look at the following two definitions of communication:

- *A process by which information is exchanged between individuals through a common system of symbols, signs, or behavior.*[3]
- *Communication is giving, receiving or exchanging ideas, information, signals or messages through appropriate media, enabling individuals or groups to persuade, to seek information, to give information or to express emotions.*[4]

These definitions offer an overview of the concept of communication. Within this chapter, however, you will be looking deeper into the "process" of communication and how infinitely complex it really is. To start with, let's take a look at both traditional and the newest forms of communication and see if you can determine rules for each.

ACTIVITY

In your opinion, what are the rules for different forms of communication? List the rules or guidelines related to each communication form listed in the table below. An example of a rule for the telephone might be identifying yourself when you call, in case the person didn't recognize your number.

Form of Communication	Rules for This Form
Face-to-face	
Phone	
Printed letters	
Email	
Texting	
Instant messaging/group chat	
Social media	

Were you able to discern different rules for the various forms of communication? Do you find yourself

---

2 Sommerville, Joseph. *The Five Keys to Interpersonal Success*. 2004.
3 In Merriam-Webster online dictionary: https://www.merriam-webster.com/dictionary/communication
4 Definitions of Communication. Communication Theory.Org. https://www.communicationtheory.org/definitions-of-communication/

following these rules when texting or sending an email or talking to someone face-to-face? These questions are something to consider as we move through this chapter.

Variables of Communication

Technology has created new rules for communication because of the different structures of communication, everything from emoji protocols, to truncated words and spelling, to etiquette and how we form communication networks. AAMOF it is important to understand communication. However, BTAIM, you might think it is a CWOT. FWIW this chapter will help you navigate the myriad ways of communicating. SLAP? *(Meaning of acronyms should be included at bottom of page)* (AAMOF = as a matter of fact, BTAIM = be that as it may, CWOT = complete waste of time, FWIW = for what it's worth, SLAP = sounds like a plan)

Figure 8.2

Although using the acronyms (symbols of communication) above allow us to do more in less space and time, we need to be careful about how we pass information to others as well as think more clearly about what is being communicated to us. Certainly, with the scope of the Internet we are seeing briefer messages, a wider reach, and greater immediacy.

You are aware that the transfer of information can be done vocally—voice, phone, face-to-face, over radio or television. It can come to us in a written format such as correspondence or printed or digital media. We obtain information visually in logos, pictures, maps, menus, and street signs. And, of course, we find ourselves learning things nonverbally by observing body language, tone of voice, gestures, and so forth.

Communication means that there is at least one sender and one recipient, and in between, there is the message. The kind of communication tool you choose to use also has an effect on the message being conveyed. Will you choose a pencil? Pen? Phone? Email? Text? Picture? Or perhaps a face-to-face opportunity? Whatever you choose as your method of communicating with one person or a group of people guides how effectively you send your message. Additionally, there are always emotions behind a message. You could just be sharing a picture of yourself on the beach or sending out a call for help on a class assignment, or perhaps feeling sad because a friend is sick. Each of these would affect how you might communicate.

Have you ever sent a message to someone too quickly? For example, you heard that a friend just broke up with her boyfriend and is terribly heartbroken. You immediately think you should send some kind of "hope you are ok" comment and decide to use Facebook to do so. Later you find out that she didn't want people to know about it at all and you kind of jumped the gun on your condolences. How did you feel? Could you have gone about it in any other way? Perhaps waited until she told you about it herself? A private email or phone call? This is one of those situations where you have to step back for a moment and clarify for yourself that what you are about to send will be received the way you intended. Learning a little about the concept of emotional intelligence (EQ) will also be helpful to your decision about how to communicate in various situations. More on that concept will be discussed in the sections on listening and miscommunication.

Additionally, there are other significant variables that play an important role in communicating. These range from ethnicity to culture to age to gender and are meaningful to what one is trying to "say" to someone else. Unfortunately, sometimes the message is lost or misconstrued because neither the sender nor the receiver has taken into account these important aspects of successful communication. You will learn more about this later in the chapter.

Context of Communication

It is also essential to understand the context of your communication. In other words, to whom are you talking? Why are you talking to this person or people? What, exactly, do you hope to achieve out of the communication you initiate? An effective communicator understands the audience to whom they are trying to send a message. This means that you use the correct venue—face-to-face conversation, phone, email, text, written letter, picture, or whatever else makes the most sense in a particular situation. This way your message can reach your audience (professor, boss, colleague, friend, parent, teammate) in a productive way, and hopefully the message you intend to convey is received accordingly.

An example of context might be the following: you need to ask your professor about a grade you received on an assignment because you think the grade was too low for the work you did. Would it be appropriate for you to send a text asking why you received the grade? Might it be better to give your professor a call and hope she is available to talk with you? Or do you think it could be more useful and productive if you found out the professor's office hours and went in to discuss your concerns in person? These are decisions you have to make carefully so you can make the most of what you are trying to communicate.

Listening

Another aspect of communication is the art of listening. Remember, communication is a two-way street. It is not enough to just send out a message. One has to listen carefully to the response, and not only listen, but understand that the audience receiving your message might have a very different take on the topic. As noted earlier, this could be due to gender, age, culture, and so forth. All of these have an effect on how well the communication is transmitted and received. Later in this chapter we will discuss the difference between just "hearing" the response and actually "listening" to the response. Optimal communication occurs when both parties actively listen. And finally, it comes down to this: communication is any act that involves a sender and at least one receiver, where a message is conveyed and hopefully the message is received correctly.

> **"We all feel better when we feel listened to. And we feel even better when we feel understood. In order to be understood, we must be listened to. Often it is more important to us to feel heard than to actually get what we said we wanted. On the other hand, feeling ignored and misunderstood is literally painful whether we are six or sixty."**[5] — *Steve Hein*

---

5   Hein, Steve. "Listening." Eqi.org. http://eqi.org/listen.htm

Many variables get in the way of messages being received correctly. One of these is emotion—both yours and that of the person with whom you are trying to communicate. Sometimes you have to use emotional information to help you make a decision about how you are communicating. What this means is that you need to be able to understand your own feelings and those of others. There are five components (self-awareness, self-regulation, motivation, empathy, and social skills) to emotional intelligence. Understanding how these components work to help you get in touch with your and others' emotional sides is an important part of listening.

Ultimately, communication is about information. The message you are sending may be as simple as one word (or even one letter), or as complex as an application for an internship. How you act on that information, how you expect others to act on it, and how it becomes knowledge are all part of the complexity of communication.

8.2 Purpose of Communication

Estimated completion time: 8 minutes.

Questions to consider:

- Does everything I say or write have a purpose?
- Do I expect a response or a result from my communication?
- Do I change how I communicate depending on what response I want or need?

> **"The difference between the right word and almost the right word is the difference between lightning and the lightning bug."**
>
> — Mark Twain[6]

Does Everything I Say or Write Have a Purpose?

There are many reasons that communication takes place. Some of our communication might be simply an attempt at being cordial and friendly. For instance, we might like to say hello to a friend down the hall, give a shout-out on Twitter to a family member living in another state, say "excuse me" to someone we've just bumped into, smile at a baby in a stroller going by, post a picture of our birthday party on Facebook, and stop to pet a new puppy in the park. Or maybe we just need some information, such as asking an instructor for guidelines for a project, telling a store owner what we are looking for, or going up to a stranger for directions to the nearest bus stop. As you can see, almost everything we do on a daily basis has something to do with communication. Additionally, we can communicate the same information to a wide range of people, and how this is received can vary greatly.

Another important purpose of communication is to forge relationships, whether these are of short or long duration or for particular purposes. What kind of relationships do you hope to develop when using various forms of communication? Are you looking for a partner for a project, or perhaps a date for the football game, or just want to nurture the relationships you have with friends already? The impact of flawed communication on relationships can be long-lasting, so it is important to be thoughtful when posting your thoughts and ideas.

---

6   The Art of Authorship: Literary Reminiscences, Methods of Work, and Advice to Young Beginners, Compiled and edited by George Bainton. 1890. Section: Mark Twain

Do I Expect a Response or a Result From My Communication?

There are times we are just sending out messages or information and not expecting a response, except perhaps a "like." For instance, your friend posts a picture of her new dog on Instagram and you click on "like." Other times we try to communicate an idea or ask a question and we do want a response, such as "What time is the exam on Friday?" This response is possibly from one person or many. There are instances when you need information, and you will either ask someone, do some web searching, or make a phone call to get the information that you need. Depending on what your need is, you must consider what form of communication will work best and get you the most satisfactory results. Your purpose for communicating is to get some kind of reply.

What Do I Bring to My Communication With Others?

You probably haven't thought of this, but whether you actively communicate or not, you are still communicating. Your facial expressions, body language, what you are wearing, your hairstyle, body art, where you choose to sit or stand in a room, the people you associate with, eye contact or lack thereof, and any other mannerisms that you have are a form of communication. We all pick up signals from each other in these nonverbal ways. So even though you might be shy, or reserved, or not interested in any interaction at all, you are still communicating some information to others.

8.3 Communication and Technology

Estimated completion time: 28 minutes.

Questions to Consider:

- Is technology vital to your ability to communicate well?
- Are there rules to follow when using communication technology?
- How do you take control of your online communication?

> **"Now we know that once computers connected us to each other, once we became tethered to the network, we really didn't need to keep computers busy. They keep us busy."**
>
> — *Sherry Turkle*[7]

Is Technology Vital to Your Ability to Communicate Well?

Over a billion people use chat rooms, mailing lists, instant messengers, social network services, newsgroups, games, wikis, blogs, and more in order to share social relationships and organize collective action. Everything is connected: people, information, events, and places, all the more so with the advent of online social media. You live in a world where the traditional forms of education, conversations, relationships, and social activity in general have been transformed by the ubiquitous presence of technology. Digital media affects every student's life and that of their families, friends, and the wider community. Most of you have grown up while this transformation has taken place. The new technologies have created dramatic changes in the relationship between people and information. Though you will come across people who don't want to believe that these new technologies are here to stay, we, as humans, will never be able to separate ourselves from our own

---

7   Turkle, Sherry. *Alone Together.* New York: Basic Books. 2011.

inventions, and trying to do so is perhaps only a step backward in an evolutionary sense. Therefore it is important that we learn to adapt our behavior to include the new inventions. Technology, after all, is an extension of the human mind, and the new technologies are only tools we have created over years of fashioning new ways to do things.

We continue to move from simple to complex tools. Advancements of technology go hand in hand with changes in communication options. The telegraph was replaced with landlines, those went out of style as the cordless phone became available, and this phone eventually morphed to a cell phone. When the Internet became accessible by cell phone, cell phones became devices that revolutionized personal communication.

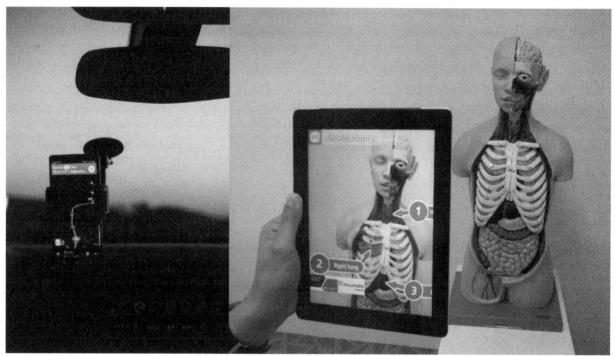

Figure 8.3 Just as mobile device roadmaps have replaced paper ones, augmented reality may replace our typical means interacting with the world. From learning about anatomy to cooking a meal to assembling a child's toy, we may reach a point in which we can't imagine living without AR. (Credit Zedinteractive / Pixabay)

The following activity is a good way for you to reflect on your own use of technology. It is always interesting to step back and actually see what platforms you use and how much time you spend using them.

ACTIVITY

Share your personal story about when you started using social media. Include what social media you use, how you use it, and how much time you spend doing so. At the end of this story, discuss what you might like to see in the future of social media. What other communication technologies do you wish were available to you, and why?

Are There Rules to Follow When Using Communication Technology?

Did you find anything significant about how you use social media? When you carefully looked at how much time you spent on the different platforms, were you surprised? It is probably a good thing to sometimes step back and take a look at how we use our communication tools, and even more importantly, we need to ask ourselves if we are using them to our advantage and not just to pass the time.

Netiquette

Just as it is important to know your responsibilities in using communication technologies, it is necessary for you to understand that there is a code of honor and etiquette to go along with them.

Here are a few pointers on how to go about being active on the Internet without offending or annoying others.

1. Don't write emails, post to social media sites, or talk in chat rooms in ALL CAPS. CAPS can be interpreted as screaming or talking in a very loud voice.
2. Don't make fun of others.
3. Apologize if someone was offended and did not "hear" what you were saying in the way you meant it.
4. When stating a strong opinion, it is not a bad idea to use the abbreviation of IMHO (in my humble opinion). It might keep people from reacting strongly right back at you.
5. Remember, no one can hear your tone of voice or see your facial expression, so use words carefully to get your message across.
6. Be respectful of your audience with the level of familiarity used.

College Netiquette

While these Netiquette guidelines are applicable in nearly every environment, communication in college may have additional or more stringent rules to consider. Always be particularly mindful of how you communicate in any official environments, such as online courses, course discussion boards, and even on social media specifically related to your college, such as a club or team page.

For example, if your political science class requires students to post in a discussion forum after each night's reading, students may have the opportunity to argue about issues or politics. Vibrant discussion, and even argument, may be acceptable, but personal attacks or insults won't advance the discussion and could result in more significant consequences. Just as you wouldn't—and couldn't—become overly animated in an in-class argument, online arguments should remain civil. The goal is to make your points with evidence and reason, not emotion and assertiveness.

Finally, just as a note of caution, college codes of conduct regarding communication often apply to *any* interaction between members of the community, whether or not they occur on campus or in a campus online environment. Any inappropriate, offensive, or threatening comments or messages may have severe consequences.

Our communication in college conveys how we feel about others and how we'd like to interact with them. Unless you know for certain they don't like it, you should use professional or semi-formal communication when interacting with college faculty and staff. For example, if you need to send a message explaining something or making a request, the recipient will likely respond more favorably to it if you address them properly and use thoughtful, complete sentences.

In a similar manner, you can make or break relationships with your classmates depending on how you communicate with them. Consider the following scenario:

Demetrius sends an email to several classmates about the details of a group assignment. He asks about availability and about which member of the group will take responsibility for which aspect of the project. He's received four responses addressing availability, but no one volunteers for the responsibilities. Demetrius replies to all with an attempt at creating a division of responsibilities by typing different names next to each role. He uses ALL CAPS to make sure his classmates notice the suggestions. Lee responds immediately. They don't like being forced into a specific role, and think Demetrius should have waited until the first group session instead of forcing his opinion on the group. Shirisha jumps in to mention that she's upset Demetrius chose to put her in a non-speaking role of recording secretary.

What mistake did Demetrius make? How might he have handled the situation more smoothly?

ACTIVITY

You most likely have considerable experience on a variety of social media platforms. Can you add three more suggestions for how to navigate these sites politely and with consideration for others?

Now, add three suggestions specifically related to considerate communication in online educational environments.

How Do You Control Your Online Communication Strategies?

> **"Whether digital media will be beneficial or destructive in the long run doesn't depend on the technologies, but on the literacy of those who use them."**
>
> — Howard Rheingold

What is important is that we have to decide what we are going to do with the new communication tools for our future. We need to understand when to log on and when to log off. These days you sometimes find yourself being bombarded with new technologies and social media platforms, and you don't know how you will keep up with them all. You have multiple sites sending you continuous notifications and find yourself scrambling to look at them and perhaps respond. Perhaps turning off those notifications will free up your mind a bit. Sitting at your desk in your dorm room and trying to do an assignment for a class can be difficult if your phone is blinking messages at you continuously.

It is probably important sometimes to take the focus away from the media itself and look at oneself. What is happening to our minds, our sense of self, and our ways of representing ourselves to others when we spend a significant portion of our time on various online sites? How do we mediate our relationships differently? What kinds of signals do we send, knowingly and unknowingly? Are we shaping the media we use, or is it shaping us? Sometimes we hide behind our on-screen identities as well as navigate social media sites in ways that make us communicate with people that are like ourselves. Do we use these new communication tools appropriately?

The following activity might help clarify how well you utilize your social media platforms.

ANALYSIS QUESTION

Go outside your usual comfort zone and friend group. Find someone with whom you disagree, and think about how what they said had an effect on you. Did they use correct etiquette when saying what they said? If you respond, what would you do to make certain your response was heard correctly and was not offensive?

Ways to Take Control of Your Online Communication

Howard Rheingold, a technology guru who coined the term "virtual community" in 1993, has been thinking and writing about the changes that technology has been making over the years. He has come to the opinion that in order for us to deal with the new communication opportunities, we must learn about what he calls "mindful participation."[8] Rheingold doesn't suggest, as many others do, that these new technologies are bad for us. He offers ways to engage online that keep us in control of our actions and make us a bit more productive about our use of online platforms. He believes in social media literacy and suggests that learning the following five literacies will make our life on the Internet more productive, less stressful, and ultimately more enjoyable. If social media is our most often used form of communication, then the following five literacies should help us manage our time online and keep us in control of the tools we use for purposes of communication.

---

8 Rheingold, Howard. *Net Smart: How to Thrive Online*. Cambridge: MIT Press. 2012.

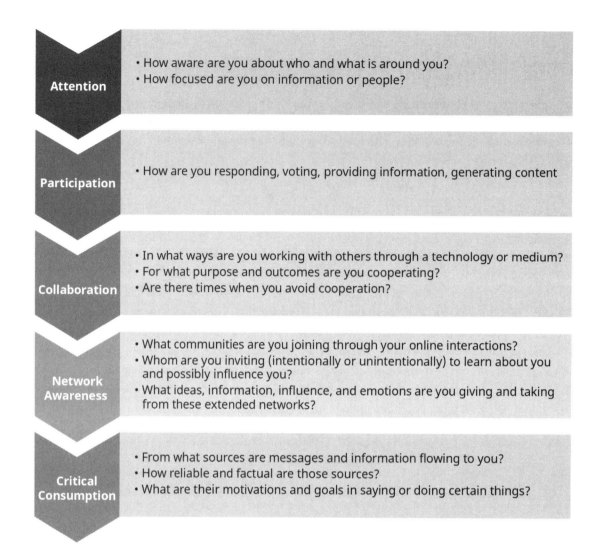

Figure 8.4 Howard Rheingold explores ways we can consider our use and consumption of media technologies, such as social media, in terms of five literacy areas. Asking ourselves questions will lead us to thoughtfully consider how an online environment may be changing us and our relationships. (Credit: Modification of work by Howard Rheingold.)

Attention

Attention is the first literacy and is the fundamental building block of how individuals think. It is sometimes difficult to focus our attention since our minds tend to wander in a random manner. It is therefore essential that you become more aware of how you are directing your attention. Consider being in a lecture hall and trying to focus on the professor and what she is saying. Is your full attention there? Are you also scrolling through some social media feed while listening to the lecture? When you are in your dorm room working on a class assignment, are you also watching your social media notifications, listening to music, talking to your roommate, and clicking on various ads on a website? On what is your attention most focused? Probably on everything and consequently on nothing. Learning how to pay attention to what is most important at the moment will help you fine-tune your skills.

Figure 8.5 Paying attention in class, in the face of many distractions, takes effort and awareness. The benefits, both for the class and for the long-term ability to retain your focus, will be extremely valuable. (Credit: Pixabay / Pexels)

Participation

And even though you might be really good at using online applications and connecting with friends, that does not necessarily mean that you always understand the implications of your participation or that you are actually participating.

Participation, the next literacy, is much broader as it recognizes the vast population of users that are connected. Participation is connecting with the tool, not people. It is a way of becoming an active citizen and not just a passive consumer. There are multiple ways to participate on a variety of social media platforms. In fact, you probably don't realize that clicking on a "like," making a short comment on a picture, or whatever else one does on a site is actually participating. Of course, the effect of your participation can vary, but it can also be very powerful. You participate when you post, fill out a survey, start your own blog, respond to others' blogs, or just watch a video on YouTube. All of these actions are a form of participation.

In college, participation with communication environments and other resources is often essential for success and for your grade. If you use learning management systems, online homework systems, polling or attendance software, or other educational media, you need to understand the levels and types of participation, as well as the implications of each. As with social media platforms, learning technology can be a powerful tool, and you'll likely engage with it throughout your academic and even your professional career.

Collaboration

The third literacy, **collaboration**, refers to your being able to work together using technology. Doing things together gives us more power than doing them alone. Think of all the times Twitter was used by multitudes of people to pass on information about major storms. When there was a bombing in Paris, people went to Twitter to let those people in the streets who'd been displaced know they had apartments and homes that they would open up to them. Of course, there are many collective intelligence projects, such as helping Coke come up with a new flavor, or GoFundMe sites to help people in need of money for health reasons. The collaborative efforts of people communicating around a big project are endless and a perfect way to use communication technologies. Tools allowing collaboration allow you to share resources and work as a team, and build on each other's ideas.

ACTIVITY

Think of a time when you collaborated with others to get something done. This could be organizing a party, planning transportation to an event, doing a school project, building a stage for a play, or any other activity that was done as a group. What forms of communication did you use to work as a team? How did the environment and the other people in the group influence tools and methods you used? Complete the table below to illustrate the challenges, opportunities, and communication approaches you might use (or have used) for each situation.

	Challenges	Opportunities	Communication Methods and Tools
Group project for an on campus (traditional) course.			
Group project for an online-only course.			
Planning an event with your extended family.			
Planning an event with your friends/peers.			

Table 8.1

Network Awareness

Network awareness is the fourth literacy. Technological networks now allow us to have a greater number of people we can contact. These networks multiply human capacity for social networking and allow connection in a matter of seconds. You can become a member of newsgroups, virtual communities, gossip sites, forums, and other organizations. Making use of these possibilities expands your ability to contribute to the vast stores of information on the Internet. At the same time, you should be conscious of the people whom you're inviting to hear you and influence you. Have you ever been intrigued, angered, or persuaded by a friend of a friend (someone you don't know at all) who commented on a social media posting? If so, you are in a relationship with that stranger, and they are affecting you.

Figure 8.6 Do you follow influencers? What is their impact on you? (Credit: The Lazy Artist / Pexels)

Critical Consumption

The last literacy, critical consumption, helps us to discern what is true and what is not. We have to learn how to differentiate fact from fiction. Humans have a difficult time trusting people in everyday life; this also translates to the millions of people on the Internet using social media. Before believing what others have written, communicating with them, or using a tool, it is wise to do some detective work. Check the claims, the author's background, sources, and accuracy.

Critical consumption is closely related to Informational Literacy, which is discussed in Chapter 7 on Thinking.

Evolving Our Strategies to Match Our Evolving Technologies

Communication has changed because of the way we are using technology. Yes, we still write and talk, but where and how? There are myriad social media platforms that you can use for communication, from Snapchat to Twitter, each with its own set of rules and limitations. These platforms have completely changed many of the ways we transfer ideas and information, find romantic partners, keep in touch with friends and family, connect with our professors and classmates, make plans with teammates, look for employment, and so much more.

When using a device for communication, there are fewer nonverbal cues we can pick up on, only what the other person is posting or showing. In certain situations, such as talking on the phone, a person can't see hand gestures but can still hear a tone of voice. When typing, however, there is no tone of voice or hand gesture or body language. Sometimes typing may not convey the same message as saying what you're feeling.

Social media has made it easier to keep in contact with many people, but it also creates missed opportunities for new relationships since we are too often looking down at our phones instead of talking with the person standing next to us.

ANALYSIS QUESTION

Technology has definitely had an effect on our society. Think about how it has this effect.

- Is that cell phone in your pocket something that has made life better?
- Are we empowering those who most often don't have access to power in our society?
- Or are we further alienating them?
- Does the ability to access global communications create people who are more open and free with their ideas?
- Is an email to a colleague in another country more significant than a snail mail letter?
- Are there any new platforms or apps that you are reluctant to try?

Socialization is an integral part of human behavior, and over time new technologies have made networking and communication more complex. The tools you have available for communication within your networks are powerful and fulfilling, but they can also stand in the way of real-time thinking, doing, relating, and communicating. The past twenty years have seen an explosion in new tools and means of communication, but the next twenty may see similarly rapid growth and change. Adaptability may be as important a skill as any method specific to a certain platform. The key is mindfully participating and knowing when to use and when not to use the new technological tools available to us, which may require learning and acceptance. In this way your communication with others will be positive and allow you to be productive in all aspects of your life.

GET CONNECTED

Information is processed and transferred faster than ever. Social media has become the place where people obtain information. This could be news on YouTube, shocking events on IGTV, or even fake rumors on Facebook spread from friends of friends. It almost seems that information can't travel fast enough today, but it's vital to take everything you see with a grain of salt and evaluate the information given based on what it is, its source, context, and credibility.

- The Verge published a how-to guide on checking facts and sources online (https://openstax.org/l/fightmisinformation) .
- Social networking addiction (https://openstax.org/l/socialnetworkingaddiction) occurs when people become so dependent on Instagram, Snapchat, Twitter, Facebook, and related platforms that all of their communication seems to take place within these virtual places. Many researchers conclude that addiction to social media is much stronger than an addiction to cigarettes or alcohol.
- Six Ways Social Media Changed the Way We Communicate (https://openstax.org/l/communication) discusses how our ability and need to share and consume information quickly can lead to changes in our relationships and ourselves. The article also provides related links.

8.4 The Context of Communication

Estimated completion time: 20 minutes.

Questions to Consider:

- Does my form of communication change in certain situations?
- Do I use an altered style of talking when I am with different people?
- What role does listening play in communication?

Does My Form of Communication Change in Certain Situations?

The circumstances surrounding a message provide the context. These include the setting you are in, the culture that guides you and whomever you are communicating with, and the purpose of the communication to begin with. Context also includes the values people have, appropriateness of the message, the timing you choose to convey your message, and the reason behind your wanting to communicate. This means considering your audience, the place, the time, and all other variables that impact communicating constructively.

Figure 8.7 Your career area, work environment, its accepted style of dress, and the relationships with your colleagues or clients all add context to your communication. (Credit (both photos): Lyncconf Games / Flickr / Attribution 2.0 Generic (CC-BY 2.0))

Generally, all communication happens for a reason. When you are communicating with people, are you always on the same wavelength? Are you wide-awake and your roommate almost asleep? Is the baseball game really important to you but totally boring to the person you are talking with? It is important that everyone involved understands the context of the conversation. Is it a party, which lends itself to frivolous banter? Is the conversation about something serious that occurred? What are some of the relevant steps to understanding context? First of all, pay attention to timing. Is there enough time to cover what you are trying to say? Is it the right time to talk to the boss about a raise? What about the location? Should your conversation take place in the elevator, over email, in a chat room? Is everyone in the conversation involved for the same reason?

The following is an activity that might help you understand what is meant by context.

ANALYSIS QUESTION

Consider the context of a family dinner. You are at the table with siblings, cousins, parents, aunts and uncles, and grandparents. A wide variety of age groups are present around the dinner table. Are there any rules about how you behave in this circumstance? What are they?

Then put yourself in the context of a chat room with people you might know and some that you do not know. Are there rules for communicating in that situation? What are they?

Sometimes we have misconceptions about what is going on in a group situation. Perhaps we think that everyone there knows what we are talking about. Or we think we know everyone's opinions on an issue or situation. Or we come into the conversation already thinking we are right and they are wrong. Communication in these instances can go very wrong. Why? We aren't listening or even preparing ourselves adequately for the conversation we hope to have. So often we are only concerned about what we have to say to an individual or a group and we don't step back long enough to reflect on what our message might mean to them. We seem to not care about how the message will be received and are often surprised by how poorly the communication actually went. Why? Because we didn't step back and think, "Hmmmm, my aunt is a really religious person and probably would be offended by a conversation about sexual intimacy." Or, "My father is having a bit of financial trouble, and this might not be the right time to bring up money I need for a new car."

Do I Use an Altered Style of Talking When I Am With Different People?

There are so many instances in our lives when we think about our needs first and blurt out what we are thinking, leading to some critical misunderstandings. It is really important not only to be concerned about our need to communicate, but to take into consideration with whom we are communicating, when and where we are communicating, and how we are going to do so in a positive way. First, you should step back and think about what you want to say and why. Then reflect on with whom you are attempting to communicate.

WHAT STUDENTS SAY

1. Of the following methods, which is your preferred method of communication?
    a. In person/face-to-face
    b. Voice call
    c. Video call
    d. Email
    e. Texting (including texting apps)
    f. Social media environments
2. Which element of communication do you find most challenging?
    a. Understanding the audience/situation and using the best form/tone to fit it
    b. Speaking in front of a group of people
    c. Writing papers or reports

d. Listening and interpreting
3. When writing a paper for a course, which aspect do you find most challenging?
    a. Coming up with an original idea/thesis/research question
    b. Finding sources and background information
    c. Evaluating the quality of sources or data
    d. Organizing the paper
    e. Writing/editing the paper
    f. Writing the bibliography/works cited list

You can also take the anonymous What Students Say (https://openstax.org/l/collegesurvey6-12) surveys to add your voice to this textbook. Your responses will be included in updates.

Students offered their views on these questions, and the results are displayed in the graphs below.

Of the following methods, which is your preferred method of communication?

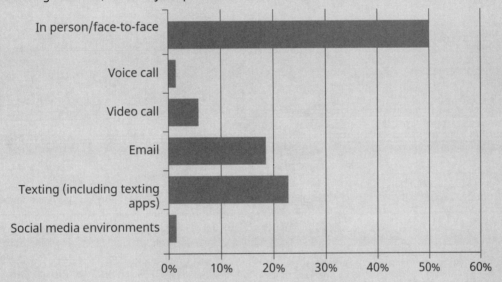

Figure 8.8

Which element of communication do you find most challenging?

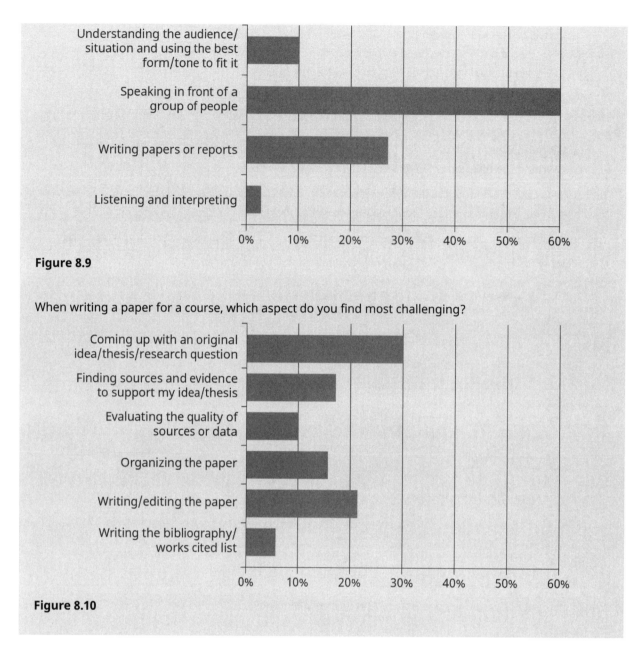

Figure 8.9

Figure 8.10

Emotional Intelligence

We've talked about emotional intelligence when it comes to listening. Recognizing your own emotions and those of others will help you avoid miscommunication as well. When you are aware of your own emotional state and you have the skills to address and adjust, your communication with others will improve. You're less likely to blurt out an angry retort to a perceived criticism, for example.

You're better able to manage communication when you recognize someone else's emotions, as well. A conversation can veer into hostile territory if someone feels attacked, or perhaps simply because they've had an emotional experience related to the conversation that you don't understand. Taking note of other people's emotional responses during a conversation and listening and speaking with empathy will help you manage the situation.

When conversations begin to feel heated, it's a good idea to pause and ask yourself why. If it's you who are feeling defensive and angry, make an effort to recognize the source of your frustration and try to take a step back, perhaps leaving the conversation until you're better able to control your emotions and communicate in a way that's more clearheaded and calm.

If it's someone else who's emotional, again, ask yourself why. Can you see reasons that this person may feel attacked, belittled, or usurped? If you can recognize their emotion and address it, you may be able to get the communication back on solid footing.

ACTIVITY

Think of what context and what communication tool you would consider in the following situations:

1. You need to let your professor know you won't be able to hand in your assignment on time. What will you say, when and where will you say it, and what form of communication will you use and why?
2. Your roommate wants to have friends over for a party and you aren't sure you are up for that. What and how do you tell your roommate?
3. The weekend is full of activities, but you are expected home for a family gathering. How do you let your parents know you aren't coming?

Listening Is a Communication Action

Our communication includes both sending and, especially, receiving messages. Unfortunately, we often don't take the time to focus on the latter part. Often we are already thinking about what we are going to say next and not listening to what is being said to us. This lack of focus occurs in intense, oppositional discussions, but it can also be common in one-on-one conversations and when someone is confiding in us. When we listen, we need to embrace the concept of empathy, meaning you understand what a person might be feeling, and understand why that person's actions made sense to them at the time. This way our ideas can be communicated in a way that makes sense to others, and it helps us understand others when they communicate with us.

Even though it is silent, listening is communication. We can often "hear" what is being said but don't really listen well enough to discern what is meant by the person trying to communicate with us. In order to listen effectively, we should consider it an active process, in the same way we think about speaking or messaging.

So what does active listening entail? There are some strategies you can use to help you become a good listener. First of all, stop talking. You can't listen if you are talking. Secondly, turn off the television, put your phone in your pocket, silence the music and, if needed, go somewhere quiet, so you can actually focus on what is being said. Next, have empathy for the person talking to you. In other words, don't begin thinking of ways to answer. Even if someone has a problem (with you or something else), avoid trying to immediately solve it; consider whether the person speaking to you really wants advice or action, or might simply want to be seen and heard. Finally, before you say anything as a reply, repeat what you heard so the other person can confirm that you heard them correctly. You would be amazed at how well these strategies work to help avoid misunderstandings and confusion.

Figure 8.11 Being a good listener takes practice and focus. To help, try to eliminate distraction and avoid giving too much advice or telling your own related stories. Even if you're only listening to a brief summary after running into someone in the hallway, do your best to internalize what they're saying. (Credit: University of the Fraser Valley / Flickr / Attribution 2.0 Generic (CC-BY 2.0))

Think about all the times you have gone through a drive-through for food or coffee. The scenario is most often the same, right? You order, let's say, medium fries, a burger with no cheese or onions, and a large soft drink. You then listen to the person inside the restaurant say back to you, "You want medium fries, a quarter pounder with no cheese or onions, and a large Coke." If that is the right order, you say yes and move on to pay. This can be seen as active listening on both sides. The following activity can help you reflect on active listening.

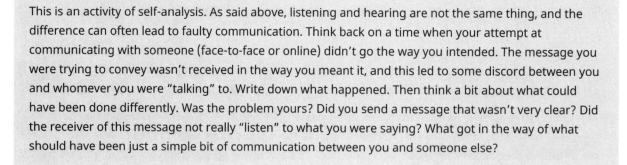

ANALYSIS QUESTION

This is an activity of self-analysis. As said above, listening and hearing are not the same thing, and the difference can often lead to faulty communication. Think back on a time when your attempt at communicating with someone (face-to-face or online) didn't go the way you intended. The message you were trying to convey wasn't received in the way you meant it, and this led to some discord between you and whomever you were "talking" to. Write down what happened. Then think a bit about what could have been done differently. Was the problem yours? Did you send a message that wasn't very clear? Did the receiver of this message not really "listen" to what you were saying? What got in the way of what should have been just a simple bit of communication between you and someone else?

As said earlier, emotions are frequently involved in communication. It would be nice if everything was logical and everyone was always coming from that place of no emotion. But that's not how it works in most instances. People have opinions, needs, desires, and outcomes they are looking for; feelings that can be hurt; and differing attitudes. The list could go on and on. What is important is that we need to be aware of our own emotions, and those of others, when attempting to communicate. Consider other people's feelings as well as your own. Have empathy. And in the midst of trying to do that, listen, don't just hear!

8.5 Barriers to Effective Communication

Estimated completion time: 18 minutes.

Questions to consider:

- Can you remember a time when you were surprised that what you communicated was not well received?
- What are some other barriers to effective communication?

"Words are the source of misunderstandings."

— *Antoine de Saint-Exupéry, The Little Prince*[9]

Meredith and Anvi are working together on a project on marketing for a communications class: Anvi will create content for a flier, and Meredith will determine the best platform for advertising. In their brainstorming session the two realized they had some outstanding questions about how much content the flier should contain and whether they needed to turn in additional documentation. Meredith left it to Anvi to clarify this material since the content of the flier was her responsibility. Meredith waited impatiently the entire class session for Anvi to ask about the assignment. With class time almost up, Meredith spoke up, telling the instructor in front of the class that Anvi had a question about the assignment.

Anvi clarified the assignment with the professor, but when Meredith tried to find her after class to talk about next steps, Anvi had gone. Meredith was surprised to receive an angry text from Anvi soon after class accusing Meredith of embarrassing her. Anvi pointed out that she'd managed to complete every assignment so far in the course and she didn't need Meredith to take over on this one.

Communication can go awry for a number of reasons. One could use jargon or technical language that is unfamiliar. There can be differences in the perception of an issue. People may speak different languages, or the colloquialisms that one uses don't make sense to everyone.

As in the case with Meredith and Anvi, cultural considerations can also affect the way people communicate. Anvi, for instance, prefers not to speak to the instructor during class because she feels that she's interrupting. She prefers to approach the instructor after class time is over. Meredith, on the other hand, usually has a task list she likes to tick off one by one to make sure everything is moving on time, and she can sometimes become insensitive to the communication styles of others.

Some barriers are likely to be emotional, often caused by topics that are sometimes considered problematic, such as sex, politics, or religion, which can interfere with effective communication. Sometimes what you are trying to communicate is embarrassing or otherwise a bit personal, and you kind of skirt around the edges of really saying what you want to say. Other emotions, such as stress, anger, depression, sadness, and the like, can have an effect on how well you communicate with another person, or they with you. Physical disabilities, such as hearing loss, can also come into play and get in the way of successful communication.

Some of our behavior and communication is based on previous encounters, and we don't see past that and start fresh. Sometimes the barrier can be a lack of interest or attention on the part of the receiver. There are also expectations about what might be said or stereotyping on the part of the sender or the receiver. Often when we communicate with people we have preconceptions about who they are, what they are thinking, and how they will react to whatever we say. These preconceptions can get in the way of productive communication. A person could have an attitude that comes with whatever is being said or written. Or perhaps there is a lack of motivation to clarify what you want to communicate, and the end result is not what you were hoping for.

---

9 Saint-Exupéry, Antoine de, and Katherine Woods. The Little Prince. New York: Harcourt Brace Jovanovich, 1961.

ACTIVITY

Take into consideration some of your own stereotypes and preconceptions, and try them out on the following scenario.

You are walking down the street and need to ask someone for change for a dollar because you need it for the parking meter. There are only a few people around you, and you have to choose whom to ask for help. Which person would you choose, and why?

- A person with tattoos all over their arms
- An elderly woman who is hunched over and walking gingerly
- A person of color who is absorbed in their own phone
- A parent with three children who is frantically trying to keep them together
- A well-dressed man, with shiny leather shoes, walking briskly to wherever he is going

Preconceptions and Assumptions

Have you ever thought about the message you are conveying to others? If you were the one standing on the street corner, what would others see? How do you play into others' preconceptions simply based on your appearance?

Of course, you should be yourself, but certain environments or situations require us to consider and, perhaps, change our appearance. Wearing a T-shirt with a "message" may be appropriate when you're at leisure, but you wouldn't wear it to a job interview.

College presents us with many situations where people's preconceived notions of our appearance may come into play. For example, while it might not be fair, faculty may have a certain perception of students who attend lecture or office hours in pajamas. Consider the implications of sitting in your instructor's office, asking for help, when they think you haven't changed your clothes since you woke up. You are absolutely free to express yourself in a certain manner, but your appearance may miscommunicate your motivation or intent. Recognizing how our own preconceptions come into play, and acknowledging those of others, generally leads to more effective interactions.

One of the biggest changes about the way we interact is the vast number of people available with whom we can communicate. This is a wonderful thing as we get to meet many people from diverse places. It can also be challenging because we are not always prepared to communicate with people from varying cultures, genders, ages, or religious and political views. Sometimes a simple lack of familiarity can lead to errors or even offense.

ACTIVITY

Think about how you communicate to different types of people. For each person in the left-most column and each example of something you need to describe, write some notes on how you might communicate, the types of words you might use, or what you may consider when speaking to them.

	Describing a sporting event you watched.	Describing an argument you got into on social media.	Describing a night out with friends.
An eight-year-old			
A 20-year-old woman			
A middle-aged man			
An elderly person			

Did your answers come from stereotypes or experience? (Or both?) Did you choose your words carefully with the child? Did you assume the man would know more about sports than the woman? Did you assume the elderly person wouldn't know about Twitter or Instagram? Perhaps being mindful in your interactions with others will help bring clarity to your communication.

Unfortunately, relying on stereotypes often results in failed communication. Our understanding of others is often masked by the stereotypes that have infiltrated our society. Think about if you bring your own stereotypes to the table. Do you think others do the same? If so, those probably get in the way of a successful conversation.

Look in more detail at the issues of stereotypes, assumptions, and avoiding offense (microaggressions) in Chapter 9.

> "Precision of communication is important, more important than ever, in our era of hair trigger balances, when a false or misunderstood word may create as much disaster as a sudden thoughtless act."
>
> — *James Thurber*[10]

How Can Identities and Experiences Lead to Communication Barriers?

Aside from our actual communication abilities and tools, we bring to each interaction many unique aspects based on who we are and where we come from. Diversity, as important and great as it is, requires us to consider the different perspectives and experiences others bring to a discussion or interaction, and to understand that our own views and contexts may be unfamiliar to others. While we shouldn't shy away from this diversity, we should exercise patience and practice when communicating with new people.

Part of this consideration is known as cultural competency, which you'll learn more about in Chapter 9. Below are several aspects of people's lives that you might consider when communicating.

---

10   Thurber, James. Lanterns and Lances. Harper and Brothers. 1961.

Identity is generally a feeling of belonging to a group. It is your self-perception and is usually related to nationality, ethnicity, religion, social class, sexual orientation, gender, generation, region or any social group that has its own distinct identity. Examples of cultural identity markers include the rituals people observe, the music that a group prefers, the style of clothing that is worn, the languages actual ethnic group one belongs to and its various foods and celebrations, or possibly the games that are a preferred sport in some communities. All of these variables can constitute a cultural identity for people. And belonging to these groups gives people an identity and a frame of reference on how to communicate and relate to the world around them.

Gender identity refers to the deeply held, internal sense of a person's gender. Sometimes, a person's genetically assigned sex does not line up with their gender identity. These individuals might refer to themselves as transgender, nonbinary, or gender-nonconforming.[11] Thus, gender is what a person identifies with.

While gender is internal, social influences and perceptions can shape a person's attitude and method of communication. For example, in some families and cultures, men are raised to be more dominant or less emotionally expressive. Their use of that approach may lead to communication problems with others. However, people's *assumptions* about men may also lead to communication problems. The same can happen with other gender identities.

What are your communication experiences with different genders? Have you seen people communicate a specific way based on the genders involved in the conversation? For example, does a classmate have a way of speaking to men that is different from their way of speaking to women? Does that difference become a barrier or issue in the communication?

Age can have a very significant impact on communication. This is a little easier to understand, as people from varying generations bring very different experiences to their contact with others. We all grow up surrounded by certain music, clothing styles, language, and cultural influences. Modes of parenting have evolved, food choices have expanded, and tragedies and world politics have occurred, and each of these had an effect on the generation that experienced them firsthand. And, of course, most of us live or have lived with multiple generations in our lives and have experienced many of the differences ourselves. Think of the times you've tried to explain what you do on your social media platforms to your grandparent (though some grandparents are pretty good at all the new technologies!). And think of how very young family members—age three or four—describe the videos they watch or the games they play.

As you can see from the above categories of cultural identity, gender, age, and our own stereotypes about people, there are many barriers that can come into play when you are trying to communicate with someone. In fact, on a college campus you probably will run into a large variety of differences in the people you meet. Many come from other countries, cultures, religions, and family backgrounds. Some may be in the country solely for the purpose of going to college, and intend to return home when they graduate. Some may have a lot of life experience, while others could be high school students in a dual enrollment program. All of that will have an effect on how they communicate, as your own upbringing and experiences have had an influence on who you are. Keep that in mind as you try to create relationships with the many people that are available to you, both face-to-face and online.

 Summary

Communication is one of the basic components of how we live our lives. It's a foundation of society and

---

11   Newman, Tim. "Sex and gender: What's the Difference?" *Medical News Today*. February 7, 2018 http://www.medicalnewstoday.com/articles/232363.php

civilization as a whole. And the better we become at navigating through all of our various communication options, the more fulfilled and productive we will become. You have the capability to communicate with myriad people and groups in faraway places, as well as just next door or the room down the hall. In all of those interactions, the sender and recipient of each message brings their own context, purpose, and perspective. Your communication will be much more effective if you think about those differences before sending and especially before *responding* to people.

Sometimes thinking so deeply about a simple conversation seems overwhelming and unnecessary, but keeping in mind the reasons you're communicating and focusing on the words you use can lead to better relationships and outcomes. Listening, practicing empathy, and working on your cultural competence will enrich you and the people around you.

Career Connection

Check the methods of communication you would most likely use for each of the following. Then write an explanation for why you have chosen the various forms of communication and how your choice had a link to the purpose of communicating with these different people.

	Face-to-Face	Email	Letter	Phone	Facebook	Instagram	Snapchat
Parent							
Peer							
Sibling							
Boss							
Doctor							
Professor							
Waitress							
Office assistant							
Significant other							

Take a close look at how you filled out the above chart. Do you find that there were definitely different purposes to how and why you used email instead of the phone, or Snapchat instead of a letter? It is good for you to reflect on your communication choices so that they are always most effective.

Look at the forms of communication you chose for "boss." Perhaps you chose face-to-face and email as the two forms of communication you would use with your boss. Think through how those might have had an effect on the success of your communication with them. Now select two other forms of communication. Would you have been able to get the same response from your boss?

Rethinking

Revisit the questions you answered at the beginning of the chapter, and consider one option you learned in this chapter that might change your answer to one of them.

1. I think my mobile device is effective and appropriate for most communication.
2. I have a good sense of how to communicate in different environments/situations.
3. I listen more than I talk.
4. I have a lot of experience with research projects and essays.

 Where do you go from here?

Staying aware of how and when you communicate is important to every aspect of your life. As you learned throughout this chapter, there are many variables that come into play when you communicate. Most of the time none of us really think about all of these before we send out some kind of communication. Perhaps you would like to learn a little more about how to be mindful of your methods of communication. It will serve you well throughout your life.

Choose a topic that interests you from the list below. Then search for sources that inform this topic and create an annotated bibliography that would be useful to someone who is interested in doing further research.

- Communication using social media can be detrimental to mental health.
- It is imperative that you pay attention to cultural norms when trying to communicate with others.
- Listening is important to successful communication, and there are steps that can be taken to hone listening skills.
- Men and women are said to communicate differently.

9 Understanding Civility and Cultural Competence

Figure 9.1 (Credit John Martinez Pavliga / Flickr / Attribution 2.0 Generic (CC-BY 2.0))

Chapter Outline

9.1 What Is Diversity, and Why Is Everybody Talking About It?
9.2 Categories of Diversity
9.3 Navigating the Diversity Landscape
9.4 Inclusivity and Civility: What Role Can I Play?

Introduction

Student Survey

How do you feel about diversity, equity, and inclusion? These questions will help you determine how the chapter concepts relate to you right now. As you are introduced to new concepts and practices, it can be informative to reflect on how your understanding changes over time. We'll revisit these questions at the end of the chapter to see whether your feelings have changed. Take this quick survey to figure it out, ranking questions on a scale of 1–4, 1 meaning "least like me" and 4 meaning "most like me."

1. I'm aware of the different categories of diversity and the various populations I may encounter.
2. I think we sometimes go too far in trying to be sensitive to different groups.
3. I think nearly everybody in our society has equal opportunity.
4. It's not my role to ensure equity and inclusiveness among my peers or colleagues.

You can also take the Chapter 9 survey (https://openstax.org/l/collegesurvey09) anonymously online.

STUDENT PROFILE

"For the vast majority of my life, I thought being an Asian-American—who went through the Palo Alto School District—meant that I was supposed to excel in academics. But, in reality, I did the opposite. I struggled through college, both in classes and in seeking experiences for my future. At first, I thought I was unique in not living up to expectations. But as I met more people from all different backgrounds, I realized my challenges were not unique.

"I began capturing videos of students sharing their educational issues. Like me, many of my peers lack the study skills required to achieve our academic goals. The more I researched and developed videos documenting this lack of skill, the more I realized that student identities are often lost as they learn according to a traditional pedagogy. I began documenting students' narratives and the specific strategies they used to overcome difficulty. Once we can celebrate a diverse student body and showcase their strengths and identities as well as the skills necessary to excel academically, my hope is that students of all backgrounds can begin to feel that they belong."

—**Henry Fan**, Foothill College and San Jose State University

About This Chapter

In this chapter you will learn about diversity and how it plays a role in personal, civic, academic, and professional aspects of our lives. By the end of the chapter, you should be able to do the following:

- Articulate how diverse voices have been historically ignored or minimized in American civic life, education, and culture.
- Describe categories of identity and experience that contribute to diverse points of view.
- Acknowledge implicit bias and recognize privilege.
- Evaluate statements and situations based on their inclusion of diverse perspectives.

9.1 What Is Diversity, and Why Is Everybody Talking About It?

Estimated completion time: 34 minutes.

Questions to Consider:

- Historically, has diversity always been a concern?
- What does it mean to be civil?
- Why do people argue about diversity?

What Would Shakespeare Say?

Figure 9.2 (Credit: Sourced originally from Helmolt, H.F., ed. History of the World. Dodd, Mead and Company, 1902 / Perry-Castañeda Library, University of Texas at Austin / Wikimedia Commons / Public Domain).

In our classroom, everyone is the same...

Consider a classroom containing 25 college students and their instructor. In this particular class, all of the students and the instructor share the same racial group—white. In fact, everyone in the class is a white American from the Midwest.

The instructor is leading the class through reading a scene from William Shakespeare's drama *Romeo and Juliet*. As students read their parts, each one is thinking carefully about the role he or she has been given.

One of the male students wonders what it would be like to read the part of Juliet; after all, men originally played the part in Shakespeare's day. The young woman reading Juliet wonders if anyone would object to her taking the role if they knew she was a lesbian. What would it be like, she wonders, if Romeo, her love interest, were also played by a woman? One reader strongly identifies as German American, but he is reading the part of an Italian. Another student has a grandmother who is African American, but he looks like every other white student in the room. No one recognizes his mixed-race heritage.

After the students finish reading the scene, the instructor announces, "In our classroom, everyone is the same, but these days when Shakespeare is staged, there is a tendency for nontraditional casting. Romeo could be black, Juliet could be Latina, Lady Montague could be Asian. Do you think that kind of casting would disrupt the experience of seeing the play?"

In this case, the instructor makes the assumption that because everyone in the class *looks* the same, they *are* the same. What did the instructor miss about the potential for diversity in his classroom? Have you ever made a similar mistake?

Diversity is more than what we can recognize from external clues such as race and gender. Diversity includes many unseen aspects of identity, like sexual orientation, political point of view, veteran status, and many other aspects that you may have not considered. To be inclusive and civil within your community, it is essential that you avoid making assumptions about how other people define or identify themselves.

In this chapter we will discover that each person is more than the sum of surface clues presented to the world. Personal experience, social and family history, public policy, and even geography play a role in how diversity is constructed. We'll also explore elements of civility and fairness within the college community.

One important objective of civility is to become culturally competent. Culturally competent people understand the complexity of their own personal identity, values, and culture. In addition, they respect the personal identities and values of others who may not share their identity and values. Further, culturally competent people remain open-minded when confronted with new cultural experiences. They learn to relate to and respect difference; they look beyond the obvious and learn as much as they can about what makes each person different and appreciated.

These concepts tie closely to Chapter 8: Communication, particularly the section on Emotional Intelligence and Overcoming Barriers to Communication.

WHAT STUDENTS SAY

1. Do you think the diversity of your school's student body is reflected in course offerings and campus activities?
   a. Yes
   b. Somewhat
   c. No
2. How comfortable are you when discussing issues of race, sexuality, religion, and other aspects of civility?
   a. Extremely comfortable
   b. Somewhat comfortable
   c. Somewhat uncomfortable
   d. Extremely uncomfortable
3. Do you generally feel welcomed and included on campus?
   a. Yes
   b. No
   c. It varies significantly by class or environment.

You can also take the anonymous What Students Say surveys (https://openstax.org/l/collegesurvey6-12) to add your voice to this textbook. Your responses will be included in updates.

Students offered their views on these questions, and the results are displayed in the graphs below.

Do you think the diversity of your school's student body is reflected in course offerings and campus activities?

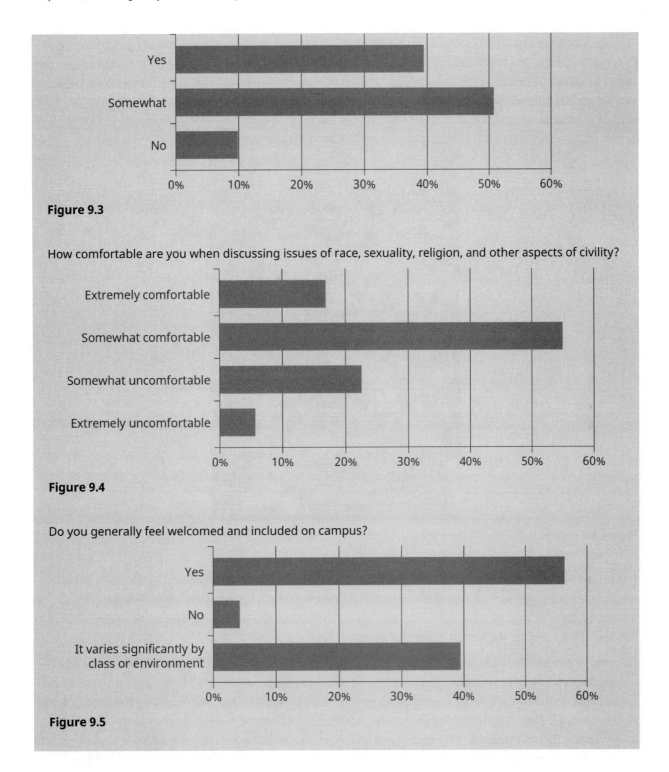

Figure 9.3

How comfortable are you when discussing issues of race, sexuality, religion, and other aspects of civility?

Figure 9.4

Do you generally feel welcomed and included on campus?

Figure 9.5

Why Diversity Matters

The United States of America is viewed the world over as a leader in democracy and democratic ideals. Our nation, young by most standards, continues to evolve to make the freedoms and opportunities available to all. Where the benefits of citizenship have been imperfect, discord over issues related to civil rights and inclusion have often been at the center of the conflict.

To understand the importance of civility and civil engagement, it is necessary to acknowledge our country's history. The United States is a country born out of protest. Colonists protesting what they felt were unfair taxes under King George III was at the foundation of the Revolutionary War. Over time, many groups have been given their civil liberties and equal access to all that our country has to offer through that same spirit of protest and petition.

Figure 9.6 (Credit: Carl Campbell / Flickr / Attribution 2.0 Generic (CC-BY 2.0))

The United States is often described as a "melting pot," a rich mixture made up of people of many colors, religions, abilities, etc. working together to make one great big stew. That is the image generations of Americans grew up learning, and it is a true one. The United States is a nation of immigrants, and cultural influences from around the world have added to its strength.

Historically, however, not all contributions and voices have been acknowledged equally or adequately. Some groups have had to struggle to have their contributions acknowledged, be treated fairly, and be allowed full participation in the civic life of the country. Entire populations of people have been oppressed as a part of the nation's history, something important for Americans to confront and acknowledge. For example, in what is known as the Trail of Tears, the U.S. government forcibly removed Native Americans from their homelands and made them walk to reservations; some had to travel more than 1,000 miles, and over 10,000 died on the journey. Further, in an act of forced assimilation, Native American children were taken from their families and placed in schools where they were not allowed to practice cultural traditions or speak their Native languages. This practice continued as late as the 1970s. As a result, many Native American languages have been lost or are at risk of being lost.

The slavery of Africans occurred in America for close to 250 years. Much of the wealth in the United States during that time came directly from the labor of enslaved people; however, the enslaved people themselves did not benefit financially. During World War II, Japanese Americans were placed into internment camps and considered a danger to our country because our nation was at war with Japan.

For many years, all women and minority men were traditionally left out of public discourse and denied participation in government, industry, and even cultural institutions such as sports. For example, the United States Supreme Court was founded in 1789; however, the court's first female justice, Sandra Day O'Connor, was not appointed until 1981, almost 200 years later. Jackie Robinson famously became the first African American major league baseball player in 1947 when he was hired by the Brooklyn Dodgers, although the major leagues were established in 1869, decades earlier. The absence of white women and minorities was not an accident. Their exclusion was based on legal discrimination or unfair treatment.

These are all examples of mistreatment, inequality, and discrimination, and they didn't end without incredible sacrifice and heroism. The civil rights movement of the 1950s and 1960s and the equal rights movement for women's rights in the 1970s are examples of how public protests work to bring attention to discriminatory practices and to create change. Because racism, anti-Semitism, sexism, and other forms of bias and intolerance still exist, civil engagement and protests continue, and policies must be constantly monitored. Many people still work to ensure the gains these communities have made in acquiring the rights of full citizenship are not lost.

Diversity refers to differences in the human experience. As different groups have gained in number and influence, our definition of diversity has evolved to embrace many variables that reflect a multitude of different backgrounds, experiences, and points of view, not just race and gender. Diversity takes into account age, socioeconomic factors, ability (such as sight, hearing, and mobility), ethnicity, veteran status, geography, language, sexual orientation, religion, size, and other factors. At one time or another, each group has had to make petitions to the government for equal treatment under the law and appeals to society for respect. Safeguarding these groups' hard-won rights and public regard maintains diversity and its two closely related factors, *equity* and *inclusion*.

ACTIVITY

Our rights and protections are often acquired through awareness, effort, and, sometimes, protest. Each one of the following groups has launched protests over discrimination or compromises to their civil rights. Choose three of the groups below and do a quick search on protests or efforts members of the group undertook to secure their rights. To expand your knowledge, choose some with which you are not familiar.

Record the name, time frame, and outcomes of the protest or movements you researched.

The groups are as follows:

- Veterans
- Senior citizens
- Blind or visually impaired people
- Muslims
- Christians
- LGBTQ+ community
- Hispanic/Latinos
- People with intellectual disabilities

- Undocumented immigrants
- Little people
- College students
- Jewish Americans
- Farm workers
- Wheelchair users

The Role of Equity and Inclusion

Equity plays a major part in achieving fairness in a diverse landscape. Equity gives everyone equal access to opportunity and success. For example, you may have seen interpreters for deaf or hard of hearing people in situations where a public official is making an announcement about an impending weather emergency. Providing immediate translation into sign language means that there is no gap between what the public official is saying and when all people receive the information. Simultaneous sign language provides equity.[1] Similarly, many students have learning differences that require accommodations in the classroom. For example, a student with attention-deficit/hyperactivity disorder (ADHD) might be given more time to complete tests or writing assignments. The extra time granted takes into account that students with ADHD process information differently.

If a student with a learning difference is given more time than other students to complete a test, that is a matter of equity. The student is not being given an advantage; the extra time gives them an equal chance at success.

The Americans with Disabilities Act (ADA, 1990) is a federal government policy that addresses equity in the workplace, housing, and public places. The ADA requires "reasonable accommodations" so that people with disabilities have equal access to the same services as people without disabilities. For example, wheelchair lifts on public transportation, automatic doors, entrance ramps, and elevators are examples of accommodations that eliminate barriers of participation for people with certain disabilities.

Without the above accommodations, those with a disability may justly feel like second-class citizens because their needs were not anticipated. Further, they might have to use their own resources to gain equal access to services although their tax dollars contribute to providing that same access and service to other citizens.

Equity levels the playing field so that everyone's needs are anticipated and everyone has an equal starting point. However, understanding equity is not enough.

---

1 https://www.nad.org/resources/american-sign-language/community-and-culture-frequently-asked-questions/

Figure 9.7 Equality is a meaningful goal, but it can leave people with unmet needs; equity is more empowering and fair. In equality portion of the graphic, people all sizes and a person who uses a wheelchair are all given the same bicycle, which is unusable for most. In the equity portion, each person gets a bicycle specifically designed for them, enabling them to successfully ride it. Credit: Robert Wood Johnson Foundation / Custom License: "May be Produced with Attribution[2]")

When equity is properly considered, there is also inclusion. *Inclusion* means that there are a multiplicity of voices, skills, and interests represented in any given situation. Inclusion has played a major role in education, especially in terms of creating inclusion classrooms and inclusive curricula. In an inclusion classroom, students of different skill levels study together. For example, students with and without developmental disabilities study in the same classroom. Such an arrangement eliminates the stigma of the "special education classroom" where students were once segregated. In addition, in inclusion classrooms all students receive support when needed. Students benefit from seeing how others learn. In an inclusive curriculum, a course includes content and perspectives from underrepresented groups. For example, a college course in psychology might include consideration of different contexts such as immigration, incarceration, or unemployment in addition to addressing societal norms.

Inclusion means that these voices of varied background and experience are integrated into discussions, research, and assignments rather than ignored.

Our Country Is Becoming More Diverse

You may have heard the phrase "the browning of America," meaning it is predicted that today's racial minorities will, collectively, be the majority of the population in the future. The graph from the Pew Research Center projects that by the year 2065, U.S. demographics will have shifted significantly. In 2019, the white population made up just over 60% of the population. In 2065, the Pew Research Center predicts that whites will be approximately 46% of the population. The majority of Americans will be the non-white majority, 54% Hispanic/Latinos, blacks, and Asians.

---

2   https://www.rwjf.org/en/library/infographics/visualizing-health-equity.html#/download

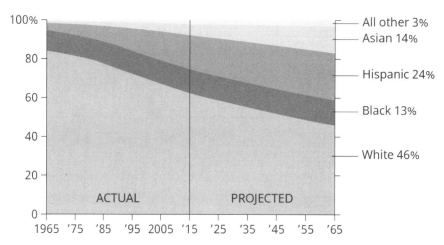

Figure 9.8 United States demographics (or statistical characteristics of populations) are changing rapidly. In just over 35 years, the country as a whole will be a "majority minority" nation, with ethnic/racial minorities making up more than half of the population. (Credit: Based on work by the Pew Research Center.)

What does this mean? It could mean that the United States begins accepting Spanish as a mainstream language since the Hispanic/Latino population will be significantly larger. It could mean a changing face for local governments. It could mean that our country will elect its second nonwhite president. Beyond anything specific, the shifting demographics of the United States could mean greater attention is paid to diversity awareness, equity, and inclusion.

ANALYSIS QUESTION

How should the United States prepare for its projected demographic shift? What changes do you suppose will take place as part of the "browning of America"?

Education: Equity for All

Education has been one of the most significant arenas for social change related to our rights as Americans. And the effects of that change have significantly impacted other power dynamics in society. You need look no further than the landmark case *Brown v. Board of Education of Topeka* (1954) to see how our nation has responded passionately in civil and uncivil ways to appeals for equity and inclusion in public education.

For much of the 20th century, African Americans lived under government-sanctioned separation better known as segregation. Not only were schools segregated, but Jim Crow laws allowed for legal separation in transportation, hospitals, parks, restaurants, theaters, and just about every aspect of public life. These laws enacted that there be "whites only" water fountains and restrooms. Only white people could enter the front door of a restaurant or sit on the main level of a movie theater, while African Americans had to enter through the back door and sit in the balcony. The segregation also included Mexican Americans and Catholics, who were forced to attend separate schools. *Brown v. Board of Education* was a landmark Supreme Court case that challenged the interpretation of the 14th Amendment to the Constitution of the United States. The case involved the father of Linda Brown suing the Topeka, Kansas, board of education for denying his daughter the right to attend an all-white school. Oliver Brown maintained that segregation left his black community with inferior schools, a condition counter to the equal protection clause contained in Section I of the 14th Amendment:

> **"All persons born or naturalized in the United States, and subject to the jurisdiction thereof, are citizens of the United States and the State wherein they reside. No State shall make or enforce any law which shall abridge the privileges or immunities of citizens of the United States; nor shall any State deprive any person of life, liberty, or property, without due process of law; nor deny to any person within its jurisdiction the equal protection of the laws."**

There was widespread heated opposition to desegregated education across the country. Passions were even more severe after *Brown v. Board of Education* was won by the plaintiff on appeal to the United States Supreme Court. In effect, the case changed the power dynamics in America by leveling the playing field for education. No longer were white schools (and their better resources) legally segregated. In principal, there was equity—equal access.

Debates in the courtrooms surrounding *Brown* were passionate but professional. Protests and debate in those communities directly affected by the decision, especially in the South, were intense, violent confrontations that demonstrated the height of incivility. One thing you may notice about uncivil behavior is the difficulty most have looking back on those actions.

Figure 9.9 After the Brown v Board of Education decision, Americans pursued their rights for equal education in other districts. In Arkansas, a group of teenagers, which would come to be known as the Little Rock Nine, were blocked from entering a formerly whites-only school. Facing angry protestors, the state governor, and even the National Guard, the nine students finally took their rightful place in the school after a judge ruled in their favor and President Eisenhower sent the 101st Airborne Division to secure the situation. (Credit: Courtesy of the National Archives, sourced from The US Army / Flickr / Attribution 2.0 Generic (CC-BY))

Educational institutions like colleges and school districts are critically important spaces for equity and inclusion, and debates around them remain challenging. Transgender students in America's schools face discrimination, harrassment, and bullying, which causes nearly 45 percent of LGBTQ+ to feel unsafe becuase of their gender expression and 60 percent of to feel unsafe due to their sexual orientation. Many of these students miss school or experience significant stress, which usually has a negative impact on their grades, participation, and overall success.[3] In essence, this hostility creates inequality. Regardless of individual state or district laws on bathroom use and overall accommodation, federal law protects *all* students from discrimination, especially that based on categories such as gender. But implementation of these federal protections varies, and, in general, many outside the transgender community do not fully unerstand, empathize with, or support transgender rights.

How can the circumstances improve for transgender students? In other societal changes throughout our nation's history, court decisions, new legislation, protests, and general public opinion combined to right past wrongs and provide justice and protection for mistreated people. For example, in 2015, the Supreme Court upheld the right to same-sex marriage under the 14th Amendment. Just as African Americans publicly debated and protested educational inequality, the gay community used discusion, protest, and debate to sway public and legal opinion. Proponents of gay marriage faced fervent argument against their position based on religion and culture; like other minority groups, they were confronted with name-calling, job insecurity, family division, religious isolation, and physical confrontation. And as has often been the case, success in achieving marriage equality eventually came through the courts.

Legal remedies are significant, but can take a very long time. Before they see success in the courts or legislatures, transgender students in America's schools will continue to undergo harsh treatment. Their lives and education will remain very difficult until people from outside their community better understand their situation.

Debates: Civility vs. Incivility

Healthy debate is a desirable part of a community. In a healthy debate, people are given room to explain their point of view. In a healthy airing of differences, people on opposing sides of an argument can reach common ground and compromise or even agree to disagree and move on.

However, incivility occurs when people are not *culturally competent*. An individual who is not culturally competent might make negative assumptions about others' values, lack an open mindset, or be inflexible in thinking. Instead of being tolerant of different points of view, they may try to shut down communication by not listening or by keeping someone with a different point of view from being heard at all. Out of frustration, a person who is uncivil may resort to name-calling or discrediting another person only with the intention of causing confusion and division within a community. Incivility can also propagate violence. Such uncivil reaction to difficult issues is what makes many people avoid certain topics at all costs. Instead of seeking out diverse communities, people retreat to safe spaces where they will not be challenged to hear opposing opinions or have their beliefs contested.

Debates on difficult or divisive topics surrounding diversity, especially those promoting orchestrated change, are often passionate. People on each side may base their positions on deeply held beliefs, family traditions, personal experience, academic expertise, and a desire to orchestrate change. With such a strong foundation, emotions can be intense, and debates can become uncivil.

Even when the disagreement is based on information rather than personal feelings, discussions can quickly

---

3   2017 National School Climate Survey, GLESN. https://www.glsen.org/research/school-climate-survey

turn to arguments. For example, in academic environments, it's common to find extremely well-informed arguments in direct opposition to each other. Two well-known economics faculty members from your college could debate for hours on financial policies, with each professor's position backed by data, research, and publications. Each person could feel very strongly that they are right and the other person is wrong. They may even feel that the approach proposed by their opponent would actually do damage to the country or to certain groups of people. But for this debate—whether it occurs over lunch or on an auditorium stage—to remain civil, the participants need to maintain certain standards of behavior.

ACTIVITY

1. Describe a time when you could not reach an agreement with someone on a controversial issue.
2. Did you try to compromise, combining your points of view so that each of you would be partially satisfied?
3. Did either of you shut down communication? Was ending the conversation a good choice? Why or why not?

Civility is a valued practice that takes advantage of cultural and political systems we have in place to work through disagreements while maintaining respect for others' points of view. Civil behavior allows for a respectful airing of grievances. The benefit of civil discussion is that members of a community can hear different sides of an argument, weigh evidence, and decide for themselves which side to support.

You have probably witnessed or taken part in debates in your courses, at social events, or even at family gatherings. What makes people so passionate about certain issues? First, some may have a personal stake in an issue, such as abortion rights. Convincing other people to share their beliefs may be intended to create a community that will protect their rights. Second, others may have deeply held beliefs based on faith or cultural practices. They argue based on deeply held moral and ethical beliefs. Third, others may be limited in their background knowledge about an issue but are able to speak from a "script" of conventional points of view. They may not want to stray from the script because they do not have enough information to extend an argument.

Rules for Fair Debate

Figure 9.10 You'll participate in classroom or workplace debate throughout your academic or professional career. Civility is important to productive discussions, and will lead to worthwhile outcomes. (Credit: Creative Sustainability / Flickr / Attribution 2.0 Generic (CC-BY 2.0))

The courtroom and the public square are not the only places where serious debate takes place. Every day we tackle tough decisions that involve other people, some of whom have strong opposing points of view. To be successful in college, you will need to master sound and ethical approaches to argument, whether it be for a mathematical proof or an essay in a composition class.

You probably already know how to be sensitive and thoughtful when giving feedback to a family member or friend. You think about their feelings and the best way to confront your disagreement without attacking them. Of course, sometimes it's easier to be less sensitive with people who love you no matter what. Still, whether in a classroom, a workplace, or your family dinner table, there are rules for debating that help people with opposing points of view get to the heart of an issue while remaining civil:

1. Avoid direct insults and personal attacks—the quickest way to turn someone away from your discussion is to attack them personally. This is actually a common logical fallacy called ad hominem, which means "to the person," and it means to attack the person rather than the issue.
2. Avoid generalizations and extreme examples—these are two more logical fallacies called bandwagon, or ad populum, and reduction to absurdity, or argumentum ad absurdum. The first is when you argue that everyone is doing something so it must be right. The second is when you argue that a belief or position would lead to an absurd or extreme outcome.
3. Avoid appealing to emotions rather than facts—it's easy to get emotional if you're debating something about which you feel passionate. Someone disagreeing with you can feel like a personal affront. This fallacy, called argument to compassion, appeals to one's emotions and happens when we mistake feelings for facts. While strong and motivating, our feelings are not great arbiters of the truth.
4. Avoid irrelevant arguments—sometimes it's easy to change the subject when we're debating, especially if we feel flustered or like we're not being heard. Irrelevant conclusion is the fallacy of introducing a topic that may or may not be sound logic but is not about the issue under debate.
5. Avoid appeal to bias—you may not have strong opinions on every topic but, no doubt, you are

opinionated about things that matter to you. This strong view can create a bias, or a leaning toward an idea or belief. While there's nothing wrong with having a strong opinion, you must be mindful to ensure that your bias doesn't create prejudice. Ask yourself if your biases influence the ways in which you interact with other people and with ideas that differ from your own.

6. Avoid appeal to tradition—just because something worked in the past or was true in the past does not necessarily mean that it is true today. It's easy to commit this fallacy, as we often default to "If it ain't broke, don't fix it." It's appealing because it seems to be common sense. However, it ignores questions such as whether the existing or old policy truly works as well as it could and if new technology or new ways of thinking can offer an improvement. Old ways can certainly be good ways, but not simply because they are old.

7. Avoid making assumptions—often, we think we know enough about a topic or maybe even more than the person talking, so we jump ahead to the outcome. We assume we know what they're referring to, thinking about, or even imagining, but this is a dangerous practice because it often leads to misunderstandings. In fact, most logical fallacies are the result of assuming.

8. Strive for root cause analysis—getting at the root cause of something means to dig deeper and deeper until you discover why a problem or disagreement occurred. Sometimes, the most obvious or immediate cause for a problem is not actually the most significant one. Discovering the root cause can help to resolve the conflict or reveal that there isn't one at all.

9. Avoid obstinacy—in the heat of a debate, it's easy to dig in your heels and refuse to acknowledge when you're wrong. Your argument is at stake, and so is your ego. However, it's important to give credit where it's due and to say you're wrong if you are. If you misquoted a fact or made an incorrect assumption, admit to it and move on.

10. Strive for resolution—while some people like to debate for the sake of debating, in the case of a true conflict, both parties should seek agreement, or at least a truce. One way to do this is to listen more than you speak. Listen, listen, listen: you'll learn and perhaps make better points of your own if you deeply consider the other point of view.

ANALYSIS QUESTION

Have you ever witnessed incivility in person or an argument in the news? Briefly describe what happened. Why do you think individuals are willing to shut down communication over issues they are passionate about?

Online Civility

The Internet is the watershed innovation of our time. It provides incredible access to information and resources, helping us to connect in ways inconceivable just a few decades ago. But it also presents risks, and these risks seem to be changing and increasing at the same rate as technology itself. Because of our regular access to the Internet, it's important to create a safe, healthy, and enjoyable online space.

Expectations for Digital Civility in the 2020s

As part of the 2020 Digital Civility research, Microsoft asked more than 12,500 teens and adults in 25 countries to predict the tone and tenor of online behavior in the next decade. Here are some of those findings.

- Situation will improve
- Situation will worsen
- Situation will stay the same

Technology and social media companies' tools and policies to encourage respectful and civil behavior while punishing bad conduct will be …

Your ability to protect your personal information and privacy online will be …

Online discussions about local, national or international politics will be …

The number of women who experience sexual harassment or abuse online will be …

The number of teens who are bullied, harassed or abused online will be …

Figure 9.11 Microsoft's Digital Civility Research survey asked people their opinions on the future of online behavior and communication. While in some cases, the respondents thought circumstances would improve, predictions about the others, such as harassment and bullying, are more bleak. (Credit: Based on work from Microsoft, "Expectations for Digital Civility 2020."[4])

In the survey conducted by Microsoft, "nearly 4 in 10 [respondents] feel unwanted online contact (39%), bullying (39%) and unwelcome sexual attention (39%) will worsen [in 2020]. A slightly smaller percentage (35%) expect people's reputations, both professional and personal, will continue to be attacked online. One-quarter (25%) of respondents see improvement across each of these risk areas in 2020."

Digital civility is the practice of leading with empathy and kindness in all online interactions and treating each other with respect and dignity. This type of civility requires users to fully understand and appreciate potential harms and to follow the new rules of the digital road. You can find a discussion on best practices for online communication, often referred to as Netiquette, in Chapter 8 on Communicating. Following, are some basic guidelines to help exercise digital civility:

- **Live the "Golden Rule"** and treat others with respect and dignity both online and off.
- **Respect differences** of culture, geography, and opinion, and when disagreements surface, engage thoughtfully.
- **Pause before replying** to comments or posts you disagree with, and ensure responses are considerate and free of name-calling and abuse.
- **Stand up for yourself and others** if it's safe and prudent to do so.

---

4 Expectations for Digital Civility. Note: Link leads to direct download.

9.2 Categories of Diversity

Estimated completion time: 16 minutes.

Questions to consider:

- What is identity?
- Can a person have more than one identity?
- Can identity be ambiguous?
- What are fluidity and intersectionality?

The multiple roles we play in life—student, sibling, employee, roommate, for example—are only a partial glimpse into our true identity. Right now, you may think, "I really don't know what I want to be," meaning you don't know what you want to do for a living, but have you ever tried to define yourself in terms of the sum of your parts?

Social roles are those identities we assume in relationship to others. Our social roles tend to shift based on where we are and who we are with. Taking into account your social roles as well as your nationality, ethnicity, race, friends, gender, sexuality, beliefs, abilities, geography, etc., who are you?

Who Am I?

Popeye, a familiar 20th-century cartoon character, was a sailor-philosopher. He declared his own identity in a circular manner, landing us right where we started: "I am what I am and that's all that I am." Popeye proves his existence rather than help us identify him. It is his title, "The Sailor Man," that tells us how Popeye operates in the social sphere.

According to the American Psychological Association, personal identity is an individual's sense of self defined by (a) a set of physical, psychological, and interpersonal characteristics that is not wholly shared with any other person and (b) a range of affiliations (e.g., ethnicity) and social roles. Your identity is tied to the most dominant aspects of your background and personality.[5] It determines the lens through which you see the world and the lens through which you receive information.

ACTIVITY

Complete the following statement using no more than four words:

I am _____.

It is difficult to narrow down our identity to just a few options. One way to complete the statement would be to use gender and geography markers. For example, "I am a male New Englander" or "I am an American woman." Assuming they are true, no one can argue against those identities, but do those statements represent everything or at least most things that identify the speakers? Probably not.

Try finishing the statement again by using as many words as you wish.

I am _____.

---

5 APA Dictionary of Psychology https://dictionary.apa.org/identity proper citation to come

> If you ended up with a long string of descriptors that would be hard for a new acquaintance to manage, don't worry. Our identities are complex and reflect that we lead interesting and multifaceted lives.

To better understand identity, consider how social psychologists describe it. Social psychologists, those who study how social interactions take place, often categorize identity into four types: personal identity, role identity, social identity, and collective identity.

Personal identity captures what distinguishes one person from another based on life experiences. No two people, even identical twins, live the same life.

Role identity defines how we interact in certain situations. Our roles change from setting to setting, and so do our identities. At work you may be a supervisor; in the classroom you are a peer working collaboratively; at home, you may be the parent of a 10-year-old. In each setting, your bubbly personality may be the same, but how your coworkers, classmates, and family see you is different.

Social identity shapes our public lives by our awareness of how we relate to certain groups. For example, an individual might relate to or "identify with" Korean Americans, Chicagoans, Methodists, and Lakers fans. These identities influence our interactions with others. Upon meeting someone, for example, we look for connections as to how we are the same or different. Our awareness of who we are makes us behave a certain way in relation to others. If you identify as a hockey fan, you may feel an affinity for someone else who also loves the game.

Collective identity refers to how groups form around a common cause or belief. For example, individuals may bond over similar political ideologies or social movements. Their identity is as much a physical formation as a shared understanding of the issues they believe in. For example, many people consider themselves part of the collective energy surrounding the #metoo movement. Others may identify as fans of a specific type of entertainment such as Trekkies, fans of the Star Trek series.

"I am large. I contain multitudes." Walt Whitman

In his epic poem *Song of Myself*, Walt Whitman writes, "Do I contradict myself? Very well then I contradict myself (I am large. I contain multitudes.)." Whitman was asserting and defending his shifting sense of self and identity. Those lines importantly point out that our identities may evolve over time. What we do and believe today may not be the same tomorrow. Further, at any one moment, the identities we claim may seem at odds with each other. Shifting identities are a part of personal growth. While we are figuring out who we truly are and what we believe, our sense of self and the image that others have of us may be unclear or ambiguous.

Many people are uncomfortable with identities that do not fit squarely into one category. How do you respond when someone's identity or social role is unclear? Such ambiguity may challenge your sense of certainty about the roles that we all play in relationship to one another. Racial, ethnic, and gender ambiguity, in particular, can challenge some people's sense of social order and social identity.

When we force others to choose only one category of identity (race, ethnicity, or gender, for example) to make ourselves feel comfortable, we do a disservice to the person who identifies with more than one group. For instance, people with multiracial ancestry are often told that they are too much of one and not enough of another.

The actor Keanu Reeves has a complex background. He was born in Beirut, Lebanon, to a white English mother and a father with Chinese-Hawaiian ancestry. His childhood was spent in Hawaii, Australia, New York, and Toronto. Reeves considers himself Canadian and has publicly acknowledged influences from all aspects of his heritage. Would you feel comfortable telling Keanu Reeves how he must identify racially and ethnically?

There is a question many people ask when they meet someone whom they cannot clearly identify by checking a specific identity box. Inappropriate or not, you have probably heard people ask, "What are you?" Would it surprise you if someone like Keanu Reeves shrugged and answered, "I'm just me"?

Malcom Gladwell is an author of five New York Times best-sellers and is hailed as one of Foreign Policy's Top Global Thinkers. He has spoken on his experience with identity as well. Gladwell has a black Jamaican mother and a white Irish father. He often tells the story of how the perception of his hair has allowed him to straddle racial groups. As long as he kept his hair cut very short, his fair skin obscured his black ancestry, and he was most often perceived as white. However, once he let his hair grow long into a curly Afro style, Gladwell says he began being pulled over for speeding tickets and stopped at airport check-ins. His racial expression carried serious consequences.

Figure 9.12 Writer Malcolm Gladwell's racial expression has impacted his treatment by others and his everyday experiences. (Credit: Kris Krug, Pop!Tech / Flickr / Attribution 2.0 Generic (CC-BY 2.0))

Gender

More and more, gender is also a diversity category that we increasingly understand to be less clearly defined. Some people identify themselves as gender fluid or non-binary. "Binary" refers to the notion that gender is only one of two possibilities, male or female. Fluidity suggests that there is a range or continuum of expression. Gender fluidity acknowledges that a person may vacillate between male and female identity.

Asia Kate Dillon is an American actor and the first non-binary actor to perform in a major television show with their roles on *Orange is the New Black* and *Billions*. In an article about the actor, a reporter conducting the interview describes his struggle with trying to describe Dillon to the manager of the restaurant where the two planned to meet. The reporter and the manger struggle with describing someone who does not fit a pre-defined notion of gender identity. Imagine the situation: You're meeting someone at a restaurant for the first time, and you need to describe the person to a manager. Typically, the person's gender would be a part of the description, but what if the person cannot be described as a man or a woman?

Figure 9.13 Asia Kate Dillon is a non-binary actor best known for their roles on *Orange Is the New Black* and *Billions*. (Credit: *Billions* Official Youtube Channel / Wikimedia Commons / Attribution 3.0 Unported (CC-BY 3.0))

Within any group, individuals obviously have a right to define themselves; however, collectively, a group's self-determination is also important. The history of black Americans demonstrates a progression of self-determined labels: Negro, Afro-American, colored, black, African American. Similarly, in the nonbinary community, self-described labels have evolved. Nouns such as *genderqueer* and pronouns such as *hir, ze,* and *Mx.* (instead of *Miss, Mrs. or Mr.*) have entered not only our informal lexicon, but the dictionary as well.

> **Merriam-Webster's dictionary includes a definition of "they" that denotes a nonbinary identity, that is, someone who fluidly moves between male and female identities.**

Transgender men and women were assigned a gender identity at birth that does not fit their true identity. Even though our culture is increasingly giving space to non-heteronormative (straight) people to speak out and live openly, they do so at a risk. Violence against gay, nonbinary, and transgender people occurs at more frequent rates than for other groups.

To make ourselves feel comfortable, we often want people to fall into specific categories so that our own social identity is clear. However, instead of asking someone to make us feel comfortable, we should accept the identity people choose for themselves. Cultural competency includes respectfully addressing individuals as they ask to be addressed.

Table Gender Pronoun Examples

Subjective	Objective	Possessive	Reflexive	Example
She	Her	Hers	Herself	She is speaking. I listened to her. The backpack is hers.
He	Him	His	Himself	He is speaking. I listened to him. The backpack is his.
They	Them	Theirs	Themself	They are speaking. I listened to them. The backpack is theirs.
Ze	Hir/Zir	Hirs/Zirs	Hirself/Zirself	Ze is speaking. I listened to hir. The backpack is zirs.

Table 9.1 The website Transstudent.org provides educational resources such as the above graphic for anyone seeking clarity on gender identity. Note that these are only examples of some gender pronouns, not a complete list.

Intersectionality

The many layers of our multiple identities do not fit together like puzzle pieces with clear boundaries between one piece and another. Our identities overlap, creating a combined identity in which one aspect is inseparable from the next.

The term intersectionality was coined by legal scholar Kimberlé Crenshaw in 1989 to describe how the experience of black women was a unique combination of gender and race that could not be divided into two separate identities. In other words, this group could not be seen solely as women or solely as black; where their identities overlapped is considered the "intersection," or crossroads, where identities combine in specific and inseparable ways.

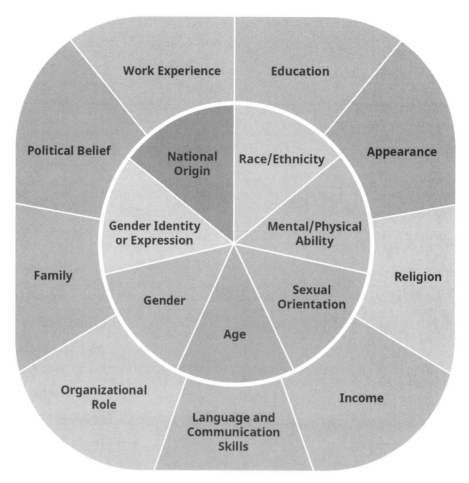

Figure 9.14 Our identities are formed by dozens of factors, sometimes represented in intersection wheels. Consider the subset of identity elements represented here. Generally, the outer ring are elements that may change relatively often, while the inner circle are often considered more permanent. (There are certainly exceptions.) How does each contribute to who you are, and how would possible change alter your self-defined identity?

Intersectionality and awareness of intersectionality can drive societal change, both in how people see themselves and how they interact with others. That experience can be very inward-facing, or can be more external. It can also lead to debate and challenges. For example, the term "Latinx" is growing in use because it is seen as more inclusive than "Latino/Latina," but some people—including scholars and advocates—lay out substantive arguments against its use. While the debate continues, it serves as an important reminder of a key element of intersectionality: Never assume that all people in a certain group or population feel the same way. Why not? Because people are more than any one element of their identity; they are defined by more than their race, color, geographic origin, gender, or socio-economic status. The overlapping aspects of each person's identity and experiences will create a unique perspective.

ANALYSIS QUESTION

Consider the intersectionality of race, gender, and sexuality; religion, ethnicity, and geography; military experience; age and socioeconomic status; and many other ways our identities overlap. Consider how these overlap in you.

Do you know people who talk easily about their various identities? How does it inform the way you interact with them?

9.3 Navigating the Diversity Landscape

Estimated completion time: 22 minutes.

Questions to consider:

- What happens when we make assumptions about others?
- Are microaggressions honest mistakes?
- How do I know if I have a diversity "problem"?
- How important is diversity awareness in the college classroom?

Avoid Making Assumptions

By now you should be aware of the many ways diversity can be both observable and less apparent. Based on surface clues, we may be able to approximate someone's age, weight, and perhaps their geographical origin, but even with those observable characteristics, we cannot be sure about how individuals define themselves. If we rely too heavily on assumptions, we may be buying into stereotypes, or generalizations.

Stereotyping robs people of their individual identities. If we buy into stereotypes, we project a profile onto someone that probably is not true. Prejudging people without knowing them, better known as prejudice or bias, has consequences for both the person who is biased and the individual or group that is prejudged. In such a scenario, the intimacy of real human connections is lost. Individuals are objectified, meaning that they only serve as symbolic examples of who we assume they are instead of the complex, intersectional individuals we know each person to be.

Stereotyping may be our way of avoiding others' complexities. When we stereotype, we do not have to remember distinguishing details about a person. We simply write their stories for ourselves and let those stories fulfill who we expect those individuals to be. For example, a hiring manager may project onto an Asian American the stereotype of being good at math, and hire her as a researcher over her Hispanic counterpart. Similarly, an elementary school teacher may recruit an Indian American sixth-grader to the spelling bee team because many Indian American students have won national tournaments in the recent past. A real estate developer may hire a gay man as an interior designer because he has seen so many gay men performing this job on television programs. A coach chooses a white male student to be a quarterback because traditionally, quarterbacks have been white men. In those scenarios, individuals of other backgrounds, with similar abilities, may have been overlooked because they do not fit the stereotype of who others suspect them to be.

Earlier in this chapter, equity and inclusion were discussed as going hand in hand with achieving civility and diversity. In the above scenarios, equity and inclusion are needed as guiding principles for those with decision-making power who are blocking opportunity for nontraditional groups. Equity might be achieved by giving a diverse group of people access to internships to demonstrate their skills. Inclusion might be achieved by assembling a hiring or recruiting committee that might have a better chance of seeing beyond stereotypical expectations.

APPLICATION

Often, our assumptions and their impacts are not life-changing, but they can be damaging to others and limiting to our own understanding. Consider the following scenarios, and answer the questions that follow.

Scenario 1:

During an in-class conversation about a new mission to explore Mars, two classmates offer opinions.

- Student A says, "We should focus on this planet before we focus on others."
- Student B responds immediately with, "If we're going to stop climate change, we'll probably find the answer through science related to space travel."

What assumption did student B make about student A's point? What else, aside from climate change, could student A have been considering?

Scenario 2:

For an important group project, an instructor designates teams of six students and gives them time to set up their work schedule for the assignment. One group of students, most of whom don't know each other well, agrees to meet two nights later. They initially propose to get together in the library, but at the last moment one member suggests an off-campus restaurant; several of the others agree right away and move on to other topics. The remaining two students look at each other uncomfortably. One interjects, suggesting they go back to the original idea of meeting in the library, but the others are already getting up to leave. It's clear that two of the students are uncomfortable meeting at the restaurant.

What might be the reason that two of the students are not comfortable meeting over dinner? What assumptions did the others make?

Being civil and inclusive does not require a deep-seated knowledge of the backgrounds and perspectives of everyone you meet. That would be impossible. But avoiding assumptions and being considerate will build better relationships and provide a more effective learning experience. It takes openness and self-awareness and sometimes requires help or advice, but learning to be sensitive—practicing assumption avoidance—is like a muscle you can strengthen.

Be Mindful of Microaggressions

Whether we mean to or not, we sometimes offend people by not thinking about what we say and the manner in which we say it. One danger of limiting our social interactions to people who are from our own social group is in being insensitive to people who are not like us. The term *microaggression* refers to acts of insensitivity that reveal our inherent biases, cultural incompetency, and hostility toward someone outside of our community. Those biases can be toward race, gender, nationality, or any other diversity variable. The individual on the receiving end of a microaggression is reminded of the barriers to complete acceptance and understanding in the relationship. Let's consider an example.

Ann is new to her office job. Her colleagues are friendly and helpful, and her first two months have been promising. She uncovered a significant oversight in a financial report, and, based on her attention to detail, was put on a team working with a large client. While waiting in line at the cafeteria one day, Ann's new boss overhears her laughing and talking loudly with some colleagues. He then steps into the conversation, saying, "Ann, this isn't a night at one of your clubs. Quiet down." As people from the nearby tables look on, Ann is humiliated and angered.

What was Ann's manager implying? What could he have meant by referring to "*your* clubs?" How would you feel if such a comment were openly directed at you? One reaction to this interaction might be to say, "So what? Why let other people determine how you feel? Ignore them." While that is certainly reasonable, it may ignore the pain and invalidation of the experience. And even if you could simply ignore some of these comments, there is a compounding effect of being frequently, if not constantly, barraged by such experiences.

Consider the table below, which highlights common examples of microaggressions. In many cases, the person speaking these phrases may not mean to be offensive. In fact, in some cases the speaker might think they are being *nice*. However, appropriate terminology and other attitudes or acceptable descriptions change all the time. Before saying something, consider how a person could take the words differently than you meant them. As we discussed in Chapter 8, emotional intelligence and empathy can help understand another's perspective.

Microaggressions

Category	Microaggression	Why It's Offensive
Educational Status or Situation	"You're an athlete; you don't need to study."	Stereotypes athletes and ignores their hard work.
	"You don't get financial aid; you must be rich."	"Even an assumption of privilege can be invalidating.
	"Did they have honors classes at your high school?"	Implies that someone is less prepared or intelligent based on their geography.
Race, Ethnicity, National Origin"	"You speak so well for someone like you."	Implies that people of a certain race/ethnicity can't speak well.
	"No, where are you *really* from?"	Calling attention to someone's national origin makes them feel separate."
	"You must be good at ____."	Falsely connects identity to ability.

Table 9.2 Have you made statements like these, perhaps without realizing the offense they might cause? Some of these could be intended as compliments, but they could have the unintended effect of diminishing or invalidating someone. (Credit: Modification of work by Derald Wing Sue[6].)

---

6   Adapted from Sue, Derald Wing, Microaggressions in Everyday Life: Race, Gender and Sexual Orientation, Wiley & Sons, 2010

Microaggressions

Category	Microaggression	Why It's Offensive
Gender and Gender Identity	"My people had it so much worse than yours did."	Makes assumptions and diminishes suffering/difficulty.
	"I'm not even going to try your name. It looks too difficult."	Dismisses a person's culture and heritage.
	"It's so much easier for black people to get into college."	Assumes that merit is not the basis for achievement.
	"They're *so* emotional."	Assumes a person cannot be emotional and rational.
	"I guess you can't meet tonight because you have to take care of your son?"	Assumes a parent (of any gender) cannot participate.
	"I don't get all this pronoun stuff, so I'm just gonna call you what I call you."	Diminishes the importance of gender identity; indicates a lack of empathy.
	"I can't even tell you used to be a woman."	Conflates identity with appearance, and assumes a person needs someone else's validation.
	"You're too good-looking to be so smart."	Connects outward appearance to ability.
Sexual Orientation	"I support you; just don't throw it in my face."	Denies another person's right to express their identity or point of view.
	"You seem so rugged for a gay guy."	Stereotypes all gay people as being "not rugged," and could likely offend the recipient.
	"I might try being a lesbian."	May imply that sexual orientation is a choice.
	"I can't even keep track of all these new categories."	Bisexual, pansexual, asexual, and other sexual orientations are just as valid and deserving of respect as more binary orientations.
	"You can't just love whomever you want; pick one."	
Age	"Are you going to need help with the software?"	May stereotype an older person as lacking experience with the latest technology.

Table 9.2 Have you made statements like these, perhaps without realizing the offense they might cause? Some of these could be intended as compliments, but they could have the unintended effect of diminishing or invalidating someone. (Credit: Modification of work by Derald Wing Sue.)

Microaggressions

Category	Microaggression	Why It's Offensive
	"Young people have it so easy nowadays."	Makes a false comparison between age and experience.
	"Okay, boomer."	Dismisses an older generation as out of touch.
Size	"I bet no one messes with you."	Projects a tendency to be aggressive onto a person of large stature.
	"You are so cute and tiny."	Condescending to a person of small stature.
	"I wish I was thin and perfect like you."	Equates a person's size with character.
Ability	(To a person using a wheelchair) "I wish I could sit down wherever I went."	Falsely assumes a wheelchair is a luxury; minimizes disabilities.
	"You don't have to complete the whole test. Just do your best."	Assumes that a disability means limited intellectual potential.
	"I'm blind without my glasses."	Equating diminished capacity with a true disability.

Table 9.2 Have you made statements like these, perhaps without realizing the offense they might cause? Some of these could be intended as compliments, but they could have the unintended effect of diminishing or invalidating someone. (Credit: Modification of work by Derald Wing Sue.)

Everyone Has a Problem: Implicit Bias

One reason we fall prey to stereotypes is our own implicit bias. Jo Handelsman and Natasha Sakraney, who developed science and technology policy during the Obama administration, defined implicit bias.

According to Handelsman and Sakraney, "A lifetime of experience and cultural history shapes people and their judgments of others. Research demonstrates that most people hold unconscious, implicit assumptions that influence their judgments and perceptions of others. Implicit bias manifests in expectations or assumptions about physical or social characteristics dictated by stereotypes that are based on a person's race, gender, age, or ethnicity. People who intend to be fair, and believe they are egalitarian, apply biases unintentionally. Some behaviors that result from implicit bias manifest in actions, and others are embodied in the absence of action; either can reduce the quality of the workforce and create an unfair and destructive environment."[7]

The notion of bias being "implicit," or unconsciously embedded in our thoughts and actions, is what makes this characteristic hard to recognize and evaluate. You may assume that you hold no racial bias, but messages from our upbringing, social groups, and media can feed us negative racial stereotypes no matter how carefully

---

7   Handlesman, Jo and Sakraney, Natasha. White House Office of Science and Technology Policy. https://obamawhitehouse.archives.gov/sites/default/files/microsites/ostp/bias_9-14-15_final.pdf.

we select and consume information. Further, online environments have algorithms that reduce our exposure to diverse points of view. Psychologists generally agree that implicit bias affects the judgements we make about others.

Harvard University's Project Implicit website offers an interactive implicit association test that measures individual preference for characteristics such as weight, skin color, and gender. During the test, participants are asked to match a series of words and images with positive or negative associations. Test results, researchers suggest, can indicate the extent to which there is implicit bias in favor of or against a certain group. Completing a test like this might reveal unconscious feelings you were previously aware you had.

The researchers who developed the test make clear that there are limitations to its validity and that for some, the results of the test can be unsettling. The test makers advise not taking the test if you feel unprepared to receive unexpected results.

APPLICATION

Take the Project Implicit (https://openstax.org/l/IAT) test and write a brief passage about your results.

Do you think the results accurately reflect your attitude toward the group you tested on? Can you point to any actions or thoughts you have about the group you tested on that are or are not reflected in the test results? Will you change any behaviors or try to think differently about the group you tested on based on your results? Why or why not?

Cultural Competency in the College Classroom

We carry our attitudes about gender, ethnicity, sexual orientation, age, and other diversity categories with us wherever we go. The college classroom is no different than any other place. Both educators and students maintain their implicit bias and are sometimes made uncomfortable by interacting with people different than themselves. Take for example a female freshman who has attended a school for girls for six years before college. She might find being in the classroom with her new male classmates a culture shock and dismiss male students' contributions to class discussions. Similarly, a homeschooled student may be surprised to find that no one on campus shares his religion. He may feel isolated in class until he finds other students of similar background and experience. Embedded in your classroom may be peers who are food insecure, undocumented, veterans, atheist, Muslim, or politically liberal or conservative. These identities may not be visible, but they still may separate and even marginalize these members of your community. If, in the context of classroom conversations, their perspectives are overlooked, they may also feel very isolated.

In each case, the students' assumptions, previous experience with diversity of any kind, and implicit bias surface. How each student reacts to the new situation can differ. One reaction might be to self-segregate, that is, locate people they believe are similar to them based on how they look, the assumption being that those people will share the same academic skills, cultural interests, and personal values that make the student feel comfortable. The English instructor at the beginning of this chapter who assumed all of his students were the same demonstrated how this strategy could backfire.

You do not have to be enrolled in a course related to diversity, such as Asian American literature, to be concerned about diversity in the classroom. Diversity touches all aspects of our lives and can enter a curriculum or discussion at any time because each student and the instructor bring multiple identities and concerns into the classroom. Ignoring these concerns, which often reveal themselves as questions, makes for an unfulfilling educational experience.

In higher education, diversity includes not only the identities we have discussed such as race and gender, but also academic preparation and ability, learning differences, familiarity with technology, part-time status, language, and other factors students bring with them. Of course, the instructor, too, brings diversity into the classroom setting. They decide how to incorporate diverse perspectives into class discussions, maintain rules of civility, choose inclusive materials to study or reference, receive training on giving accommodations to students who need them, and acknowledge their own implicit bias. If they are culturally competent, both students and instructors are juggling many concerns.

How do you navigate diversity in the college classroom?

Academic Freedom Allows for Honest Conversations

Academic freedom applies to the permission instructors and students have to follow a line of intellectual inquiry without the fear of censorship or sanction. There are many heavily contested intellectual and cultural debates that, for some, are not resolved. A student who wants to argue against prevailing opinion has the right to do so based on academic freedom. Many point to a liberal bias on college campuses. Conservative points of view on immigration, education, and even science, are often not accepted on campus as readily as liberal viewpoints. An instructor or student who wants to posit a conservative idea, however, has the right to do so because of academic freedom.

Uncomfortable conversations about diversity are a part of the college classroom landscape. For example, a student might use statistical data to argue that disparities in degrees for men and women in chemistry reflect an advantage in analytical ability for men. While many would disagree with that theory, the student could pursue that topic in a discussion or paper as long as they use evidence and sound, logical reasoning.

"I'm just me."

Remember the response to the "What are you?" question for people whose racial or gender identity was ambiguous? "I'm just me" also serves those who are undecided about diversity issues or those who do not fall into hard categories such as feminist, liberal, conservative, or religious. Ambiguity sometimes makes others feel uncomfortable. For example, if someone states she is a Catholic feminist unsure about abortion rights, another student may wonder how to compare her own strong pro-life position to her classmate's uncertainty. It would be much easier to know exactly which side her classmate is on. Some people straddle the fence on big issues, and that is OK. You do not have to fit neatly into one school of thought. Answer your detractors with "I'm just me," or tell them if you genuinely don't know enough about an issue or are not ready to take a strong position.

Seek Resources and Projects That Contribute to Civility

A culturally responsive curriculum addresses cultural and ethnic differences of students. Even in classrooms full of minority students, the textbooks and topics may only reflect American cultural norms determined by the mainstream and tradition. Students may not relate to teaching that never makes reference to their socio-economic background, race, or their own way of thinking and expression. Educators widely believe that a culturally responsive curriculum, one that integrates relatable contexts for learning and reinforces cultural norms of the students receiving the information, makes a difference.

The K-12 classroom is different than the college classroom. Because of academic freedom, college instructors are not required to be culturally inclusive. (They *are* usually required to be respectful and civil, but there are different interpretations of those qualities.) Because American colleges are increasingly more sensitive to issues regarding diversity, faculty are compelled to be inclusive. Still, diversity is not always adequately addressed. In his TED "Talk Can Art Amend History?" the artist Titus Kaphar tells the story of the art history class that influenced him to become an artist and provides an example of this absence of diversity in the college classroom. Kaphar explains that his instructor led his class through important periods and artists throughout history, but failed to spend time on black artists, something that Kaphar was anxiously awaiting. The instructor stated that there was just not enough time to cover it. While the professor probably did not intend to be noninclusive, her choice resulted in just that. Kaphar let his disappointment fuel his passion and mission to amend the representation of black figures in historical paintings. His work brings to light the unnoticed black figures that are too often overlooked.

Figure 9.15 In *Twisted Tropes,* Titus Kaphar reworks a painting to bring a black figure to the forefront of an arrangement in which she had previously been marginalized. (Credit: smallcurio / Flickr / Attribution 2.0 Generic (CC-BY 2.0))

Any student can respond to a lack of diversity in a curriculum as Titus Kaphar did. Where you find diversity missing, when possible, fill in the gaps with research papers and projects that broaden your exposure to diverse perspectives. Take the time to research contributions in your field by underrepresented groups. Discover the diversity issues relevant to your major. Are women well-represented in your field? Is there equity when it comes to access to opportunities such as internships? Are veterans welcomed? Do the academic societies in your discipline have subgroups or boards focused on diversity and equity? (Most do.) Resources for expanding our understanding and inclusion of diversity issues are all around us.

Directly Confront Prejudice

To draw our attention to possible danger, the Department of Homeland Security has adopted the phrase, "If you see something, say something." That credo can easily be adopted to confront stereotypes and bias: "If you hear something, say something." Academic freedom protects students and instructors from reprisal for having unpopular opinions, but prejudice is never correct, nor should it be tolerated. Do not confuse hate speech, such as sexist language, anti-Semitism, xenophobia, and acts that reflect those points of view, with academic freedom. Yes, the classroom is a place to discuss these attitudes, but it is not a place to direct those sentiments toward fellow students, educators, or society in general.

Most higher education institutions have mission statements and codes of conduct that warn students about engaging in such behavior. The consequences for violators are usually probation and possibly dismissal. Further policies such as affirmative action and Title IX are instituted to evaluate and maintain racial and gender equity.

APPLICATION

No one knows when a racist or sexist attack is coming. The Barnard Center for Research on Women has created a video suggesting ways to be an ally to people victimized by intolerant behavior (https://openstax.org/l/dontbeabystander) .

Affirmative Action and Higher Education

Affirmative action is a policy that began during the John F. Kennedy administration to eliminate discrimination in employment. Since that time, it has expanded as a policy to protect from discrimination in a number of contexts, including higher education. Most notably in higher education, affirmative action has been used to create equity in access. Institutions have used affirmative action as a mandate of sorts in admission policies to create diverse student bodies. Colleges sometimes overlook traditional admissions criteria and use socioeconomic and historical disparities in education equity as criteria to admit underrepresented groups. Affirmative action is a federal requirement to be met by entities that contract with the federal government; most colleges are federal government contractors and must adhere to the policy by stating a timeline by which its affirmative action goals are met.

Many interpret "goals" as quotas, meaning that a certain number of students from underrepresented groups would be admitted, presumably to meet affirmative action requirements. Opposition to affirmative action in college admissions has been pursued in several well-known court cases.

Regents of the University of California v. Bakke

This 1978 case resulted in a U.S. Supreme Court decision to allow race to be used as one of the criteria in higher education admission policies as long as quotas were not established and race was not the only criterion for admission. The case stemmed from Alan Bakke, an applicant to the University of California at Davis Medical School, suing the university because he was not admitted but had higher test scores and grades than minority students who had been accepted. Lawyers for Bakke referenced the same equal protection clause of the 14th Amendment used to desegregate public schools in *Brown v. Board of Education*. The "reverse discrimination" denied him equal protection under the law.

Fisher v. University of Texas

In 2016, the U.S. Supreme Court decided another affirmative action case regarding Fisher v. University of Texas. Abigail Fisher also argued that she had been denied college admission based on race. The case ended in favor of the university. Justice Kennedy, in the majority opinion, wrote:

> "A university is in large part defined by those intangible "qualities which are incapable of objective measurement but which make for greatness." Considerable deference is owed to a university in defining those intangible characteristics, like student body diversity, that are central to its identity and educational mission."

In each of the above landmark cases, affirmative action in college admission policies were upheld. However, cases of reverse discrimination in college admission policies continue to be pursued.

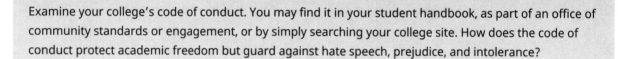

ANALYSIS QUESTION

Examine your college's code of conduct. You may find it in your student handbook, as part of an office of community standards or engagement, or by simply searching your college site. How does the code of conduct protect academic freedom but guard against hate speech, prejudice, and intolerance?

Title IX and Higher Education

Title IX of the Education Amendments of 1972 states, "No person in the United States shall, on the basis of sex, be excluded from participation in, be denied the benefits of, or be subjected to discrimination under any education program or activity receiving Federal financial assistance." As with affirmative action, Title IX applies to institutions that receive federal funding, such as public and charter schools, for-profit schools, libraries, and museums in the United States and its territories.

According to the Office for Civil Rights, educational programs and activities receiving federal funds must operate in a nondiscriminatory manner. Title IX addresses recruitment, admissions, and counseling; financial assistance; athletics; sex-based harassment; treatment of pregnant and parenting students; discipline; single-sex education; and employment.

Before the enactment of Title IX, there were few if any protections provided for women college students. To give some perspective, consider this description of the circumstances:

"Young women were not admitted into many colleges and universities, athletic scholarships for women were rare, and math and science was a realm reserved for boys. Girls square danced instead of playing sports, studied home economics instead of training for 'male-oriented' (read: higher-paying) trades. Girls could become teachers and nurses, but not doctors or principals; women rarely were awarded tenure and even more rarely appointed college presidents. There was no such thing as sexual harassment because 'boys will be boys,' after all, and if a student got pregnant, her formal education ended. Graduate professional schools openly discriminated against women."[8]

---

8 WInslow, Barbara. "The Impact of Title IX." Gilder-Lerhman Institute. https://faculty.uml.edu/sgallagher/The_Impact_of_Title_IX-_GilderLehrman.pdf

The protections of Title IX have been invoked in college athletics to ensure women's athletic programs are sustained. In addition, schools must make efforts to prevent sexual harassment and violence. Gender discrimination under Title IX extends to the protection of transgender students so that they are treated as the gender they identify with.

> ### ANALYSIS QUESTION
>
> Based on the cases against affirmative action in higher education, are admissions policies that use race, along with other factors, as admissions criteria fair? What other options do you think would create equity in admissions?

9.4 Inclusivity and Civility: What Role Can I Play?

Estimated completion time: 10 minutes.

Questions to consider:

- Is it my fault that I have privilege?
- How long will diversity, equity, and inclusion efforts continue?
- What is to be gained by cultural competency?

Privilege Is Not Just for White People

Privilege is a right or exemption from liability or duty granted as a special benefit or advantage. Oppression is the result of the "use of institutional privilege and power, wherein one person or group benefits at the expense of another,"[9] according to the University of Southern California Suzanne Dworak Peck School of Social Work.

Just as everyone has implicit bias, everyone has a certain amount of privilege, too. For example, consider the privilege brought by being a certain height. If someone's height is close to the average height, they likely have a privilege of convenience when it comes to many day-to-day activities. A person of average height does not need assistance reaching items on high store shelves and does not need adjustments to their car to reach the brake pedal. There's nothing wrong with having this privilege, but recognizing it, especially when considering others who do not share it, can be eye-opening and empowering.

Wealthy people have privilege of not having to struggle economically. The wealthy can build retirement savings, can afford to live in the safest of neighborhoods, and can afford to pay out of pocket for their children's private education. People with a college education and advanced degrees are privileged because a college degree allows for a better choice of employment and earning potential. Their privilege doesn't erase the hard work and sacrifice necessary to earn those degrees, but the degrees often lead to advantages. And, yes, white people are privileged over racial minorities. Remember Malcolm Gladwell's explanation of how he was treated when people assumed he was white as opposed to how people treated him when they assumed

---

9 Golbach, Jeremy. "A Guide to Discussion Identity, Power, and Priveledge." https://msw.usc.edu/mswusc-blog/diversity-workshop-guide-to-discussing-identity-power-and-privilege/

he was black?

It is no one's fault that they may have privilege in any given situation. In pursuit of civility, diversity, equity, and inclusion, the goal is to not exploit privilege but to share it. What does that mean? It means that when given an opportunity to hire a new employee or even pick someone for your study group, you make an effort to be inclusive and not dismiss someone who has not had the same academic advantages as you. Perhaps you could mentor a student who might otherwise feel isolated. Sharing your privilege could also mean recognizing when diversity is absent, speaking out on issues others feel intimidated about supporting, and making donations to causes you find worthy.

> **In pursuit of civility, diversity, equity, and inclusion, the goal is to not exploit privilege but to share it.**

When you are culturally competent, you become aware of how your privilege may put others at a disadvantage. With some effort, you can level the playing field without making yourself vulnerable to falling behind.

APPLICATION

Think about a regular activity such as going to a class. In what ways are you privileged in that situation? How can you share your privilege with others?

"Eternal vigilance is the price of civility."

The original statement reads, "Eternal vigilance is the price of liberty." History sometimes credits that statement to Thomas Jefferson and sometimes to Wendell Holmes. Ironically, no one was paying enough attention to document it accurately. Still, the meaning is clear—if we relax our standards, we may lose everything.

Civility is like liberty; it requires constant attention. We have to adjust diversity awareness, policies, and laws to accommodate the ever-changing needs of society. Without the vigilance of civil rights workers, society could have lapsed back into the Jim Crow era. Without activists such as Betty Friedan, Gloria Steinem, and Flo Kennedy remaining vigilant, women might not have made the gains they did in the 1970s. Constant attention is still needed because in the case of women's earning power, they only make about 80 cents for every dollar a man makes. Constant vigilance requires passion and persistence. The activism chronologies of Native Americans, African Americans, Asian Americans, the LGBTQ+ community, immigrants, students, labor, and other groups is full of stops and starts, twists and turns that represent adjustments to their movements based on the shifting needs of younger generations. As long as there are new generations of these groups, we will need to pursue diversity, equity, and inclusion.

Your Future and Cultural Competency

Where will you be in five years? Will you own your own business? Will you be a stay-at-home parent? Will you be making your way up the corporate ladder of your dream job? Will you be pursuing an advanced degree? Maybe you will have settled into an entry-level job with good benefits and be willing to stay there for a while.

Wherever life leads you in the future, you will need to be culturally competent. Your competency will be a valuable skill not only because of the increasing diversity and awareness in America, but also because we live in a world with increasing global connections.

If you do not speak a second language, try to learn one. If you can travel, do so, even if it's to another state or region of the United States. See how others live in order to understand their experience and yours. To quote Mark Twain, "Travel is fatal to prejudice, bigotry, and narrow-mindedness." The more we expose ourselves to different cultures and experiences, the more understanding and tolerance we tend to have.

The United States is not perfect in its practice of diversity, equity, and inclusion. Still, compared to much of the world, Americans are privileged on a number of fronts. Not everyone can pursue their dreams as freely as Americans do. Our democratic elections and representative government give us a role in our future.

Understanding diversity and being culturally competent will make for a better future for everyone.

Summary

Understanding diversity, especially in the context of our country's history, is an important part of being an engaged citizen who can help us to adapt to a changing world. Diversity goes hand in hand with the concepts of equity and inclusion, which increase the chances of equal opportunity and representation. Sometimes creating inclusive communities upsets the social order with which people are familiar. Change can be difficult, and people are passionate. These passions can disrupt communities and communication with uncivil behavior, or people can "fight fair" and use strategies that allow for the smooth exchange of ideas.

Everyone has a personal identity made up of various aspects and experiences—intersectionality. Some elements of identity place people in a diversity category. Some categories are expansive and well understood; others are new and may face scrutiny. Policies and laws have been put in place to protect underrepresented citizens from discrimination. These standards are constantly being challenged to make sure that they allow for the shifting demographics of the United States and shifting values of its citizens.

Cultural competency, which includes our ability to adapt to diversity, is a valuable skill in our communities and workplaces. The more culturally competent we are, the more we can help safeguard diversity and make equitable and inclusive connections on a global scale.

Career Connection

Keisha went to a temp agency to sign up for part-time work. The person in charge there gave her several tests on office skills. She checked Keisha's typing speed, her ability to handle phone calls, and her writing skills. Keisha also took a grammar test and a test about how to handle disputes in the office. The tester also had Keisha answer questions about whether it was OK to take home office supplies and other appropriate things to do and not to do.

The tester told Keisha that she scored very well on the evaluations, but she never called Keisha back for a job or even an interview. Keisha knows that she presented herself well, but wonders if she was not called back because she wears her hair in dreadlocks or because she has been told that her name sounds African American?

Reflection questions:

- Can this student say that she was discriminated against?

- What would you do to determine why you were not called back for a job?
- Should Keisha ask about how her name and appearance were received?

 ## Rethinking

Revisit the questions you answered at the beginning of the chapter, and consider one option you learned in this chapter that might make you rethink how you answered each one. Has this chapter prompted you to consider changing any of your feelings or practices?

Rank the following questions on a scale of 1–4. 1 = "least like me" and 4 = "most like me."

1. I'm aware of the different categories of diversity and the various populations I may encounter.
2. I think we sometimes go too far in trying to be sensitive to different groups.
3. I think nearly everybody in our society has equal opportunity.
4. It's not my role to ensure equity and inclusiveness among my peers or colleagues.

 ## Where do you go from here?

This chapter touched on many elements of civility and diversity, and mentioned a wide array of groups, identities, and populations. But the chapter certainly did not explore every concept or reflect every group you may encounter. In a similar way, you can't know everything about everyone, but you can build cultural competency and understanding to make people feel included and deepen your abilities and relationships.

Sometimes learning about one group or making one person feel comfortable can be as important as addressing a larger population. To that end, consider researching or discussing one of the following topics to increase your level of civility and understanding:

- Appropriate terminology and ways to address members of certain populations. For example, ways to properly describe people with certain disabilities, or discuss issues around racial or gender identity.
- Discussions or debates related to civility and intersectionality, such as whether "Latinx" should be used instead of "Latino/Latina," or whether certain sports team mascots can be considered offensive.
- Major historical figures or events related to a certain group.
- Academic majors and research centers/groups related to aspects of diversity.
- Historical events at your college or in your city related to civil rights.

10 Understanding Financial literacy

Figure 10.1 Financial success depends on getting a good start and avoiding setbacks and wrong turns. It's a lifelong process, more like a marathon than a sprint. (Credit: Bengt Nyman / Flickr / Attribution 2.0 Generic (CC-BY 2.0))

Chapter Outline

10.1 Personal Financial Planning
10.2 Savings, Expenses, and Budgeting
10.3 Banking and Emergency Funds
10.4 Credit Cards and Other Debt
10.5 Education Debt: Paying for College
10.6 Defending against Attack: Securing Your Identity and Accounts

Introduction

Student Survey

How financially literate are you? This survey will help you determine how the chapter concepts relate to you right now. As we are introduced to new concepts and practices, it can be informative to reflect on how your understanding changes over time. We'll revisit these questions at the end of the chapter to see whether your feelings have changed. Take this quick survey to figure it out, ranking the statements on a scale of 1–4, 1 meaning "least like me" and 4 meaning "most like me."

1. I actively and regularly plan and/or monitor my finances.
2. I understand the benefits and risks of credit.
3. I have a plan to repay my student loans.
4. I regularly take steps to protect my identity and assets.

You can also take the Chapter 10 survey (https://openstax.org/l/collegesurvey10) anonymously online.

STUDENT PROFILE

"A big part of the college experience for many students is the art of the student loan process. This has been both a painful and challenging experience for me over the course of the first semester. The biggest struggle for me has been simply understanding what everything means and what I'm supposed to do. Another challenge has been determining how exactly I'm going to pay these loans back while also saving for rent, utilities, additional expenses, and a study abroad fund with a part-time job that I don't even have yet."

—**Hanna Moyster**

About This Chapter

In this chapter, you will learn to reach your personal life goals by implementing financial planning and strategies to protect yourself, manage your money today, and put yourself in a better position for tomorrow. How you act today impacts your tomorrow.

By the end of this chapter, you should be able to do the following:

1. Align your personal and financial goals through smart financial planning.
2. Create a saving and spending plan and track your performance.
3. Plan for emergencies.
4. Identify best practices and risks associated with credit cards and other debt.
5. Determine the best opportunities for you to finance your college education.
6. Articulate specific ways to secure your identity and accounts.

What Would You Do?

Everything was working out for Elan. They got into the college they wanted to, and some friends were planning to attend as well. They felt like an adult, and were looking forward to new freedoms and opportunities. Elan's parents let them get a credit card after high school graduation. Elan shared an apartment with their friends just off campus, and was able to get where they needed to go because they had a car. Elan had also saved over $1,000 from gifts and a summer job. They needed a new laptop.

Elan planned to stay within set limits. They went to the store found a very knowledgeable salesperson, Jermain, who said he knew exactly what Elan needed. Jermain pointed out that the laptop in Elan's budget would do schoolwork just fine, but it was not as powerful as the best top-of-the line unit with advanced gaming features. Plus, the better computer came with new headphones! Jermain suggested that Elan could later sell the computer to incoming students. (Most freshmen bought used computers if they did not have one when they came to school.) The high-powered computer was $2,000, though, and Elan didn't have that much money. Maybe they should use the credit card? Maybe their new part-time job would pay for it. But Jermain arranged for a small down payment and monthly payments of only $100. That did not seem too bad to Elan. The future looked bright!

At least, that's what Elan thought. They soon realized that working more hours meant fewer hours to study. Meanwhile, Elan's rent and gas usage went up, and, as a young car owner, their insurance was through the roof. Only three months into the first semester, Elan missed a payment on the laptop and accrued a late fee. They put the next laptop payment on the credit card. Soon, Elan was alternating payments between the credit card, laptop, and car, building up interest and late charges. Now Elan was having trouble paying their rent and started getting calls from creditors. Everything had seemed so promising. Elan didn't know where they had gone wrong.

Elan comes to you and shares the situation. They ask, "What could I have done differently?"

This chapter offers you insight into your finances so that you can make good decisions and avoid costly mistakes. We all face chances to spend money and try to get what we want. Many think only about now and not next month, next year, or ten years from now, but our behavior now has consequences later. Not everyone can own all the latest technology, drive their dream car, continually invest for their retirement, or live in the perfect home at this moment. But by understanding the different components of earning money, banking, credit, and budgeting, you can begin working toward your personal and financial goals. We'll also discuss a related topic, safeguarding your accounts and personal information, which is critical to protecting everything you've worked for. By the end of this chapter, you will have good insights for Elan . . . and you!

10.1 Personal Financial Planning

Estimated completion time: 13 minutes.

Questions to consider:

- What simple steps do I take to create a financial plan?
- How do I use financial planning in everyday life?
- How is the financial planning process implemented for every purchase?

If you fail to plan, you are planning to fail.

Honestly, practicing money management isn't that hard to figure out. In many ways it's similar to playing a video game. The first time you play a game, you may feel awkward or have the lowest score. Playing for a while can make you OK at the game. But if you learn the rules of the game, figure out how to best use each tool in the game, read strategy guides from experts, and practice, you can get really good at it.

Money management is the same. It's not enough to "figure it out as you go." If you want to get good at managing your money, you must treat money like you treat your favorite game. You have to come at it with a well-researched plan. Research has shown that people with stronger finances are healthier[1] and happier,[2] have better marriages,[3] and even have better cognitive functioning.[4]

WHAT STUDENTS SAY

1. What is your top immediate financial priority?
   a. Minimizing debt
   b. Get a better job
   c. Pay for college
   d. Move out on my own

---

1 https://www.sciencedirect.com/science/article/pii/S0277953613002839
2 https://academic.oup.com/geronj/article-abstract/38/5/626/578092
3 https://onlinelibrary.wiley.com/doi/abs/10.1111/j.1741-3729.2012.00715.x and http://onlinelibrary.wiley.com/doi/10.1111/j.1741-3729.2012.00715.x/abstract
4 https://science.sciencemag.org/content/341/6149/976%20

e. Get a car
   f. Increase my savings or money on hand
2. Which aspect of your finances concerns you the most?
   a. The amount of debt I have or will have
   b. Getting a job that will pay well enough
   c. Being financially independent
   d. Supporting my family
   e. Planning/saving for the future
3. When considering how to pay for college, which of the following do you know *least* about?
   a. Grants
   b. Scholarships
   c. Loans
   d. Work-study programs

You can also take the anonymous What Students Say surveys to add your voice to this textbook. Your responses will be included in updates.

You can also take the anonymous What Students Say surveys (https://openstax.org/l/collegesurvey6-12) to add your voice to this textbook. Your responses will be included in updates.

Students offered their views on these questions, and the results are displayed in the graphs below.

What is your top immediate financial priority?

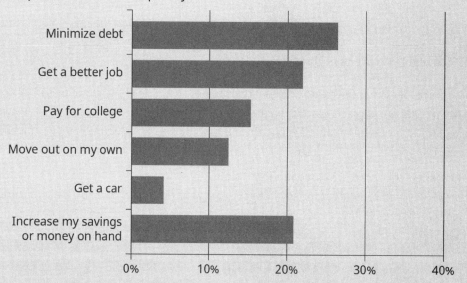

Figure 10.2

Which aspect of your finances concerns you the most?

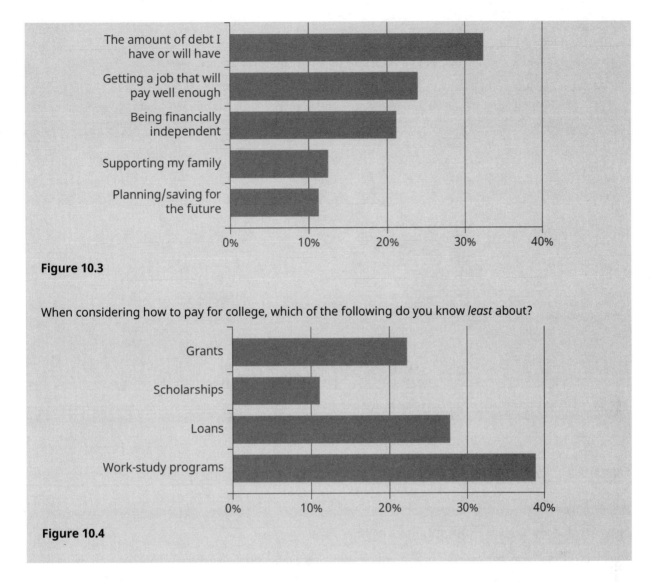

Figure 10.3

Figure 10.4

Financial Planning Process

Personal goals and behaviors have a financial component or consequence. To make the most of your financial resources, you need to do some financial planning. The financial planning process consists of five distinct steps: goal setting, evaluating, planning, implementing, and monitoring. You can read in more depth about SMART goals in chapter 3.

Financial Planning in Five Steps

1. Develop Personal Goals
    - What do I want my life to look like?

2. Identify and Evaluate Alternatives for Achieving Goals for My Situation
    - What do my savings, debt, income, and expenses look like?
    - What creative ways are available to get the life I want?

3. Write My Financial Plan
    - What small steps can I take to start working toward my goals?

4. Implement the Plan
    - Begin taking those steps, even if I can only do a few small things each week.
5. Monitor and Adjust the Plan
    - Make sure I don't get distracted by life. Keep taking those small steps each week. Make adjustments when needed.

Figure 10.5 Steps of financial planning.

How to Use Financial Planning in Everyday Life

The financial planning process isn't only about creating one big financial plan. You can also use it to get a better deal when you buy a car or computer or rent an apartment. In fact, anytime you are thinking about spending a lot of money, you can use the financial planning process to pay less and get more.

To explore financial planning in depth, we'll use the example of buying a car.

1. Develop Goals

First, what do you really need? If you're looking for a car, you probably need transportation. Before you decide to buy a car, consider alternatives to buying a car. Could you take a bus, walk, or bike instead? Often one goal can impact another goal. Cars are typically not good financial investments. We have cars for convenience and necessity, to earn an income and to enjoy life. Financially, they are an expense. They lose value, or depreciate, rather than increasing in value, like savings. So buying a car may slow your savings or retirement plan goals. Cars continually use up cash for gas, repairs, taxes, parking, and so on. Keep this in mind throughout the planning process.

2. Identify and Evaluate Alternatives for Achieving Goals in Your Current Situation.

For this example, let's assume that you have determined the best alternative is to buy a car. Do you need a new car? Will your current car last with some upkeep? Consider a used car over a new one. On average, a new car will lose one-fifth of its value during its first year.[5] Buying a one-year-old car is like getting a practically new car for a 20 percent discount. So in many cases, the best deal may be to buy a five- or six-year-old car. Sites such as the Kelley Blue Book website (KBB.com) and Edmunds.com can show you depreciation tables for the cars you are considering. Perhaps someone in your family has a car they will sell you at a discount.

Do you know how much it will cost in total to own the car? It will help to check out the total cost of ownership tools (also on KBB.com and Edmunds.com) to estimate how much each car will cost you in maintenance, repairs, gas, and insurance. A cheap car that gets poor gas mileage and breaks down all the time will actually cost you more in the long run.

Figure 10.6 Weighing all the factors is critical when deciding on any purchase, especially a major one like a car. (Credit: Greg Gjerdingen / Flickr / Attribution 2.0 Generic (CC-BY 2.0))

5   Krome, Charles. "Car Depreciation." 2018, Carfax. https://www.carfax.com/blog/car-depreciation

3. Write Down Your Financial Plan

Goal	Item	Details	Budget	Timeline
Transportation/Car	2014 Toyota Camry	Black, A/C, power windows, less than 60,000 miles	Car $12,000 (max) Down payment $3,000 Insurance $100/mo Sales tax $900 + Licensing $145 Cash needed $4,145	Have $3600 in savings for this. Save $50/week. Purchase in approximately 11 weeks.
Computer	Used or refurbished laptop	Dell w/ Windows, minimum 13", 128G hard drive, HD Graphics	$300 Use free Windows update from school. Use free Wi-Fi at school.	Sell current laptop for $100. Buy refurbished from Dell site for $289. $189 on credit card. Pay off when statement comes.

Table 10.1 Examples of financial plans for a car and a computer.

4. Implement Your Plan

Once you've narrowed down which car you are looking for, do more online research with resources such as Kelley Blue Book to see what is for sale in your area. You can also begin contacting dealerships and asking them if they have the car you are looking for with the features you want. Ask the dealerships with the car you want to give you their best offer, then compare their price to your researched price. You may have to spend more time looking at other dealerships to compare offers, but one goal of online research is to save time and avoid driving from place to place if possible.

When you do go to buy the car, bring a copy of your written plan into the dealership and stick to it. If a dealership tries to switch you to a more expensive option, just say no, or you can leave to go to another dealership. Remember Elan in our opening scenario? He went shopping alone and caved to the pressure and persuasion of the salesperson. If you feel it is helpful, take a responsible friend or family member with you for support.

5. Monitor and Adjust the Plan to Changing Circumstances and New Life Goals

Life changes, and things wear out. Keep up the recommended maintenance on the car (or any other purchase). Keep saving money for your emergency fund, then for your next car. The worst time to buy a car is when your current car breaks down, because you are easier to take advantage of when you are desperate. When your car starts giving you trouble or your life circumstances start to change, you will be ready to shop smart again.

A good practice is to keep making car payments once the car loan is paid off. If you are paying $300 per month for a car loan, when the loan is paid off, put $300 per month into a savings account for a new car instead. Do it long enough and you can buy your next car using your own money!

Use the Financial Planning Process for Everything

The same process can be used to make every major purchase in your life. When you rent an apartment, begin with the same assessment of your current financial situation, what you need in an apartment, and what goals it will impact or fulfill. Then look for an apartment using a written plan to avoid being sold on a more expensive place than you want.

You can even use the process of assessing and planning for small things such as buying textbooks or weekly groceries. While saving a few bucks each week may seem like a small deal, you will gain practice using the financial planning process, so it will become automatic for when you make the big decisions in life. Stick to your plan.

10.2 Savings, Expenses, and Budgeting

Estimated completion time: 19 minutes.

Questions to consider:

- How is the flow of money best measured?
- How do I keep things balanced?

> **"Do not save what is left after spending; instead spend what is left after saving."**
>
> —Warren Buffett[6]

What is the best way to get to the Mississippi River from here? Do you know? To answer the question, even with a map app, you would need to know where you are starting from and exactly where on the river you want to arrive before you can map the best route. Our financial lives need maps, too. You need to know where you are now and where you want to end up in order to map a course to meet the goal.

You map your financial path using a spending and savings plan, or budget, which tracks your income, savings, and spending. You check on your progress using a balance sheet that lists your *assets*, or what you own, and your *liabilities*, or what you owe. A balance sheet is like a snapshot, a moment in time, that we use to check our progress.

---

6   Buffett, Warren. The Essays of Warren Buffett: Lessons for Corporate America. 1991. Cardozo Law Review.

Budgets

The term *budget* is unpleasant to some people because it just looks like work. But who will care more about your money than you? We all want to know if we have enough money to pay our bills, travel, get an education, buy a car, etc. Technically, a budget is a specific financial plan for a specified time. Budgets have three elements: income, saving and investing, and expenses.

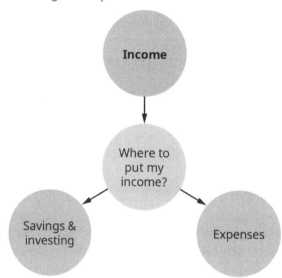

Figure 10.7 A budget is a specific financial plan for a finite amount of time. For example, you can set a budget for your family for a year.

Income

Income most often comes from our jobs in the form of a paper or electronic paycheck. When listing your income for your monthly budget, you should use your *net pay*, also called your disposable income. It is the only money you can use to pay bills. If you currently have a job, look at the pay stub or statement. You will find *gross pay*, then some money deducted for a variety of taxes, leaving a smaller amount—your net pay. Sometimes you have the opportunity to have some other, optional deductions taken from your paycheck before you get your net pay. Examples of optional deductions include 401(k) or health insurance payments. You can change these amounts, but you should still use your net pay when considering your budget.

Some individuals receive disability income, social security income, investment income, alimony, child support, and other forms of payment on a regular basis. All of these go under income. During school, you may receive support from family that could be considered income. You may also receive scholarships, grants, or student loan money.

Saving and Investing

The first bill you should pay is to yourself. You owe yourself today and tomorrow. That means you should set aside a certain amount of money for savings and investments, before paying bills and making discretionary, or optional, purchases. Savings can be for an emergency fund or for short-term goals such as education, a wedding, travel, or a car. Investing, such as putting your money into stocks, bonds, or real estate, offers higher returns at a higher risk than money saved in a bank. Investments include retirement accounts that can be automatically funded with money deducted from your paycheck. Automatic payroll deductions are an effective way to save money before you can get your hands on it. Setting saving as a priority assures that you will work to make the payment to yourself as hard as you work to make your car or housing payment. The money you "pay" toward saving or investing will earn you back your money, plus some money earned on your money. Compare this to the cost of buying an item on credit and paying your money plus interest to a creditor. Paying yourself first is a habit that pays off!

Pay yourself first! Put something in savings from every paycheck or gift.

Expenses

Expenses are categorized in two ways. One method separates them into fixed expenses and variable expenses. Rent, insurance costs, and utilities (power, water) are fixed: they cost about the same every month and are predictable based on your arrangement with the provider. Variable expenses, on the other hand, change based on your priorities and available funds; they include groceries, restaurants, cell phone plans, gas, clothing, and so on. You have a good degree of control over your variable expenses. You can begin organizing your expenses by categorizing each one as either fixed or variable.

A second way to categorize expenses is to identify them as either needs or wants. Your needs come first: food, basic clothing, safe housing, medical care, and water. Your wants come afterward, if you can afford them while sticking to a savings plan. Wants may include meals at a restaurant, designer clothes, video games, other forms of entertainment, or a new car. After you identify an item as a need or want, you must exercise self-control to avoid caving to your desire for too many wants.

ACTIVITY

List the last ten purchases you made, and place each of them in the category you think is correct.

Item	Need Expense $	Want Expense $

Table 10.2

Item	Need Expense $	Want Expense $
Totals		

Table 10.2

How do your total "need" expenses compare to your total "want" expenses? Should either of them change?

Budgets are done in a chart or spreadsheet format and often look like the ones below. Pay attention to how the first budget differs from the second.

Income (use net monthly pay)		
	Paycheck	$2200
	Other	$300
	Total Income	**$2500**
Saving and Investing		
Savings Account		$120
Investments		$240
	Amount Left for Expenses	$2140
Expenses (Monthly)		
	Housing	$750
	Car Payment/Insurance	$450
	Groceries	$400
	Restaurants/Food Delivery	$100
	Internet	$60
	Phone	$60
	Medical Insurance and Copays	$120

	Gas	$200
	Total Expenses	**$2140**
Balance (Amount left for expenses minus total expenses)		$0

Table 10.3 This budget balances because all money is accounted for.

Income (use net monthly pay)		
	Paycheck	$2200
	Other	$300
	Total Income	**$2500**
Saving and Investing		
Savings Account		$120
Investments		$240
	Amount Left for Expenses	**$2140**
Expenses (Monthly)		
	Housing	$750
	Car Payment/Insurance	$450
	Groceries	$400
	Restaurants/Food Delivery	$225
	Internet	$60
	Phone	$75
	Medical Insurance and Copays	$120

Table 10.4 Note that Restaurants, Phone, and Gas are more expensive in this budget, so the total expenses are more than the amount left for them.

	Gas	$250
Total Expenses		**$2330**
Balance (Amount left for expenses minus total expenses)		**-$190**

Table 10.4 Note that Restaurants, Phone, and Gas are more expensive in this budget, so the total expenses are more than the amount left for them.

Balancing Your Budget

Would you take all your cash outside and throw it up in the air on a windy day? Probably not. We want to hold on to every cent and decide where we want it to go. Our budget allows us to find a place for each dollar. We should not regularly have money left over. If we do, we should consider increasing our saving and investing. We also should not have a negative balance, meaning we don't have enough to pay our bills. If we are short of money, we can look at all three categories of our budget: income, savings, and expenses.

We could increase our income by taking a second job or working overtime, although this is rarely advisable alongside college coursework. The time commitment quickly becomes overwhelming. Another option is to cut savings, or there's always the possibility of reducing expenses. Any of these options in combination can work.

Another, even less desirable option is to take on debt to make up the shortfall. This is usually only a short-term solution that makes future months and cash shortages worse as we pay off the debt. When we budget for each successive month, we can look at what we actually spent the month before and make adjustments.

Tracking the Big Picture

When you think about becoming more financially secure, you're usually considering your *net worth*, or the total measure of your wealth. Earnings, savings, and investments build up your assets—that is, the valuable things you own. Borrowed money, or debt, increases your liabilities, or what you owe. If you subtract what you owe from what you own, the result is your net worth. Your goal is to own more than you owe.

When people first get out of college and have student debt, they often owe more than they own. But over time and with good financial strategies, they can reverse that situation. You can track information about your assets, liabilities, and net worth on a balance sheet or part of a personal financial statement. This information will be required to get a home loan or other types of loans. For your net worth to grow in a positive direction, you must increase your assets and decrease your liabilities over time.

Assets (Owned) – Liabilities (Owed) = Net Worth

ANALYSIS QUESTION

Can you identify areas in your life where you are losing money by paying fees on your checking account or interest on your loans? What actions could you take to stop giving away money and instead set yourself up to start earning money?

Good Practices That Build Wealth	Bad Practices That Dig a Debt Hole
Tracking all spending and saving	Living paycheck to paycheck with no plan
Knowing the difference between needs and wants	Spending money on wants instead of saving
Resisting impulse buying and emotional spending	Using credit to buy more that you need and increasing what you owe

Table 10.5

GET CONNECTED

You can write down your budget on paper or using a computer spreadsheet program such as Excel, or you can find popular budgeting apps that work for you.[7] Some apps link to your accounts and offer other services such as tracking credit cards and your credit score. The key is to find an app that does what you need and use it.

Here are some examples:

- Mint (https://www.mint.com/)
- Mvelopes (https://www.mvelopes.com/)
- Wally (http://wally.me/)
- Goodbudget (https://goodbudget.com/)

10.3 Banking and Emergency Funds

Estimated completion time: 24 minutes.

Questions to consider:

- How do I plan appropriately for a financial emergency?

---

7 http://www.techtimes.com/articles/80726/20150902/best-budgeting-apps-for-college-students-mint-you-need-a-budget-and-more.htm

- What do I need to keep in mind when it comes to the banking system?

Emergency Funds

> **"Time and unexpected events [affect us] all."**
> —King Solomon

Plan on the unplanned happening to you. It happens to all of us: a car repair, a broken computer, an unplanned visit to the doctor, a friend or relative in desperate need, etc. How will you pay for it? A recent study found that over 60 percent of households could not pay cash for a $400 unexpected expense.[8] Could you?

What Is an Emergency Fund?

An emergency fund is a cash reserve that's specifically set aside for unplanned expenses or financial emergencies[9]. Some common examples include car repairs, home repairs, medical bills, and a loss of income. In general, emergency savings can be used for large or small unplanned bills or payments that are not part of your routine monthly expenses and spending.

Why Do I Need an Emergency Fund?

Without savings, even a minor financial shock could set you back, and if it turns into debt, it can potentially have a lasting impact.

Research suggests that individuals who struggle to recover from a financial shock have less savings to help protect against a future emergency. They may rely on credit cards or loans, which can lead to debt that's generally harder to pay off. They may also pull from other savings, such as retirement funds, to cover these costs.

How Much Money Should I Keep in My Emergency Fund?

There is no magic or "official" amount to keep in an emergency fund, but you can look at your own life to get an idea to start with. How much could you put into a bank account to have for emergencies? Some students and their parents will not have a problem paying for most emergencies, but many students are on their own. What can you save up over time? A common recommendation for graduates with full-time jobs is perhaps three to six months' worth of expenses. This may not be practical for you. A large sampling of students in financial literacy classes recommend approximately $1,000.

One thousand dollars can cover a lot of small to medium unexpected expenses, such as last-minute textbooks, computer repair or replacement, car repair, or a prescription or doctor's visit. The emergency fund is best kept separate from other money for living expenses to protect it as emergency money. While you could keep cash, an emergency fund is often best kept in a bank, in order to avoid theft or loss and still have easy access by debit card or ATM. Pizza is not an emergency!

---

8 Board of Governors of the Federal Reserve System. "Report on the Economic Wellbeing of US Households, 2018" https://www.federalreserve.gov/publications/2019-economic-well-being-of-us-households-in-2018-dealing-with-unexpected-expenses.htm
9 Consumer Financial Protection Bureau. "An Essential Guide to Building an Emergency Fund." https://www.consumerfinance.gov/start-small-save-up/an-essential-guide-to-building-an-emergency-fund/?utm_source=newsletter&utm_medium=email&utm_campaign=SSSU_YSFT&utm_content=FY20_Jan_P

Figure 10.8 Emergency funds can cover the cost of a broken phone. (Credit: Simon Clancy / Flickr / Attribution 2.0 Generic (CC-BY 2.0))

How Do I Create an Emergency Fund?

Emergency funds can be created quickly if you have the money, or over time if you need to save a little from each paycheck, loan, or gift. You can use a financial planning tool similar to the one in section 10.1. Follow these steps:

- Set an emergency fund goal.
- Identify an amount to keep on hand.
- Determine how to fund it, monthly or all at once.
- Decide where you will keep your fund (e.g., a savings account), and set specific dates to deposit money in it.
- Start now!

ANALYSIS QUESTION

How do you feel when you do not have enough money for something? Will you stop spending on some wants while you build up your emergency fund?

Safety and Success: Bank on It!

The banking system in the United States is one of the safest and most regulated banking systems in the world. A host of federal and state agencies regulate financial institutions to keep them from accidentally or purposefully losing customer money.

Banks, Credit Unions, and Online Banking

In the United States, financial institutions (FIs) are divided into multiple types of companies. The banking system is generally divided into banks and credit unions, which have similar offerings and are both regulated and insured by the federal government.

Choosing a Bank or Credit Union

When choosing a bank or credit union, it is important to understand what you are looking for and what benefits each company provides. Generally, large national banks offer the most advanced technology and a large network of branches. There are also smaller community banks that serve specific groups of people and may offer products to meet the specific needs of the community. For example, a community bank that serves Latino customers might make it easier to send money to family in South American countries, while a bank that focuses on small businesses will promote products specifically needed by business owners.

Credit unions differ from banks in that they don't have a profit motive. Instead, they are not-for-profit organizations that are owned by the people who bank with them. Each member of a credit union gets one vote for the board of directors, which runs the credit union. This means that whether you have $5 in your account or $5 million, you get the same vote. Credit unions tend to offer better rates and lower fees, on average, than banks.

There is no single best answer for what bank or credit union you should choose. The most vital question to ask and answer about a financial institution is whether it meets both your current and your future needs. Use figure 10.3 to compare different options and determine the best one for you.

Many banks and credit unions do not publish the interest rates paid on deposit accounts or charged on loans. While some colleges have their own bank or credit union right on campus, you should consider visiting at least one other bank or one credit union to compare. You may also explore at least one online bank, which will publish interest rates on their website. Consider interest rates, access to automated teller machines (ATMs), online transfers, automatic paycheck deposits, branch locations if you will use one, and other services important to you. Since you will select a bank or credit union that is insured, do not feel pressure to use any specific institution.

Comparison Chart for Choosing a Bank/Credit Union

Item	Local Bank	Credit Union	Online Only Bank
	Yes/No/Amount	Yes/No/Amount	Yes/No/Amount

Table 10.6

Comparison Chart for Choosing a Bank/Credit Union

Item	Local Bank	Credit Union	Online Only Bank
Checking Accounts			
• Monthly Fees			
• Methods to Avoid Fees			
Savings Accounts			
• Interest Percentage			
• Monthly Fees			
• Methods to Avoid Fees			
Loans			
• Auto Loans			
• Home Loans			
• Credit Cards			
Nearest Branch Location*			
• Near Home?			
• Near School or Work?			
• Convenient ATMs?			
Online Banking Services*			
• Transfer Funds between Accounts			
• Open New Accounts			
• Pay Bills			

Table 10.6

Comparison Chart for Choosing a Bank/Credit Union

Item	Local Bank	Credit Union	Online Only Bank
• Fees			
• Budgeting/Daily Transaction Access			
Additional Services or Fees			

* Branch locations are less important if you use online banking for most banking activity.

Table 10.6

Banking Products and Services

Banks and credit unions offer a similar set of financial products or services, called account types. The difference between the account types lies primarily in how easy it is to put money into or take money out of an account. Regulations set maximum numbers of transactions (deposits or withdrawals) for each type of account at a bank or credit union.

How you use these accounts is less about the rules and more about how long you plan to keep the money in the account. The main reason to use a bank is to keep your money safe and available. Banks may offer other services that benefit you, such as certificates of deposit (which allow you to earn higher interest over a longer time), retirement accounts, and car and home loans.

Checking

Checking accounts allow you to deposit money and take money out anytime you want. There are no government limits on the number of transactions, although a bank or credit union might begin to charge you if you make too many transactions. Checking accounts often don't pay any interest or pay an extremely low rate of interest. They are used to keep money safe and pay bills conveniently.

Checking accounts are ideal for depositing paychecks, cashing paper checks, buying everyday items, and paying your bills. The money you have in your checking account should be money you plan to spend by the end of the month. Any money you don't plan to spend within a month should be transferred from your checking account to a savings account. Your savings account should be the *first* bill that you pay each month. You can still add extra at the end of the month!

Savings Accounts

Savings accounts allow you a specific number of transactions each month or each quarter. If you go over the maximum number of transactions, the bank won't let you take any more money out or put any more money into the account until the next month. Savings accounts pay a small amount of interest on your money, but usually not enough to keep up with inflation or overcome banking fees (see below).

This actually causes your savings to go backwards. If you earn 2 percent on a savings account but inflation is 3 percent per year, you are losing 1 percent of purchasing power each year. For this reason, money in a savings account should be money you plan to spend within the next 12–48 months. The only exception to this is money you have saved for an emergency, called an emergency fund. Since you never know when an emergency (such as losing your job) is going to happen, you want the money to be available to you in a savings account.

Figure 10.9 Banks and credit unions can be accessed in many forms, both physical and online. (Credit David Hilowitz / Flickr / Attribution 2.0 Generic (CC-BY 2.0))

Debit Cards

When you get a checking account, you'll also get a debit card, or check card. This card allows you to access the money in your checking account (and savings account at an ATM) using a plastic card similar to a credit card. But it is not a credit card.

A debit card only uses money available in your account. Paying with a debit card is like paying with a paper check, but more immediate and convenient. You will have the option of selecting overdraft protection, which means the bank or credit union will allow you to buy stuff even if you don't have enough money in your account; they'll just charge you a fee, perhaps $25, for each event. This can be compared to a high-interest loan. Depending on how many things you buy in a week, overdraft protection could add many fees to your statement and use up your cash so it will not be available for your planned expenses. Consider opting out of overdraft protection and carefully keeping track of your account balance. This way you can only spend the money that you have.

Be aware that by using your debit card at an ATM associated with a different bank, you can incur fees—sometimes from both banks!

Debit cards offer a lot of security benefits over carrying around cash, including the ability to cancel a lost or stolen debit card. While the legal protections on debit cards are not as great as the legal protections on credit cards, you can't go into debt using a debit card. This inability to go into significant debt is a major advantage for those who struggle with debt.

Banking Fees

Banks and credit unions charge fees to operate. Many charge fees for a checking or savings account, overdrafts, and other services. You should seek to avoid fees for which you receive no extra services or when you can get similar services elsewhere for free. Two areas that are most subject to fees are services and "triggered" events. Triggered events are primarily caused by actions such as overdrawing your account (an overdraft). Overdraft fees are avoidable. The best way to avoid an overdraft fee is to continually monitor your bank balance and only spend money that you have.

Standard bank fees can often be avoided by taking one or more measures as specified by the bank, such as maintaining a minimum balance or using direct deposit. Avoid getting paid on a payroll or prepaid card unless you know all related costs or have a reason to want to be paid in that manner. Payroll cards often lead to ATM and banking fees, so federal law requires employers to offer you an alternative.[10] Ask at your financial institution for assistance in setting up an account or accounts that are best for you.

Online and Mobile Banking

There are other important banking tools you should also consider. Online and mobile banking are among the most important activities in banking. You should list all the things you might want to do regularly with your bank accounts and make sure you can do them through the bank's website and app. This might include making payments on loans, transferring money between your checking and savings accounts, paying bills through automated bill pay, and creating new savings accounts.

Learn the rules of your account, and keep track of how you use it. This can help you keep costs down and develop a positive banking relationship.

Earning Interest and Compound Interest

Interest refers to money paid for the privilege of borrowing money. When banks use our money for their investments, they pay us interest. (Remember, our bank accounts are insured, so you can't lose your money even when the banks use it.) When you take out a loan using the bank's money, you pay the bank interest.

Compound interest means that you earn interest on the money that you deposit, called the principal, first. After that, you earn money on your money *plus* all the interest that has been paid to your account. Your earnings are reinvested. Interest on interest! You are being paid on the basis of other people's money—the interest that they paid you. Over time, this compound interest results in more and more money in your account. The same principle holds true for investing. Banks sometimes have investment services that pay higher interest but include risk to your money, which you typically access after completing your degree or certificate and obtaining full-time work. If you are employed full time and have access to investment, perhaps in a company-sponsored retirement account, see a brief section below on Investing and Buying Power.

Consider the example below, and notice that the amount of interest paid each year is larger than the year before. That is compound interest. The only money deposited by the account owner was the first $2,000.

---

10   Dratch, Dana. "It pays to know these five things about payroll cards." Credit Cards.com. https://www.creditcards.com/credit-card-news/payroll_cards-fees-employer-1271.php

Year	Starting Deposit or Beginning Amount from End of Last Year	Annual Interest Rate	Interest Paid over Period (1 year) (Interest x Beginning Amount)	Total at End of Year / Beginning Amount for Next Year
1	$2,000.00	6%	$120	$2,120.00
2	$2,120.00	6%	$127.20	$2,247.20
3	$2,247.20	6%	$134.83	$2,382.03
4	$2,382.03	6%	$142.92	$2,524.95

Table 10.7

In this example, at the end of four years, the account owner has put in $2,000 and has added $524.95 of other people's money in earned interest! You can use online financial calculators to try scenarios for saving, buying a car or home, and even building a retirement account. One source is bankrate.com (http://www.bankrate.com) . Look under Calculators. Do not pursue marketing efforts on the sites suggested or used for examples in this chapter. Stick to the tools used.

ANALYSIS QUESTION

What happens to the amount of compound interest when you save for a longer time? When should you start saving?

10.4 Credit Cards and Other Debt

Estimated completion time: 15 minutes.

Questions to consider:

- What do I need to know about student loans?
- How dangerous is debt?
- What should I think about when getting and using a credit card?

Yes, taking on too much debt can (and does) have disastrous effects on people's personal finances, but if used appropriately, debt can be a tool to help you build wealth. Debt is like fire. You can use it to keep yourself warm, cook food, and ward off animals—but if you don't know how to control it, it'll burn your house down.

The Danger of Debt

When you take out a loan, you take on an obligation to pay the money back, with interest, through a monthly payment. You will take this debt with you when you apply for auto loans or home loans, when you enter into a marriage, and so on. Effectively, you have committed your future income to the loan. While this can be a good idea with student loans, take on too many loans and your future self will be poor, no matter how much money you make. Worse, you'll be transferring more and more of your money to the bank through interest payments.

Compounding Interest

While compounding works to make you money when you are earning interest on savings or investments, it works against you when you are paying the interest on loans. To avoid compounding interest on loans, make sure your payments are at least enough to cover the interest charged each month. The good news is that the interest you are charged will be listed each month on the loan account statements you are sent by the bank or credit union, and fully amortized loans will always cover the interest costs plus enough principal to pay off what you owe by the end of the loan term.

The two most common loans on which people get stuck paying compounding interest are credit cards and student loans. Paying the minimum payment each month on a credit card will just barely cover the interest charged that month, while anything you buy with the credit card will begin to accrue interest on the day you make the purchase. Since credit cards charge interest daily, you'll begin paying interest on the interest immediately, starting the compound interest snowball working against you. When you get a credit card, always pay the credit card balance down to $0 each month to avoid the compound interest trap.

Student loans are another way you can be caught in the compound interest trap. When you have an unsubsidized student loan or put your loans into deferment, the interest continues to rack up on the loans. Again, you'll be charged interest on the interest, not just on the original loan amount, forcing you to pay compound interest on the loan.

Sacrificing Your Future Fun

When you graduate college, you are most likely to graduate with student loan debt and credit card debt.[11] Many students use credit cards and student loans to allow them to pay for fun today, such as trips, clothing, and expensive meals.

Getting into debt while in college forces you to sacrifice your future fun. Say you take out $100,000 in student loans instead of the $50,000 you need, doubling your monthly payment. You are not just making an extra $338 payment; you are also sacrificing anything else you can do with that money. You sacrifice that extra $338 a month, every month, for the next twenty-five years. You can't use it to go to the movies, pay down other debt, save for a home, take a vacation, or throw a party. When you sign those papers, you sacrifice all those opportunities every month for decades. As a result, when you take out a loan, you should make sure it's a good loan.

How Much Good Debt to Take On

A drink of water is refreshing on a hot day and is required to stay alive. Too much water, however, and you will

---

11   Debt.org. "Demographics of Debt." https://www.debt.org/faqs/americans-in-debt/demographics/

drown.

During college and for the first few years after graduation, most students should only have two loans: student loans and possibly a car loan. We've already discussed your student loans, which should be equal to or less than your first year's expected salary after graduation.

When you get a car, you should keep your car payment to between 10 and 20 percent of your monthly take-home pay. This means if your paycheck is $200 per week, your car payment should be no more than $80–$160 each month.

In total, you want your debt payments (plus rent if you are renting) to be no more than 44 percent of your take-home pay. If you are planning to build wealth, however, you want to cap it at 30 percent of take-home pay.

Signs You Have Too Much Debt

You can consider yourself in too much debt if you have any of the following situations:

- You cannot make your minimum credit card payments.
- Your money is gone before your next paycheck.
- Bill collectors are contacting you.
- You are unable to get a loan.
- Your paycheck is being garnished by creditor.
- You are considering a debt consolidation loan with extra fees added.
- Your items are repossessed.
- You do not know your debt or financial situation.

Getting and Using a Credit Card

One of the most controversial aspects of personal finance is the use of credit cards. While credit cards can be an incredibly useful tool, their high interest rates, combined with the how easily credit cards can bury you in debt, make them extremely dangerous if not managed correctly.

Reflect on Elan from the chapter introduction and how he felt. How would you (or did you) feel to hold a new credit card with a $2,000 spending limit?

Benefits of a Credit Card

There are three main benefits of getting a credit card. The first is that credit cards offer a secure and convenient method of making purchases, similar to using a debit card. When you carry cash, you have the potential of having the money lost or stolen. A credit card or debit card, on the other hand, can be canceled and replaced at no cost to you.

Additionally, credit cards offer greater consumer protections than debit cards do. These consumer protections are written into law, and with credit cards you have a maximum liability of $50. With a debit card, you are responsible for transfers made up until the point you report the card stolen. In order to have the same protections as with credit cards, you need to report the card lost or stolen within 48 hours. The longer you wait to report the loss of the card, or the longer it takes you to realize you lost your card, the more money you may be responsible for, up to an unlimited amount.[12]

The final benefit is that a credit card will allow you to build your credit score, which is helpful in many aspects of life. While most people associate a credit score with getting better rates on loans, credit scores are also important to getting a job, lowering car insurance rates, and finding an apartment.[13]

What Is a Good Credit Score?

Most credit scores have a 300–850 score range. The higher the score, the lower the risk to lenders. A "good" credit score is considered to be in the 670–739 score range.

Credit Score Ranges	Rating	Description
< 580	Poor	This credit score is well below the average score of US consumers and demonstrates to lenders that the borrower may be a risk.
580-669	Fair	This credit score is below the average score of US consumers, though many lenders will approve loans with this score.
670-739	Good	This credit score is near or slightly above the average of US consumers, and most lenders consider this a good score.
740-799	Very Good	This credit score is above the average of US consumers and demonstrates to lenders that the borrower is very dependable.
800+	Exceptional	This credit score is well above the average score of US consumers and clearly demonstrates to lenders that the borrower is an exceptionally low risk.

Table 10.8

Components of a Credit Score and How to Improve Your Credit

Credit scores contain a total of five components. These components are credit payment history (35 percent), credit utilization (30 percent), length of credit history (15 percent), new credit (10 percent), and credit mix (10 percent). The main action you can take to improve your credit score is to stop charging and pay all bills on time. Even if you cannot pay the full amount of the credit card balance, which is the best practice, pay the minimum on time. Paying more is better for your debt load but does not improve your score. Carrying a balance on a credit card does not improve your score. Your score will go down if you pay bills late and owe more than 30 percent of your credit available. Your credit score is a reflection of your willingness and ability to do what you say you will do—pay your debts on time.

---

12   Federal Trade Commission. "Lost Or Stolen Credit, ATM, and Debit Cards." 2012.
13   Purposeful Finance. "Four Surprising Ways Your Credit Score Will Affect Your Life." https://www.purposefulfinance.org/home/Articles/2016/four-surprising-ways-your-credit-score-will-affect-your-life

How to Use a Credit Card

All the benefits of credit cards are destroyed if you carry credit card debt. Credit cards should be used as a method of paying for things you can afford, meaning you should only use a credit card if the money is already sitting in your bank account and is budgeted for the item you are buying. If you use credit cards as a loan, you are losing the game.

Every month, you should pay your credit card off in full, meaning you will be bringing the loan amount down to $0. If your statement says you charged $432.56 that month, make sure you can pay off all $432.56. If you do this, you won't pay any interest on the credit card.

But what happens if you don't pay it off in full? If you are even one cent short on the payment, meaning you pay $432.55 instead, you must pay daily interest on the entire amount from the date you made the purchases. Your credit card company, of course, will be perfectly happy for you to make smaller payments—that's how they make money. It is not uncommon for people to pay twice as much as the amount purchased and take years to pay off a credit card when they only pay the minimum payment each month.

What to Look for in Your Initial Credit Card

1. Find a Low-Rate Credit Card
   Even though you plan to never pay interest, mistakes will happen, and you don't want to be paying high interest while you fix a misstep. Start by narrowing the hundreds of card options to the few with the lowest APR (annual percentage rate).
2. Avoid Cards with Annual Fees or Minimum Usage Requirements
   Your first credit card should ideally be one you can keep forever, but that's expensive to do if they charge you an annual fee or have other requirements just for having the card. There are many options that won't require you to spend a minimum amount each month and won't charge you an annual fee.
3. Keep the Credit Limit Equal to Two Weeks' Take-Home Pay
   Even though you want to pay your credit card off in full, most people will max out their credit cards once or twice while they are building their good financial habits. If this happens to you, having a small credit limit makes that mistake a small mistake instead of a $5,000 mistake.
4. Avoid Rewards Cards
   Everyone loves to talk about rewards cards, but credit card companies wouldn't offer rewards if they didn't earn them a profit. Rewards systems with credit cards are designed by experts to get you to spend more money and pay more interest than you otherwise would. Until you build a strong habit of paying off your card in full each month, don't step into their trap.

10.5 Education Debt: Paying for College

Estimated completion time: 35 minutes.

Questions to consider:

- What choices should you consider when taking on student debt?
- How do you match debt to postgraduate income?
- What types of financial aid are available?
- How do you apply for financial aid?
- What are the best repayment strategies?

> "An investment in knowledge always pays the best interest."
>
> —Benjamin Franklin, *The Way to Wealth*: Ben Franklin on Money and Success

As you progress through your college experience, the cost of college can add up rapidly. Worse, your anxiety about the cost of college may rise faster as you hear about the rising costs of college and horror stories regarding the "student loan crisis." It is important to remember that *you* are in control of your choices and the cost of your college experience, and you do not have to be a sad statistic.

Education Choices

Education is vital to living. Education starts at the beginning of our life, and as we grow, we learn language, sharing, and to look both ways before crossing the street. We also generally pursue a secular or public education that often ends at high school graduation. After that, we have many choices, including getting a job and stopping our education, working at a trade or business started by our parents and bypassing additional schooling, earning a certificate from a community college or four-year college or university, earning a two-year or associate degree from one of the same schools, and completing a bachelor's or advanced degree at a college or university. We can choose to attend a public or private school. We can live at home or on a campus.

Each of these choices impacts our debt, happiness, and earning power. The average income goes up with an increase in education, but that is not an absolute rule. The New York Federal Reserve Bank reported in 2017 that approximately 34 percent of college graduates worked in a job that did not require a college degree,[14] and in 2013, CNN Money reported on a study from Georgetown University's Center on Education and the Workforce showing that nearly 30 percent of Americans with two-year degrees are now earning more than graduates with bachelor's degrees.[15] Of course, many well-paying occupations do require a bachelor's or master's degree. You have started on a path that may be perfect for you, but you may also choose to make adjustments.

College success from a financial perspective means that you must:

- Know the total cost of the education
- Consider job market trends
- Work hard at school during the education
- Pursue ways to reduce costs

Most importantly: Buy only the amount of education that returns more than you invest.

According to *US News & World Report*, the average cost of college (including university) tuition and fees varies widely. In-state colleges average $9,716 while out-of-state students pay $21,629 for the same state college. Private colleges average $35,676. The local community college averages approximately $3,726. On-campus housing and meals, if available, can add approximately $10,000 per year.[16] See the table below, and create your own chart after you research.

---

14 https://www.forbes.com/sites/prestoncooper2/2017/07/13/new-york-fed-highlights-underemployment-among-college-graduates/#55be172f40d8

15 https://www.communitycollegereview.com/blog/studies-show-community-college-may-offer-superior-roi-to-some-four-year-schools

16 https://www.usnews.com/education/best-colleges/paying-for-college/articles/what-you-need-to-know-about-college-tuition-costs

Sample College Costs

Type of School	Annual Tuition without Housing	Tuition If Living on Campus	Total Cost at Planned Completion
Community College (2 yr.)	$3,726	Live at Home	$7,452
Public University, In State (4 yr.)	$9,716	Live at Home	$38,864
Public University, In State (4 yr.)		$19,716	$78,864
Public University, Out of State (4 yr.)	$21,629	$31,629	$126,516
Private College (4 yr.)	$35,676	$45,676	$182,704

Table 10.9

You may need to adjust your college plan as circumstances change for you and in the job market. You can modify plans based on funding opportunities available to you (see next sections) and your location. You may prefer a community-college-only education, or you may complete two years at a community college and then transfer to a university to complete a bachelor's degree. Living at home for the first two years or all of your college education will save a lot of money if your circumstances allow. Be creative!

Key to Success: Matching Student Debt to Postgraduation Income

Students and parents often ask, "How much debt should I have?" The problem is that the correct answer depends on your personal situation. A big-firm attorney in a major city might make $120,000 in their first year as a lawyer. Having $100,00 or even $200,000 in student debt in this situation may be reasonable. But a high school teacher making $40,000 in their first year would never be able to pay off the debt.

The amount of debt you take on should be tied to the income you expect.

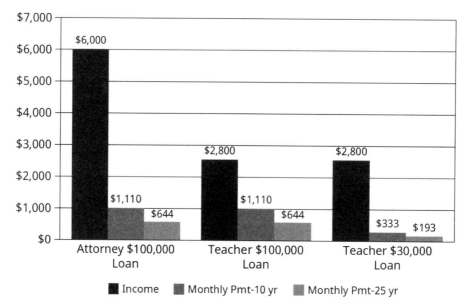

Figure 10.10 Each field of employment brings with it an average income and assumed debt. This graph shows the impact of an attorney's income versus debt, and then compares a teacher who took a $100,000 loan with one who took a $30,000 loan. Note the teacher's income is the same in both cases. (Credit: Based on information from National Association of Colleges and Employers and US Bureau of Labor Statistics.)

Research Your Starting Salary

Begin by researching your expected starting salary when you graduate. Most students expect to make significantly more than they will actually make.[17] As a result, your salary expectations are likely much higher than reality. Ask professors at your college what is typical for a recent graduate in your field, or do informational interviews with human resource managers at local companies. Explore the US Bureau of Labor Statistics' Occupational Outlook Handbook (https://openstax.org/l/OOH) . PayScale (https://openstax.org/l/salariesbyoccupation) also has a handy tool for getting general information based on your personal experience and location. Search websites and talk to employees of companies that interest you for future employment to identify real starting salaries.

Undergraduate Degree: 1 x Annual Salary

For students working toward a bachelor's or associate degree, both forms of undergraduate degrees, you should try to keep your student loans equal to or less than your expected first year's salary. So if, based on research, you expect to make $40,000 in your first year out of college, then $33,000 in student loans would be a reasonable amount for you to pay out of a monthly budget with some sacrifice.

Advanced Degrees: 1–2 x Annual Salary

Once you've graduated with your bachelor's degree, you may want to get an advanced degree such as a master's degree, a law degree, a medical degree, or a doctorate. While these degrees can greatly increase your income, you still need to match your student debt to your expected income. Advanced degrees can often

---

17 Hess, Abigail. "College Grades expect to earn $60,000." 2019. CNBC. https://www.cnbc.com/2019/02/15/college-grads-expect-to-earn-60000-in-their-first-job----few-do.html

double your expected annual salary, meaning your total debt for all your degrees should be equal to or less than twice your expected first job income. A lower number for the debt portion of your education would be more manageable.

Your goal should be to pay for college using multiple methods so your student loan debt can be as small as possible, rather than just making low monthly payments on a large loan that will lead to a higher overall cost.

Types of Financial Aid: How to Pay for College

The true cost of college may be more than you expected, but you can make an effort to make the cost less than many might think. While the price tag for a school might say $40,000, the net cost of college may be significantly less. The net price for a college is the true cost a family will pay when grants, scholarships, and education tax benefits are factored in. The net cost for the average family at a public in-state school is only $3,980. And for a private school, free financial aid money reduces the cost to the average family from $32,410 per year to just $14,890.

If you haven't visited your college's financial aid office recently, it's probably worth it to talk with them. You must seek out opportunities, complete paperwork, and learn and meet criteria, but it can save you thousands of dollars.

Type of College	Average Published Yearly Tuition and Fees
Public Two-Year College (in-district students)	$3,440
Public Four-Year College (in-state students)	$9,410
Public Two-Year College (out-of-state students)	$23,890
Private Four-Year College	$32,410

Table 10.10

Grants and Scholarships

Grants and scholarships are free money you can use to pay for college. Unlike loans, you never have to pay back a grant or a scholarship. All you have to do is go to school. And you don't have to be a straight-A student to get grants and scholarships. There is so much free money, in fact, that billions of dollars go unclaimed every year.[18]

While some grants and scholarships are based on a student's academic record, many are given to average students based on their major, ethnic background, gender, religion, or other factors. There are likely dozens or hundreds of scholarships and grants available to you personally if you look for them.

Federal Grants

Federal Pell Grants are awarded to students based on financial need, although there is no income or wealth limit on the grant program. The Pell Grant can give you more than $6,000 per year in free money toward

---

18   https://www.usatoday.com/story/college/2015/01/20/29-billion-unused-federal-grant-awards-in-last-academic-year/37399897/

tuition, fees, and living expenses.[19] If you qualify for a Pell Grant based on your financial need, you will automatically get the money.

Federal Supplemental Educational Opportunity Grants (FSEOGs) are additional free money available to students with financial need. Through the FSEOG program, you can receive up to an additional $4,000 in free money. These grants are distributed through your school's financial aid department on a first-come, first-served basis, so pay close attention to deadlines.

Teacher Education Assistance for College and Higher Education (TEACH) Grants are designed to help students who plan to go into the teaching profession. You can receive up to $4,000 per year through the TEACH Grant. To be eligible for a TEACH Grant, you must take specific classes and majors and must hold a qualifying teaching job for at least four years after graduation. If you do not fulfill these obligations, your TEACH Grant will be converted to a loan, which you will have to pay back with both interest and back interest.

There are numerous other grants available through individual states, employers, colleges, and private organizations.

State Grants

Most states also have grant programs for their residents, often based on financial need. Eleven states have even implemented free college tuition programs for residents who plan to continue to live in the state. Even some medical schools are beginning to be tuition free. Check your school's financial aid office and your state's department of education for details.

College/University Grants and Scholarships

Most colleges and universities have their own scholarships and grants. These are distributed through a wide variety of sources, including the school's financial aid office, the school's endowment fund, individual departments, and clubs on campus.

Private Organization Grants and Scholarships

A wide variety of grants and scholarships and are awarded by foundations, civic groups, companies, religious groups, professional organizations, and charities. Most are small awards under $4,000, but multiple awards can add up to large amounts of money each year. Your financial aid office can help you find these opportunities.

Employer Grants and Scholarships

Many employers also offer free money to help employees go to school. A common work benefit is a tuition reimbursement program, where employers will pay students extra money to cover the cost of tuition once they've earned a passing grade in a college class. And some companies are going even further, offering to pay 100 percent of college costs for employees. Check to see whether your employer offers any kind of educational support.

---

19 https://studentaid.ed.gov/sa/types/grants-scholarships/pell

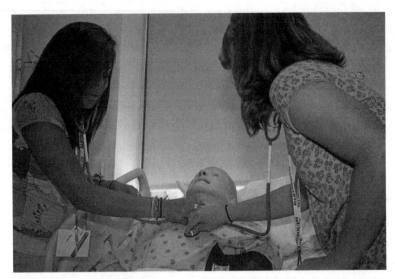

Figure 10.11 Employers in certain fields, such as healthcare, may offer their own grants and scholarships. (Credit: Ano Lobb / Flickr / Attribution 2.0 Generic (CC-BY 2.0))

Additional Federal Support

The federal government offers a handful of additional options for college students to find financial support.

Education Tax Credits

The IRS gives out free money to students and their parents through two tax credits, although you will have to choose between them. The American opportunity tax credit (AOTC) will refund up to $2,500 of qualifying education expenses per eligible student, while the lifetime learning credit (LLC) refunds up to $2,000 per year regardless of the number of qualifying students.

While the AOTC may be a better tax credit to choose for some, it can only be claimed for four years for each student, and it has other limitations. The LLC has fewer limitations, and there is no limit on the number of years you can claim it. Lifetime learners and nontraditional students may consider the LLC a better choice. Calculate the benefits for your situation.

The IRS warns taxpayers to be careful when claiming the credits. There are potential penalties for incorrectly claiming the credits, and you or your family should consult a tax professional or financial adviser when claiming these credits.

Federal Work-Study Program

The Federal Work-Study Program provides part-time jobs through colleges and universities to students who are enrolled in the school. The program offers students the opportunity to work in their field, for their school, or for a nonprofit or civic organization to help pay for the cost of college. If your school participates in the program, it will be offered through your school's financial aid office.

Student Loans

Federal student loans are offered through the US Department of Education and are designed to give easy and inexpensive access to loans for school. You don't have to make payments on the loans while you are in school, and the interest on the loans is tax deductible for most people. Direct Loans, also called Federal Stafford Loans, have a competitive fixed interest rate and don't require a credit check or cosigner.

Direct Subsidized Loans

Direct Subsidized Loans are federal student loans on which the government pays the interest while you are in school. Direct Subsidized Loans are made based on financial need as calculated from the information you provide in your application. Qualifying students can get up to $3,500 in subsidized loans in their first year, $4,500 in their second year, and $5,500 in later years of their college education.

Direct Unsubsidized Loans

Direct Unsubsidized Loans are federal loans on which you are charged interest while you are in school. If you don't make interest payments while in school, the interest will be added to the loan amount each year and will result in a larger student loan balance when you graduate. The amount you can borrow each year depends on numerous factors, with a maximum of $12,500 annually for undergraduates and $20,500 annually for professional or graduate students.

There are also aggregate loan limits that apply to put a maximum cap on the total amount you can borrow for student loans.

Direct PLUS Loans

Direct PLUS Loans are additional loans a parent, grandparent, or graduate student can take out to help pay for additional costs of college. PLUS loans require a credit check and have higher interest rates, but the interest is still tax deductible. The maximum PLUS loan you can receive is the remaining cost of attending the school.

Parents and other family members should be careful when taking out PLUS loans on behalf of a child. Whoever is on the loan is responsible for the loan forever, and the loan generally cannot be forgiven in bankruptcy. The government can also take Social Security benefits should the loan not be repaid.

Private Loans

Private loans are also available for students who need them from banks, credit unions, private investors, and even predatory lenders. But with *all* the other resources for paying for college, a private loan is generally unnecessary and unwise. Private loans will require a credit check and potentially a cosigner, they will likely have higher interest rates, and the interest is not tax deductible. As a general rule, you should be wary of private student loans or avoid them altogether.

Repayment Strategies

Payments on student loans will begin shortly after you graduate. While many websites, financial "gurus," and talking heads in the media will encourage you to pay off your student loans as quickly as possible, you should give careful consideration to your repayment options and how they may impact your financial plans. Quickly paying off your student loans or refinancing your student loans into a private loan may be the worst option available to you.

Payment Plans

The federal government has eight separate loan repayment programs, each with their own way of calculating the payment you owe. Five of the programs tie loan payments to your income, which can make it easier to afford your student loans when you are just starting off in your career. The programs are described briefly below, but you should seek the help of a licensed fiduciary financial adviser familiar with student loans when making decisions related to student loan payment plans.

The standard repayment plan sets a consistent monthly payment to pay off your loan within 10 years (or up to 30 years for consolidated loans). You can also choose a graduated repayment plan, which will begin with lower payments and then increase the payment every two years. The graduated plan is also designed to pay off your student loans in 10 years (or up to 30 years for consolidated loans). A third option is the extended repayment plan, which provides a fixed or graduated payment for up to 25 years. However, none of these programs are ideal for individuals planning to seek loan forgiveness options, which are discussed below.

Beyond the "normal" repayment options, the government offers five income-based repayment options: (1) the Pay As You Earn (PAYE) repayment plan, (2) the Revised Pay As You Earn (REPAYE) repayment plan, (3) the Income-Based Repayment (IBR) plan, (4) the Income-Contingent Repayment (ICR) plan, and (5) the Income-Sensitive Repayment (ISR) plan. Each program has its method of calculating payments, along with specific requirements for eligibility and rules for staying eligible in the program. Many income-based repayment plans are also eligible for loan forgiveness after a set period of time, assuming you follow all the rules and remain eligible.

Loan Forgiveness Programs

Many income-based repayment options also have a loan forgiveness feature built into the repayment plan. If you make 100 percent of your payments on time and follow all the other plan rules, any remaining loan balance at the end of the plan repayment term (typically 20 to 30 years) will be forgiven. This means you will not have to pay the remainder on your student loans.

This loan forgiveness, however, comes with a catch: taxes. Any forgiven balance will be counted and taxed as income during that year. So if you have a $100,000 loan forgiven, you could be looking at an additional $20,000 tax bill that year (assuming you were in the 20 percent marginal tax rate).

Another option is the Public Service Loan Forgiveness (PSLF) program for students who go on to work for a nonprofit or government organization. If eligible, you can have your loans forgiven after working for 10 years in a qualifying public service job and making 120 on-time payments on your loans. A major advantage of PSLF is that the loan forgiveness may not be taxed as income in the year the loan is forgiven.

Consider Professional Advice

The complexity of the payment and forgiveness programs makes it difficult for nonexperts to choose the best strategy to minimize costs. Additionally, the strict rules and potential tax implications create a minefield of potential financial problems. In 2017, the first year graduates were eligible for the PSLF program, 99 percent of applicants were denied due to misunderstanding the programs or having broken one of the many requirements for eligibility.[20]

---

20 https://www.forbes.com/sites/zackfriedman/2019/05/01/99-of-borrowers-rejected-again-for-student-loan-forgiveness/

Your Rights as a Loan Recipient

As a recipient of a federal student loan, you have the same rights and protections as you would for any other loan. This includes the right to know the terms and conditions for any loan before signing the paperwork. You also have the right to know information on your credit report and to dispute any loan or information on your credit file.

If you end up in collections, you also have several rights, even though you have missed loan payments. Debt collectors can only call you between 8 a.m. and 9 p.m. They also cannot harass you, threaten you, or call you at work once you've told them to stop. The United States doesn't have debtors' prisons, so anyone threatening you with arrest or jail time is automatically breaking the law.

Federal student loans also come with many other rights, including the right to put your loan in deferment or forbearance (pushing pause on making payments) under qualifying circumstances. Deferment or forbearance can be granted if you lose your job, go back to school, or have an economic hardship. If you have a life event that makes it difficult to make your payments, immediately contact the student loan servicing company on your loan statements to see if you can pause your student loan payments.

The Consumer Financial Protection Bureau (CFPB) has created a series of sample letters (https://openstax.org/l/debtcollectors) you can use to respond to a debt collector. You can also file a complaint (https://openstax.org/l/consumercomplaint) with the CFPB if you believe your rights have been violated.

Applying for Financial Aid, FAFSA, and Everything Else

Take this first step—you will need to do it. The federal government offers a standard form called the Free Application for Federal Student Aid (FAFSA), which qualifies you for federal financial aid and also opens the door for nearly all other financial aid. Most grants and scholarships require you to fill out the FAFSA, and they base their decisions on the information in the application.

The FAFSA only requests financial aid for the specific year you file your application. This means you will need to file a FAFSA for each year you are in college. Since your financial needs will change over time, you may qualify for financial aid even if you did not qualify before.

You can apply for the FAFSA through your college's financial aid office or at studentaid.gov (https://openstax.org/l/fafsa) if you don't have access to a financial aid office. Once you file a FAFSA, any college can gain access to the information (with your approval), so you can shop around for financial aid offers from colleges.

Maintaining Financial Aid

To maintain your financial aid throughout your college, you need to make sure you meet the eligibility requirements for each year you are in school, not just the year of your initial application. The basic requirements include being a US citizen or eligible noncitizen, having a valid Social Security number, and registering for selective service if required. Undocumented residents may receive financial aid as well and should check with their school's financial aid office.

You also must make satisfactory academic progress, including meeting a minimum grade-point average, taking and completing a minimum number of classes, and making progress toward graduation or a certificate. Your school will have a policy for satisfactory academic progress, which you can get from the financial aid office.

What to Do with Extra Financial Aid Money

One expensive mistake that students make with financial aid money is spending the money on noneducation expenses. Students often use financial aid, including student loans, to purchase clothing, take vacations, or dine out at restaurants. Nearly 3 percent spend student loan money on alcohol and drugs.[21] While this seems like fun now, these noneducation expenses are major contributors to student loan debt, which will make it harder for you to afford a home, take vacations, or save for your retirement after you graduate.

When you have extra student loan money, consider saving it for future education expenses. Just like you will need an emergency fund all your adult life, you will want an emergency fund for college when expensive books or travel abroad programs present unexpected costs. If you make it through your college years with extra money in your savings, you can use the money to help pay down debt.

> **ANALYSIS QUESTION**
>
> A closer look: How much student loan debt do you currently have, and how much do you think you'll have by the end of college? How could this debt impact your future?

10.6 Defending against Attack: Securing Your Identity and Accounts

Estimated completion time: 24 minutes.

Questions to consider:

- How should you manage passwords and online security?
- What's the best way to deal with identity theft?
- How can you get help and avoid scams?

Identity theft is one of the fastest growing crimes in the United States, and the FBI estimates that more than 10 million new victims are harmed each year.[22] Among the problems contributing to this rapid increase in identity theft are the significant amount of data stored online and the poor security practices of both individuals and companies. In 2017, Equifax announced that their security had been breached and the data of every adult in the country was likely compromised.[23]

Passwords and Security

The first line of defense to prevent identity theft is to create strong passwords and take other security measures with your online accounts. An important factor in the strength of a password is the length of the

---

21 https://studentloanhero.com/featured/smart-dumb-money-moves-students/
22 https://archives.fbi.gov/archives/news/stories/2004/october/preventidt_102104
23 https://www.purposefulfinance.org/home/Articles/2017/understanding-the-equifax-security-breach

password.[24] This means a password of 12 characters or more is desirable. Consider using pass phrases, or short sentences, rather than passwords. You should vary your pass phrases for each site so a hacker that gets your password can only use it for a single site. Government agencies and security experts are recommending password management software such as LastPass to help with remembering all of these differing passwords.

Another important strategy is to implement two-factor authentication (TFA) on all your online accounts. TFA adds another method of identifying you in addition to your password. Many TFA systems use your cell phone and will text you a code to allow you to log in to your account. A criminal would then need both your password and access to your cell phone to log in. Check the settings on your email, bank website, and other accounts to see how to enable two-factor authentication.

Preventing and Dealing with Identity Theft

Setting strong passwords and enabling two-factor authentication will help keep criminals out of your online banking, email, and other important accounts. Many criminals use lower-tech methods of stealing your identity, however, including tricking or scaring you into giving out information or simply digging through your trash to find account statements.

Never Give Info to Someone Who Contacts You

Never provide a person with personal information unless you initiated the contact. If someone calls you asking for personal information, tell them you'll call them back. Then ignore the phone number or website they give you, and instead look up the phone number for the organization on their official website. A legitimate company or government agency will never require you to stay on the line with them to solve the problem.

Shred Everything

You should also purchase an inexpensive cross-cut shredder and get in the habit of shredding all paperwork and mail before you throw it away. A good rule of thumb is that if the paper has your name on it, you should shred it before throwing it out.

Order Your Credit Report Annually

At least once per year, you should get your credit report from the credit reporting agencies through annualcreditreport.com, which is the only website approved by the Federal and State governments. The three major agencies -- Transunion, Equifax, and Experian -- all provide the legally mandated free report through this website. Learn how to read a credit report from one of these agencies.

Look for incorrect information or accounts you don't recognize. If you see accounts you didn't open on your credit report, file a report with the local police and the local FBI field office. You can also file a complaint with the Federal Trade Commission and Internet Crime Complaint Center.

---

24   Information Security Institute. "Password Security:Complexity Versus Length." 2019. https://resources.infosecinstitute.com/password-security-complexity-vs-length/

ANALYSIS QUESTION

Think about your account passwords and your habits related to your identity security. Identify mistakes you have made in the past with your security. What can you start doing today to protect yourself from identity theft or financial fraud?

ACTIVITY

Credit Report Review

Using the sample credit reports below, write an analysis of the person's credit and how they are managing and using debt. Go through the factors that affect credit, and determine how this person is doing with each factor. What in the report is beneficial, and what is harmful? Carefully review each page for accuracy. Pay particular attention to the personal information, negative credit, and any notes about the person or their credit activity.

Example of a Negative Account – Missed Payments

Account Name

First USA bank N A

Account #

44171259XXXX

Recent Balance

$1,684

Date Opened

03/2012

Personal Statement/Comments

Account Type

Credit card – revolving terms

Terms

Bank credit cards

On Record Until

02/2023

Credit Limit/Original Amount

$8,850

High Balance

$2,695

Balance

$2,695

Balance Updated

02/2016

Monthly Payment

—

Address ID Number

0963215875

Contact Information

1665 Center Ave
Fresno, CA 93710
(800) 658-4235

Recent Payment

—

Status/Account Status

Past due 60 days

Past Due Amount

$50

Date of Status/Status Updated

02/2016

First Reported

04/2012

Payment Status

60 days late

Responsibility

Individual

Payment History

2016
Feb. 60
Jan. 30

2015
Dec. OK
Nov. OK
Oct. OK
Sep. OK
Aug. OK
Jul.

Figure 10.12 A sample credit report. (Credit: Based on information from Experian (https://openstax.org/l/experianreport) .)

Creating Strong Alliances: Getting Help and Avoiding Scams

As a college student, you are a prime target for predatory practices designed to make the adviser or company rich at your expense.

As you've read through this chapter, it may have dawned on you that this personal finance stuff is a lot more complicated than it seems. There are people who have devoted their entire educations and careers to mastering single areas of personal finance, such as taxes, investing, and estate planning. When you feel it's time to get professional help, there are many qualified professionals who can assist you. Not everyone who calls themselves a financial adviser is actually looking out for your best interest, however.

The terms *financial adviser*, *financial planner*, *wealth manager*, and many other impressive-sounding job titles are not regulated by the government. Anyone can put these job titles on their business cards. You need to be able to differentiate between a qualified professional and those who are untrained product salespeople, predatory financial businesses, or outright scams.

Predatory Practices Aimed at College Students

As a college student, you are a prime target for predatory practices designed to make the adviser or company rich at your expense.

Annuities and Life Insurance

Annuities and life insurance products are often aggressively sold to college students. They are generally inappropriate for college students and even most college graduates because they have high fees and lower returns than many other investment options, and the benefits are rarely needed by young people.[25]

Investment Schemes

Regulators identify specialized investments, such as promissory notes, real estate, oil and gas, and gold, as a major threat to investors. Investing systems, including stock picking and buying or selling strategies, are also a concern. Academic research has continually disproven these strategies.[26]

If someone is pitching you on their special system or secret strategy, be extremely skeptical. Legitimate investments are regulated by government agencies and are therefore never a secret.

---

25   North American Securities Administrators Association. Top Investor Threats. ttp://www.nasaa.org/top-investor-threats /
26   Kadan, Maduriera, Wang and Zach. "Stock Picking, Industry Picking, and Market Timing in Sell-Side Research." Singapore Management University. 2012.

Scam or Scheme	Characteristics or Promises	Issues and Reasons to Avoid
"Cash Value" Life Insurance Often sold as "7702 Plans"	Cash value life insurance and similar programs promise that a certain amount of the insurance premiums are set aside as a fund that can be used for expenditures such as college.	If they are ever paid out, the consumer must pay taxes and may also pay fees up to 50 percent, losing much of the built-up value.
Investment Schemes	These highly optimistic "sure thing" / "can't miss" opportunities are specifically geared toward quick rewards or paying for college. They are often specialized investments such as real estate, gold, or oil.	Sellers often rely on students' lack of resources and experience to prevent them from thoroughly investigating the opportunity or properly evaluating the contract terms.
Advertising, Sales, or Data Entry Opportunities "I make $40 an hour working from home. . . ."	Offers of high pay for what seems like little work are likely too good to be true. "Car wrap" opportunities (driving around with ads on your car), data entry, and online sales opportunities are typical examples.	The advertised salaries are often very difficult to achieve and come with significant conditions. Some "pay first" programs utilize fake checks to mislead students.
Financial Aid Services or Debt Consolidation	These services offer to find advantageous financial aid packages for a fee.[27]	The offers usually do not return as beneficial a package as they promise, and most financial aid can be discovered without paying for it.

Table 10.11

---

27   Boswell, Brian. "Don't Get Suckered By These College Savings Plans." Forbes.com. 2019.

Scam or Scheme	Characteristics or Promises	Issues and Reasons to Avoid
Phone Scams "The IRS has detected tax fraud. . . ." "This will be an attempt to avoid an initial appearance before a grand jury for a criminal offense. . . ."	Phone scammers use threatening, official-sounding messages to scare recipients. They often demand immediate return calls or request account or identifying information. These scams are not unique to college students.	As official as they sound, these are scams. The perpetrators will use any account information you provide to invade your privacy or steal your money.
Too-Good-to-Be-True Credit Cards	Credit cards with very low introductory interest rates, a promise of points, or other impressive-sounding benefits may be offered to students on college campuses, especially during events.	Low rates can explode into high rates or incur fees after a brief period or a single late payment. This is not technically fraudulent, but be very careful when reading the terms.
Freebie or Social Media Survey Scams	Many legitimate companies will offer free products or ask students to complete surveys, but high-risk offerings will ask for personal information or account information.	Free products or compensation may not arrive, and even if they do, they may not offset the risk of giving up account information.
Fake Universities or Degree Programs (Diploma Mills)	Offers may sound very legitimate and similar to real colleges. They often promise significant financial aid or degrees in just weeks or months.[28]	A certificate from a school with no accreditation or a poor reputation is a waste of time and money. Be certain that any college or certificate program is formally accredited; review the credentials of current faculty, and determine the job placement of alumni.

Table 10.11

---

28   Creel, Wes. "How Cn I Tell if a Degree is Legitiamte or a Scam." Abound/Finish College.

Sources of Good Information and Help

With all the high-cost, predatory, and scam financial advice out there, it is important to know where to turn for help.

Personal Finance Classes

One option is to look for a personal finance class, which will take the concepts found in this chapter and expand on them for an entire semester. Your college may have a financial literacy, personal finance, or money management class available.

Be wary of personal finance or investing classes offered through other sources, however, as many include hidden sales agendas and aggressive pitches to buy a company's financial products. Never make an investment decision, buy a product, or sign a contract at a class, and always seek advice from others on any opportunity.

Websites and Government Resources

There are a ridiculous number of websites available to the public to help with your personal finances. When choosing a website for help, lean toward sites run by a legitimate government agencies or nonprofit organizations.

The first place you should look for help with finances is the official website of related government agencies. If you have a question about insurance, look to your state's insurance commissioner website. If you are having problems with your apartment, contact your city's housing authority.

Government agencies not only have the authoritative word on any legal matter, but are also generally unbiased. The downside to government websites is that they can be hard to understand, with legal wording taken directly from the law. Some government agencies are also prohibited from giving advice to the public, leaving it up to you to apply the information they provide.

There are also many nonprofit organizations that have been established to assist the public with finances. Nonprofit organizations may have information that is easier to understand, and they may also be able to offer personal advice.

Official Government Websites

- Personal Finance: Consumer Financial Protection Bureau, consumerfinance.gov
- Taxes: Internal Revenue Service, irs.gov
- Retirement: Social Security Administration, ssa.gov
- Investing: Securities Exchange Commission, sec.gov
- Investing: North American Securities Administrators Association, nasaa.org (state and provincial investment regulators)

Nonprofit Organization Websites

- National Endowment for Financial Education, nefe.org
- National Foundation for Credit Counseling, nfcc.org
- Consumer Reports, consumerreports.org (national consumer advocacy organization)
- Purposeful Finance, purposefulfinance.org (a nonprofit organization run by this chapter's author)

Your College's Financial Aid Office

The financial aid or student aid office of your college may also be a good place to look for financial help, especially surrounding student loans. It is important to realize, however, that a conflict of interest exists between you and the financial aid adviser. Your college's financial aid office is charged with helping you find the money to go to college, but it isn't charged with making sure you don't take on too much student debt. It is possible to get good advice on getting money to pay for college that is also bad advice for your future finances.

College financial aid counselors are also generally not trained in other areas of finance and should not be relied on for advice on investing, taxes, noncollege debt, or other financial matters. To get help with these areas, consult a qualified professional who can guide you with fewer conflicts of interest, such as the professionals listed below.

> ### ANALYSIS QUESTION
>
> Talk with your parents or other family members about their experience with finances, including financial advisers, taxes, legal issues, and investing. When could they have used professional advice in their past? Did they have bad experiences with getting advice that wasn't best for them? How has a lack of *good* advisers harmed your family financially (even if just because they could have had more money)?

Summary

There are a lot of benefits to good financial management. Primarily, it generally allows you to do more of what you want with your life. When you have poor financial habits, too much of your money goes into other people's pockets. But when you have good financial management habits, you can afford to do more because you have worked hard, separated needs from wants, saved and invested, and avoided credit card and debt pitfalls.

Career Connection

Search the articles at PurposefulFinance.org and find one you deem interesting.

Why do you find it interesting, and how can you apply it to your life? How does the article relate to the concepts in this chapter?

Rethinking

Revisit the questions you answered at the beginning of the chapter, and consider one concept or practice you learned in this chapter that might change your answer to one of them.

1. I actively and regularly plan and/or monitor my finances.

2. I understand the benefits and risks of credit.
3. I have a plan to repay my student loans.
4. I regularly take steps to protect my identity and assets.

Where do you go from here?

Financial literacy is a topic that many college students struggle with, but good financial planning habits will benefit you long after your college days are behind you. What would you like to learn more about? Choose a topic from the list below, and create an annotated bibliography that would direct further research.

- Marrying personal finance goals with financial planning
- Creating a saving and spending plan
- Best practices concerning credit cards
- Financing a college education

11 Engaging in a Healthy Lifestyle

Figure 11.1 Movement, in all its forms, is an important element of health and wellness. Movement contributes to balance, cardiovascular health, strength, and flexibility; it can also help clear your mind in the midst of study and stress. (Credit: Steven Pisano / Flickr / Attribution 2.0 Generic (CC-BY 2.0))

Chapter Outline

11.1 Taking Care of Your Physical Health
11.2 Sleep
11.3 Taking Care of Your Emotional Health
11.4 Taking Care of Your Mental Health
11.5 Maintaining Healthy Relationships
11.6 Your Safety

Introduction

Student Survey

How do you feel about health and wellness? These questions will help you determine how the chapter concepts relate to you right now. As we are introduced to new concepts and practices, it can be informative to reflect on how your understanding changes over time. We'll revisit these questions at the end of the chapter to help you identify opportunities for improved health. Take this quick survey to figure it out, ranking questions on a scale of 1–4, 1 meaning "least like me" and 4 meaning "most like me."

1. I eat enough fruits and vegetables every day.
2. I get enough sleep.
3. I have, for the most part, healthy relationships with friends and family.
4. I feel like I know how to manage stress.

You can also take the Chapter 11 survey (https://openstax.org/l/collegesurvey11) anonymously online.

STUDENT PROFILE

"My freshman year of college, I started at a pretty big university. I had what some call "social anxiety" and even cried before getting out the car on my first day. That year was a struggle for me, and I constantly had to fight with myself to step out of my comfort zone in order to succeed. I knew that if I made positive changes to my life then I would easily succeed in school. I joined a group of students who were a support system for me during my first year of college. Together we studied together and even worked out together. It helped me be more involved on my campus and less worried. Being connected with other students has taught me a lot of ways to cope with common problems many students face.

"My first advice would be first and foremost, always make sure you are being kind to yourself. It's not advisable to work 40 hours a week and also try to be a full time student. You need to set up a realistic home and school life so that way you are balanced with your assignments and other responsibilities. You need to give your body and your brain time to rest so you can absorb as much as you want to without restrictions. I found it useful to start working out to make sure that I'm dedicating the time I should be to myself and not working myself until exhaustion. Little things like exercise, yoga and meditation can do amazing things for your body as well as your mind. If you take care of your body, your body will take care of you."

–**Felicia Santiago**, Delgado Community College

About this Chapter

This chapter explores the many ways your health is impacted by your lifestyle choices. The goal of this material is to help you do the following:

- Describe actions you can take to improve your physical health.
- Identify ways to maintain and enhance your emotional health.
- Understand mental health risks and warning signs.
- Articulate reasons and ways to maintain healthy relationships.
- Outline steps you can take to be more safety conscious.

Recent headlines were buzzing with news about a 17-year-old boy who lost his eyesight because of a poor diet. While the boy ate enough food and his weight was considered normal, when doctors investigated, they discovered he didn't eat enough **nutrient-rich** food. A self-described picky eater, the teen's daily diet consisted of sausage, deli ham, white bread, Pringles, and french fries. His food choices led to numerous nutritional deficiencies of several essential vitamins and minerals, causing nutritional optic neuropathy.[1]

Have you heard the saying "you are what you eat"? If so, likely a parent or someone who loves you said it while coaxing you to eat your vegetables. Are we really what we eat, and what does this phrase actually mean? While the example of the boy who lost his vision may be extreme, the food we eat does impact our physical and mental health. What's at the end of our fork can keep us healthy or eventually make us sick. Every 27 days, our skin replaces itself and our body makes new cells from the food we eat.[2] And according to Dr. Libby Weaver, every three months we completely rebuild and replace our blood supply. What you eat becomes you.

It's not only what you eat that impacts your health but also how much you exercise, how effectively you deal

---

1 Harrison, Warburton, Lux, and Atan. Blindness caused by a junk food diet. *Annals of Intern Med.* September 3, 2019.
2 https://www.webmd.com/beauty/cosmetic-procedures-overview-skin#1

with stress, how well you sleep, your work habits, and even your relationships—these things all have an impact on your well-being.

There are two primary reasons we become unhealthy. First, we do not deliver enough nutrients for our cells to operate properly, and second, our cells are bombarded with too many toxins. Keeping it simple, good health is proper nutrients in, toxins out. Toxins come from a host of sources—certain foods, the environment, stressful relationships, smoking, vaping, and alcohol and drug use. And if we don't sleep and exercise enough, toxins can hang around long enough to cause us harm.

As a first-year college student you will make many choices without parental oversight, including the food you eat and the way you take care of your body and brain. Some choices put you on a path to health, and other choices can lead you down a path toward illness. There is a strong connection between success in college and your ability to stay healthy.

Health is more than a strong body that doesn't get sick. Health also includes your overall sense of well-being (mental, emotional) and healthy relationships. Good health is about making positive choices in all of these areas, and avoiding destructive choices. It's about learning to be smart, to set boundaries, to watch out for your safety, and to take care of the one body that will carry you through life.

While health and wellness are often interchanged, it is important to differentiate the two concepts. Health **is** a state of physical, mental, and social well-being, while wellness is a process through which people become aware of and make choices toward a healthy and fulfilling life.

11.1 Taking Care of Your Physical Health

Estimated completion time: 26 minutes.

Questions to consider:

- What is healthy eating?
- Why is it important to stay hydrated?
- How important is exercise to a healthy body?
- Are you getting enough sleep to be healthy?
- What are toxins, and how can they affect your health?

You have one body. Treat it well so as to maximize its ability to serve you throughout your life. Often physical health gets moved to the bottom of the priority list when we are busy. Taking care of your physical health doesn't mean six-pack abs or training for a marathon. It means honoring your physical needs so your body can function properly, feeding your cells the nutrients that will keep your body working well your entire life, and minimizing exposure to toxins to reduce your risk of disease.

Healthy Eating

While it's not the only thing that contributes to great health, what you eat makes a huge difference. We have 37 trillion cells in our body. The only way they function optimally is with good nutrition. As a college student, you will be surrounded by temptations to eat poorly or even to overeat. It's now up to you to make wise choices in the face of these temptations. Your dining hall is likely full of many healthy foods and just as many unhealthy foods. You may grab food on the run while racing to class or order a pizza at midnight while studying for a test. Lobby vending machines or a stash of snacks in your room should not turn into a substitute for real meals. The downside of fast food and easy access treats is that many are loaded with sugar, salt, or both.

The United States Department of Agriculture (USDA) updated their Healthy Plate Guidelines in 2011. MyPlate illustrates five different food groups considered the building blocks for a healthy diet—vegetables, fruits, protein, grains, and dairy.

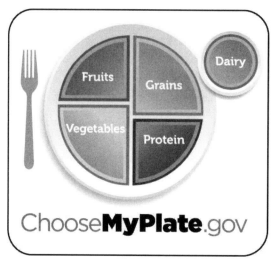

Figure 11.2 Eating healthy is a journey shaped by many factors, including our state of life, situations, preferences, access to food, culture, traditions, and the personal decisions we make over time. The USDA recommends that vegetables and fruits make up the largest portions of your diet, and dairy the smallest portion. All your food and beverage choices count. MyPlate offers ideas and tips to help you create a healthier eating style that meets your individual needs and improves your health. (Credit: USDA / Public Domain)

It's also important to know what is not a healthy plate. A healthy plate is low in refined carbohydrates (donuts, pastries, pasta, cookies), low in sugar, and low in saturated fat (although we need healthy fats like avocado and nuts). You can learn more at https://www.choosemyplate.gov/.

While the USDA's MyPlate was revised to reflect some key findings at that time, nutritionists at Harvard felt it didn't offer the most complete picture when it comes to basic nutrition guidelines. They created The Healthy Eating Plate, which is based on what they consider to be the best available science. Similar to MyPlate, half the plate is vegetables and fruit. Aim for eight servings of veggies or fruits a day, more veggies than fruits. It's important to note that the Harvard version was created without the political pressure from food industry lobbyists (for example, the dairy industry). Note that grains are further defined as whole grains, protein is now healthy protein, and water is emphasized over dairy/milk. What other differences do you see?

This table (https://openstax.org/l/healthyeatingplate) provides more detail on how The Healthy Eating plate compares to USDA's MyPlate.

Healthy eating also includes choosing organic fruits and vegetables when possible. By choosing organic, you help lower the amount of toxins your body encounters (since conventional fruits and vegetables are often sprayed with pesticides). Organic foods may not be readily available on your campus or in your local grocery store, so strive to choose the best options possible given availability and your budget. Many college and universities are adding organic food as a result of student demand. If healthy eating is something you are passionate about, consider organizing an effort to influence the dining options on your campus. When shopping on your own, the Dirty Dozen list provided by the Environmental Working Group (EWG) is a good guide of which produce is most important to eat organic, as these are the fruits and vegetables with the most pesticide residue. The EWG also compiles a Clean 15 list (https://openstax.org/l/producepesticideguide) of the vegetables and fruits with the least amount of pesticides.

Whole Foods vs. Processed Foods

Choose whole foods. Whole foods are any foods that have not been processed, packaged, or altered in any way. Whole foods are an essential part of a healthy diet because they contain the vitamins and minerals our bodies need.

Examples of whole foods include the following:

- **Vegetables:** Carrots, broccoli, kale, avocados, cauliflower, spinach, peppers
- **Fruits:** Apples, bananas, blueberries, strawberries, grapes, melons, peaches
- **Grains:** Brown rice, oatmeal, barley, buckwheat, quinoa, millet
- **Beans:** Black, pinto, kidney, black-eyed peas, chickpeas

Minimize **non-whole foods**. These are foods that have been processed, such as cookies, hot dogs, chips, pasta, deli meat, and ice cream. Even seemingly healthy foods like yogurt, granola, and protein bars are processed and should be checked for added sugar and other unhealthy ingredients.

The average American eats 62 percent of their daily calories from processed foods.[3] In order for your body to be as healthy as possible, it's extremely important to include lots of whole foods in your diet.

> "When you eat junk food you think junk thoughts."
>
> — Michael Bernard Beckwith

How to Read a Food Label

The U.S. government requires food manufacturers to put a label on every processed food product. This is so we, as consumers, know what we are putting into our bodies and can make good dietary choices. A quick review of the label will provide a lot of important information about what you are eating, yet most people don't take the time to read the label. This is a big mistake.

Think of the front of the package as a marketing billboard. Don't be fooled by the marketing. Every day millions of dollars are spent to persuade us to eat foods that are not healthy for us. Through visuals (like the strawberry on the bottle of dressing below) and words (like natural, healthy, or gluten free), the food industry wants us to make assumptions about the nature of a food product without looking at the facts. For example, many people eat protein bars thinking they are a healthy choice, but protein bars can have up to 30 grams of sugar! Understanding the nutrition information and ingredients will help you make healthier choices. When you take the time to read the labeled ingredients, you are no longer being marketed to—you are staring at the facts.

---

3 Dr. Joel Furhman https://www.mensjournal.com/features/joel-fuhrman-the-doctor-is-out-there-20121107/

Nutrition Facts

8 servings per container
Serving size   2/3 cup (55g)

Amount per serving
Calories   **230**

	% Daily Value*
Total Fat 8g	**10%**
Saturated Fat 1g	**5%**
Trans Fat 0g	
Cholesterol 0mg	**0%**
Sodium 160mg	**7%**
Total Carbohydrate 37g	**13%**
Dietary Fiber 4g	**14%**
Total Sugars 12g	
Includes 10g Added Sugars	**20%**
Protein 3g	
Vitamin D 2mcg	10%
Calcium 260mg	20%
Iron 8mg	45%
Potassium 240mg	6%

* The % Daily Value (DV) tells you how much a nutrient in a serving of food contributes to a daily diet. 2,000 calories a day is used for general nutrition advice.

Figure 11.3 This label displays the key nutritional information about a common container of fruit salad. Though fruit is generally healthy, be aware of the amount of calories and sugars, and particularly the serving size to which those amounts are tied. Note that the US government has updated food label requirements and this version of the label will soon be the only one you'll see. (Credit U.S. Food and Drug Administration / Public Domain)

Look at the label on the back of what appears to be a healthy item: fruit salad or fruit cocktail. One of the first things to look for is the amount of sugar. 12 grams equals just under 2.5 teaspoons. The serving size indicated is 2/3 cups, so if you have double that amount, it's the equivalent of spooning out 5 teaspoons of sugar. The lower the sugar the better.

It's also important to avoid high amounts of sodium, to minimize saturated fats, and to avoid all trans fats. Trans fats are unhealthy substances made through the process of solidifying liquid oils to increase the shelf life of foods. Also called partially hydrogenated oil, trans fats are often found in margarine, microwave popcorn, crackers, cookies, and frozen pizza. Saturated fat usually comes from animal products like butter and meat fat. Saturated fat tends to raise the level of cholesterol in the blood, and while some is OK, moderation is best.

Dietary fiber is a good thing; the higher the number the better. Fiber has virtually no calories, but it holds water in your stomach, makes you feel full, and helps with digestion. Vitamins are very important. Aim to get to 100 percent of your recommended daily value through the food you eat throughout the day.

Next, look at the ingredient list that can be found at the bottom of the nutrition label. A long list of ingredients likely contains fillers and preservatives you should avoid. If you can't pronounce an ingredient, you can generally assume it is not a healthy option. And it's not only what you eat, it's what you don't eat. As a rule, the fewer the ingredients, the better.

This video on how to read a food label (https://openstax.org/l/foodlabels) is a helpful overview on what else to look for.

You can also download the **Fooducate** app, which allows you to scan the bar code of any food item and quickly see a report card and suggestions for healthier alternatives.

> ### ANALYSIS QUESTION
>
>
> Take a few minutes to write down everything you ate in the last two days. Now review your list and estimate what percent of your food intake came from whole foods. How did your meals compare to The Healthy Plate? Where is there opportunity for healthier choices? How can these changes benefit you?

What You Drink

What is your go-to drink when you are thirsty? Soda? Juice? Coffee? How about water? Most of your blood and every cell in your body is composed of water. In fact, water makes up 60 to 80 percent of our entire body mass, so when we don't consume enough water, all kinds of complications can occur. To function properly, all the cells and organs in our body need water. Proper hydration is key to overall health and well-being. By the time you feel thirsty, you are already dehydrated. Dehydration is when your body does not have as much water and fluids as it needs. Researchers at Virginia Polytechnic discovered that mild dehydration (as little as losing 1 to 2 percent of body water) can impair cognitive performance.[4] Water increases energy and relieves fatigue, promotes weight loss, flushes toxins, improves skin complexion, improves digestion, and is a natural headache remedy (your brain is 76 percent water). Headaches, migraines, and back pains are commonly caused by dehydration. Your body will also let you know it needs water by messaging through muscle cramps, achy joints, constipation, dry skin, and of course a dry mouth.

Aside from feeling thirsty, the easiest way to tell if you are dehydrated is to check your urine. If it is a dark shade of yellow, your urine is over-concentrated with waste. This happens because water helps flush out waste and when you're hydrated there's a higher ratio of water to waste, turning your urine a lighter color.

One of the best habits you can develop is to drink a large glass of water first thing in the morning. Your body becomes a little dehydrated as you sleep. Drinking water first thing in the morning allows your body to

---

4 University of Virginia https://www.ncbi.nlm.nih.gov/pmc/articles/PMC4207053/

rehydrate, which helps with digestion and helps move the bowels for regularity in the morning. It also helps to eliminate the toxins your liver processed while you slept.

Check out this video (https://openstax.org/l/drinkwater) for more benefits of drinking water.

Staying hydrated is important to keep your body healthy, energized, and running properly. As a general guideline, aim to drink eight glasses of water a day, although a more helpful guide is to drink half your body weight in ounces (for example, if you weigh 150 lb, try to drink 75 oz of water a day). One of the best ways to remind yourself to drink throughout the day is to buy a reusable bottle and bring it everywhere you go. There are two reasons to use a refillable water bottle instead of a plastic bottle:

1. **Your own health.** Most plastic water bottles have a chemical called bisphenol A (BPA), which is added to plastics to make them more durable and pliable. BPA is known to disrupt hormones and has been linked to sperm dysfunction.
2. **The health of the planet.** Do you know that every time you drink from a plastic water bottle and casually toss it in the trash, it can stay on the planet approximately 450 years?[5] Even when you recycle, the complex nature of recycling doesn't guarantee your plastic bottle will make it through the process. Americans purchase about 50 billion water bottles per year, averaging 13 bottles a month for each of us. By using a reusable water bottle, you can save an average of 156 plastic bottles annually.[6]

"But I don't like the taste of water!" It may take time, but eventually you will. Add a little more each day, and eventually your body will feel so fantastic fully hydrated that you will have water cravings. In the meantime, you can visit the dining hall in the morning and add lemon, lime, berries, watermelon, cucumbers, or whatever taste you enjoy that will add a little healthy flavor to the water.

While water is undeniably the healthiest beverage you can drink, it is unrealistic to assume that is all you will drink. Be careful to minimize your soda intake, as most sodas are loaded with sugar or artificial sweeteners (which can be even worse than sugar). And unless you are squeezing your own fruit juice, you are also likely drinking a lot of sugar. Many fruit juices sold in supermarkets contain only a small percentage of real fruit juice, and have added sugar and other unhealthy sweeteners like high-fructose corn syrup. A 12-oz glass of orange juice can contain up to 9 teaspoons of sugar, about the same as a 12-oz can of Coke! Hot or cold herbal teas are a wonderful addition to your diet.

Exercise

Many people exercise to maintain or lose weight, but weight loss is only one potential benefit of exercise. Regular exercise can improve the quality of your sleep, strengthen your bones, increase your energy levels, and reduce your risk of high blood pressure, diabetes, and even some forms of cancer.[7] Regular exercise is key to living a long, healthy life.

There are three basic types of exercise—flexibility, strength training, and cardiovascular.

1. **Flexibility** is the range in motion of the joints in your body, or the ability for your muscles to move freely. Without adequate flexibility, daily activities can become difficult to do. Stretching increases your body's flexibility, improves circulation, and sends more blood to your muscles. Just a few minutes a day of deep stretching can have a powerfully positive impact on your health. Yoga and Tai Chi are other wonderful ways to improve your flexibility.
2. **Strength** is the body's ability to produce force. Strength training helps improve muscle strength and

---

5 https://www.telegraph.co.uk/news/2018/01/10/stark-truth-long-plastic-footprint-will-last-planet/
6 https://www.earthday.org/2018/03/29/fact-sheet-single-use-plastics/#_ftn5
7 Harvard Medical School https://www.health.harvard.edu/newsletter_article/Exercise_as_medicine

muscle mass, which will become increasingly important as you age. Increased muscle helps your body burn calories more efficiently. Strength training also helps maintain bone strength. In addition to lifting weights, other ways to build strength include push-ups, pull-ups, squats, lunges, and yoga.

3. **Cardiovascular** is the body's ability to use oxygen efficiently during exercise. As one's ability to use oxygen improves, daily activities can be performed with less fatigue. Great cardiovascular modes of exercise include jogging, swimming, biking, and HIIT (high intensity interval training). HIIT is short bursts of intense activity followed by a rest period. With HIIT, you can squeeze a lot of benefit into a short period of time. Click here for an example of HITT workouts (https://openstax.org/l/hiitworkout) .

Figure 11.4 Your college may offer a variety of unique and interesting exercise programs and classes, which you can take advantage of to learn new things and stay fit. (Credit: Jo Allebon / Flickr / Attribution 2.0 Generic (CC-BY 2.0))

Research indicates that regular aerobic exercise can support memory and cognition. In these studies, aerobic exercise generally increases the number of new neurons created in the brain's memory center and also reduces inflammation.[8] Inflammation in the brain may contribute to the development of dementia and other neurodegenerative conditions. It might be good timing to take a jog before you sit down to study for a test!

It's important to move throughout the day, and every day. Aim to exercise for 150 minutes a week. You don't have to be the king or queen of CrossFit; it's the daily movement that is most important. While it is best to integrate all three types of exercise, the best exercise is the one you will actually do. Find and commit to a form of exercise you will enjoy.

Toxins

We live in an increasingly toxic world. Since the Industrial Revolution, we have released thousands of man-made chemicals into the environment. These chemical toxins are in our food (pesticides, conventional fertilizers), in food packaging, in household products, and in our personal care products. Many of these chemicals have been linked to infertility, asthma, migraines, ADHD, and cancer.

The complicated thing about these chemicals is that their effects can take years or even decades to appear.

The chemicals build up over time *and they interact with each other*, which can result in problems that are not considered by "single chemical" testing (which is the majority of the limited testing that is done).

Now the good news—there are simple things you can do right now to limit the amount of toxins in your environment. First, it is best to avoid any products with "artificial colors" or "fragrance."

- **Artificial colors:** Synthetic dyes like Yellow 10, Blue 1, and Red 28 may contain carcinogens and neurotoxins and can be absorbed by your skin and go directly into your bloodstream.
- **Fragrance:** Have you ever walked down the cleaning and laundry soap aisle and been assaulted by so many fragrances you couldn't get to the next aisle fast enough? Claiming trade secrets, companies don't have to tell us what's in "fragrance," which can include highly toxic ingredients, hormone disruptors, and carcinogens. Fragranced products come in the form of soaps, cleaners, air fresheners, hand sanitizers, laundry detergents, and personal care products. Studies have repeatedly shown that the synthetic fragrances and other toxic chemicals included in these products are causing a range of health problems.[9]

There is a long and ever-growing list of common chemicals to avoid, but it's hard to remember the names when you are shopping. That's where a handy app like Healthy Living from the EWG comes in.

Simply scan the bar code of any products you use and learn about any potential health hazards.

> "Many Americans are surprised to learn that the ingredients in their makeup, shampoo and body lotion are largely unregulated and, in some cases, harmful to their health. The fact is that companies can put potentially dangerous ingredients into the products they sell without ever having to prove they are safe."
>
> — Heather White, Environmental Working Group Executive Director

Your skin is your largest organ, and in seconds will absorb what you put on it. It's important to be wary of conventional skin care products that could potentially leak toxins into your body. Think of your skin as one giant mouth. If you wouldn't eat the ingredients in your products, think twice before applying them to your skin.

ANALYSIS QUESTION

Are your eating and sleeping habits currently affecting your ability to have a super-successful college experience? Describe the health and wellness changes a commitment to eating clean and sleeping well will bring about, and how you will benefit in the short and long term.

11.2 Sleep

Estimated completion time: 19 minutes.

Questions to consider:

- How much sleep is enough?
- What are the impacts of sleep deprivation?

---

9   https://www.ewg.org/

- Which strategies and support can enhance sleep?

How often do you wake up filled with energy, eager to embrace the day? How often do you wake up still tired, with heavy eyes that just don't want to open? Your answer to these questions has a direct bearing on the quality of your decisions, your ability to use good judgement, the extent to which you can focus in the classroom, and ultimately your long-term health.

A great night's sleep begins the minute you wake up. The choices you make throughout the day impact how quickly you fall asleep, whether you sleep soundly, and whether your body is able to successfully complete the cycle of critical functions that only happen while you sleep.

Sleep is the foundation of amazing health, yet almost 40 percent of adults struggle to get enough sleep.[10] Lack of sleep affects mental and physical performance and can make you more irritable. The diminished energy that results from too little sleep often leads us to make poor decisions about most things, including food. Think about the last time you were really tired. Did you crave pizza, donuts, and fries—or a healthy salad? Studies have shown that people who sleep less are more likely to eat fewer vegetables and eat more fats and refined carbohydrates, like donuts.[11]

With sufficient sleep it is easier to learn, to remember what you learned, and to have the necessary energy to make the most of your college experience. Without sufficient sleep it is harder to learn, to remember what you learned, and to have the energy to make the most of your college experience. It's that simple.

What Happens When We Sleep?

Sleep is a time when our bodies are quite busy repairing and detoxifying. While we sleep we fix damaged tissue, toxins are processed and eliminated, hormones essential for growth and appetite control are released and restocked, and energy is restored. Sleep is essential for a healthy immune system. How many colds do you catch a year? How often do you get the flu? If you are often sick, you do not have a healthy immune system, and sleep deprivation may be a key culprit.

A review of hundreds of sleep studies concluded that most adults need around eight hours of sleep to maintain good health. Some people may be able to function quite well on seven and others may need closer to nine, but as a general rule, most people need a solid eight hours of sleep each night. And when it comes to sleep, both quantity and quality are important.

When sleep is cut short, the body doesn't have time to complete all the phases needed for the repair and detoxification.

A tiny lobe called the pineal gland helps us fall asleep. The pineal gland secretes melatonin to calm the brain. The pineal gland responds to darkness. If you are watching TV until the minute you go to bed and then sleep with the artificial light from smartphones and other devices, your brain is tricked into thinking it is still daylight; this makes it difficult for the pineal gland to do its job. In addition, if the TV shows you watch before bed are violent or action-packed, your body will release cortisol (the stress hormone). Anything that creates stress close to bedtime will make it more difficult to fall asleep. A bedtime practice of quiet activities like reading, journaling, listening to music, or meditation will make it much easier to fall asleep.

---

10   https://news.gallup.com/poll/166553/less-recommended-amount-sleep.aspx
11   Cleveland Clinic, https://health.clevelandclinic.org/lack-sleep-make-crave-junk-food/

What Happens If You Don't Get Enough Sleep?

Lack of sleep has a big impact on your overall state of health and well-being. Studies have linked poor sleep to a variety of health problems. The U.S. Centers for Disease Control and Prevention have identified sleep deprivation as a public health epidemic.

A lack of sleep can change the way your genes express themselves. One notable study involved a group of healthy adults limited to six hours of sleep for one week. Researchers then measured the change in gene activity compared to the prior week when these same people were getting a full eight hours of sleep a night. The lack of sleep caused the activity of 711 genes to become distorted. About half of the genes were switched off by a lack of sleep, and these genes were associated with the immune system. The other half of the genes experienced increased activity from a lack of sleep, and these were genes associated with the promotion of tumors, genes associated with long-term chronic inflammation, and stress genes.[12]

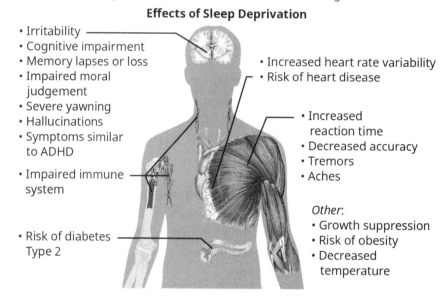

Figure 11.5 **The Effects of Sleep Deprivation** This visual depicts many of the ways we are affected by insufficient sleep. (Credit: Häggström, Mikael (2014). "Medical gallery of Mikael Häggström 2014". *WikiJournal of Medicine*. Public Domain.)

Some of the health risks of insufficient sleep include the following:

Increased risk of heart attack and stroke: In his book *Why We Sleep*, Matthew Walker, PhD, shares Japanese research showing that male workers who average six hours of sleep or less are 400 to 500 percent more likely to suffer one or more cardiac arrests than those getting more than six hours of sleep each night. Another study of women between the ages of 20 and 79 found that those who had mild sleep disturbance such as taking longer to fall asleep or waking up one or more times during the night were significantly more likely to have high blood pressure than those who fell asleep quickly and slept soundly.[13]

Impaired cognitive function: Even one night of sleeping less than six hours can impact your ability to think clearly the next day.

Increased risk of accidents: Sleep deprivation slows your reaction time, which increases your risk of accidents. You are three times more likely to be in a car crash if you are tired. According to the American Sleep

---

12 Archer, https://www.ncbi.nlm.nih.gov/pubmed/23440187
13 Matthew Walker, PhD *Why We Sleep*

Foundation, 40 percent of people admitted to falling asleep behind the wheel at least once. A Governor's Highway Safety Association report estimates there are 6,400 fatal drowsy driving crashes each year. Fifty percent of these crashes involve drivers under the age of 25.[14]

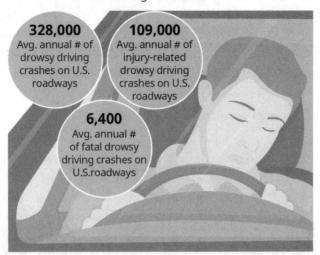

Figure 11.6 Driving while drowsy puts you, your passengers, and many others in danger. (Credit: Modification of work by Governors Highway Safety Association.)

Driving after 20 hours without sleep is the equivalent of driving with a blood-alcohol concentration of 0.08 percent—the U.S. legal limit for drunk driving.

Weight gain/increased risk for obesity: Sleep helps balance your appetite by regulating hormones that play a role in helping you feel full after a meal. Also, cortisol is released during times of anxiety, and exhaustion causes your body to produce more cortisol. This can stimulate your appetite.

Increased risk of cancer: Tumors grow up to three times faster in laboratory animals with severe sleep dysfunctions. Researchers believe this is because of disrupted melatonin production, as melatonin has both antioxidant and anticancer activity.

Increased emotional intensity: The part of the brain responsible for emotional reactions, your amygdala, can be 60 percent more reactive when you've slept poorly, resulting in increased emotional intensity.

For more information on the advantages and health risks of sleep watch this TED Talk (https://openstax.org/l/sleepsuperpower) by Matt Walker, PhD, Director of the Sleep Center at U California Berkeley.

Tips to Improve the Quality of Your Sleep

Now that you are more aware of the ways insufficient sleep harms your body, let's review some of the things you can do to enhance your sleep.

Make sleep a priority.

It can be challenging in college, but try to get on a schedule where you sleep and wake at the same time every day to get your body accustomed to a routine. This will help your body get into a sleep rhythm and make it easier to fall asleep and get up in the morning.

Sleep in a cool, quiet, dark room.

Create a sleeping environment that is comfortable and conducive to sleep. If you can control the temperature in your room, keep it cool in the evening. Scientists believe a cool bedroom (around 65 degrees) may be best for sleep, since it mimics our body's natural temperature drop. Exposure to bright light suppresses our body's ability to make melatonin, so keep the room as dark as possible. A 2010 study in *The Journal of Clinical Endocrinology & Metabolism* found that individuals exposed to room light "during the usual hours of sleep suppressed melatonin by greater than 50%."[15] Even the tiniest bit of light in the room (like from a clock radio LCD screen) can disrupt your internal clock and your production of melatonin, which will interfere with your sleep. A sleep mask may help eliminate light, and earplugs can help reduce noise.

Avoid eating late or drinking alcohol or caffeine close to bedtime.

It is best to finish eating at least two hours before bedtime and avoid caffeine after lunch. While not everyone is affected in the same way, caffeine hangs around a long time in most bodies. Although alcohol will make you drowsy, the effect is short-lived and you will often wake up several hours later, unable to fall back to sleep. Alcohol can also keep you from entering the deeper stages of sleep, where your body does most of the repair and healing. A 2013 *Scientific Research* study concluded that "energy drinks, other caffeinated beverages and alcoholic beverages are risk factors of poor sleep quality." It's important to finish eating hours before bedtime so your body is able to heal and detoxify and it is not spending the first few hours of sleep digesting a heavy meal.

Start to wind down an hour before bed.

There are great apps to help with relaxation, stress release, and falling asleep. Or you can simply practice 4-7-8 breathing to calm your nervous system—breathe in to the count of 4, hold your breath for a count of 7, and release your breath slowly to the count of 8.

Consider the Insight Timer (http://insighttimer.com) app, or any of the free apps (https://openstax.org/l/sleepapps) listed by the American Sleep Association.

Exercise for 30 minutes a day.

One of the biggest benefits of exercise is its effect on sleep. A study from Stanford University found that 16 weeks in a moderate-intensity exercise program allowed people to fall asleep about 15 minutes faster and sleep about 45 minutes longer. Walking, yoga, swimming, strength training, jumping rope—whatever it is, find an exercise you like and make sure to move your body every day.

Improve your diet.

Low fiber and high saturated fat and sugar intake is associated with lighter, less restorative sleep with more wake time during the night. Processed food full of chemicals will make your body work extra hard during the night to remove the toxins and leave less time for healing and repair.

Sleep affects how we look, feel, and function on a daily basis and is vital to our health and quality of life. When you get the sleep your body needs, you look more vibrant, you feel more vibrant, and you have the energy to live your best life.

Now, with a better understanding of the benefits of getting the recommended hours of nightly sleep and the health risks of not getting enough sleep, what changes can you make to improve the quality and quantity of your sleep?

---

15   JCEM, https://www.ncbi.nlm.nih.gov/pmc/articles/PMC3047226/

What If I'm Doing All These Things and I Still Have Trouble Sleeping?

People that have trouble falling asleep also often have low magnesium levels (sources suggest that over half of the adults in the United States are magnesium deficient). You can ask your doctor to check your magnesium levels, but you can also focus on eating magnesium-rich foods to help. One of the best magnesium-rich snacks is pumpkin seeds. Other great sources are almonds, sesame seeds, and walnuts.

Difficulty sleeping may be a sign that you have a clinical sleep problem, such as insomnia or sleep apnea. If you are doing all the right things and still have trouble falling or staying asleep, talk to your doctor.

These are some resources for insomnia:

- Healthy Sleep (https://openstax.org/l/gettingsleep) , Harvard Medical School Division of Sleep Medicine
- Insomnia Treatment (https://openstax.org/l/insomniatreatment) , American Association of Sleep Medicine
- Sleep Medicine (https://openstax.org/l/behaviroalsleepmedicine) , Society of Behavioral Sleep Medicine

ANALYSIS QUESTION

Do you have a ritual to shut down your day and calm your mind? If yes, can you identify two ways to improve upon your current ritual? If no, what three things can you put in place to prepare your body and mind for a restorative night's sleep?

11.3 Taking Care of Your Emotional Health

Estimated completion time: 16 minutes.

Questions to consider:

- What are some of the ways to tell if you are holding onto stress?
- How do mindfulness and gratitude encourage emotional health?

Identifying and Managing Stress

According to a 2018 report from the American College Health Association, in a 12-month period 42 percent of college students reported that they have felt so depressed it was difficult to function, and 63 percent reported feeling overwhelming anxiety.[16] Your ability to manage stress, maintain loving relationships, and rise to the demands of school and work all impact your emotional health.

Stress is not always bad. In fact, some stress is helpful. Good stress is stress in amounts small enough to help you meet daily challenges. It's also a warning system that produces the fight-or-flight response, which increases blood pressure and your heart rate so you can avoid a potentially life-threatening situation. Feeling stressed can be perfectly normal, especially during exam time. It can motivate you to focus on your work, but it can also become so overwhelming you can't concentrate. It's when stress is chronic (meaning you always feel stressed) that it starts to damage your body.

---

16   American College Health Association 2018 report https://www.acha.org/documents/ncha/NCHA-II_Spring_2018_Reference_Group_Executive_Summary.pdf

What Chronic Stress Does to Your Body

Do you find it difficult to concentrate or complete your work? Are you frequently sick? Do you have regular headaches? Are you more anxious, angry, or irritable than usual? Do you have trouble falling asleep or staying awake? If you answered yes to any or all of these questions, you may be holding on to too much stress.

Stress that hangs around for weeks or months affects your ability to concentrate, makes you more accident-prone, increases your risk for heart disease, can weaken your immune system, disrupts your sleep, and can cause fatigue, depression, and anxiety.[17] To learn more about what stress does to your body, click here: apa.org/helpcenter/stress.

Some people refer to the time we are living in as the age of overload. It's easy to get worn down by social media and the constant news cycle, and to be overwhelmed by too many choices. We live in a fast-paced, always-on world with a lot of pressures. The military created the VUCA acronym for the world we currently live in. VUCA stands for volatile, uncertain, complex, and ambiguous, and as a result of living in this VUCA world, many of us are in a constant state of overdrive.

You will have stress. Stress is inevitable. It's how you deal with it that can make all the difference. One of the most important things you can do is to keep perspective on your stressors. When feeling stressed, ask yourself, on a scale of 1 to 100, how stressful a situation is this? Will I even remember this three years from now? When facing potential stressors, the way you view what you're experiencing can intensify your stress or minimize it.

There are many ways to manage stress. Take a look at some of the ideas in the stress toolkit below. Which ones have you tried? Which ones do you want to try? It's helpful to have different tools for different situations—for example, a calming yoga pose in your dorm room and deep breathing in the classroom.

Mindfulness and Gratitude

Deep breathing, mindfulness, and a practice of gratitude are some of the most effective ways to manage stress and take care of your emotional health.

Mindfulness

Mindfulness means being present with your thoughts, feelings, bodily sensations, and surrounding environment. Mindfulness is also without judgement—meaning there is no right or wrong way to think or feel in a given moment. When we practice mindfulness, our thoughts tune into what we're sensing in the present moment rather than rehashing the past or imagining the future.[18]

Anything that keeps you present in the moment and gives your prefrontal cortex (the reasoning and thinking part of your brain) a break is practicing mindfulness. Mindfulness can be a slow walk; looking intently at the grass, trees, flowers, or buildings; and being aware of what you are sensing and feeling. Mindfulness can be sitting quietly—even sitting still in a quiet place for as little as a few minutes can reduce heart rate and blood pressure.[19]

Developing a practice of mindfulness is easier than you may think:

---

17 *The University of Maryland Medical Center UMMC,* https://www.umms.org/ummc
18 Moran, Joan; University of California at Los Angeles, http://newsroom.ucla.edu/stories/gratitude-249167
19 The Greater Good Science Center, UC Berkeley https://ggia.berkeley.edu/practice/

- **Slow down.** From brushing your teeth, to washing your face, to shampooing your hair—can you take the speed out of getting ready in the morning? Focus on the activity, pay attention to what you are doing, stay present (this means don't think about what happened last night or what's in store for the day, just stay focused on the activity), and take your time.
- **Focus on your breath.** How fast are you breathing? Is your breath coming from your chest or your belly? Can you feel the air come through your nose on the inhale? Can you slow down the exhale? Can you feel your body relax when you slow the exhale?
- **Connect to your environment.** Walk for a few minutes, focused on the world around you—look at the leaves on the trees or the light at the corner, listen to the sounds around you, stay with your surroundings, and observe what you see and hear around you.

"**We can't change the world, at least not quickly, but we can change our brains. By practicing mindfulness all of us have the capacity to develop a deeper sense of calm.**"

— *Rick Hanson, author, Resilient*

Deep Breathing

When people hear mindfulness they often think meditation. While meditation is one method of mindfulness, there are many others that may be simpler and easier for you to practice. Deep breathing helps lower stress and reduce anxiety, and it is simple yet very powerful. A daily mindful breathing practice has been shown to reduce test anxiety in college students.[20] A 2-4-6-8 breathing pattern is a very useful tool that can be used to help bring a sense of calm and to help mild to moderate anxiety. It takes almost no time, requires no equipment, and can be done anywhere:

- Start by quickly exhaling any air in your lungs (to the count of 2).
- Breathing through your nose, inhale to the count of 4.
- Hold your breath for a count of 6.
- Slowly exhale through your mouth to the count of 8.

This is one round. Do not repeat the quick exhale again. Instead start round two with an inhale through your nose to the count of 4, hold for 6, and exhale to 8. Repeat for three more rounds to relax your body and mind.

With practice, 2-4-6-8 breathing will become a useful tool for times when you experience tension or stress.

Meditation

Dan Harris, a news reporter at ABC, fell into drug use and suffered a major panic attack on national television. Following this embarrassing period in his life, he learned to meditate and found that it made him calmer and more resilient. He's now on a mission to make meditation approachable to everyone. Dan used to be a skeptic about meditation but now says that if he learned to meditate, anyone can learn to meditate! Dan reminds us that we ARE going to get lost, and our mind IS going to stray, and that's ok. Simply notice when you're lost and start over. Every time your mind strays and your start over, it is like a bicep curl for your brain. Start with 3 minutes and slowly work your way up to 15 or 20. To hear more about Dan's journey, watch this video (https://openstax.org/l/danharris) , and for a simple meditation to get started, you can try one of the videos on the meditation Youtube channel (https://openstax.org/l/meditation) .

Some great meditation apps include Insight Timer, CALM, and Headspace.

Gratitude

Too often people think it is the external factors that bring us joy and happiness, when really it's all related to internal work. According to UCLA's Mindfulness Awareness Research Center, "Having an attitude of gratitude changes the molecular structure of the brain, and makes us healthier and happier. When you feel happiness, the central nervous system is affected. You are more peaceful, less reactive and less resistant."[21]

Numerous studies show that people who count their blessings tend to be happier and less depressed. In a UC Berkeley study, researchers recruited 300 people who were experiencing emotional or mental health challenges and randomly divided them into three groups. All three groups received counseling services. The first group also wrote a letter of gratitude every week for three weeks. The second group wrote about their thoughts and feelings with negative experiences. The third group received only counseling. The people in the group who wrote gratitude letters reported significantly better mental health for up to 12 weeks after the writing exercise ended.

This would suggest that a healthy emotional self-care practice is to take note of good experiences or when you see something that makes you smile. Think about why the experience feels so good. According to Rick Hanson, author of *Resilient*, "Each day is strewn with little jewels. The idea is to see them and pick them up. When you notice something positive, stay with the feeling for 30 seconds. Feel the emotions in your whole body. Maybe your heart feels lighter or you're smiling. The more you can deepen and lengthen positive experiences the longer those positivity neurons in your brain are firing—and the longer they fire the stronger the underlying neural networks become. Repeat that process a half dozen times a day and you'll feel stronger, more stable and calmer within a few weeks."

Build a Stress Toolkit

Practice self-compassion	Laugh with friends
Eat clean food	Listen to music

Mindfulness
  Meditation
  Deep breathing (2-4-6-8)
  A walk in nature
	Drink calming tea

	Watch a funny movie

Exercise/Movement
  Yoga, Tai chi
  Dance
  HIIT
  Run, Spin, Lift
	Write in a gratitude journal

	Change phone screen to this picture
	Change passwords to calming words
Epsom salt baths	Keep something in your backpack that reminds you to take a deep breath every time you see it
Hugs	

Figure 11.7 Do you have a stress toolkit filled with a variety of stress-coping tools to help you navigate any stressful situation? (Credit: Modification of work by Robin Benzrihem)

---

21   2016 Study Journal of PLoS One, https://journals.plos.org/plosmedicine/article?id=10.1371/journal.pmed.1000316

ACTIVITY

Take a look at some of the suggested tools for your stress toolkit. Which ones have you tried? Have they been effective in helping you manage stress? Ask two friends or family members about their favorite stress-management strategies. What has worked for you and others that is not on this list? Identify two new tools you would like to explore and articulate how you will determine if they work for you, and then you can confidently add them to your stress toolkit.

11.4 Taking Care of Your Mental Health

Estimated completion time: 16 minutes.

Question to consider:

- What is mental health?
- How can I take care of it?

The World Health Organization ranks mental health conditions as the leading cause of disability in the United States. One in four adults experience a diagnosable mental health disorder in any given year, yet more than half will not seek treatment. The primary reason people don't seek the help they need is shame and fear of judgment from friends, family, and coworkers. It is important to remove any stigma associated with mental health and encourage those who need help to seek support.

WHAT STUDENTS SAY

1. In your opinion, which of the following is the most significant health issue facing college students?
    a. stress and/or exhaustion
    b. drinking and/or substance abuse
    c. unhealthy eating
    d. unhealthy relationships
    e. safety
2. Which of the following best describes your experience or outlook regarding healthy eating while in college?
    a. I'm generally able to eat healthy food most of the time.
    b. I have difficulty eating healthy food because of lack of choices on campus.
    c. I don't have enough money to eat healthy food.
    d. I don't have enough time to focus on eating healthy food.
    e. I need to learn more about healthy eating.
    f. It's not something I'm very concerned about.
3. When you are facing an issue regarding your emotions, stress, mental health, or relationships, what do you typically do?

a. Wait for it to pass or work through it.
b. Talk to a health professional.
c. Talk to friends or family.
d. Talk to another trusted person such as a teacher, RA, or religious person.
e. Use a method such as meditation, exercise, or something similar.

You can also take the anonymous What Students Say (https://openstax.org/l/collegesurvey6-12) surveys to add your voice to this textbook. Your responses will be included in updates.

Students offered their views on these questions, and the results are displayed in the graphs below.

In your opinion, which of the following is the most significant health issue facing college students?

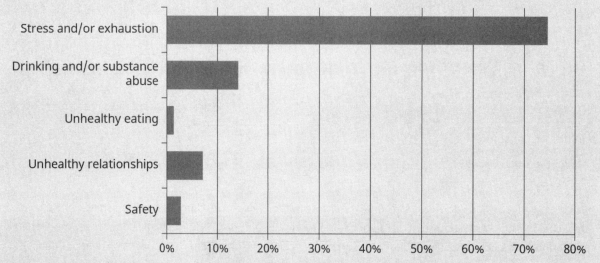

Figure 11.8

Which of the following best describes your experience or outlook regarding healthy eating while in college?

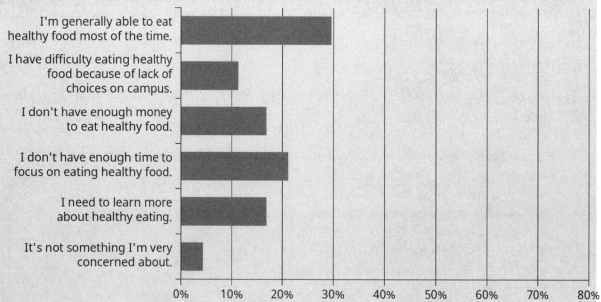

Figure 11.9

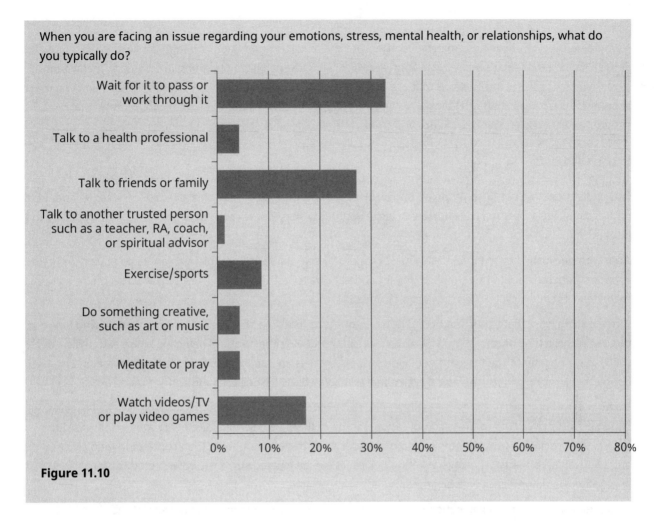

Figure 11.10

What Is Mental Health?

Mental health is "the level of psychological well-being or an absence of mental illness. It is the state of someone who is functioning at a satisfactory level of emotional and behavioral adjustment."[22]

According to NAMI (National Alliance on Mental Illness), a mental illness is a condition that affects a person's thinking, feeling, or mood. The condition may affect a person's ability to relate to others and function throughout the day.

A mental health condition isn't the result of one event; it is most often the result of multiple overlapping causes. Environment, lifestyle, and genetic predisposition can all be factors in whether someone develops a mental health condition. Traumatic life events or stressful experiences may make some people more susceptible, and brain biochemistry may play a role as well. Mental health conditions show up in many ways. Anxiety, depression, and eating disorders are some of the most common.

Anxiety Disorders

We all experience the occasional feeling of anxiety, which is quite normal. New situations, meeting new people, driving in traffic, and public speaking are just a few of the common activities that can cause people to feel anxious. It is important to seek help when these feelings become overwhelming, cause fear, or keep us

---

22   Wikipedia, https://en.wikipedia.org/wiki/Mental_health

from doing everyday activities. Anxiety disorders are the most common mental health concern in the United States, and while there are many types of anxiety disorders, they all have one thing in common: "persistent, excessive fear or worry in situations that are not threatening."[23] Physically, your heart may race, and you may experience shortness of breath, nausea, or intense fatigue. Talk with a mental health care professional if you experience a level of anxiety that keeps you from your regular daily activities.

Eating Disorders

Eating disorders are not uncommon among students. Stress or anxiety may create a desire for some students to overeat, while others may develop a concern about body shape or weight and significantly reduce their food intake.

Anorexia nervosa is a potentially fatal illness marked by self-starvation. People with anorexia usually have an irrational concern about body shape or weight and eat a very restricted diet. They may also feel the need to exercise all the time, even when they are sick or exhausted.

Binge eating is frequent consumption of large amounts of food in a short period of time. People who binge regularly (more than once a week) and feel a lack of control over their eating may have binge eating disorder (BED). It is important to seek treatment if you suspect there is an issue with binge eating. Treatment can address any underlying psychological issues that will help control urges to binge eat.

Bulimia involves cycles of excessive eating followed by eliminating food through vomiting or with laxatives. Eating disorders can lead to many complications, some of them very serious, like heart conditions and kidney failure. It is crucial for anyone with an eating disorder to stabilize their health, then continuing medical care and counseling to reach full recovery. Eating disorders can be treated successfully with medical care, psychotherapy, counseling, or coaching.

If you think you might have an eating disorder, visit a doctor or your campus health center. The National Eating Disorders Association (https://www.nationaleatingdisorders.org) also offers information, help, and support.

Depression

Most people feel sad at times. This is a normal reaction to loss or struggles we face. Being sad is not the same as having depression. When intense sadness lasts for several days or even weeks and you are no longer interested in activities you once enjoyed, it may be depression. Depression can lead to a variety of emotional and physical problems and can decrease a person's ability to function at work and at home.

Depression does not have a single cause. It can follow a life crisis or physical illness, but it can also occur spontaneously. Several factors including trauma, a significant life change, brain injury, and drug and alcohol misuse may contribute to depression. Depression is a treatable medical condition. Talk with a mental health care professional if you experience an ongoing level of sadness that keeps you from your regular daily activities.

Suicidal Behavior

Suicide is when people direct violence at themselves with the intent to end their lives, and they die because of

---

23   NAMI, https://www.nami.org/NAMI/media/NAMI-Media/Images/FactSheets/Anxiety-Disorders-FS.pdf

their actions.[24]

People who contemplate suicide often experience a deep feeling of hopelessness. They often don't feel they can cope with challenging life events and are not able to see solutions to problems. In the moment, they are unable to see that the challenges are really only temporary. Most survivors of suicide attempts go on to live wonderful, full lives.

Depression is a key risk factor for suicide, along with substance abuse, chronic debilitating pain, mental health disorders, and a family history of suicide.

These are some of the warning signs to help you determine if a friend or loved one is at risk for suicide, especially if the behavior is new, has increased, or seems related to a painful event:

- talking about wanting to die or to kill themselves
- looking for a way to kill themselves, like searching online or buying a gun
- talking about feeling hopeless or having no reason to live
- talking about feeling trapped or in unbearable pain
- talking about being a burden to others
- increasing the use of alcohol or drugs
- acting anxious or agitated; behaving recklessly
- sleeping too little or too much
- withdrawing or isolating themselves
- showing rage or talking about seeking revenge
- extreme mood swings[25]

Help is available all day, every day, for anyone who might be in crisis. By offering immediate counseling to everyone that may need it, crisis centers provide invaluable support at the most critical times. If you or someone you know has warning signs of suicide, get help as soon as possible. Family and friends are often the first to recognize any warning signs and can help take the first step in finding treatment.

If someone is telling you that they are going to kill themselves, do not leave them alone. The National Suicide Prevention Lifeline at 1-800-273-TALK (8255) is available 24 hours a day, 7 days a week. A Crisis Text Line is also available 24/7 by texting HOME to 741741, 85258, or 686868. There are also near-term plans to implement a 988 suicide hotline number that will work similarly to 911.

Additional Resources

Because entering college is such a big transition, it is important to know what health services are available on your campus. Some help may be beyond the scope of a college counseling program, and if this is the case, your college health center can refer you to off-campus resources to support you.

Regardless of where you attend college, OK2TALK and NAMI offer online, text, and phone support.

- OK2TALK (https://ok2talk.org) is a community for young adults struggling with mental health problems. It offers a safe place to talk.
- Call the NAMI helpline at 800-950-6264, or txt NAMI to 741741.

Your brain requires a constant supply of energy to function. What you eat and are exposed to have a direct impact on its processes, your mood, and your ability to make good decisions. A majority of college students

---

24 NIMH, https://www.nimh.nih.gov/health/publications/suicide-faq/index.shtml
25 https://suicidepreventionlifeline.org/how-we-can-all-prevent-suicide/; https://www.nimh.nih.gov/health/publications/suicide-faq/index.shtml

feel anxious, lonely, or depressed at some point during the year. We all have bad days, and sometimes bad days string into weeks. It's OK to feel bad. What's important is to acknowledge and work through your feelings, and find a friend or a counselor to talk to.

11.5 Maintaining Healthy Relationships

Estimated completion time: 18 minutes.

Questions to consider:

- How does self-care benefit relationships?
- Why is community so important to healthy relationships?
- What is sexual health?

Relationships are key to happy and healthy lives. According to Dr. Robert Waldinger, director of the Harvard Study of Adult Development, people with the best health outcomes were people who "leaned into relationships, with family, with friends, with community."

Figure 11.11 Healthy relationships involve trust, respect, and support. (Credit: Garry Knight / Flickr / Attribution 2.0 Generic (CC-BY 2.0))

The quality of our relationships is important, however. What makes a relationship healthy? Relationships come in many forms: lovers, family, friends, coworkers, team members, and neighbors. Think of a relationship where you have mutual respect and trust, supporting each other in tough times, celebrating the good times, and communicating with ease and honesty. This is a healthy relationship. Do you have someone in mind? On the other hand, if communication is often tense or strained, confidences are broken, or you don't feel listened to, appreciated, or valued, these are signs of an unhealthy relationship. Unhealthy relationships can have both immediate and longer-term health impacts. If you are unhappy in a relationship, try to improve the relationship, or end it. Do not stay in a relationship for the wrong reasons, such as fear of being alone or guilt.

If a partner tries to force you to do something sexually, harms you physically, or is verbally abusive, you are in an unhealthy relationship. Even if you believe the person loves you, it does not make up for the harm they are doing to you. End the relationship.

Take a moment to assess the health of your relationships. Who are the people who make you smile, who boost your confidence, who truly listen when you need to talk, and who want only the best for you? Investing in these relationships is likely to make you happier and healthier. Relationships are two-way streets. How committed are you to your relationships? How much effort do you put into nurturing your relationships?

Self-Care

Healthy relationships start with healthy individuals. Self-care is learning to take good care of yourself and to prioritize your own needs. Self-care involves any activity that nurtures and refuels you, such as taking a walk in the woods, going to a yoga class, attending a sporting event, reading a good book, or spending time with friends. When you are feeling calm and nourished, you are going to look forward to your day, and despite how busy it is, you will prioritize time with friends and family. If you don't take care of and learn to love yourself, you will never be able to bring your best self to any relationship.

An important dynamic you bring to any relationship is how you feel about yourself. Self-esteem is about loving yourself and being happy for who you are. Building healthy self-esteem impacts how you see yourself, which can drastically improve your relationships. While low self-esteem won't keep us from romantic love, it can act as a barrier to a healthy relationship. If you do not believe you are good enough, how can you expect your partner to think so?

When you feel secure in yourself, this allows you and your partner to feel more secure about the relationship. If you have insecurities, it may show in your relationship as jealousy, defensiveness, or tension that leads to unnecessary arguments. Healthy self-esteem goes hand in hand with self-confidence, and feeling confident about yourself will translate into a stronger and more satisfying relationship. If you are experiencing low self-esteem, you may give your partner too much credit or stay in a relationship that is not healthy for you. If you find yourself changing your personality for someone else, that is never a sign of a healthy relationship.

You can reverse negative self-talk and build your self-esteem. If you catch yourself thinking you are unlovable, unattractive, or not good enough, it's important to start talking to yourself in a positive way and to celebrate all that is uniquely you.

Self-care includes self-forgiveness. We all make mistakes. A misstep isn't the end of the world. Pick yourself up, put things in perspective, acknowledge any lessons to be learned, focus on all that makes you special, and move forward. Be kind to yourself.

The Importance of Community

The Nicoya Peninsula in Costa Rica is home to some of the highest number of centenarians (people who are 100 years old or older) in the world. Costa Ricans in general report a high level of life satisfaction. Dan Buettner, author of the Blue Zones study of the longest living populations in the world, explains that Costa Rica "is a place where religion, family, and social interaction are the main values, unlike trying to get ahead, or financial security, or status. Their cities are set up so they're bumping into each other all day long. They walk to the markets, where they have conversations with people."[26]

In Costa Rica, multiple generations live together under the same roof or nearby where they can be involved in each other's lives. Neighbors are like extended family, and people often stop in for a visit and go out of their way to help one another.

While this isn't the way many of us live in the United States, the lessons from the Blue Zone study underscore the importance of community and the health benefits of connecting to and staying close to a community.

---

26 https://www.bluezones.com/2017/10/costa-rica-singapore-two-happiest-places-earth/

What communities do you belong to? Is your dorm a community? A sports team? A club or people you volunteer with? When you start seeing the social circles you connect to as communities and prioritize your time to develop more closeness with those communities, you will experience many physical, mental, and emotional health benefits.

Figure 11.12 Joining clubs in college can be an outstanding way to join and build communities. (Credit: SupportPDX, Cerritos College / Flickr / Attribution 2.0 Generic (CC-BY 2.0))

According to an analysis of research on college students (Joe Cuseo, *The Most Potent, Research-Based Principles of College Success*), college students who have a higher sense of belonging and are more involved in their college community are more successful. Additionally, college students who are involved in extracurricular, volunteer, and part-time work experiences outside the classroom (less than 20 hours per week) earn higher grades than students who do not get involved in any out-of-class activities at all.

APPLICATION

Make a list of the communities you belong to. Your list should include formal communities—for example, sports teams, fraternities or sororities, and membership in clubs and other organizations. Your list should also include informal communities—for example, your neighbors or the people you always see at your favorite exercise class.

Next to each community, write how being a member of this community benefits you and how your involvement benefits the community. Now, make a new list of your personal interests and passions. How well do these align with the communities you already belong to? Are there new communities that would be a good fit for you?

If you are struggling to identify communities you already belong to, think about your passions, causes you care about, and ways you love to spend your time. Find a group or club that aligns with your interests. If you can't find one that already exists, start a new club!

Research has shown that friends provide a sense of meaning or purpose in our lives, and that having a healthy social life is important to staying physically healthy. In a meta-analysis of the research results from 148 studies of over 300,000 participants, researchers found that social relationships are important in improving our lifespan. Social support has been linked to lower blood pressure and better immune system functioning. The meta-analysis also showed that social support operates on a continuum: the greater the extent of the relationships, the lower the health risks.[27]

According to a 2018 report from the American College Health Association, in a 12-month period, 63 percent of college students have felt very lonely. If you are feeling lonely or having a hard time making friends, know that the majority of people around you have also felt this way. Joining a group or a club of people who share your interests and passions is one of the best ways to make great friends and stay connected.

Sexual Health

Affection, love, and sexual intimacy all play an important role in healthy relationships, and a responsible approach to intimacy is essential for sexual health. Whether you are already sexually active or become sexually active in the future, your choices can affect your safety as well as the health and safety of your sexual partners. It's important to understand what you can do to protect yourself from sexually transmitted infections (STIs).

Common Sexually Transmitted Infections

Infection	Symptoms	Diagnosis and Treatment
Human papillomavirus (HPV)	• HPV can be passed even when an infected person has no signs or symptoms. • Most people with HPV do not know they are infected. • Symptoms can include genital warts, abnormal Pap test results, and cancer.	• There is no test for HPV. • There is a vaccine to prevent it. • There is no treatment for HPV, although there are treatments for the health problems it can cause. • Routine Pap tests can identify problems.
Chlamydia	• Symptoms include a burning sensation when urinating and/or discharge from the penis or vagina; however, most people who have chlamydia have no symptoms. • In women, it can cause damage to the reproductive system.	• Testing usually involves a urine sample or vaginal swab. • It can be cured with the right treatment.

Table 11.1 STI data, symptoms, diagnosis, and treatment information courtesy of Centers for Disease Control and Prevention, https://www.cdc.gov/std

---

27   Holt-Lunstad, *PLoS Medicine,* https://journals.plos.org/plosmedicine/article?id=10.1371/journal.pmed.1000316

Common Sexually Transmitted Infections

Infection	Symptoms	Diagnosis and Treatment
Genital herpes	• Genital herpes is caused by two types of viruses, herpes simplex type 1 and herpes simplex type 2. • The virus can be released through sores or through the skin even when sores are not visible. • Get examined by your doctor if you notice an unusual sore, a smelly discharge, or burning when urinating.	• It can be diagnosed through the symptoms, testing a sample from the sore(s), or a blood test. • There is no cure for herpes; however, there are medicines that can prevent or shorten outbreaks.
Gonorrhea	• Symptoms can include a burning sensation when urinating, abnormal discharge from the penis or vagina, and bleeding between periods. • Rectal infection symptoms include itching, burning, and bleeding.	• Get examined by your doctor if you or your sexual partner notice any of these symptoms. • Testing is usually a urine sample and possibly a throat or rectum swab. • It can be cured with the right treatment. • Medication will stop the infection, but it will not undo any permanent damage caused by the disease.
Human immunodeficiency virus (HIV)	• HIV damages the body's immune system cells. • The most advanced stage of HIV infection is commonly referred to as AIDS (acquired immunodeficiency syndrome). • It most often spreads through fluid exchange via unprotected sex or by sharing drug needles with an infected person. • Women can pass HIV to their babies during pregnancy or childbirth.	• Medications such as pre-exposure prophylaxis (PrEP) can reduce risk when taken consistently and with other prevention measures. • People can live with the disease for many years, especially if they are diagnosed and treated early. • Early diagnosis is also important to reduce the risk of transmitting HIV to others.

Table 11.1 STI data, symptoms, diagnosis, and treatment information courtesy of Centers for Disease Control and Prevention, https://www.cdc.gov/std

How You Can Protect Yourself against STIs

The surest way to protect yourself against STIs is to practice abstinence. This means not having any vaginal, anal, or oral sex. There are many things to consider before having sex, and it's okay to say no if you are not ready. If you do decide to have sex, you and your partner should both get tested beforehand and make sure you always use a condom. It's not safe to stop using condoms unless you've both been tested, know your status, have another form of birth control, and are in a mutually monogamous relationship. *Mutual monogamy* means that you and your partner both agree to only have sexual contact with each other. This can help protect against STIs as long as you've both been tested and know you're STI-free. Visit this website to find a confidential STI testing location near you (https://openstax.org/l/gettested) .

Before you have sex, talk with your partner about how you will prevent STIs and pregnancy. If you think you're ready to have sex, you need to be ready to protect your body and your future. You should also talk to your partner ahead of time about what you will and will not do sexually. Your partner should always respect your right to say no to anything that doesn't feel right. Sex should always be consensual and respectful.

It's important to discuss treatment with your doctor and begin treatment as soon as possible if you find out you have an STI. If you are living with an STI, it's important to tell your partner before you have sex. Although it may be uncomfortable to talk about your STI, open and honest conversation can help your partner make informed decisions to protect his or her health.

11.6 Your Safety

Estimated completion time: 22 minutes.

Questions to consider:

- What makes a person safety conscious?
- How can you improve your personal safety?

Safety Consciousness

To be safety conscious means you have an awareness of potential hazards and an alertness to danger. Simply, you are conscious of being safe. This includes being smart about your physical surroundings and careful with drug and alcohol use.

A drug is a chemical substance that can change how your body and mind work and how you feel. Some drugs are illegal (like cocaine or heroin), and while others may be legal, they can still harm your body and brain. Even prescription medicines can be abused when taken to get high or to a point of dependency.

Why do people abuse drugs? The answer varies for different people, but most want to feel good and escape any bad feelings they are experiencing. Or they want to improve in an area of their life—for example, to get better grades. This may lead them to start taking drugs for more energy, to stay awake longer, or to stay focused while studying. This short-term boost is not worth the health risks and the potential for addiction.

Alcohol

The statistics are sobering. Thirty-two percent of college students who drank alcohol reported doing something they later regretted, 27 percent forgot where they were or what they did, and 11 percent physically hurt themselves.[28] Many people consume alcohol to relax, socialize, or celebrate, but there are serious health effects attributed to too much alcohol consumption.

You do not need to be an alcoholic for alcohol to interfere with your health and life, and the potential to become addicted to alcohol is a serious problem that can affect anyone.

Alcohol is classified as a drug and is a known depressant, making it the most widely used drug in the world. Alcohol interferes with the brain's communication pathways and can affect the way the brain looks and works. These disruptions can change your mood and behavior and make it harder to think clearly and move with coordination. This is why it is critical to never drive a vehicle if you have been drinking. Drinking can weaken your immune system and damage your heart, increasing your risk for stroke and high blood pressure. Heavy drinking also harms the liver and pancreas.

The National Institute on Alcohol Abuse and Alcoholism offers the following guidelines:

- **Moderate alcohol consumption:** up to one drink per day for women and up to two drinks per day for men
- **Binge drinking:** typically occurs after four drinks for women and five drinks for men in a two-hour period that brings blood alcohol concentration levels to 0.08 g/dL
- **Heavy drinking:** drinking five or more drinks on the same occasion on each of five or more days in the past 30 days

Alcohol is a part of the social scene on many college campuses. If you choose to drink, you can avoid the devastating consequences of alcohol addiction by drinking responsibly and in moderation. The quality of your schoolwork can suffer dramatically if you drink beyond moderation. Too much alcohol can result in missing classes, performing poorly on exams, and falling behind in assignments. Have you ever decided to drink instead of study even though you had a big test the next day? Have you missed a class because you were too hungover to get out of bed? Did you hand in a project or paper late or not at all due to a series of nights spent drinking? If you answered yes to any of these questions, you are at risk of negatively impacting your success in college because of alcohol.

Tobacco and Vaping

Cigarettes and other forms of tobacco are also drugs. Tobacco contains nicotine, which excites the parts of the brain that make you feel good. Nicotine gives you a mild rush of pleasure and energy but soon wears off, which makes you want more. The more frequently you smoke, the faster your body and brain get addicted.

Tobacco is not healthy. Cigarette smoke causes lung cancer and emphysema. If you live with someone who smokes, you are also susceptible to these diseases, even if you are a nonsmoker. This is called secondhand smoke. Smokers are more likely to suffer heart attacks. Chewing tobacco can lead to cancer of the mouth. If you currently smoke, there are medicines and various treatments, as well as hotlines, to help you quit.

Electronic cigarettes are marketed as a way to help people stop smoking. Unfortunately, while they do contain less nicotine, they have many health risks.

E-cigarettes are battery-operated devices that people use to inhale an aerosol containing nicotine, flavors, and other chemicals. When you smoke an e-cigarette (also called vaping), the nicotine is absorbed from the lungs into the bloodstream, where it stimulates the adrenal glands to release the hormone epinephrine. Epinephrine

---

28   American College Health Association, 2018 https://www.acha.org/documents/ncha/NCHA-II_Spring_2018_Reference_Group_Executive_Summary.pdf

(also known as adrenaline) stimulates the central nervous system and increases blood pressure, breathing, and heart rate. Like other addictive substances, nicotine activates the brain's reward circuits and increases dopamine. This pleasure causes some people to use nicotine with increased frequency, despite risks to their health and well-being.

The FDA (Food and Drug Administration) has alerted the public to reports of serious lung illnesses and several deaths associated with vaping. While the manufacturers of e-cigarettes would like us to believe they are less harmful than cigarettes, nicotine is a highly addictive drug. It is best to stay away from it in any form. E-cigarettes are not an FDA-approved smoking cessation aid, and there is no conclusive scientific evidence on the effectiveness of e-cigarettes to help stop smoking.

Smoking e-cigarettes also exposes the lungs to chemicals. A study of some e-cigarette products found that the vapor contains known carcinogens and toxic chemicals, and the device itself can contain toxic metals.

If you are still in your teens or early adulthood, these years are critical for brain development. If you use nicotine in any form, or for that matter any substances, you are putting yourself at risk for long-lasting effects.

Marijuana

Marijuana comes from the cannabis plant. It can be rolled up and smoked like a cigarette, called a joint. It can also be smoked in a pipe, and edibles are becoming increasingly common. Marijuana can make you feel relaxed, silly, or for some people, nervous.

Marijuana makes it harder to pay attention and to remember things that just happened a few minutes ago. If you smoke before class, it is going to make it more challenging to learn. A recent study showed that if you begin regular marijuana use as a teen, you can lose an average of eight IQ points, and you do not get them back, even if you stop using.[29]

Using marijuana makes the heart beat fast and raises your risk of having a heart attack. Marijuana smoke can hurt your lungs. One of the biggest risks is drugged driving, which is driving when you are high. Marijuana makes it harder to pay attention on the road, and your reactions to traffic signs and sounds are slowed. It is dangerous to smoke and drive.

Prescription Pain Medicine

Pain medicines help relieve pain from surgery or injuries. Prescription pain medicines are legal and helpful to use when ordered by a doctor to treat a specific medical problem within a specific time frame. It is vitally important to take any prescriptions according to your doctor's instructions, and to carefully read all risks and food/medicine counteractions.

Unfortunately, people sometimes take pills without a doctor's prescription to get high, believing they are safer than street drugs. Make no mistake, prescription pain pill abuse can be just as dangerous as heroin or cocaine. Drug dealers sell these pills just like they sell heroin or cocaine. The abuse of oxycodone has become well documented—sometimes it goes by the brand names OxyContin or Percocet. Hydrocodone is also often abused and is best known under the brand name Vicodin.

Prescription pain pill abuse can lead to many problems. Pain medicine abuse can slow down or even stop your breathing. Signs of a pain medicine overdose are cold and sweaty skin, confusion, shaking, extreme sleepiness, and trouble breathing. More people overdose from pain medicines every year than from heroin and cocaine combined. If your doctor prescribes any pain relief pills for you, it is important to ask a lot of questions and understand why your doctor is prescribing them. If after consideration you decide to take pain-relief pills, stop taking them as soon as you possibly can. The longer you take them, the higher the possibility of getting addicted.

Cocaine and Heroin

Cocaine and heroin are both powders, often snorted up the nose, smoked, or mixed with water and injected with a needle. It is easy to become addicted to both drugs, and many people who seek treatment find it hard to stay off the drug. It is not uncommon to feel strong cravings for heroin or cocaine years after seeking treatment. People who inject the drug using a shared needle put themselves at further risk of contracting blood-borne viruses, such as hepatitis or HIV.

Cocaine can make people feel full of energy for a period of time, but it can also bring about feelings of restlessness and anger. Cocaine raises blood pressure and makes the heart beat faster, which could lead to a heart attack or stroke.

Heroin brings a rush of good feelings after it's taken. The feeling then wears off, and users often feel a strong urge to take more. The reason so many people overdose on heroin is because they can't tell how strong it is until they take it. Heroin can slow or stop your breathing. It can kill you. Signs of a heroin overdose are slow breathing; blue lips and fingernails; cold, clammy skin; and shaking.

There are medicines that can help people recover from addiction, but the best course is to not start. Avoid any temptation to try heroin or cocaine. Experimentation can be deadly.

Methamphetamine (Meth)

Meth is a white powder that is sometimes made into a pill or rock. Meth powder can be eaten or snorted up the nose. Like cocaine and heroin, it can also be mixed with liquid and injected into your body with a needle. Crystal meth is smoked in a small glass pipe.

Meth at first causes a rush of good feelings, but then users feel edgy, overly excited, angry, or afraid. Meth causes many problems. It can make your body temperature so hot that you pass out and could die. If you look at pictures of meth users, you will notice how quickly the drug ages them. Teeth become stained, break, and rot. As the teeth go bad the mouth looks sunken. Meth users burn a lot of energy and don't eat well, which leads to weight loss and a sickly appearance. The skin turns dull, and sores and pimples that won't heal are common. Meth use can quickly lead to addiction and cause cognitive or emotional problems that don't go away or that come back again even after you quit using. For instance, some users feel, hear, or see things that aren't there and think that people are out to get them.

This is a dangerous drug that should be avoided at all costs.

Other Drugs

There are many other drugs of abuse, including Ecstasy, K2 (or Spice), LSD, PCP, and roofies. It's best to avoid all of them.

If your use of drugs or alcohol is interfering with your life and negatively impacting your health, school, relationships, or finances—it's time to quit and find help.

The first semester is an especially critical and vulnerable time for most first-year students. It is often a time of heavy drinking and partying. The transition to college is often difficult, and while partying may feel like it is helping to ease the transition, the health risks are real: about one-third of first-year students fail to enroll for their second year.

If you are concerned about your drug or alcohol use, or you need help quitting, visit the student health center or talk with your college counselor. If you need additional resources, the following can help:

- Drug Information Online (https://openstax.org/l/drugindex)
- Drug and Alcohol Treatment Hotline: 1-800-662-HELP

Personal Safety

For many students, their first year in college is also the first time they have lived away from home, or for commuting students, often the most time they have spent away from home. This new freedom can feel really exciting. College should be a time for fun, experimentation (in healthy ways), and growth. It's important to be smart about your safety and conscious that you don't put yourself in any high-risk situations. It's also important to know what to do if any problems arise. Here are some ways to remain safe while enjoying your college experience:

1. **Speak up.**
   If you are worried about a friend's well-being, ask them if they are OK. If you see inappropriate behavior, let someone know. Get an RA or other authority involved if someone looks like they are in trouble or an activity looks like it is leading to trouble. In general, speak up if you notice something going on that concerns you.
2. **Learn your campus emergency system.**
   Many colleges and universities have blue-light phones with direct access to campus security. If your campus has blue-light phones, take the time to find out where they are. If you are not familiar with the emergency system on your campus, visit your public safety department (or website) to understand how you can call for help in an emergency. Add campus security to your phone contacts.

Figure 11.13 Emergency phones and related systems are present on many campuses. Learn your system and note the locations of these devices as you travel. If you commute via public transportation, such as a train or bus, learn the safety procedures and devices available for those systems. (Credit: KOMO News / Flickr / Attribution 2.0 Generic (CC-BY 2.0))

3. **Protect your drink.**
   A risk at bars and at college campus parties is the use of date-rape drugs to assist sexual assaults. Date-

rape drugs often have no color, smell, or taste, so you can't tell if you are being drugged. The drugs can make you weak and confused so you are unable to refuse sex or defend yourself.

It is easy for anyone to slip a date-rape drug in your drink. Never leave your drink unattended, and never accept a drink from someone you do not trust.

4. **Be alert and stay charged.**
   Always be aware of the people in your surrounding area. Notice anyone who looks out of place, and avoid dark and unpopulated areas. Make sure to charge your cell phone before you go out for the evening.
5. **Avoid walking alone at night, and don't accept rides from strangers.**
   Going out with a group is the best way to make sure everyone gets home safely. In the event you find yourself alone at the end of the night, know ahead of time what escort services your school offers. Or use services like Uber and Lyft, and MAKE SURE you get in the car that matches the license plate on the app. It's also wise to install safety apps. These apps can automatically alert police and your emergency contacts in the event of an emergency. Always let your roommates and friends know your plans for the evening and when you expect to return.

GET CONNECTED

Luckily, there are tech opportunities to keep yourself safe. Three good apps for the job are:

Noonlight (https://www.noonlight.com) is an app that connects all your devices to trigger an alarm with a live, 24/7 staff in case of any emergency: heart attack, car wreck, assault, or any other event that requires emergency attention.

Kitestring (https://www.kitestring.io) is an app you alert when you are headed out to a potentially risky situation, like a first date or meeting someone for the first time. The app texts you to check in, and if you don't respond, it alerts your emergency contacts to the situation.

Circle of 6 (https://www.circleof6app.com) makes it easy for you to alert the six people in your circle any time you need help.

If You Are a Victim of a Crime

Most college students report feeling safe on campus. College administrators are fully committed to making your campus experience as safe as possible. If you are attacked, it is important to know what to do:

- **If possible, get to a safe place.** Move to a well-lit area to call for help.
- **Call 911** or have someone call 911 for you.
- **Follow the operator's instructions.** 911 operators will instruct you until police or paramedics arrive.
- **Contact a trusted friend or family member.** You will want emotional support and also somewhere to go after all the official procedures are complete.
- **Take time to heal.** If you are a victim of crime or assault, it can be traumatic. The healing process will take time. Check with your campus mental health services about how they can help in your recovery.

If You Are a Victim of Sexual Assault or Rape

Sexual assault is any type of sexual activity you don't agree to. This can include inappropriate touching, sexual intercourse, attempted rape, and rape. Most people are surprised to learn that 80 percent of rapes are committed by someone the victim knows.

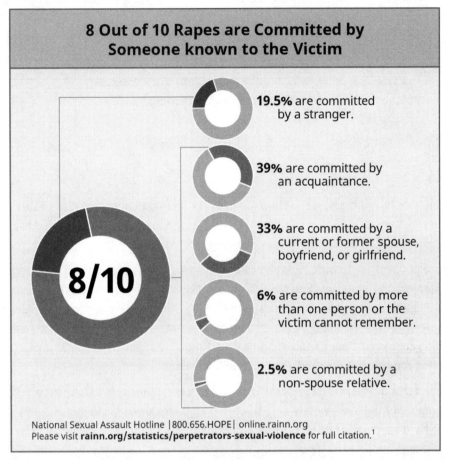

Figure 11.14 The majority of rapes are committed by people known to the victim, which can have a significant effect on prevention and reporting. (Credit: Modification of work by RAINN (https://openstax.org/l/sexualviolencestats))

Take the following steps if you or someone you know has been raped:

- Get medical care. Go to the nearest rape crisis center, hospital, or student health service center. Do not go to the bathroom, shower, brush your teeth, wash your hands, or change clothes before you go. It's important to preserve any evidence.
- Ask the hospital or center to take a urine sample to test for date-rape drugs.
- Call the police from the hospital. Tell the police exactly what you remember. File a report.
- Arrange for follow-up counseling. A counselor can help you work through the many emotions you may feel following a sexual assault, which is important to the healing process. You can get help from the **National Sexual Assault Hotline at 800-656-HOPE**.

Under Title IX legislation, sexual harassment and sexual violence are forms of gender discrimination and are prohibited. This includes off-campus incidents or incidents that involve people who are not students. If you experience a hostile environment, sexual harassment, or sexual assault, schools have a responsibility to stop the discrimination, prevent its recurrence, and address its effects. Schools also have a responsibility to protect people who report sexual harassment or assault from retaliation from other students, school administrators, or faculty.

The Clery Act, a federal law that intersects with Title IX, requires colleges and universities to do the following for survivors of campus sexual assault:

- Notify survivors of counseling resources.
- Notify survivors of the option to report a case to the school and law enforcement.
- Provide requested accommodations, such as changing dorms or classes.
- Notify survivors of the final outcome of a disciplinary proceeding.

Summary

In this chapter you have been introduced to the wide range of factors that impact your health. Health is much more than keeping your physical body in good shape. Good health also includes your mental and emotional health, quality relationships, and prioritizing your personal safety.

The contributors to physical health include eating clean, non-processed food; staying hydrated; moving your body daily; and getting sufficient sleep. You now understand why it is necessary to prioritize sleep, and that quality sleep is also dependent on the way you eat and exercise. You have identified ways to improve what you eat and how you sleep. With these changes you should be able to fall asleep with ease, stay asleep all night, and wake up feeling energized. Your mind will be clear and sharp. and you'll get more done in less time, massively increasing your productivity and your success in college.

You now understand that a certain level of stress is to be expected. Chronic stress, however, is damaging to the body, so it's important to have a variety of tools to manage stress. Practicing mindfulness, deep breathing, and gratitude can have a powerful impact on your emotional, mental, and physical health.

At the beginning of this chapter, you were introduced to a simple way of thinking about your health—nutrients in, toxins out. This means eating plenty of fruits and vegetables and avoiding junk food, soda, and other sugary beverages. If you move often throughout the day, drink plenty of clean water, and prioritize your sleep, you will help your body detoxify. Reduce your exposure to toxins by paying attention to what you put in and on your body. If you wouldn't eat it, don't put it on your skin or hair. A helpful way to remember to take care of your health is to follow the rule of eights: aim each day for eight hours of sleep, eight servings of fruits and vegetables, eight glasses of water, eight minutes of mindfulness, and eight meaningful connections, and incorporate any one of these eight ways to move—walking, aerobic exercise, strength training, yoga, Tai Chi, stretching, HIIT, or dancing.

Career Connection

Is putting in longer hours at work an effective strategy for meeting workplace demands? Read this article about managing your energy instead of your time (https://openstax.org/l/manageyourenergy) .

Rethinking

Revisit the questions you answered at the beginning of the chapter, and consider one option you learned in this chapter that might make you rethink how you answered each one. Has this chapter prompted you to consider changing any of your habits?

Rank the following questions on a scale of 1–4. 1 = "least like me" and 4 = "most like me."

1. I eat enough fruits and vegetables every day.
2. I get enough sleep.
3. I have, for the most part, healthy relationships with friends and family.
4. I feel like I know how to manage stress.

Where do you go from here?

It's easy to lose focus on your own health and wellness during the tumultuous first year in college. But the benefits of developing strategies to improve and maintain your emotional, physical, and mental health will only increase as you age. What would you like to learn more about? Choose a topic from the list below, and create an annotated bibliography that would direct further research.

- simple strategies to improve physical health
- daily opportunities to maintain and improve emotional well-being
- mental health risks and warning signs
- steps to take to be more safety conscious

12 Planning for Your Future

Figure 12.1 Credit: Stig Nygaard / Flickr / Attribution 2.0 Generic (CC-BY)

Chapter Outline

12.1 Why Worry about a Career While I'm in College?
12.2 Your Map to Success: The Career Planning Cycle
12.3 Where Can You Go from Here?

Introduction

Student Survey

How ready are you to plan your career? Take this quick survey to figure it out, ranking questions on a scale of 1–4, 1 meaning "least like me" and 4 meaning "most like me."

1. I am feeling certain about my major (or my ability to choose a major soon).
2. I know what kinds of jobs I can get with my major.
3. I have a good idea of what I need to do in each year of college to achieve career success as I graduate.
4. I am aware of what resources are on campus to help me create a career plan.

You can also take the Chapter 12 survey (https://openstax.org/l/collegesurvey12) anonymously online.

STUDENT PROFILE

"A lesson I have learned throughout my college career is that changing majors is okay. Fresh out of high school, I always wanted to be an FBI agent. I wanted to be in those forensic shows—like *Criminal Minds*—that we all see on TV. So I decided to go to college and major in criminal justice with an emphasis in forensic science. When I started to take criminal justice classes, I noticed that my passion and determination were focused on something else: helping others and changing people's lives so they do not have to struggle as much as I did. I quickly decided to talk to a career counselor and let him know that I wanted to change majors. We discussed the long-term plans and where I would see myself in the future. I changed my major to a related one, sociology. And with that, I want to be a counselor, as I want to help others achieve their goals."

—Carlos Espinosa

About This Chapter

In earlier chapters of this book (1, 3, 4), you learned more about setting the foundation for college and career success by gaining a deeper understanding of why you are attending college, how to set goals and priorities, and how to begin your academic and life planning. By the time you complete this chapter, you should be able to do the following:

- Learn what a career is and how it applies to you.
- Identify resources on campus that can help you explore careers and develop a plan.
- Increase your self-awareness relative to your career aspirations, and map productive steps forward.

12.1 Why Worry about a Career While I'm in College?

Estimated completion time: 12 minutes.

Questions to Consider:

- What should I consider when choosing a career?
- How do I separate career myths from reality?

CAREER (noun)

Definition of career (Entry 1 of 2)

1: a profession for which one trains and which is undertaken as a permanent calling

a *career* in medicine

—often used before another noun

a *career* diplomat

2: a field for or pursuit of consecutive progressive achievement especially in public, professional, or business life

Washington's *career* as a soldier[1]

Throughout your life, you've probably heard about getting a "good job" after you graduate. Everyone might define that differently. Many people say a good job is one where you can make a lot of money, but is that true? And is that true for you?

Consider the definition of "career" above. Does it seem exciting? Are there parts that sound intimidating? How can you navigate both parts of the responsibility of having a career? Many people believe that just because they have had a job, they know how to have a career. Getting a job is a single transaction. Crafting a career

---

1   https://www.merriam-webster.com/dictionary/career

takes more strategy and time.

What Is the Difference Between a Job and a Career?

A universal definition of a job is "work that you do in exchange for money." It can also be a particular role or title. Going back to our definition of career above, a career is something for which we train, something that we intend to do permanently—which in actuality means long-term and over time, not necessarily for the rest of your life. It is a field or area in which we have achievement. It occurs progressively and usually consecutively. Here is how some current college students have defined "career":

- "A career is long-term; you do it until you can't anymore."
- "Something you love . . . a dream job."
- "What you plan and strive for while you work."
- "When you are more invested in the activities of the job than just getting a paycheck."[2]

Shira

When Shira was in college, she had a *job* at a local ice-cream stand. She made very good money in the summertime, so she could work less during the school year. She also learned a lot about customer service and working with her coworkers as a team. Shira eventually took on more responsibility as a supervisor, creating work schedules and interviewing prospective new employees. She really enjoyed this part of her *job* because she liked tasks involving helping people do well at work. Her boss, customers, and coworkers told her she was good at it. Unbeknownst to her at the time, this was the beginning of Shira's *career* in human resources.

How did this happen? As she took classes in psychology and business, Shira saw her courses in organizational psychology and management as applicable to her work. She enjoyed learning about how people interact in the workplace. She learned about human resources, which is typically defined as the department of a business or organization that deals with the hiring, administration, and training of people. She wanted to learn even more, so she got an internship in the human resources department of a bank before she graduated and loved it.

After getting her Bachelor of Science degree in psychology, Shira got her first career-oriented job, as a recruiting specialist at a health insurance company. After about two years of working diligently, Shira got promoted to a job as a human resource generalist, with responsibility for recruiting strategy and process; recruiting specialists now report to her. In addition to working full-time, Shira also is active in her local chapter of the Society for Human Resource Management and will begin studying to take the national certification exams offered through this organization, giving her a highly sought-after professional credential. Within 5 to 10 years, Shira hopes to become a human resources director.

---

2 Canisius College Student Interviews, Buffalo, NY, September 2019

Figure 12.2 (Credit: University of Essex / Flickr / Attribution 2.0 Generic (CC-BY 2.0)

Shira's career path is a straightforward one. She learned a lot about herself early in her college career. She got some experience and studied academic subjects she was interested in. Shira was nervous and uncertain at times, but she remained positive and adjusted her course as needed. She worked hard and made plans to be sure she could get a "good job."

WHAT STUDENTS SAY

1. What is your most significant concern about starting your career after college?
    a. I didn't choose the right major
    b. I won't have enough experience or knowledge to get a good job
    c. I might have to compromise my interests or goals
    d. Something about my career path, my past, or my decisions will impact my ability to be hired.
2. With what do you feel you need the most help in preparing for your career?
    a. Choosing the best major/pathway
    b. Gaining experience that will lead to success
    c. Standing out from others with similar majors or experience
    d. Writing a resume/profile and/or building a portfolio

You can also take the anonymous What Students Say surveys (https://openstax.org/l/collegesurvey6-12) to add your voice to this textbook. Your responses will be included in updates.

Students offered their views on these questions, and the results are displayed in the graphs below.

What is your most significant concern about starting your career after college?

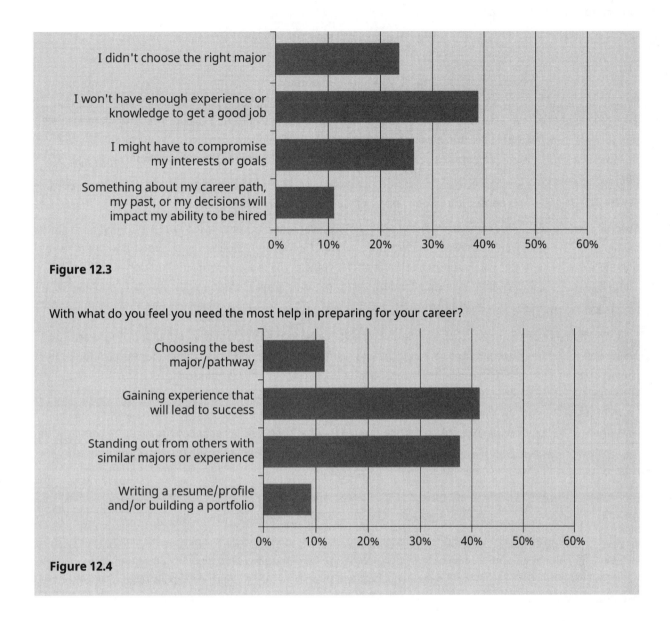

Figure 12.3

Figure 12.4

Career Myths and Realities

Because you are a student, many people will want to give you advice as you make your way through college. Older family members like to talk about how things were when they were in and graduated from college. Your parents might have very definite ideas about what you should major in and the best way to get a job (or perhaps they don't know at all, and you wish they did). Your friends, particularly those already in college, might tell you what their experience is, but maybe yours will be very different. Then there are all kinds of things you hear about in the news as to whether there are jobs out there. The economy can be very confusing at times. The stock market is up, then down. Government statistics tell us that the unemployment rate is lower than ever before, but many people say it is still very difficult to get a job. Students have seen their parents or grandparents get laid off, then hear that there is a new company in town that will hire thousands of people. Any and all of these things can be true, and all at the same time. So what does that mean for college students looking to begin their careers?

MYTH #1: "Because I am getting a college degree, I will have no problem getting hired and making a lot of money."

REALITY: As you learned in chapters 1 and 10, your chances of making more money over the course of your lifetime are greater when you have a college degree. However, employers expect more than just a diploma. They also expect that you did well in your studies and engaged in activities and experiences that demonstrate you can put learning into context in a work setting. Internships, practicums, service learning, community-based research, part-time or summer jobs, and more prove to employers that you are capable and eager to begin your career.

MYTH #2: "There is one perfect job for me" or "I will be happy if I find the right career."

REALITY: Finding the right career is not like waving a magic wand or a ticket to living your best Instagram life all of the time. There are jobs and careers for which you might be well-suited based on a combination of features and attributes. The better you know yourself, the better you can make a good match. Additionally, those features and attributes change over time, and by learning good career planning skills, you can adapt easily.

MYTH #3: "I can't get a good job with (fill in the name of a major)."

REALITY: There are some majors that traditionally result in jobs that earn more than others do. These are usually because the education for these occupations is often rigorous, and both training for and working in the occupation require a high level of skill and knowledge, even over time (engineering, computer science, accounting). However, anybody can get a "good" job with their major. The key is to understand what knowledge, skills, and abilities are required for the jobs you would like and to take action to make sure you have them. People who have a problem getting employment in their field after college may not have fully understood the requirements for being hired, they may have been unable to make the sacrifices necessary for that to happen, or they may have had unrealistic expectations.

MYTH #4: "I should base my major on 'hot' careers that will pay well."

REALITY: Just because a major or career field is "hot" doesn't mean that you will enjoy it or even be any good at it. Better to choose a career based on your interests, abilities, values, and personality. Additionally, which careers and fields are popular and well-paying can change quickly based on supply of candidates and economic situations. Thus, those who choose a hot field must be eager to learn new skills to keep up with the evolution of such a career.

MYTH #5: "It is too late to change my career."

REALITY: It is almost *never* "too late" to make a career change. There are millions of people who have made career changes, some by going to college in their 30s, 40s, 50s, or even older. In many cases, the best time to make a change is when you are older, because you have more to offer employers, have gained different experiences, and have become more settled in your personal life. Many college students find they are well-positioned to make the most of their college studies when they are more mature.

MYTH #6: "No one will hire me because I am 'just a student'; I won't be able to compete with people with more experience."

REALITY: Employers often like to hire recent graduates or people who are early in their careers because their learning is fresh, and they know how to learn new material and adapt quickly. Additionally, many employers believe that hiring new graduates allows them to train people the way that they would like. New graduates of all ages show persistence and flexibility by having earned a college degree and shown willingness to start something new.

MYTH #7: "I should be passionate about my work. If not, I am doing something wrong."

REALITY: "Do what you love and you'll never work a day in your life" and "Do what you love and the money will follow" are terrible advice. No one loves their work every minute of every day, and passion is a very high standard to meet. There are many things about which we might be passionate that would make for jobs that are completely unsuitable for us. What most people who are happy with their work have in common are that they can do it well; it has some impact on people, organizations, information, or things; and they find satisfaction in it. It is often through discovering this that passion for one's work follows.

MYTH #8: "My career path should follow a neat, straight line."

REALITY: For almost everyone, a career path is more like a winding road than a straight highway. Recall the story of Shira building a career off of her summer job, and know that Shira's experience is one path of many. Not everyone has a clear idea of how to find a job that fulfills an interest and then how to move from that job to a career. It is not always so straightforward. For example, there is great value in choosing a major in the natural sciences, social sciences, arts, or humanities, but sometimes these fields do not obviously transfer to a career. Yet with the right guidance, practice, and commitment, these majors provide many routes to a fulfilling career and life. Based on information, experiences, and skills you gather along the way, you will find that you need and want to adapt and adjust. There is no "right" or "wrong" way to get into a career.

MYTH #9: "There are not many jobs out there with good pay and benefits, so why bother looking?"

REALITY: The way in which we work has changed in the last twenty years. There are many more flexible work arrangements available. The "gig economy" refers to jobs that are independent of being an employee and are often time-limited. These positions give people multiple options for generating personal income and are good options for a "side hustle." At the present time, the job market is also considered to be a "job seeker's market," meaning employers are having difficulty finding candidates for their openings. Every day, thousands of people get jobs that advance their status.

ACTIVITY

Consider the various events or conversations you've experienced in the past few years that have led you toward a career goal. Have any of the myths or their counterparts listed above impacted your choices? Are you called to reconsider any previous decisions? Why or why not? Are there additional preconceptions you might have that could potentially block you from moving forward with your ideal plans?

What Should I Be?

Have you ever heard statements like these?

- "You are so good at math . . . you should be an accountant."
- "Your best grades have always been in art, but it isn't really practical to become an artist."
- "You like kids so much! You should be a teacher!"

Many people tend to first think of careers based on images they see in society or the media. Prestigious and high-visibility occupations are what many young people aspire to when they are young. How many of you first wanted to be a doctor, firefighter, entertainer, professional athlete, or teacher? As we grow up and get to know the world better, we are exposed to a greater universe of jobs. However, young people in middle and high school also tend to look at careers based on the subjects they are good at (or not good at) in school. These self-perceptions and interests can last long into adulthood. But education and the work world can be extremely different environments with different purposes and expectations. The realities of jobs and careers we choose are vastly more complex than the courses we like or don't and whether we perform well in them in high school. Though we may have some images for "what we are" and "who we should be," there are also many different options, and the choices can be overwhelming. How do we ensure that we make career decisions that are productive for us?

12.2 Your Map to Success: The Career Planning Cycle

Estimated completion time: 42 minutes.

Questions to Consider:

- What steps should I take to learn about my best opportunities?
- What can I do to prepare for my career while in college?
- What experiences and resources can help me in my search?

Figure 12.5 You can use the Career Planning Cycle to consider and reconsider your approach and progress in choosing and moving toward a career. (Credit: Based on work by Lisa August.)

The Career Planning Cycle helps us apply some concrete steps to figuring out where we might fit into the work world. If you follow the steps, you will learn about who you truly are, and can be, as a working professional.

You will discover important knowledge about the work world. You will gain more information to help you make solid career decisions. You will get experience that will increase your qualifications. You will be more prepared to reach your professional goals. And the good news is that colleges and universities are set up nicely to help you utilize this process.

Learn About Yourself

To understand what type of work suits us and to be able to convey that to others to get hired, we must become experts in knowing who we are. Gaining **self-knowledge** is a lifelong process, and college is the perfect time to gain and adapt this fundamental information. Following are some of the types of information that we should have about ourselves:

- **Interests:** Things that we like and want to know more about. These often take the form of ideas, information, knowledge, and topics.
- **Skills/Aptitudes**: Things that we either do well or can do well. These can be natural or learned and are usually skills—things we can demonstrate in some way. Some of our skills are "hard" skills, which are specific to jobs and/or tasks. Others are "soft" skills, which are personality traits and/or interpersonal skills that accompany us from position to position.
- **Values:** Things that we believe in. Frequently, these are conditions and principles.
- **Personality:** Things that combine to make each of us distinctive. Often, this shows in the way we present ourselves to the world. Aspects of personality are customarily described as qualities, features, thoughts, and behaviors.

In addition to knowing the things we can and like to do, we must also know how well we do them. What are our strengths? When employers hire us, they hire us to do something, to contribute to their organization in some way. We get paid for what we know, what we can do, and how well or deeply we can demonstrate these things. Think of these as your Knowledge, Skills, and Abilities (KSAs). As working people, we can each think of ourselves as carrying a "tool kit." In our tool kit are the KSAs that we bring to each job. As we gain experience, we learn how best to use our tools. We gain more tools and use some more often than others, but all the tools we gather during our career stay with us in some form.

ACTIVITY

Consider the top KSAs you currently have in your tool kit. Consider at least one in each category that you would like to develop while you're in college.

Because you're expected to spend your time in college focusing on what you learn in your classes, it might seem like a lot of extra work to also develop your career identity. Actually, the ideal time to learn about who you are as a worker and a professional is while you are so focused on learning and personal development, which lends itself to growth in all forms. College helps us acquire and develop our KSAs daily through our coursework and experiences. What might be some ways you can purposefully and consciously learn about yourself? How might you get more information about who you are? And how might you learn about what that means for your career? Awareness of the need to develop your career identity and your vocational worth is the first step. Next, undertaking a process that is mindful and systematic can help guide you through. This process will help you look at yourself and the work world in a different way. You will do some of this in this course.

Then, during your studies, some of your professors and advisors may integrate career development into the curriculum, either formally or informally. Perhaps most significantly, the career center at your school is an essential place for you to visit. They have advisors, counselors, and coaches who are formally trained in facilitating the career development process.

Often, career assessment is of great assistance in increasing your self-knowledge. It is most often designed to help you gain insight more objectively. You may want to think of assessment as pulling information out of you and helping you put it together in a way that applies to your career. There are two main types of assessments: formal assessments and informal assessments.

Formal Assessments

Formal assessments are typically referred to as "career tests." There are thousands available, and many are found randomly on the Internet. While many of these can be fun, "free" and easily available instruments are usually not credible. It is important to use assessments that are developed to be reliable and valid. Look to your career center for their recommendations; their staff has often spent a good deal of time selecting instruments that they believe work best for students.

Here are some commonly used and useful assessments that you may run across:

- **Interest Assessments:** Strong Interest Inventory, Self-Directed Search, Campbell Interest and Skill Survey, Harrington-O'Shea Career Decision-Making System
- **Personality Measures:** Myers-Briggs Type Indicator, CliftonStrengths (formerly StrengthsQuest), Big Five Inventory, Keirsey Temperament Sorter, TypeFocus, DiSC
- **Career Planning Software:** SIGI 3, FOCUS 2

GET CONNECTED

If you would like to do some formal assessment on your own, either in addition to what you can get on campus or if you don't believe you have reliable access to career planning, this site developed by the U.S. Department of Labor (https://www.careeronestop.org/) has some career exploration materials that you may find helpful.

Informal Assessments

Often, asking questions and seeking answers can help get us information that we need. When we start working consciously on learning more about any subject, things that we never before considered may become apparent. Happily, this applies to self-knowledge as well. Some things that you can do outside of career testing to learn more about yourself can include:

Self-Reflection:

- Notice when you do something that you enjoy or that you did particularly well. What did that feel like? What about it made you feel positive? Is it something that you'd like to do again? What was the impact

that you made through our actions?
- Most people are the "go to" person for something. What do you find that people come to you for? Are you good with advice? Do you tend to be a good listener, observing first and then speaking your mind? Do people appreciate your repair skills? Are you good with numbers? What role do you play in a group?
- If you like to write or record your thoughts, consider creating a career journal that you update regularly, whether it's weekly or by semester. If writing your own thoughts is difficult, seek out guided activities that help prompt you to reflect.
- Many colleges have a career planning course that is designed to specifically lead you through the career decision-making process. Even if you are decided on your major, these courses can help you refine and plan best for your field.

Enlist Others:
- Ask people who know you to tell you what they think your strengths are. This information can come from friends, classmates, professors, advisors, family members, coaches, mentors, and others. What kinds of things have they observed you doing well? What personal qualities do you have that they value? You are not asking them to tell you what career you should be in; rather, you are looking to learn more about yourself.
- Find a mentor—such as a professor, an alumnus, an advisor, or a community leader—who shares a value with you and from whom you think you could learn new things. Perhaps they can share new ways of doing something or help you form attitudes and perceptions that you believe would be helpful.
- Get involved with one or more activities on campus that will let you use skills outside of the classroom. You will be able to learn more about how you work with a group and try new things that will add to your skill set.
- Attend activities on and off campus that will help you meet people (often alumni) who work in the professional world. Hearing their career stories will help you learn about where you might want to be. Are there qualities that you share with them that show you may be on a similar path to success? Can you envision yourself where they are?
- No one assessment can tell you exactly what career is right for you; the answers to your career questions are not in a test. The reality of career planning is that it is a discovery process that uses many methods over time to strengthen our career knowledge and belief in ourselves.

ACTIVITY

Choose one of the suggestions from the list, above, and follow through on it. Keep a log or journal of your experience with the activity and note how this might help you think about your future after college.

Explore Jobs and Careers

Many students seem to believe that the most important decision they will make in college is to choose their major. While this is an important decision, even more important is to determine the type of knowledge you would like to have, understand what you value, and learn how you can apply this in the workplace after you graduate. For example, if you know you like to help people, this is a value. If you also know that you're interested in math and/or finances, you might study to be an accountant. To combine both of these, you would gain as much knowledge as you can about financial systems and personal financial habits so that you can provide greater support and better help to your clients.

The four factors of self-knowledge (interests, skills/aptitudes, values, and personality), which manifest in your KSAs, are also the factors on which employers evaluate your suitability for their positions. They consider what you can bring to their organization that is at once in line with their organization's standards and something they need but don't have in their existing workforce.

Along with this, each job has KSAs that define it. You may think about finding a job/career as looking like the figure below.

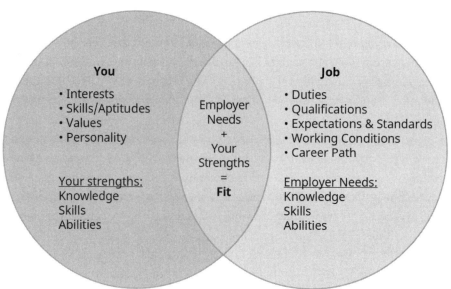

Figure 12.6 Your fit for a job lies at the intersection of your attributes and the elements of the position. When your strengths align with the employer needs, both can mutually benefit.

The importance of finding the right fit cannot be overstated. Many people don't realize that the KSAs of the person and the requirements of the job have to match in order to get hired in a given field. What is even more important, though, is that when a particular job fits your four factors of self-knowledge *and* maximizes your KSAs, you are most likely to be satisfied with your work! The "fit" works to help you not only get the job, but also enjoy the job.

So if you work to learn about yourself, what do you need to know about jobs, and how do you go about learning it? In our diagram, if you need to have self-knowledge to determine the YOU factors, then to determine the JOB factors, you need to have workplace knowledge. This involves understanding what employers in the workplace and specific jobs require. Aspects of workplace knowledge include:

- **Labor Market Information:** Economic conditions, including supply and demand of jobs; types of industries in a geographic area or market; regional sociopolitical conditions and/or geographic attributes.
- **Industry Details:** Industry characteristics; trends and opportunities for both industry and employers; standards and expectations.
- **Work Roles:** Characteristics and duties of specific jobs and work roles; knowledge, skills, and abilities necessary to perform the work; training and education required; certifications or licenses; compensation;

promotion and career path; hiring process.

This "research" may sound a little dry and uninteresting at first, but consider it as a look into your future. If you are excited about what you are learning and what your career prospects are, learning about the places where you may put all of your hard work into practice should also be very exciting! Most professionals spend many hours not only performing their work but also physically being located at work. For something that is such a large part of your life, it will help you to know what you are getting into as you get closer to realizing your goals.

How Do We Gain Workplace Knowledge?

- Understand that there is a wide range of occupations and industries that fit together so that we can see how all jobs contribute to the workplace. With the use of formal career assessments, it will be easy to see where you fit in using the map below.

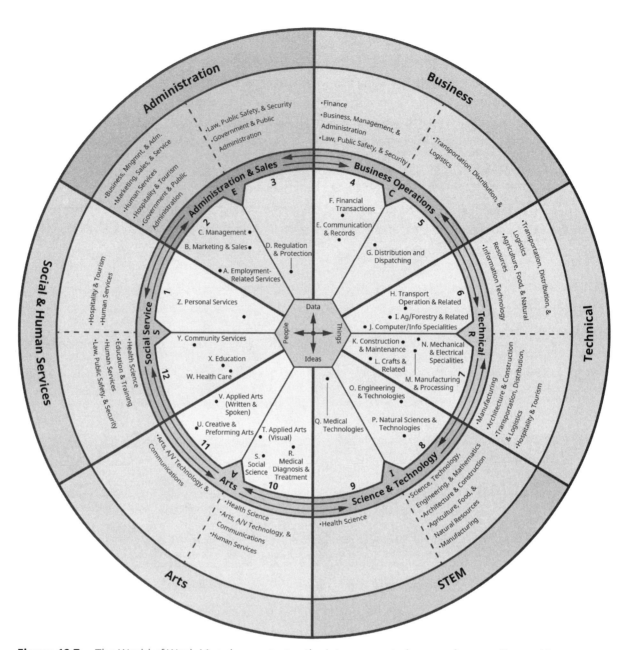

Figure 12.7 The World of Work Map demonstrates the interconnected areas of occupation and interest. You can use it to help navigate your exploration of workplace knowledge. (Credit: Based on Work by ACT.)

- Learn the "textbook" definitions of what is involved in the jobs you are considering. In Chapter 4, you used the Occupational Outlook Handbook (https://openstax.org/l/OOH) to learn more about the requirements for occupations. Its sister site (http://www.mynextmove.org) , will help show you more specific job titles.
- Read online information that is relevant to the professions you are interested in. Good sources for this include professional associations. Just "googling" information is risky. Look for professional and credible information. The Occupational Outlook Handbook has links to many of these sources. Your career center can also guide you.
- Whether you are just choosing your major or are already in a major and want to know what options it offers in terms of future work, look for this specific information. Your department may have this information; your campus career center definitely will. One very good site is What Can I Do With This

Major? (https://openstax.org/l/majorexplorer)
- Join professional clubs on campus. Many of these organizations have guest speakers who come to meetings and talk about what their jobs are like. Often, they also sponsor field trips to different companies and organizations.
- As mentioned earlier, attend campus networking events and programs such as job fairs and recruiting information sessions so that you can talk to people who actually do the work and get their insights.

Something to keep in mind as you make choices about your major and career is that the training is not the job. What you learn in your college courses is often foundational information; it provides basic knowledge that you need for more complex concepts and tasks. For example, a second-year student who is premed has the interests and qualities that may make her a good physician, but she is struggling to pass basic chemistry. She starts to think that medical school is no longer an appropriate goal because she doesn't enjoy chemistry. Does it make sense to abandon a suitable career path because of one 15-week course? In some ways, yes. In the case of medical school, the education is so long and intensive that if the student can't persevere through one introductory course, she may not have the determination to complete the training. On the other hand, if you are truly dedicated to your path, don't let one difficult course deter you.

The example above describes Shantelle. They weren't quite sure which major to choose, and they were feeling pressure because the window for making their decision was closing. They considered their values and strengths—they love helping people and have always wanted to pursue work in medical training. As described above, Shantelle struggled in general chemistry this semester and found that they actually didn't enjoy it at all. They've heard nightmare stories about organic chemistry being even harder. Simultaneously, Shantelle is taking Intro to Psychology, something they thought would be an easier course but that they enjoy even though it's challenging. Much to their surprise, they found the scientific applications of theory in the various types of mental illness utterly fascinating. But given that their life dream was to be a physician, Shantelle was reluctant to give up on medicine because of one measly chemistry course. With the help of an advisor, Shantelle decided to postpone choosing a major for one more semester and take a course in clinical psychology. Since there are so many science courses required for premed studies, Shantelle also agreed to take another science course. Their advisor helped Shantelle realize that it was likely not a wise choice to make such an important decision based on one course experience.

Focus Your Path

When you know yourself and know what to expect from a workplace and a job, you have information to begin to make decisions. As we've discussed throughout this book, you're not attending college solely to get a job. But this is likely one of your goals, and your time in school offers a tremendous opportunity to both prepare for your career (or *careers*) and make yourself more attractive to organizations where you want to work. Successfully learning the content of your classes and earning good grades are among the most important. Beyond these priorities, you'll learn the most about yourself and your potential career path if you engage in activities that will help you make decisions. Simply sitting back and thinking about the decision doesn't always help you take action.

Take Advantage of Every Resource You Can While in School

Your college has a wealth of departments, programs, and people dedicated to your success. The more you work to discover and engage with these groups, the more successfully you'll establish networks of support and build skills and knowledge for your career.

Make plans to drop by your career services or a related office early in your time in school. There, you'll learn about events you can attend, and you'll get to know some of the people there who can help you. The department may offer the formal assessments discussed earlier in this chapter, including aptitude testing, which can help you discover some of your areas of strength and give you insight into some high-potential career destinations. Career services may also have skills/interest inventories. These can help you match your attributes and ambitions with potential careers and suggest additional resources to explore.

Your college is also likely to have a resource that goes far beyond the campus itself: the alumni association. College alumni often maintain a relationship with the school and with their fellow graduates. Just by attending the same college, you have something in common with them. You chose the same place, maybe for similar reasons, and you might be having similar experiences. Often, alumni are eager to help current students by offering their professional insights and making career connections. You can find out about alumni events on your campus website, at the career center, and in the alumni department. These events can be fun and beneficial to attend, especially those involving networking opportunities. Note that specific departments or campus organizations may have their own alumni groups, whether formal or informal. Try to find former students who majored in your field or who have a job similar to the one you'd like one day. Remember, members of alumni organizations make a choice to be involved; they want to be there. It's very likely they'll be interested in offering you some help, mentoring, or even introductions to the right people.

Figure 12.8 Alumni often hold many events at colleges, some of which you can attend to build your network and learn about career paths. (Credit: University of the Fraser Valley / Flickr / Attribution 2.0 Generic (CC-BY 2.0))

Alumni may often attend events at your college, such as visiting guest speakers, art show openings, homecoming, or sporting events. You can find and talk with them there (under the right circumstances) and enjoy the event at the same time.

Networking is such a critical part of professional life that nearly every city or region has organizations and events devoted to it. Meetups are occasions for people with shared interests, skills, and professions to gather together and talk about their experiences and insights. The events might involve a brief talk or demonstration, a discussion or question-and-answer period, and then plenty of time for mingling. You can likely find these events with a quick search. But before you go, carefully review the guidelines and limits on who can attend.

Some meetups may not be open to students or others not formally employed in a field; they may also be held in bars or involve alcohol, preventing those under 21 from attending. Don't be offended by these barriers—the meetup organizers have specific goals and members to consider—but if you find one you can attend, try it out.

You can also network with people right at your college. Many of your college faculty likely have (or had) other roles and positions. A computer science professor may have worked for a tech company before moving into academia. Accounting faculty, especially certified public accountants, might take on tax work every spring. Nursing faculty likely maintain a role with a hospital or other medical office. Learn from them what the job is like and how you can better prepare for it. And don't forget to talk to adjunct instructors; they may have an entirely separate career on top of their teaching role that gives them access to a network of potential mentors and employers.

Finally, you'll likely encounter graduate students or preprofessional students, some of whom may be in the workforce or have work experience. While they themselves are still working on their education, they may have insights, connections, and ideas regarding your career.

Try Things Out

In the first two steps of the Career Planning Cycle, you gather information. You may have some ideas about jobs and careers that you may like, but you also may wonder if you will really like them. How will you know? How can you be more certain? Take an interest or a skill, and try it out in an experience. By putting it to work for you in any one of a number of different environments, you can get practice and learn more about who you are and just how much you can do. It's a great idea to try out a new skill or career field before you commit to it fully. You might find out that the field isn't right for you, but you also may find that you are heading in the right direction and want to keep pursuing it. Experiences help you become more qualified for positions. One exciting aspect of college is that there is a huge variety of learning experiences and activities in which to get involved. The following are some ways that you can try things out and get experience.

Community Involvement, Volunteering, and Clubs

You're in college to develop yourself as an individual. You'll gain personally satisfying and enriching experience by becoming more involved with your college or general community. Organizations, clubs, and charities often rely on college students because of their motivation, knowledge, and increasing maturity. The work can increase your skills and abilities, providing valuable experience that will lead to positive results.

Participate in clubs and volunteer in areas that appeal to your interests and passions. It's just as important that you enjoy them and make a difference as it is to increase career potential through networking and skill-building. But of course, it's great to do both.

Once you join a club or related organization, take the time to learn about their leadership opportunities. Most campus clubs have some type of management structure—treasurer, vice president, president, and so on. You may "move up the ranks" naturally, or you may need to apply or even run for election. Some organizations, such as a campus newspaper, radio station, or dance team, have skill-based semiprofessional or roles such as advertising manager, sound engineer, or choreographer. These opportunities may not always be available to you as freshmen, but you can take on shorter-term roles to build your skills and make a bigger impact. Managing a fundraiser, planning an event, or temporarily taking on a role while someone else is busy are all ways to engage further.

Volunteering can be an important way to access a profession and get a sense for whether you will enjoy it or not, even before you do an internship. And in certain arenas, such as politics, it might be the *only* readily accessible approach, especially if you have no prior experience. In all of these cases, you can build important skills and increase your experience working with people in your chosen field. Spend time reflecting on and recording your experiences so that you're better prepared to talk about them and utilize what you learned.

Internships and Related Experiences

Many employers value experience as much as they do education. Internships and similar fieldwork allow you to use what you've learned and, sometimes more importantly, see how things work "in the real world." These experiences drive you to communicate with others in your field and help you understand the day-to-day challenges and opportunities of people working in similar areas. Even if the internship is not at a company or organization directly in your field of study, you'll focus on gaining transferable skills that you can apply later on.

Speaking to career or academic counselors and planning your major will help you learn about internship requirements and recommendations. You'll find out how, where, and when to apply, the level of commitment required, and any limitations or guidelines your college indicates. If you're going to receive credit for your internship or fieldwork, it must be directly related to your field of study.

When you intern, you are usually treated like you work there full-time. It's not just learning about the job; it's *doing* the job, often similarly to an entry-level employee. The level of commitment may vary by the type of internship and may be negotiable based on your schedule. Be very clear about what's required and what you can handle given your other commitments, because you want to leave a very good impression. (Internship managers are your top resource for employment references and letters of recommendation.)

Note that while internships and similar positions may seem to involve low-level work, you maintain your rights and should be treated properly. Getting coffee, organizing shelves, and copying papers are often part of the work. Your internship should be structured with duties, responsibilities, and goals for learning that are mutually agreed upon by both you and the internship site, as well as approved by an internship supervisor from your college or university. This will help ensure a positive and productive experience for both you and your internship sponsor.

Students who take internships generally report them to be worthwhile experiences. In a survey of students taken by the National Association of Colleges and Employers, approximately 75 percent of students responding to the survey said their professionalism/work ethic, teamwork/collaboration, and oral/written communication skills were "very" to "extremely" improved by their internship/coop experience, and 66 percent said the same of their critical thinking/problem-solving skills.[3]

---

3   *2018 Student Survey Report*. National Association of Colleges and Employers. https://www.naceweb.org/career-readiness/internships/students-internships-positively-impact-competencies/

ACTIVITY

Go to Internships.com (https://www.internships.com) and enter a specific keyword and location in the fields on the homepage, such as "airline" and "Bend, OR." How many opportunities came back? How many piqued your interest?

Now, try to choose a broader, less specific keyword. For example, instead of "airline," try "aviation" on the second search. If the first keyword was "physical therapy," you might try "health care" for a broader search in the same field. Did you receive more opportunities the second time? Do you see ones that aren't exactly in your field but that still seem interesting?

On sites like these, you can play with the options and filters to find a wide array of internship possibilities in related fields. In the example above, a future physical therapist who took an internship in another area of health care would certainly still learn a lot.

There are many and varied types of experiential learning opportunities that can help you learn more about different career opportunities. These are fully discussed in chapter 4. The table below provides a brief overview.

Internship and Experiential Learning Terminology

Internship	A period of work experience in a professional organization, in which participants (interns) are exposed to and perform some of the tasks of actual employees. Internships are usually a relatively high commitment, and may be paid and/or result in college credit.
Externship/Job Shadowing	Usually a briefer and lower-commitment experience than internships, in which participants are observing work activities and perhaps undertaking small projects. Unpaid and not credit-bearing.
Fieldwork	A period or trip to conduct research or participate in the "natural environment" of a discipline or profession. Fieldwork may involve visiting a work site, such as a hospital or nursing home, or being a part of a team gathering data or information.
Apprenticeship	A defined period of on-the-job training in which the student is formally doing the job and learning specific skills. Unlike most internships, apprenticeships are usually formal requirements to attain a license or gain employment in skilled trades, and they are growing in use in health care, IT, transportation, and logistics.
Undergraduate Research	Even as an undergrad, you may find opportunities to partake in actual research in your field of study. Colleges often have strict guidelines on types and levels of participation, and you will likely need to apply. The benefits include firsthand knowledge of a core academic activity and exposure to more people in your field.

Table 12.1

Internship and Experiential Learning Terminology

Related Employment	It may be possible to get a regular, low-level paying job directly in your field of study or in a related place of work. While it's not essential, simply being around the profession will better inform and prepare you.
Clinicals, Student Teaching, and Related Experiences	Health care, education, and other fields often have specific requirements for clinicals (learning experience in health care facilities) or student teaching. These are often components of the major and required for both graduation and licensure.
Service Learning	Students learn educational standards through tackling real-life problems in their community. Involvement could be hands-on, such as working in a homeless shelter. Students could also tackle broad issues in an indirect manner, such as by solving a local environmental problem.

Table 12.1

Productive Downtime

Throughout this book, we've discussed all the work required for a successful and productive college experience. And in this chapter, we've outlined a wide range of extracurricular activities that are likely necessary to achieve your career goals. But as we've also made clear, balance and rest are critical for success and well-being. Everyone needs time off.

So, when you have a school break, relax. Spend time with the people who motivate and help you—family and friends—or take a trip if that's possible. If you work during school and school breaks, the decrease in your school responsibilities should help recharge your batteries.

Another way you might spend your time off from school is to find an employment and/or experiential opportunity, especially during a longer time off. Winter break may afford a weeklong volunteer opportunity or a brief externship. Summer break is particularly helpful for formal internships and other experiences.

Figure 12.9 Internships present a range of opportunities to work and learn in the authentic environment of your career or interest area. (Credit: Bureau of Land Management / Flickr / Attribution 2.0 Generic (CC-BY 2.0))

If you do seek a summer internship or related activity, be aware that they can be very competitive. With many college students off for the summer, they may be targeting the same opportunities as you are. Work with your academic or career advisors to start the process early and put yourself in the best position to get an internship. Consider all of the application components, including essays, portfolio items, and letters of recommendation; all of these may take time to generate. If possible, pursue multiple opportunities to increase your chances. Just be clear on the application policies, and be sure to inform them if you take another position.

Summer jobs, whether related to your field or not, may also be hard to come by without prior planning. If you go away to school and need a job at home over the summer, be sure to connect with the potential employer early. Get them the application, resume, and any certifications or recommendations with plenty of time for them to process and contact you for clarification or follow-up. Employers who regularly employ college students will likely be comfortable working via email or by phone, but ask if an in-person interview is necessary, and see if you can schedule it during a spring break or as soon as you get back from school. Even if you don't go away to school, plan and connect early. You wouldn't want all the other students to come home and take your opportunity when you've been there all along.

While you're not focused on your schoolwork, or even after you graduate, you can keep learning. Beyond the different types of degrees and certificates discussed in the Academic Pathways chapter, you'll be more prepared and more attractive to a potential employer if you demonstrate a continued thirst and effort to gain knowledge and "remain current." Find the leaders in your field and read their articles or books (your future employers may be familiar with them). Or consider more formal summer courses, short-courses, or online learning opportunities. Each profession has its own resources. For example, in the software and computing field, Thinkful (http://www.thinkful.com) offers courses and mentoring for students and professionals.

Transferable Skills

Whether or not your internship or other experiences are directly connected to your career, you should focus as much as possible on building and improving transferable skills. These are abilities and knowledge that are useful across an array of industries, job types, and roles. They can be transferred—hence the name—from where you learned them to another career or area of study.

Examples of transferable skills include communication, personnel management/leadership, teamwork, computation/quantitative literacy, information technology, research/analysis, foreign language, and so on. If you search for lists of transferable skills, you'll see that some sites only include compilations of a few very broad areas, such as communication, while others provide longer and more specific lists, such as breaking down communication into writing, verbal, and listening skills. Employers believe that transferable skills are critical to the success of their recent college graduate new hires. The top four career competencies that employers want are critical thinking/problem solving, teamwork/collaboration, professionalism/work ethic, and oral/written communication.[4] If you remember the statistics noted above, students said that all four of these skills were significantly improved through their internship experiences.

These are considered *skills* because they are not simply traits or personality elements; they are abilities and intelligences you can develop and improve. Even if you're a great writer before starting an internship, you may need to learn how to write in a more professional manner—becoming more succinct, learning the executive summary, conforming to templates, and so on. Once you establish that skill, you can not only mention it on a resume or interview, but also discuss the *process* by which you improved, demonstrating your adaptability and eagerness to learn.

Not everyone can land an internship or perform fieldwork. Perhaps you need to work nearly full-time while in school. If so, focus on developing transferable skills in that environment. Take on new challenges in areas where you don't have experience. For example, if you work in retail, ask your manager if you can help with inventory or bookkeeping (building quantitative literacy skills). If you're a waiter, help the catering manager plan a party or order food (building organizational skills). Remember, extending yourself in this way is not simply a means to enhance your resume. By taking on these new challenges, you'll see a side of the business you hadn't before and learn things that you can apply in other situations.

Whether or not it's required as a part of your internship or other experience, be sure to reflect on your time there—what you did, what you learned, where you excelled, where you didn't excel. Maintaining a journal of some sort will enable you to share your experiences and employ your transferable skills in your college courses and other activities. Jot down some anecdotes, events, and tasks you performed. Any materials or documents you produced can go into your portfolio, and the record of your experience will serve you well while searching for a job. Consider that it is customary to be asked during a job interview to share a personal strength and a weakness. Sharing a strength is often more expected and, thus, easier to plan for. While it may seem reasonable to say that your weakness is that you're always late, it's better to provide a weakness within the context of work experience. For example, if you have had a part-time job where one of your colleagues was always slacking off and putting the load on others, you may have felt frustrated and even expressed your anger. Rather than view this as a negative, consider the positive benefit and craft this into a solid answer to the likely interview question. For example, "I have found that I'm rather impatient with colleagues who take shortcuts to a solution and don't really apply themselves. My weakness is impatience. However, rather than call it out in a negative way, I share my observation as constructive feedback and let it go. My colleague can take it or leave it, but I'm not carrying it with me." If you wrote about this experience around the time that it occurred, it will be easier to shape into a thoughtful response later. Continuing to work on your transferable skills will allow you to improve them and make a better impression on faculty, advisors, and potential employers.

---

4 National Association of Colleges and Employers. "The Four Career Competentices Employers Value Most." 2019. https://planww.naceweb.org/career-readiness/competencies/the-four-career-competencies-employers-value-most/

What to Do to Get Ready

Being prepared to find a job means putting evidence of your KSAs together in a way that employers will understand. It is one thing to say you can do something; it is another to show that you can. The following are things that you will want to compile as a part of your college career.

Resumes and Profiles: The College Version

You may already have a resume or a similar profile (such as LinkedIn), or you may be thinking about developing one. Usually, these resources are not required for early college studies, but you may need them for internships, work-study, or other opportunities. When it comes to an online profile, something that is a public resource, be very considerate and intentional when developing it.

Resume

A resume is a summary of your education, experience, and other accomplishments. It is not simply a list of what you've done; it's a showcase that presents the best you have to offer for a specific role. While most resumes have a relatively similar look and feel, there are some variations in the approach. Especially when developing your first résumé or applying in a new area, you should seek help from resources such as career counselors and others with knowledge of the field. Websites can be very helpful, but be sure to run your résumé by others to make sure it fits the format and contains no mistakes.

A resume is a one-page summary (two, if you are a more experienced person) that generally includes the following information:

- Name and contact information
- Objective and/or summary
- Education—all degrees and relevant certifications or licenses
    - While in college, you *may* list coursework *closely related* to the job to which you're applying.
- Work or work-related experience—usually in reverse chronological order, starting with the most recent and working backward. (Some resumes are organized by subject/skills rather than chronologically.[5])
- Career-related/academic awards or similar accomplishments
- Specific work-related skills

While you're in college, especially if you went into college directly after high school, you may not have formal degrees or significant work experience to share. That's okay. Tailor the résumé to the position for which you're applying, and include high school academic, extracurricular, and community-based experience . These show your ability to make a positive contribution and are a good indicator of your work ethic. Later on in this chapter, we'll discuss internships and other programs through which you can gain experience, all of which can be listed on your resume. Again, professionals and counselors can help you with this.

If you have significant experience outside of college, you should include it if it's relatively recent, relates to the position, and/or includes transferable skills (discussed above) that can be used in the role for which you're applying. Military service or similar experience should nearly always be included. If you had a long career with one company quite some time ago, you can summarize that in one resume entry, indicating the total years worked and the final role achieved. These are judgment calls, and again you can seek guidance from experts.

---

5 Writing@CSU. "Organizing Your Resume." https://writing.colostate.edu/guides/page.cfm?pageid=1517&guideid=77

> **Henry Townsend**
> htownse@stlu.mi.edu
>
> 2438 McNair Avenue, Apartment 3
> St. Louis, Missouri
>
> *Summary*
> Highly organized audiology major with excellent communication skills and extensive customer service background. Currently focused on gaining clinical experience and leadership skills.
>
> *Education*
> **St. Louis University**, St. Louis, Missouri
> *Major*: Communication Disorders, Focus on Audiology; Expected Graduation 2022
> *Activities*: Pep Band, Concert Band, Comms Club
>
> **Spring Lakes High School**, Crimson, Virginia, 2018
> *Cumulative G.P.A*: 3.6
> Rotary Public Service Award
> Founder and President, Hip Hop Health -- hospital patient music program
>
> *Experience*
> **Student Relations Coordinator**
> St. Louis Children's Hospital   2019-Present
>
> **Circulation Clerk**
> St. Louis University Library   2018-Present
>
> **Service Desk Representative**
> Forte Equipment Rental, Virginia Beach   2017-2019
>
> *Skills*
> American Sign Language, Near Fluent
> Google Sheets and Slides, Highly Proficient
> Zendesk and Salesforce, Highly Proficient

Figure 12.10 Resumes summarize your accomplishments, education, skills, and experience.

Digital Profiles

An online profile is a nearly standard component of professional job seeking and networking. LinkedIn is a networking website used by people from nearly every profession. It combines elements of résumés and portfolios with social media. Users can view, connect, communicate, post events and articles, comment, and recommend others. Employers can recruit, post jobs, and process applications. Alternatives include Jobcase, AngelList, Hired, and Nexxt. These varying sites work in similar ways, with some unique features or practices.

Some professions or industries have specific LinkedIn groups or subnetworks. Other professions or industries may have their own networking sites, to be used instead of or in addition to LinkedIn. Industry, for example, is a networking site specifically for culinary and hospitality workers.

As a college student, it might be a great idea to have a LinkedIn or related profile. It can help you make connections in a prospective field, and provide access to publications and posts on topics that interest you. Before you join and develop a public professional profile, however, keep the following in mind:

- **Be professional.** Write up your profile information, any summary, and job/education experience separately, check for spelling and other errors, and have someone review *before* posting. Be sure to be completely honest and accurate.
- **Your profile isn't a contest.** As a college student, you may only have two or three items to include on your profile. That's okay. Overly long LinkedIn profiles—like overly long resumes—aren't effective anyway, and a college student's can be brief.
- **Add relevant experience and information as you attain it.** Post internships, summer jobs, awards, or work-study experiences as you attain them. Don't list *every* club or organization you're in if it doesn't pertain to the professional field, but include some, especially if you become head of a club or hold a competitive position, such as president or member of a performance group or sports team.
- **Don't "overconnect."** As you meet and work with people relevant to your career, it is appropriate to connect with them through LinkedIn by adding a personal note on the invite message. But don't send connection invites to people with whom you have no relationship, or to too many people overall. Even alumni from your own school might be reluctant to connect with you unless you know them relatively well.
- **Professional networking is not the same as social media.** While LinkedIn has a very strong social media component, users are often annoyed by too much nonprofessional sharing (such as vacation/child pictures); aggressive commenting or arguing via comments is also frowned upon. As a student, you probably shouldn't be commenting or posting too much at all. Use LinkedIn as a place to observe and learn. And in terms of your profile itself, keep it professional, not personal.
- **LinkedIn is not a replacement for a real resume.**

There's no need to rush to build and post an online professional profile—certainly not in your freshman year. But when the time is right, it can be a useful resource for you and future employers.

Social Media and Online Activity Never Go Away

While thinking about LinkedIn and other networks, it's a good time to remember that future employers, educational institutions, internship coordinators, and anyone else who may hire or develop a relationship with you can see most of what you've posted or done online. Companies are well within their rights to dig through your social media pages, and those of your friends or groups you're part of, to learn about you. Tasteless posts, inappropriate memes, harassment, pictures or videos of high-risk behavior, and even aggressive and mean comments are all problematic. They may convince a potential employer that you're not right for their organization. Be careful of who and what you retweet, like, and share. It's all traceable, and it can all have consequences.

For other activities on social media, such as strong political views, activism, or opinions on controversial topics, you should use your judgment. Most strong organizations will not be dissuaded from working with you because you're passionate about something within the realm of civility, but any posts or descriptions that seem insensitive to groups of people can be taken as a reason not to hire you. While you have freedom of speech with regard to the government, that freedom does not extend to private companies' decisions on whether to hire you. Even public institutions, such as universities and government agencies, can reject you for unlawful activity (including threats or harassment) revealed online; they can also reject you if you frequently post opinions that conflict with the expectations of both your employer and the people/organizations they serve.

With those cautions in mind, it's important to remember that anything on your social media or professional network profiles related to federally protected aspects of your identity—race, national origin, color, disability, veteran status, parental/pregnancy status, religion, gender, age, or genetic information (including family medical history)—cannot be held against you in hiring decisions.

Building Your Portfolio

Future employers or educational institutions may want to see the work you've done during school. Also, you may need to recall projects or papers you wrote to remember details about your studies. Your portfolio can be one of your most important resources.

Portfolio components vary according to field. Business students should save projects, simulations, case studies, and any mock companies or competitions they worked on. Occupational therapy students may have patient thank-you letters, summaries of volunteer activity, and completed patient paperwork (identities removed). Education majors will likely have lesson plans, student teaching materials, sample projects they created, and papers or research related to their specialization.

Other items to include a portfolio:

- Evidence of any workshops or special classes you attended. Include a certificate, registration letter, or something else indicating you attended/completed it.
- Evidence of volunteer work, including a write-up of your experience and how it impacted you.
- *Related* experience and work products from your time prior to college.
- Materials associated with *career-related* talks, performances, debates, or competitions that you delivered or took part in.
- Products, projects, or experiences developed in internships, fieldwork, clinicals, or other experiences (see below).
- Evidence of "universal" workplace skills such as computer abilities or communication, or specialized abilities such as computation/number crunching.

A portfolio is neither a scrapbook nor an Instagram story. No need to fill it with pictures of your college experience unless those pictures directly relate to your career. If you're studying theology and ran a religious camp, include a picture. If you're studying theology and worked in a food store, leave it out.

Certain disciplines, such as graphic design, music, computer science, and other technologies, may have more specific portfolio requirements and desired styles. You'll likely learn about that in the course of your studies, but be sure to proactively inquire about these needs or seek examples. Early in your college career, you should be most focused on gathering components for your portfolio, not formalizing it for display or sharing.

Preparing to Network

Throughout this chapter, we have discussed how important relationships are to your career development. It can sometimes be a little intimidating to meet new people in the professional environment. But with preparation and understanding, these encounters can be not only helpful, but also rewarding. Here are some ideas to consider when meeting new people who can be helpful to your career:

- **Be yourself.** You're your own best asset. If you're comfortable with who you are and where you come from, others will be, too.
- **Remember, you're in college and they know it.** Don't try to impress everyone with what you *know*; alumni or faculty know more. Instead, talk about what you're *learning*—your favorite class, the project you're most proud of, or even the ones by which you've been most challenged.
- **Be polite, not too casual.** If your goal is to become a professional, look and sound the part.
- **Listen.**
- **Think of some questions ahead of time.** Don't aim for difficult questions or anything too personal, but asking people how they got into their career, with whom they studied in college, what their job is like, and similar questions will both start conversations and provide you with meaningful insight.
- **Don't stress.** Remember, if alumni, even highly successful ones, are speaking to you, it's usually because they want to. An encounter over finger food or a brief meetup in the Rad Tech department office isn't going to make or break your job prospects.
- **If appropriate and timely, ask if you can keep in touch.** Be prepared with a polished email address and phone number. For example, if your current address is "fortnitefan@gmail.com," consider creating a second account that's more professional.
- **Say thank you.** No need to go on and on, but thank them for any advice they give or simply for taking the time to talk with you

> While you're in college, don't try to impress everyone with what you *know*. Instead, talk about what you're *learning*.

Making Your Case through the Words of Others: Letters of Recommendation

Whether you go on to graduate school or directly into the workforce (or both at the same time), decision makers will want to learn more about you. Your grades, interviews, test scores, and other performance data will tell them a lot. But sometimes they'll want to hear from others.

Letters of recommendation are often a standard component of convincing people you're the right person to join their organization. Some positions or institutions require a certain quantity of letters and may have specific guidance on who should write them. Other companies will accept them as additional evidence that you're a great candidate. Either way, gathering such letters or having a few people whom you can ask for them will put you in a better position. Note that internships, especially competitive ones, may also require letters of recommendation.

Figure 12.11 When you ask someone to write you a letter of recommendation, be prepared to share information about your goals, your accomplishments, and why you are asking the person in particular. Don't assume that they know which strengths or experience of yours to highlight. (Credit: US Embassy Jerusalem / Flickr / Attribution 2.0 Generic (CC-BY 2.0))

Whom to ask for a letter? They're usually written by instructors, department chairs, club advisors, managers, coaches, and others with whom you've had a good relationship. Maybe it's someone who taught two or three of your courses, or someone you helped in a volunteer or work-study capacity.

Just by taking the time to write the letter, a faculty member is sending a message: "The person about whom I'm writing impressed me." So the first step is to make a good impression on the person you're asking to write a letter. You may do this in many ways. Getting a good grade in the class is important, but a faculty member may be more impressed by your perseverance, improvement over time, or creativity in meeting challenges.

How to ask? Be straightforward and direct. The appeal is best made in person, but be prepared for the person you're asking to ask for some time to make the decision. People who get frequent requests may have a policy or even a form to fill out. They may ask you to provide more information about yourself so that they can write an original letter. If they do so, be thorough but prompt—you don't want to keep them waiting. *And if you have a deadline, tell them.*

When to ask? If you encounter a faculty member early in your college career who you think would be the best person to write a letter for you, ask them what they think toward the end of your course or soon after. They may feel it's too early or not specific enough to simply hand you a general letter at that time. If so, ask if you can come back when you are applying to internships, jobs, or grad schools.

If you wait until you're applying or you're about to graduate, you may have a more specific subject or reason for a letter. Be sure to tell the writer where you're applying and what type of career you're going into, so they can tailor the recommendation to that area.

Thank-you notes. They wrote you a letter, so you should write them one in return. A brief and personal thank-you note is appropriate and necessary.

Steps to Success

> "Things change—circumstances change. Learn to adapt. Adjust your efforts and yourself to what is presented to you so you can respond accordingly. Never see change as a threat—do not get intimidated by it. Change can be an opportunity to learn, to grow, to evolve, and to become a better person."
>
> —Rodolfo Costa[6]

Preparing for Change and Being Open to Opportunities

Earlier in this text, we discussed managing change, adapting to the unexpected, and handling setbacks. These are critical skills that, while difficult during the process, ultimately build a better—and more employable—you. While you can't prepare for every obstacle or surprise, you can be certain that you'll encounter them.

You may go through all of college, and even high school, with one job in mind. You may apply early to a specific program, successfully complete all the requirements, and set yourself on a certain career path. And then something may change.

Figure 12.12 Career fairs are important before (and sometimes after) you graduate, both to explore opportunities and to make actual connections that can lead to a position. Be prepared before you go—with your resume, portfolio, a plan, and questions to ask. Focus on the best opportunities, but be very open to learning about industries or companies you may not have considered. (Credit: COD Newsroom / Flickr / Attribution 2.0 Generic (CC-BY 2.0))

As described above, changes in your interests or goals are a natural part of developing your career; they're nothing to be ashamed of. Most college students change majors several times. Even once they graduate, many people find themselves enjoying careers they didn't envision. Ask the people around you, and many will share stories about how they took a meandering or circuitous path to their profession. Some people end up in jobs or companies that they didn't know existed when they started school.

What's most important is that you build on your successes and failures, consider all your experiences, and

---

6 Costa, Robert. Advice My Parents Gave Me: Aand Other Lessons I Learned from My Mistakes. 2011.

pursue your purpose and overarching personal goals. For example, if you want to become a police officer but cannot complete all of the degree requirements on time, taking a job as a security officer or even an unrelated job in the meantime might lead to a great deal of satisfaction and set you on a different path. If, after that, you still want to pursue law enforcement, you can build it into your plan—managing your priorities, gaining the required experience and credentials, and applying for jobs closer to your chosen career.

This early in your college experience, you shouldn't be too worried about how to conduct job interviews or explain employment gaps or changing directions. However, you may need or want to explain the thinking behind your future plans to academic advisors, internship managers, your peers, and your family. You should feel free to do so openly, but you'll probably be better prepared if you revisit some of the ideas discussed earlier in this chapter. Consider how a shift in your plans, whether slight or significant, reflects who you are now and who you hope to be in the future. Knowing yourself as an emerging and new professional by discovering and developing your interests, skills, values, personality, and strengths is something that everyone should do on an ongoing basis throughout their lives. Explore job opportunities or career paths available to people in your new major or discipline area. Think about whether you need to handle any financial impacts, such as paying for additional education or delaying employment.

Employers, for their part, are often unfazed by changes or even mistakes. Remember, when they ask about your greatest weakness or failure, they want to hear something genuine. Just like the alumni you meet or the faculty you're asking for recommendations, interviewers may be more impressed by how and what you've *learned* rather than how you followed a preplanned path. Remember, most jobs are a continuous thread of situations to think through, information to analyze, and problems to solve. Your ability to solve your own problems, and reflect and discuss them later, will show that you're ready to do the same for an employer.

12.3 Where Can You Go from Here?

Estimated completion time: 7 minutes.

Hopefully you've noticed that we've ended each chapter of this book with a subsection called "Where Do You Go from Here?" In many of those cases, the story or reflection was aimed at giving you some ideas about how you could apply the topics and skills from that chapter to college and your career. Now we're at the last chapter, and the question is even more personal and a little different: Where *can* you go? Where do you want to go? And, perhaps more importantly, why?

The provided ideas and methods regarding choosing your career are proven winners. Learning about yourself, whether through simple reflection or formal analysis, is important to find your place. But consider the importance and reality of change and your openness to it. Regardless of your major, you will embark on a job and a career that will change many times over the course of your life. You'll likely change responsibilities, roles, companies, and even industries. Even if you join a company one week after graduation and stay with it until you retire, the job and the company won't remain the same. The world moves far too quickly for that, which is a good thing. All of those changes are opportunities to improve yourself and get closer to the "why" of your work: your purpose.

Your purpose is the answer to all types of questions that people may ask you. "Do you like your job?" "How did you get into that?" "Is it worth it?" But more importantly, your purpose is the answer to all types of questions that you should ask *yourself*. If you keep asking yourself those questions and give yourself time to answer, you'll have the best understanding of not only what you want to do, but why.

You may find out that no single job or career is going to fulfill your purpose. If your foremost goal—your ideal—is being a good parent, your job might simply be the financial means to help accomplish that. If you want to eradicate poverty, you may do that through a job plus volunteer work plus a management position at a foundation.

Don't think, however, that you can't fulfill your purpose within your career. It may take a few tries and restarts, but you can make a widespread impact in a number of ways. Furthermore, if you're having trouble entering a career-oriented purpose through the "front door," your skills and abilities might get you in through the side door. For example, if your purpose is to help eradicate racial and socioeconomic differences in America, you can work toward that in dozens of ways. At first it may seem that being a social worker, political activist, civil rights lawyer, or educator is the primary entryway—the front door. But what if none of these work out for you? What if you don't fit any of these molds, but you're the best salesperson most people have ever met? Every sales job you've taken, you've blown past your goal and earned top awards and bonuses. You've come so far that giving up your career would be financially devastating. So how can you use your skills and experience toward your purpose? Well, you could volunteer to use your sales skills to raise money or convince lawmakers to change things. Or you could get a job where you're selling products or services that help people in the exact situations you are trying to improve. You could sell low-cost telecommunication systems to towns and school systems so that residents have better access to the Internet, helping them learn and stay connected. You could sell building safety systems to keep people secure. You could sell educational technology, financial services, or even low-cost solar paneling to improve the lives and independence of people in impoverished areas. Your work would be similar to what you've done your whole life, but you would feel personally fulfilled and connected to a purpose.

In psychology, advertising, education, and other disciplines, researchers and professionals use a concept called Maslow's Hierarchy of Needs. In essence, it's a progression that starts with satisfying our most basic, physical needs (food, shelter) and moves through our more social and societal needs (cooperation, belonging) to our highest needs—feeling fulfilled and complete. (This brief description oversimplifies a rather detailed theory.)

Given this base introduction, consider how Maslow's theory applies to your future. At the bottom, your most basic needs are fulfilled by a job. It pays the bills, keeps you secure, and puts food on your table. At the next level is your career. Your career is more consistent; you invest more in it and probably are more heavily rewarded. In your career, you'll likely build up relationships over time, both professional and personal, creating a sense of community and belonging. Some people will come to associate you with your career, and you may feel partly defined by it. But it likely won't fulfill you all on its own.

At the highest level, the level that allows you to become more fulfilled and complete, is your purpose. That's the piece you strive for, the piece that helps you navigate your path. It's what you may see yourself still moving toward in a later part of your life. It's what you most want or even need to accomplish.

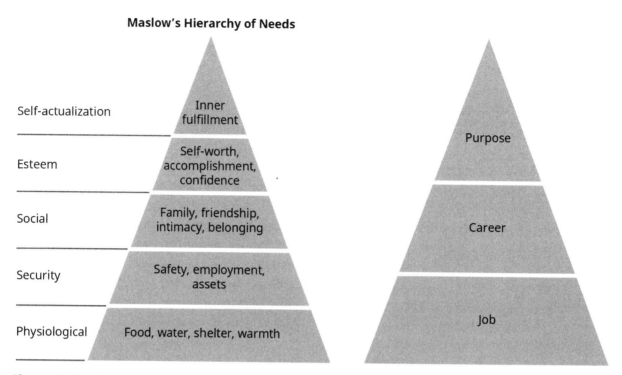

Figure 12.13 This adapted version of Maslow's hierarchy aligns different aspect of your pathway with the different levels and type of needs we have as humans.

Just as you'll likely have more than one job and even more than one career, you will have more than one purpose. You will even have them at the same time. You can be 100 percent driven to be the best possible therapist and 100 percent driven to be the best possible older sibling, all while being 100 percent driven to continually deepen your knowledge of yoga. Your time and your focus will be split between them, but they will still each fulfill you. As you get older and gain experiences, both positive and negative, your priorities may change. But you'll be successful as long as you adhere to the principles we've discussed and the qualities, values, and abilities you've identified in yourself. College offers you the opportunity to keep asking yourself the best, most challenging questions, all while you have many people dedicated to helping you find the answers. Those answers may surprise you, but the important thing is to keep asking and keep learning.

Appendix A

A Conducting and Presenting Research

Turning Information into Knowledge

Estimated completion time: 35 minutes.

Questions to consider:

- What is the difference between information and knowledge?
- What is information literacy?
- What are the steps to a good research study?

What Is the Difference between Information and Knowledge?

Life is a series of problems needing solutions. We need to find information that matters and then discover why it matters. Curiosity, then, is a response to an environment of exploration, manifesting in wanting to know "why" or "how." How do you make sense of the world? How does information translate to knowledge? Connecting ideas, thinking critically, acting responsibly, and communicating effectively are all essential to lifelong learning and active engagement in today's world. You need to become proficient, ethical users and producers of information in a globally connected world. It is important to be able to reason, manage resources, work productively with others, acquire and evaluate information effectively, organize information, interpret and communicate the information, and work with an ever-evolving variety of technologies. In other words, you need to become information-savvy consumers and producers. You need to be able to adapt to, understand, evaluate, and make use of technology so you can be citizens that shape our society, rather than being its pawns. What you learn is often what you will want to communicate to others.

What Is Information Literacy?

Human beings are passionate, curious, and always seeking to connect with each other and make sense of things. Learning is more effective when new information is meaningful and linked to some personal experience or prior knowledge. Learning is about both context and content. It is necessary to learn how to assess, evaluate, and connect in order to make information become knowledge. Information literacy skills are the hallmark of the ability to do research. What is important is for you to learn how to find information that "matters" and then figure out why it might matter.

Information literacy is a link between the life experiences of you as a student, the academic world of scholarship, and the postcollege real world of application of learning. An information-literate person has the ability to ask questions and knows the difference between ignorance and understanding. (When do I need information?) Information literacy builds a lifelong ability to determine where information is kept (Where is the best place to find this?) and in what forms knowledge is stored (Which knowledge products will likely have what I need?).

Information literacy relies on the use of a critical mind to discern credible from not credible, valid from not valid. It is actually the core of the first-year experience. It lasts, while the specifics of particular courses fade over time. After all, the nature of research, the core of higher education, is a learning process: "How do I learn about something?" Communication skills are essential to your ability to both learn and share what you've learned.

What Are the Steps to a Good Research Study?

Research is a part of life. In fact, you conduct research daily. You look things up whenever you want a hotel or a good restaurant in a new city, or a recipe for cookies you'd like to make for a party. Sometimes you use Google for answers, and other times you ask people to help you answer your question. At times you might need to visit specific websites to find good information on the kind of used car you should buy or tickets to a sporting event or concert you hope to attend. All of this is part of research at its most basic level—asking a question and then answering it. Research can be defined as an activity that produces new knowledge. However, it is not timeless. Questions change, and so do answers. New questions bring new light to bear on any topic or issue. For example, consider the way we have controlled the use of pesticides. Over time, we moved from acceptance to shock and now horror at some of the side effects. It is new information on pesticides that has influenced our change in thinking. And the reason we know this information is that someone did the research and then communicated it to our community through newscasts, newspapers, online sites, and so forth.

We often accept ideas as fact. For instance, how do we come to believe such things as "Three out of four dentists recommend . . . " or "McDonald's french fries are preferred three to one over . . ."? Or that heroin is addictive, or that putting infants in car seats prevents fatal injuries, or that drinking while pregnant can be harmful? It is important to know that these statements are the result of questions that led to serious research. Understanding the methods used to do research will help us understand how we come to know what we know. In cases such as these, someone was interested in knowing the answer to a particular question, planned a research study, and then published the findings. When people do this kind of research, their purpose is not only to find an answer but also to communicate what they found to the rest of us. They are communicating new knowledge.

Research is exploration and the search for possible answers to questions. Most students think research is about finding answers, but it is more about the questions we ask that lead us to the answers. Good research starts with good questions. Researchers ask themselves a question, create a possible answer in the form of a hypothesis, and then begin a process of gathering information with a methodology. If we understand how important questions are to doing research, we are then better able to determine the credibility and validity of the information sources we use. When evaluating sources, we can ask: Why should I believe this author? What does she know that makes her someone I should pay attention to? And when deciding on credibility, we can ask: What did the author do to convince me his answer is the correct one? Did the evidence really match the question the author was asking? Thus, information literacy is the ability to evaluate sources on the basis of what questions were asked, determine if those are the best questions to ask, assess whether the answers offered really answer the questions, and decide if the author is prepared to answer those questions well. Remember the literacies that Howard Rheingold suggested in the "Communicating" chapter. Using these as guides leads us to mindfully explore the vast array of information available to us. And when we do so, we won't find ourselves taking information at face value and passing it on as though it were valid, like some of the "fake news" that is prevalent today.

So let's start the process of doing research. The activity below will help you begin the process. After this, you will be introduced to the simple steps you need to take to do the research and then communicate your findings appropriately.

Pick a topic you might like to research or have already been assigned to research for a class. Then take a close look at the list of knowledge products below, and rank them in order of which ones you would most likely use for a research paper. After ranking them, explain why you put them in that order.

- **Books:** histories, pictures, topic overviews
- **Journals:** research studies, expert opinions, analyses, lists of other information sources

- **Magazines:** basic and recent information, pictures, reviews
- **Newspapers:** very recent information, place-specific information, reviews
- **Films, videos, television, music:** pictures, speeches, sound
- **Internet sources:** current or historical information from a variety of sources or individuals, data or commentary compiled by individuals or specific organizations or companies, graphics, sound, music, animation, video, pictures
- **Conversations, interviews:** opinions, direct experiences, personal viewpoints, attitudes, histories
- **Government publications:** reports, studies, statistics, laws, regulations
- **Documents:** reports, laws, statistics, facts
- **Diaries:** personal stories, histories, opinions, reflections

These can also categorized by types of knowledge products. For your research, you have to choose wisely among these, too. There are *scholarly* knowledge products, which are mostly written for scholars in a particular field. The author is identified, and credentials are available. Sources are documented, and technical language is often used. Secondly, some knowledge products might be considered *professional*. These are written for professionals in a field, the author is most often identified, sources are not always documented, and the language may or may not be technical. Finally, there are *popular* knowledge products, which communicate a broad range of information. The author is often not identified, sources are often not documented, and language is not technical. Because they are commercial products packaged for wide sales, they often use color and have numerous ads.

When you are faced with a research assignment, it is important for you to be able to create successful search strategies. You need to find sources for specific purposes and audiences and be able to critically evaluate these sources. When doing research, you also have to incorporate the information you find for specific purposes, acknowledge the sources, and provide citations. To make this easier to understand, think of scholarly writing as a simple story told with a particular set of conventions (rules). What are these conventions? They are: a research question, a hypothesis, a methodology, a review of the literature, an interpretation of your work, and an analysis of the significance of what you've found.

Research Question

First of all, you need a topic. This is often the most difficult part of the whole process. So begin by thinking of something that is really interesting to you. Let's take music for an example. You need to ask some questions about music to start the process. Some examples of questions are:

- What does music mean?
- What is the function of music?
- What is the value of music?
- What is the significance of music?
- How is music made?
- What causes music to happen?

The easiest way to come up with questions regarding whatever topic you choose is to start with basic questioning words: *who, what, why, when, where, how, might, could, can, should, will, must, did,* and so forth. You can ask better questions, and this will help you narrow down your hypothesis. For instance, *why* does music change over time? *Who* will play this music? *How* did this music come about? *Why should* we listen to this music?

Pick a topic and try to describe it:

1. Name your topic: *I am studying* _____
2. Suggest a question: *Because I want to find out who/how/why/whether/when/what* _____
3. State a rationale for the question: *In order to understand who/what/where/how/why/whether* _____

Going through this exercise every time you are tasked with writing a research paper will help you clarify what you want to accomplish and why.

Hypothesis

Scholars use information to answer one or more questions inspired by a topic of interest. Usually, a scholarly question identifies a problem and a solution. Such questions are usually written in the form of a hypothesis, which is a statement about the relationship between two things that identifies both a problem and an answer or solution. An example of a hypothesis would be: Different genres of music have an effect on the mood of the people listening to them. The questions asked to get to this hypothesis might be: Does music have an effect on mood? Do people listen to music to make them feel better? What kind of music is used as a way to energize the listener? Is there one type of music that is better than others for calming someone down?

Your hypothesis must reflect what is known about a research topic in such a way that your research project will add new knowledge and insight to what is already known. In order to arrive at a hypothesis that achieves this goal, you must learn as much as possible about your topic so you can narrow down your hypotheses to what you don't know. Then your research project will produce new knowledge. *Your hypothesis is about what you don't know*. However, you might find that you can't prove your hypothesis. You might find evidence that contradicts it, and you will have to reflect on why your hypothesis might have been wrong.

Find two newspaper articles to analyze. Read through them and answer the following:

1. What questions are being answered in the articles?
2. What questions do you think need to be answered?
3. What was the hypothesis that the writer of these articles was working from?

It is important to be able to find the hypothesis that a writer has constructed to tell you a story. You have to make sure you understand what they are trying to "prove" and what questions they asked in order to do so.

Methodology

Education is about discovery. This means that you need to learn how to question, evaluate, and determine the worth, credibility, and relevance of what you, as a student, find. Thus, when doing research, you need that hypothesis to begin the rest of your research.

The next step is to come up with key words or concepts that describe your topic. Start by preparing an outline for yourself. List the key words (for instance, on the topic of music, some key words might be *music*, *instruments*, *genres*, *musicians*, and so on). Then create a list of narrower terms, which are more specific things that you want to know about your topic, such as *time frames*, *geography*, *population*, and *age groups*. Finally, you can list broader terms that are the larger subjects that include your key words. For music these could be *cultural expression*, *jazz*, *hip-hop*, *singers*, and so forth. Your methodology will be a compilation of the sources you decide to review. It is an orderly approach to problem solving and gathering useful data, using such sources and strategies as interviews, public documents, surveys, experiments, the Internet, and many more.

The kind of methodology you decide to use depends on the type of research you will be conducting. You could do *exploratory research*, which basically answers the question "Does something exist?" This "something" could be an event, a thing, or an idea, such as a concert or music designed for relaxation. Or perhaps you want to do *descriptive research*, which is the kind of study that defines something by describing its characteristics, behaviors, or actions. For instance, you could describe a genre of music, how it was created, and what instruments are usually used to compose this type of music. A third type of research you may want to do is called *prediction research*, which involves identifying relationships that make it possible for us to speculate about one thing by knowing about something else. Music has taken many turns over time, and you might want to suggest that the next phase of music might all be electronically produced. And finally, you could choose to do *explanatory research*. This type of research examines cause-and-effect relationships. For example, there is music created to tell a particular story in a specific manner. This might be true of rap music. To study this, you would use explanatory research to describe this phenomenon.

Review of the Literature

One other piece of the research puzzle is a review of the literature. The literature in a particular field is its *discourse*, which is actually a conversation over time about a topic. When you do your literature review, you are inserting yourself in the middle of such a conversation and getting information only from that particular time and perspective. For instance, if you want to study the effects of music on children, you will find a wide variety of sources that will give you information about the topic. You will discover that many people have been interested in the issue and have done studies trying to find out the answer. These studies have been done over many years, and the perspectives involved have changed accordingly. The discourse continues over time, and you can insert information into the conversation by conducting your own research.

Thus, a review of the literature finds, evaluates, and integrates past research. It is a critical synthesis of research literature that:

- shows how previous studies relate to one another.
- shows similarities and differences between studies.
- discriminates between relevant and irrelevant information.
- indicates weaknesses in previous work.

The purpose of the literature review is to synthesize many specific events and details into a comprehensive whole. Synthesis results from weaving together many smaller generalizations and interpretations into a coherent main theme. You will find that a literature review is always required of an assigned research paper for a course. The purpose is to enable you to critically analyze a segment of an already published body of knowledge. A comprehensive literature review encompasses the following elements:

- Start the introduction by describing the problem or issue you are addressing, then focus on your research hypotheses or questions.
- Explicitly state the significance of the topic in the introduction.
- Present the review as an essay, not an annotated list.
- Emphasize the findings of previous research you have found.
- Point out the trends and themes in the literature.
- Point out the gaps in the literature.
- Express opinions about the quality and importance of the research you have found.
- Use the review to suggest that there is a need for more study.

Avoiding Plagiarism

You certainly have heard about plagiarism and how important it is not to let yourself participate in it. It is so easy to read through many other people's work and grab a sentence here and there to put into your own paper. As you're struggling to come up with ideas, you may also find yourself borrowing from others. Neither of these is a good idea.

Plagiarism often starts with the note-taking stage of the research process. Thus, when taking notes, be sure to distinguish between paraphrases and direct quotations. When you are copying an exact quotation, be extremely precise. Note all the information you will need for the citation. It is a good idea to make a system for yourself, perhaps color coding, when doing your research. Make direct quotations one color and your own paraphrasing of ideas another color. Both quotations and paraphrases need to be cited with sources, both within the paper and at the end.

Learning how to use the ideas of others to add weight to your own ideas involves effort and a commitment to academic honesty. It is not always clear exactly how or when to use sources, and sometimes you might need advice or guidance. Since your professors are most familiar with the expectations of their disciplines, they are the best people to ask. Your college likely offers support in the writing lab or online. If you need more guidance, the Purdue Online Writing Lab (OWL) has a section on safe practices for researching and drafting (https://openstax.org/l/avoidingplagiarism), where you can find excellent advice on identifying plagiarism and preventing yourself from plagiarizing.

While the process of writing authentically and avoiding plagiarism must be focused from the start, you can avoid a world of trouble by double-checking your near-final work with a source identification site or plagiarism detector. Doing so can help you avoid any unintentional reuse of others' work and may simply identify a source you forgot to cite. Chegg Writing (https://www.chegg.com/writing) allows you to upload or paste in your paper for a detailed source evaluation. Note that this is only a check step; you must follow best practices to ensure that you don't plagiarize.

Validity and Credibility

Before you move on to interpreting your data and addressing the significance of what you found, you need to understand the concepts of validity and credibility. There are many ways you can check the validity of a piece of information. Can you find contradictory or confirmatory data? Can you find evidence that disputes what you are reading? If so, use this information. It is always useful to mention opposing ideas. Ultimately, doing so might strengthen your own ideas. Is the topic within the expertise of the person offering the information? Was the method chosen to convey this information the best method to use? The credibility of the author is another important aspect of checking your sources. In other words, evaluate the authors. Are they experts on the topic? Do they have credentials to write on this particular topic? Has this author written anything else on this topic?

Evidence is the way we show that we are using the experiences, values, research, and perspectives of others. To be information literate is to apply the concepts of subjective and objective evidence to our selection, use, and evaluation of information. When we read a website or view a television program, can we recognize that a particular set of values and perspectives is being used? Are we able to identify when evidence is being used? Can we determine that the evidence being used shows a relevant connection between values, perspectives, and conclusions? Are enough different values and perspectives being presented that the conclusions can be considered objective? It is important to learn how to determine the validity and credibility of sources.

The Internet presents its own challenges when it comes to discovering valid and credible information. When looking at a website, you should be able to answer the following questions: Who is responsible for the site (i.e., who is the author)? What can you find out about the responsible party? Where does the site's information come from (e.g., opinions, facts, documents, quotes, excerpts)? What are the key concepts, issues, and "facts" on the site? And finally, can the key elements of the site be verified by another site or source? In other words, if you want to find some information online, you shouldn't just Google the topic and then depend on the first website that pops up.

For certain topics and types of information, you may need to dig deeper. Take into account the funding behind a website. Look up the author, and see if they have written anything else and if there are any obvious biases present in that writing. As an example, if you find a website about vaccinations and autism, and this website was put up by a parent group that opposes vaccinations, you have found information that has biases built in from the start. The point of view presented is most likely one-sided, and thus you need to look for more balanced sources to learn if there is in fact some relationship between childhood vaccinations and the onset of autism. This is just an example; you can find sources ranging from reasonably trustworthy to totally untrustworthy on any topic.

Interpretation

Interpretation is the task of drawing inferences from the facts that you collect in your research. It is a search for the broader meaning of your research findings. This is where you try to make sense of what you discovered. In this part of your research, you should discuss the most important knowledge you gained about your topic from your sources. Here is where you go back to your hypothesis and research questions to discuss your findings and whether or not your hypothesis is correct.

Significance

Remember that earlier it was stated, "Life is a series of problems needing solutions." Consequently, an increased amount of inquiry leads to progress as we continue to expand our knowledge base on a variety of topics. Whatever you find in your research study has significance, as it adds to our knowledge in a particular area. In this section of your writing, it is important to describe the process by which you located your information and then provide advice to other researchers on how to effectively and efficiently find information on this topic. This allows for the continuation of inquiry and the development of more data and knowledge. This is where you communicate to others the new knowledge you discover in your research.

I Did the Research—How Do I Present It?

Estimated completion time: 12 minutes.

Questions to consider:

- How do I communicate my research findings?
- What are the elements of a good oral presentation?
- How do I successfully prepare a visual presentation?

Oral Presentations

When giving an oral presentation, you should pay special attention to voice, body, and attitude. If you take the following tips into consideration, you should do a fine job of conveying your ideas to an audience.

Voice

Voice is more than the sum of the noises you make as you speak. Pay attention to inflection, which is the change in pitch or loudness of your voice. You can deliberately use inflection to make a point, to get people's attention, or to make it very obvious that what you are saying right now is important. You can also change the volume of your voice. Speak too softly, and people will think you are shy or unwilling to share your ideas; speak too loudly, and people will think you are shouting at them. Control your volume to fit the audience.

Some people have a tendency to rush through their presentations. This means they speed up their speech, and the audience has a difficult time following along. Take care to control the speed at which you give a presentation so that everyone can listen comfortably. Also, to add to the comfort of the listeners, it is always nice to use a conversational tone in a presentation.

Body

This includes such components as stance, gesture, and eye contact—in other words, overall body language. How do you stand when you are giving a presentation? Do you move around and fidget? Do you look down at the ground or stare at your note cards? Are you chewing gum or sticking your hands in and out of your pockets nervously? Obviously, you don't want to do any of these things. Make eye contact as often as possible. Stand in a comfortable manner, but don't fidget. Use gestures sparingly to make certain points.

Attitude

Attitude is everything. Your enthusiasm for your presentation will prime the audience. If you are bored by your own words, the audience will be yawning. If you are jazzed by what you have to offer, they will sit up in their seats and listen intently. Also, be interested in your audience. Let them know that you are excited to share your ideas with them because they are worth your effort.

Visual Presentations

You might also think about using technology to make your presentation. Perhaps you will do a slide presentation in addition to orally communicating your ideas to your class or another group. Keep in mind that the best presentations are those with minimal words or pictures on the screen, just enough to illustrate the information conveyed in your oral presentation. Do a search on lecture slides or presentation slides to find myriad suggestions on how to create them effectively. You may also create videos to communicate what you found in your research. Today, there are many different ways to take the information you found and create something memorable with which to share your knowledge.

When you are making a presentation that includes a visual component, pay attention to three elements: design, method, and function.

Design

The design includes such elements as size, shape, color, scale, and contrast. You have a vast array of options for designing a background or structuring the visual part of your presentation, whether online or offline.

Method

The method is how you visually present your ideas. Will it be better to show your ideas by drawing a picture, including a photograph, using clip art, or showing a video? Or will it be more powerful to depict your ideas through a range of colors or shapes? These decisions you make will alter the impact of your presentation. Will you present your ideas literally, as with a photograph, or in the abstract, as in some artistic rendition of an idea? For instance, if you decide to introduce your ideas symbolically, a picture of a pond surrounded by tall trees may be the best way to present the concept of a calm person.

Function

The function is the purpose of the visual part of your presentation. Are you telling a story? Communicating a message? Creating movement for the audience to follow? Summarizing an idea? Motivating people to agree with an idea? Supporting and confirming what you are telling your audience? Knowing the function of the visual element of your presentation will make your decisions about design and method more meaningful and successful.

B | Recommended Readings

No list of this nature can be all-inclusive, so read online summaries and ask around before you devote time and effort to resources related to thinking. Even a bad book can teach valuable lessons (such as how to be more selective), but you also don't want to waste your limited time.

- *Thinkertoys: A Handbook of Creative-Thinking Techniques* by Michael Michalko. A former U.S. Army officer discusses idea generation and the creative thinking process to jumpstart ideas.
- *A Whack on the Side of the Head: How You Can Be More Creative* by Roger von Oech. Here, von Oech offers scenario-based discussion starters to prompt alternative thinking to solve problems.
- *Thinking, Fast and Slow* by Daniel Kahneman. Nobel Prize winner Kahneman explores intuition and emotional decision-making.
- *Essentialism: The Disciplined Pursuit of Less* by Greg McKeown. Working on the ironic concept that *less* is the new *more*, McKeown outlines how to embrace a stripped-down, back-to-basics approach to business, customer service, thinking, and life in general, in direct contrast to the typical *bigger is better* mentality.
- *Blink: The Power of Thinking without Thinking* by Malcolm Gladwell. Gladwell, a writer for the *New Yorker* magazine, presents the science of thinking on the fly—how some people are better than others at sifting through all the available information and only accessing what matters most in making important decisions. It may appear that these "gut reactions" are instantaneous, but Gladwell argues that a great deal of thinking goes into these seemingly snap decisions.
- *Critical Thinking: Tools for Taking Charge of Your Professional and Personal Life* by Richard Paul and Linda Elder. A well-respected educator and proponent of critical thinking, Paul is one of the founders of the Foundation for Critical Thinking (FCT), and this book presents his ideas about clear thinking in all aspects of business, education, and personal relationships.
- *Freakonomics: A Rogue Economist Explores the Hidden Side of Everything* by Steven D. Levitt and Stephen J. Dubner. A wildly popular mesh of economic theory (in layman's terms) and pop psychology, *Freakonomics* takes a look at topics not found in most economics lessons, including drug dealing and sumo wrestling.
- *The Organized Mind: Thinking Straight in the Age of Information Overload* by Daniel J. Levitin. Based on the concept that organizing your mind (ideas, workspace, life) is half the battle, Levitin proposes techniques to improve critical thinking through an ordered approach.

Appendix C

C | Activities and Artifacts From the Book

This appendix provides reproductions of tables, forms, and related materials from throughout the book. You can print them or copy them for completion and inclusion in your records or to turn in and use in class.

Chapter 1 Welcome to College

The Five Whys: Your Turn

Why are you in college?	I am in college to . . .
Why do you . . .	I . . .
Why do you . . .	I . . .
Why do you . . .	I . . .
Why do you . . .	I . . .

Table C1

Chapter 2 Knowing Yourself as a Learner

Parts of the learning process	Growth characteristic	What will you do to adopt a growth mindset?
Challenges	Embraces challenges	
Obstacles	Persists despite setbacks	
Effort	Sees effort as a path to success	
Criticism	Learns from criticism	
Success of Others	Finds learning and inspiration in the success of others	

Table C2

Does it ...?	Yes	No	What you can do to turn the assignment into something that is better suited to you as a learner?
Does it allow you to make decisions about your own learning?			In essence, you are doing this right now. You are making decisions on how you can make your assignment more effective for you.
Does it allow you to make mistakes without adversely affecting your grade?			Hints: *Are there ways for you to practice? Can you create a series of drafts for the assignment and get feedback?*
Is it centered on solving a problem?			Hint: *Can you turn the assignment into something that solves a problem? An example would be making a presentation that actually educated others rather than just covered what you may have learned.*
Is it related to your chosen occupation in any way?			Hint: *Can you turn the assignment into something you might actually do as a part of your profession or make it about your profession? Examples might be creating an informative poster for the workplace or writing a paper on new trends in your profession.*
Does it allow you to manage the time you work on it?			More than likely the answer here will be "yes," but you can plan how you will do it. For more information on this, see the chapter on time management.
Does it allow interaction with your instructor as a learning partner?			Hint: *Talking to your instructor about the ideas you have for making this assignment more personalized accomplishes this exact thing.*

Table C3

Chapter 3 Managing Your Time and Priorities

	Always	Usually	Sometimes	Rarely	Never
I like to be given strict deadlines for each task. It helps me stay organized and on track.					
I would rather be 15 minutes early than 1 minute late.					

Table C4

	Always	Usually	Sometimes	Rarely	Never
I like to improvise instead of planning everything out ahead of time.					
I prefer to be able to manage when and how I do each task.					
I have a difficult time estimating how long a task will take.					
I have more motivation when there is an upcoming deadline. It helps me focus.					
I have difficulty keeping priorities in the most beneficial order.					

Table C4

Chapter 4 Planning Your Academic Pathways

Take a moment to practice setting long- and short-term goals. Your short-term goal should help you progress toward your long-term goal. Include a plan for when and how you will know if you're on track or if you need to adjust your goals to match new priorities.

My Long-Term Goal:

My Short-Term Goal:

My Plan for Checking My Progress:

Table C5

Example Semester # 1:	Example Semester # 2:
List your planned courses here:	*List your planned courses here:*
List your planned activities here:	*List your planned activities here:*

Example Summer Plans:

List your planned courses here:

List your planned activities here:

Example Semester # 1:	Example Semester # 2:
List your planned courses here:	*List your planned courses here:*
List your planned activities here:	*List your planned activities here:*

Example Summer Plans:

List your planned courses here:

List your planned activities here:

Figure C.1 This two-year version of the planning document may need to be adopted for colleges operating on a quarter, trimester, or other schedule. (Downloadable versions are available at OpenStax.org.)

Appendix C

Chapter 5 Reading and Notetaking

Topic/Objective:		Name:
		Class/Period:
		Date:
Essential Question:		

Questions:	Notes:

Summary:

Figure C.2 The Cornell Method provides a straightforward, organized, and flexible approach

Chapter 8 Communicating

Form of Communication	Rules for This Form
Face-to-face	
Phone	
Printed letters	
Email	
Texting	
Instant messaging/group chat	
Social media	

Table C6

	Challenges	Opportunities	Communication Methods and Tools
Group project for an on campus (traditional) course.			
Group project for an online-only course.			
Planning an event with your extended family.			
Planning an event with your friends/peers.			

Table C7

	Describing a sporting event you watched.	Describing an argument you got into on social media.	Describing a night out with friends.
An eight-year-old			
A 20-year-old woman			

Table C8

	Describing a sporting event you watched.	Describing an argument you got into on social media.	Describing a night out with friends.
A middle-aged man			
An elderly person			

Table C8

	Face-to-Face	Email	Letter	Phone	Facebook	Instagram	Snapchat
Parent							
Peer							
Sibling							
Boss							
Doctor							
Professor							
Waitress							
Office assistant							
Significant other							

Table C9

Index

A
Academic advisors, 138
accommodations, 214
alcohol, 393
alumni, 418
Americans with Disabilities Act, 290
anxiety, 385
associate's degree, 126

B
bachelor's degree, 127
budget, 328

C
Clinicals, 133
College Terms, 19
Compound interest, 340
cramming, 198
Creativity, 224
credentials, 130
credit cards, 343
critical consumption, 269
Critical thinking, 236
curriculum maps, 137

D
debt, 342
degrees, 125
depression, 386
diet, 368
drugs, 393

E
Eating disorders, 386
Electives, 128
emotional intelligence, 274
Equity, 290
exercise, 372

F
Fieldwork, 133
four-year degree, 127

G
General education, 128
graduate degrees, 129
grit, 38

H
Health, 367
hidden curriculum, 24

I
Identity theft, 355
imposter syndrome, 29
inclusion, 291
Income, 328
information literacy, 246
Interest, 340
interleaving, 208
Internships, 420
intersectionality, 303

K
KSAs, 411

L
LinkedIn, 426
Long-term memory, 196

M
Major courses, 128
Maslow's Hierarchy of Needs, 433
master's degrees, 129
Memory, 193
mental health, 385
mental illness, 385
mindset, 49
minor, 132
Mnemonics, 205

N
negative bias., 47
negative self-talk, 48
Netiquette, 263
Network awareness, 268
Networking, 418
nutrition, 367

P
plagiarism, 440
portfolio, 428
Post-baccalaureate, 130
practice test, 209
practicums, 133
preprofessional programs, 132
presentations, 442
profile, 426
purpose, 432

R
Reliable sources, 248
research, 435
resume, 425

S
safety, 393
Self-care, 389
service learning, 135
Short-term memory, 194
social media literacy, 265
spacing, 208
stereotypes, 305
suicide, 387

T
Test anxiety, 217
transferable skills, 423

U
unconventional ideas, 230

W
wellness, 367
Working memory, 194
workplace knowledge, 414